The Curriculum

SUNY Series
FRONTIERS IN EDUCATION
Philip G. Altbach, Editor

The Frontiers in Education Series features and draws
upon a range of disciplines and approaches in the
analysis of educational issues and concerns, helping to
reinterpret established fields of scholarship in education
by encouraging the latest synthesis and research.

Other books in this series include:

Class, Race, & Gender in American Education

—Lois Weis (ed.)

*Excellence and Equality: A Qualitatively Different Perspective on
Gifted and Talented Education*

—David M. Fetterman

Change and Effectiveness in Schools: A Cultural Perspective

—Gretchen B. Rossman, H. Dickson Corbett,
and William A. Firestone

The Curriculum

Problems, Politics, and Possibilities

EDITED BY

Landon E. Beyer

AND

Michael W. Apple

State University of New York Press

Published by
State University of New York Press, Albany

© 1988 State University of New York

For information, address State University of New York
Press, State University Plaza, Albany, N.Y., 12246

Library of Congress Cataloging-in-Publication Data

The Curriculum : problems, politics, and possibilities / edited by
    Landon E. Beyer and Michael W. Apple.
        p.   cm. — (SUNY series, frontiers in education)
    Includes index.
    ISBN 0-88706-817-0. ISBN 0-88706-818-9 (pbk.)
    1. Curriculum planning—United States.   2. Education—United
States—Curricula.   3. Educational sociology—United States.
4. Education—United States—Aims and objectives.   I. Beyer, Landon
E., 1949-   .   II. Apple, Michael W.   III. Series.
LB2806.15.C87 1988
375'.001'0973—dc19   87-33556
                                                                   CIP

10   9   8   7   6   5   4   3

CONTENTS

Acknowledgments

All books depend on the efforts of many more people than those whose names appear as editors and authors. The same is true for this volume as well. Yet, aside from some important people whom we shall thank in the next paragraph, *The Curriculum: Problems, Politics, and Possibilities* could not have been created were it not for the committed action of the progressive teachers, administrators, and students with whom we have been fortunate to interact over the years. Their continuing attempts to create an education worthy of its name at the theoretical and practical levels provided a good deal of encouragement for this project.

We would like to thank a number of other people who have provided support during the writing and editing of this book. Philip Altbach showed again why he is such a superb editor and friend. Lois Patton and many other people at SUNY Press demonstrated why the Press is a pleasure to work with. Diane Falkner at the University of Wisconsin and Diane Harrington at Cornell College are clearly among the best secretaries with which one could work. Their editing and typing efforts, and their patience and understanding, are very much appreciated.

LEB
MWA

Introduction

ONE

Values and Politics in the Curriculum

Landon E. Beyer and *Michael W. Apple*

O ver the past few decades, educators have witnessed a slowly growing but significant change in the way they approach their work. This change is only visible over the long haul, yet few things have had such an important impact. We are referring here to the transformation of curriculum theory and practice from a concern with *what* should be taught and *why* we should teach it to those problems associated with *how to* organize, build, and above all now, evaluate curriculum and teaching. The difficult ethical and political questions of content, of what knowledge is of most worth, have been pushed to the background in our attempts to define technically oriented methods that will "solve" our problems once and for all. Professional curriculum debate now tends to be over procedures, not over what counts as legitimate knowledge. This shift is occurring not only in education. As a number of commentators have documented, in many areas of our cultural and political lives, technique is winning out over substance.[1]

The concern with technique is not inconsequential, of course. "How to's" play a valued role in curriculum design and teaching. However, in the process, the field itself and the people who make decisions about what happens inside schools have become increasingly subject to the dynamics of what is best called *deskilling*. The sensibilities and skills that were and are so very critical for justifying our educational programs, for understanding why we

3

should be doing *x* rather than *y*, and for building a more democratic set of educational institutions, atrophy and hence are ultimately lost.[2]

This is especially serious today because, as we will note later, public education is under a concerted attack from right wing forces that wish to substitute an ethic of private gain and an accountant's profit and loss sheet for the public good. What education is *for* is shifting.[3] In the face of such a well-financed and well-organized attack, many committed and hard-working educators often no longer have the resources (both monetary and conceptual) to argue back effectively. In this way, schools become more like miniature factories dominated by concerns for input and output, efficiency, and cost savings. The more democratic visions of education and the multitude of creative strategies educators have developed over the years to put them into practice wither. We are now in danger of losing them from our collective memory.

The Curriculum: Problems, Politics, and Possibilities wants to preserve that collective memory and wants to build on that memory to provide a set of resources so that those educators who are deeply concerned with what is happening to curricula, teachers, and students in schools can better act on the questions of what, why, and how to. It aims at reintegrating the ethical, personal, and political into curriculum discourse and decisionmaking. In order to do this, the volume must be both critical of some existing and long-lasting tendencies (for there is currently a good deal of negative pressure on education and no small amount of less-than-exciting school practices) and at the same time be supportive of the more thoughtful and democratic tendencies that exist or are currently emerging.

One of our major goals in this volume is to stimulate thoughtful practice and more politically sensitive curriculum inquiry. Many people in the field with a good deal of experience would undoubtedly agree with this, for the literature abounds with material on the "reflective practitioner," and some of it is very good. However, we wish to go further. Our objective is perhaps best embodied in the concept of *praxis*. This involves not only the justifiable concern for reflective action, but thought and action combined and enlivened by a sense of power and politics. It involves both conscious understanding of and action in schools on solving our daily problems. These problems will not go away by themselves, after all. But it also requires critically reflective practices that alter the material and ideological conditions that cause the problems we are facing as educators in the first place.

As we have argued elsewhere, to do this we need to think about education *relationally*.[4] We need to see it as being integrally connected to the cultural, political, and economic institutions of the larger society, institutions that may be strikingly unequal by race, gender, and class.[5] Schools embody and reproduce many of these inequalities. They may alleviate some of them, in part due to the committed labor of so many teachers, administrators, community activists, and others. However, as the literature on the hidden curriculum and on "cultural reproduction" has demonstrated, schools unfortunately may re-create others.[6] Because of this, part of our concern in curriculum must be with these connections between our educational institutions and differential cultural, political, and economic power.

Even though stressing the political nature of curriculum and teaching is essential, not all of our curriculum dilemmas can be totally understood this way. The problems associated with selecting from that vast universe of possible knowledge, of designing environments to make it accessible, of making it meaningful to students, all of these *are* political in fundamental ways. But an array of other crucial and complementary ways of thinking about the dilemmas we confront needs to be fully integrated into our relational and political sensitivity if we are not to lose our way.

In thinking about curriculum, a number of general issues confront us if we take the importance of thoughtful practice seriously. While no list can ever do justice to the complexity of curriculum deliberations, the following gives some flavor of the complex questions about which we have to make decisions.

1. *Epistemological.* What should count as knowledge? As knowing? Should we take a behavioral position and one that divides knowledge and knowing into cognitive, affective, and psycho-motor areas, or do we need a less reductive and more integrated picture of knowledge and the mind, one that stresses knowledge as process?
2. *Political.* Who shall control the selection and distribution of knowledge? Through what institutions?
3. *Economic.* How is the control of knowledge linked to the existing and unequal distribuiton of power, goods, and services in society?
4. *Ideological.* What knowledge is of most worth? Whose knowledge is it?
5. *Technical.* How shall curricular knowledge be made accessible to students?
6. *Aesthetic.* How do we link the curriculum knowledge to the biography and personal meanings of the student? How do we act "artfully" as curriculum designers and teachers in doing this?
7. *Ethical.* How shall we treat others responsibly and justly in education? What ideas of moral conduct and community serve as the underpinnings of the ways students and teachers are treated?
8. *Historical.* What traditions in the field already exist to help us answer these questions? What other resources do we need to go further?

The last set of historical questions is something to which the two of us have given considerable thought. We are very conscious of the work that has made it possible for the current generation of critically minded curriculum people to become more sophisticated in raising the issues on the preceding

5

list. Many past and continuing efforts have been made to bring these issues to our attention by a number of significant figures in the field. Among the most important of these individuals have been Dwayne Huebner, James Macdonald, Maxine Greene, Elliot Eisner, and Joseph Schwab. Be it Schwab's emphasis on the ultimately deliberative nature of curriculum, Huebner's eloquent insistence that we focus on language, environment, and politics, Macdonald's struggles to put the person first, Eisner's attempts to provide an aesthetic approach to curriculum, or Greene's empassioned advocacy of a curriculum theory based on literature and the poetics and politics of personal knowing—all have provided a foundation and resources for the quest for a more adequate, and more humane, grounding for curriculum theory and practice that so many people concerned with curriculum are now undertaking.[7] All recognize the inherent complexity of education and reject the comforting illusion that we can ever find the one right set of techniques that will guarantee certainty of outcome. Finally, all of them take education seriously, as worthy of our very best thought. Education is a process that must embody the finest elements of what makes us human, that frees us in the process of teaching us what is of value. For all of them, it is not something that is reducible to techniques of standardized testing, systems management, behaviorism, and competency based instruction, to being a mirror of economic and industrial needs defined by the few, and so forth.

Our attempt to integrate contemporary thought in the curriculum field within the larger social whole has a democratic as well as historical context that needs to be respected, even cherished. The hallmark of too much curriculum reform work has been its insistence on a hierarchical, top-down model of conceptualization, development, and implementation that we find intellectually and politically dishonest. In most cases, "new curricula" and standardized techniques of teaching, management, and accountability have been developed by academics in higher education, research and development agencies, and state and federal departments of education that are then superimposed on the work of teachers so as to "improve" classroom practice and curriculum deliberation.[8] As opposed to such a stratified model, this volume argues that meaningful curriculum reform must occur within those institutions, and by those people, most intimately connected to the lives of students: teachers, administrators, students, and community members whose work in schools aids the process of genuinely transforming educational practice.[9]

One of the connecting threads of this volume is the extent to which the authors included here are involved not just in the production of critically oriented theory and research—although surely this is not to be taken lightly or undervalued—but in the concrete, daily political and educational struggles in teaching, curriculum development and design, the preparation of future teachers and administrators, and the like. As educators and political actors, the authors included in this volume are keenly aware of the responsibilities they bear in helping effect substantial changes in the lives of teachers and students and of those most oppressed by current social inequalities — especially as they occur on the basis of race, gender, ethnicity, age, social class, sexual orientation, and cultural affinity. The chapters included in this volume are eloquent witness to the position that scholarship, aesthetic awareness, ethical obligation, and political involvement can be separated only at the expense of a more just, humane, and decent school environment and social order.

By asking all of us to see education relationally, to recognize its intimate connections to the inequalities in the larger society, we are self-consciously aligning ourselves with a program aimed at what Marcus Raskin has called "the common good." This program of criticism and renewal asserts the political and ethical principle that "no inhuman act should be used as a short cut to a better day," and, especially, that at each step of the way any social program — be it in the economy, in education, or elsewhere — "will be judged against the likelihood that it will result in linking equity, sharing, personal dignity, security, freedom, and caring."[10] This means that those pursuing such a program "must . . . assure themselves that the course they follow, inquire into, [and] analyze . . . will dignify human life, recognize the playful and creative aspects of people," and see others not as objects but as "coresponsible" subjects involved in the process of democratically deliberating over the ends and means of all of their institutions.[11]

Compare this language — the language of equity, sharing, personal dignity, security, freedom, and caring — with the dominant educational discourse today. The language of efficiency, standards, competency, cost effectiveness, and so on impoverishes our imagination and limits our educational and political vision. It also, and very importantly, distances us from the more personal and situational language of teachers who must make informed, flexible, and humane decisions in very uncertain and trying circumstances. One should inquire, in fact, into the possibility that such attempts at bureaucratizing and rationalizing the work of curriculum and teaching is part of a much longer history in which the paid labor that has been defined as largely women's work (we should remember that 87 percent of elementary school teachers and 67 percent of teachers overall are women) has been constantly subject to pressures to bring it under external bureaucratic control and to eliminate the elements of connectedness and caring that such work has often embodied.[12]

And, finally, the dominance of the language of efficiency cuts us off from a significant part of our own past in curriculum work. One cannot read Dewey, Rugg, and other men and women who helped form a more socially sensitive tradition in curriculum without recognizing the utter import that the impulse toward the common good, toward a democratized polity and a democratizing culture, played in their own educational theories and proposals.[13] While a number of the authors in this volume rightly wish to go beyond some of the political limitations of the positions advocated by these earlier educators, there can be no doubt that the same impulse provides the impetus for their own efforts. Without such a critical and democratic impulse, one becomes a trainer not an educator.

The substantiation of alternative ideas, forms of language, and images of possibility are central components of the personal and political issues that form the core of this volume. Thus, while celebrating and building on the ideas and struggles of those who preceded us, we also share a commitment to what Raymond Williams has called "the practice of possibility" as this may be realized in democratically organized practices in schools.[14]

What sets this volume apart from others is something else as well, however. An interest in the historical antecedents of the curriculum field and the development of alternatives that are at once politically informed and educationally appropriate has also prevented this volume from unilaterally dismissing those areas of curriculum scholarship that some critics might regard as traditional, conventional, or in the mainstream. Much of this scholarship is, to be sure, in need of critical interrogation, political analysis, and conceptual clarification. Yet we do not wish to follow totally a disturbing tendency toward rejecting the whole of the mainstream literature in the field — perhaps especially by some of those who have correctly sought to develop alternative theories and practices. This rejection, although partly correct and certainly understandable, is questionable on at least two grounds. First, such rejectionism uniformly dismisses all previous work when this is clearly not justified. Even though portions of it need to be challenged and superceded, we still have much to learn from those writing in this mode, as this volume amply attests. Second, this tendency to reject what has come before is itself symptomatic of the ahistoricism that tends to characterize our field. Although we may reject the aims and values of a good deal of conventional work in curriculum, we discount and overlook it at our own peril.

If curriculum design, and all educational decisionmaking, is to be a democratically based deliberative practice that is both critical of existing inequalities and powerful in envisioning alternative possibilities, then it should be open to the best of conventional work. Simply because a good deal of current educational research may have an interest in technical control and certainty,[15] this does not mean that we cannot learn something from it, for we are dealing with very complex institutions, and good empirical work (conceived of in its very broadest sense) can be essential. As Schwab insightfully states, the work of curriculum design and implementation is complicated. Sounding quite Deweyan, he states, "It treats both ends and means and must treat them as mutually determining one another." For him, then, deliberation must try to identify with respect to both [ends and means] what facts may be relevant. It must try to ascertain the relevant facts in the concrete case. It must try to identify the desiderata in the case. It must generate alternative solutions. . . . It must then weigh alternatives and their costs and consequences against one another, and choose, not the *right* alternatives, for there is no such thing, but the *best* one.[16]

Now Schwab may see the process of curriculum debate as more "rational" than it really can and should be. He may also underplay the growing recognition that "facts" are not there simply to be found. They are constructed by the educational and ideological agendas of the people who ask the questions that generate such data. Yet his points about being open to as much, often contradictory, information as possible and weighing this in regard to *both* ends and means are not to be dismissed. Not all past and current "conventional" curriculum work is wrong and some of it may be very helpful in our attempt to "generate alternative solutions" and "weigh alternatives and their costs and consequences against each other." What is crucial here, of course, is that this "weighing" is done with regard to the values we noted before, the values of equity, sharing, personal dignity, security, freedom, and caring. And this can only be done if we look honestly and openly at the kind of society in which we now live, the patterns of differential power and benefits that now exist inside and outside of education, and the ways some of our current perspectives make it increasingly difficult for us to face this reality.

Perhaps this point can be made clearer if we reflect on the ways slogan systems tend to dominate our work in education. We have seen, for example, in the last several years, the phrases "open education," "back to basics," "effective teaching," and so on, paraded as the definitive cure for whatever educational ailments allegedly plague us at the moment. Currently, the main slogan vying for popular approval seems to be a commitment to "excellence," and the provision of programs and materials committed to its realization. Such slogans are used in an attempt to garner support for the particular points of view or interests embodied by the group promoting them. In the current conservative climate, "excellence" has often served as an excuse to cut budgets, tighten centralized controls, and attempt to redefine the goals of the schools as primarily those needed by business and industry. It does contain progressive possibilities. After all, none of us would object to schools doing "excellent" teaching. However, in the social struggle over the means and ends of "excellence," over its very definition, the voice of women, people of color, labor, and others seems to have been muted. The voice of "efficient management" has been heightened.[17]

The chapters in this volume provide the sort of analytic sophistication

9

necessary to think through the issues, ideas, and values that attend the development of such slogans, so that we might see more clearly what these overused, often amorphous language forms actually mean. At the same time, the authors included herein are concerned with uncovering the personal, political, social, and ideological roots of such slogans, so that educators and others may make more informed and reflective judgments about the political interests that guide educational policies and practices.[18]

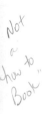

For those looking for a "how to" book that sets out the universal aims, processes, and orientations that should guide curricular deliberation and classroom practice, this volume may not be entirely satisfying. We have not attempted to set out such a complete and directive work for several reasons. First, such an attempt would belie the very commitment to democratic participation and organization that lies at the heart of this book's political sensibility. While the authors whose work appears here do offer suggestions for ways of thinking about curriculum design and development, the restructuring of classrooms, enlivening teaching practices, and so on, they cannot go much further than providing such suggestions. The actual work involved in redesigning curriculum and teaching practices, the details of how and where this is to be done, must be worked out *collaboratively* with those teachers, administrators, community members, and students with whom most of us interact every day. Second, "how to" questions — for logical and political reasons — can only be dealt with after the sort of "why" questions explored here are addressed and at least tentatively resolved. How we go about the concrete activities involved in curriculum and teaching will be affected by our answers to the critical questions raised in this volume. Because, as we noted, all too often educators have assumed that "how to" questions can supplant more normatively oriented investigations and inquiries, this volume seeks to redress this mistaken notion by highlighting the importance of the "prior questions" raised in the ensuing chapters.

This is not, of course, to suggest that the kinds of issues represented here are more important, or more valuable, than the more concrete, physical, and intellectual work engaged in by teachers and others. Indeed, the political nature of our commitments demands that we actively collaborate with others in the exploration of alternative practices. Only through such collaboration can the principle of the integration of theory and practice, of educational praxis, be actually implemented.

Because the curriculum field is one of those areas that contains representative, perennial questions and areas of inquiry, *The Curriculum: Problems, Politics, and Possibilities* is organized around these major thematic issues that tend to characterize the field, issues that themselves respond to the list of questions and concerns we introduced earlier. This volume suggests ways in which the progressive and critical perspective that has informed a good deal of recent curriculum thought can be harnessed in formulating alternative responses to the characteristic problems of our field. Within each of the six major divisions comprising this collection, we show how this more critical perspective can provide ways of thinking about a central issue that not only offer real choices, but that make clear the valuative, political, and ethical dimensions of those choices. In providing a more contextual and progressive analysis of the defining issues of curriculum studies, this book will extend the range and viability of that body of inquiry in a way that broadens the parameters of the curriculum field generally. And by including a diversity of views within the divisions of this work, we acknowledge the important questions and perspectives raised by such a diverse body of writing.

These perennial issues include: (1) the nature of curriculum as a field of study, both historically and within the current social and political context; (2) the problems posed in thinking about how to plan and organize curricula for schools; (3) the criteria with which to include specific content areas within the formal curriculum; (4) the constraints on curriculum development and theory imposed by the workplace of teaching; (5) the influence of technology on curriculum work; and (6) the problems involved in curriculum evaluation. These issues are largely constitutive of curriculum inquiry today and form the major divisions of this collection.

The Organization of this Book

Part I: Curriculum: Its Past and Present

In Chapter 2 of this volume, Herbert M. Kliebard outlines the general history of the curriculum field, indicating those interest groups, values, and assumptions that have historically struggled for control of the school curriculum. This chapter serves as a reminder of the historical legacy of our field and situates the more particular debates that follow.

Yet, the history of the field is not only represented in these major "professional" interest groups. There were other, lesser known and even more politically active, segments of the community who attempted to build alternatives to the dominant models of education. Among the most important of these was the Socialist Sunday School Movement, a group of teachers and parents who believed that only by creating different institutions could more democratic visions be taught to their children. In Chapter 3, Kenneth N. Teitelbaum explores the more particular political history of this lesser known part of curriculum, indicating the ways in which nonmainstream groups have sought to frame curriculum form and content in ways that further their own commitments. The general aim of this chapter is to provide a historical example of

11

what has been done by committed groups of people who have recognized the inherently political nature of curriculum and teaching.

Only parts of this past have lasted and made an impact on schools today. What *are* schools like today? Summarizing recent investigations of the typical classroom in the United States, Kenneth A. Sirotnik indicates the current situations in classrooms in Chapter 4. He gives us an empirical picture of some of the realities of curriculum and teaching. This reality provides some of the basis for the criticism and prospects for renewal that follow.

Part II: Curriculum and Planning

Chapter 5 outlines the central models and theories of curriculum planning. In it, George J. Posner provides an analytic discussion of the major ways of thinking about curriculum planning we have inherited and their implications for teaching. Beyond this, Posner provides a basis for the exploration of alternative theories and models that may be necessary for future more progressive curriculum work.

Beyond the conceptual boundaries of curriculum planning, we must become more sensitive to the politics of organizing and planning. This is the aim of Chapter 6 by Dennis L. Carlson. In organizing any human activity, certain procedures and parameters are constructed that may serve social and political interests differentially. Any decision about how to plan educational experiences contains at least tacit commitments that serve to support or undermine particular individuals and groups, thereby affecting their position in larger social arenas. Carlson provides a more political and critical review of some of the dominant ways in which activities are often now being organized and planned.

Part III: Curriculum and Knowledge Selection

What knowledge should be taught? In Chapter 7, Philip H. Steedman explores and critiques some central epistemological assumptions that guide our understanding of the role of the formal curriculum in furthering claims to knowledge. The nature of objectivity, validity, and certainty are treated, along with the implications of a more contextualized view of knowledge for curriculum work. A central problem addressed here is the possibility of knowledge in a "postempiricist" scientific world and its utilization within school curricula.

In addition to epistemological issues, our assumptions about the nature of knowledge have implications for our understanding of persons and their relation to possible knowledge forms. Chapter 8, by Thomas E. Barone, presents us with a humanistic criticism of some of the positivistic assumptions criticized in the previous essay, outlining important ways in which our conceptions of knowledge have depersonalized and dehumanized our "search for

12

knowledge." Barone argues for a greater reliance on "aesthetic" and "poetic" ways of dealing with curriculum.

Yet, once we raise the issue of the importance of personal meaning, of increasing our responsiveness to other forms of knowing, we need to ask *why* it is that the forms of knowledge that curriculum designers employ and that we teach to students as most important *are* so limited. This is a question about power. Because of this, Chapter 9 explores the politics of content selection in curriculum. While the previous two chapters in this section outline important conceptual and humanistic concerns regarding the formal curriculum, here George H. Wood discusses the linkages between knowledge and larger patterns of influence, status, and power. It provides one of the important boundaries within which curriculum as knowledge selection must be articulated.

Part IV: Curriculum and the Work of Teachers

Curricula are usually put into practice by teachers. In Chapter 10, Gail McCutcheon explores possible ways to conceptualize the relationship between the curriculum and the work of teachers. As with Chapter 5 on curriculum planning, this chapter details conceptually the array of possibilities for thinking about curriculum and teaching. McCutcheon provides an analytic starting point for building an approach to curriculum and teaching, and outlines the dominant orientations to what is a central issue in the curriculum field.

Chapter 11 documents the ways in which teachers' work is caught in larger transformations that are changing the nature of the workplace. It is written by Sara E. Freedman, a leader of the Boston Women's Teachers' Group. These changes have important social class and gender connections and are related to the deskilling, depowering, and depersonalizing of teaching. This has special relevance for this book, because changes in the teacher's workplace are part of a larger social and cultural dynamic that is affecting all levels of education.

The final chapter in this section, by Landon E. Beyer, approaches the problem of the relationship between curriculum and teaching as part of the larger issue of how knowledge, cultural creation, and social change can become fused in actual practice. Beyer shows how the curriculum and teachers' work can be seen as a species of cultural action aimed at broader social change. Basic issues include the role of the teacher in promoting democratic participation and the possibilities for cultural action aimed at wider changes.

Part V: Curriculum and Technology

Curriculum, as Huebner reminds us, is about the accessibility of knowledge, about making traditions available to students.[19] How is knowledge often

13

made accessible to students? This is usually done through texts, teacher talk, and increasingly through technology. The first chapter in this section outlines some of the problems associated with the technicization of curriculum work. Douglas D. Noble provides a detailed history of the growth of certain aspects of educational technology, especially the computer. Here again we see the importance of understanding where we have come from, of knowing why certain things are made available, if we are to know the limits and possibilities of our actions in education.

Of equal import are the ways in which a variety of forms of technology may be reasonably and productively employed in schools. This is the task of Michael J. Streibel. While the previous chapter raises a number of important questions about the history and legitimacy of technology in education, such questions do not imply that technology is always and uniformly determined by this past. Although he is critical of some of the uses to which computers are put in schools, Streibel looks specifically at some of the more educationally productive and humane ways in which technological forms have been and could be incorporated into school practice.

Even with what Streibel tells us, however, we still confront differential power and social pressures to use technology in specific ways in school. The computerization of schooling needs to be seen in its current economic and political context if we are to be realistic about who will benefit from its use in classrooms. In Chapter 15, Michael W. Apple addresses some of these economic and political dynamics. Linking growing technicism in curriculum with what is happening to people's jobs in the larger society and to teachers themselves, Apple broadens the sort of debate that must go on in thinking about how computers should be employed.

Part VI: Curriculum and Evaluation

Chapter 16, by George Willis, outlines some of the more humanistic problems involved in programs of evaluation. Particular perspectives on evaluation embody presuppositions about those who are the subjects in evaluative studies. The use of statistical analysis, for example, promotes a view of the participants that is decidedly different from that prompted by case study or ethnographic methodologies. Questions explored by Willis include the picture of humanness that is embedded in evaluative activities, the role of value orientations in deciding evaluative possibilities, and the relevance of the information that evaluations provide.

The final chapter in this section, written by Michael W. Apple and Landon E. Beyer, discusses the politics of evaluation, enlarging the debate begun in Chapter 16. Because the process of evaluation places certain values on school activities, and because these values are embedded in a larger social

and historical context, they necessarily embody commitments that have political consequences. Dominant models of evaluation are subjected to ethical
and political criticism and a new, more socially conscious, form of evaluation
is proposed.

Notes

1. For further discussion of this, see Michael W. Apple, *Ideology and Curriculum*
(Boston: Routledge and Kegan Paul, 1979).
2. The concept of deskilling is elaborated in greater detail in Michael W. Apple,
Education and Power (Boston: Routledge and Kegan Paul, 1982), especially
Chapter 5.
3. Michael W. Apple, *Teachers and Texts: A Political Economy of Class and Gender
Relations in Education* (New York: Routledge and Kegan Paul, 1986).
4. Apple, *Ideology and Curriculum, op. cit.*; and Landon E. Beyer, "Beyond Elitism
and Technicism: Teacher Education as Practical Philosophy," *Journal of Teacher
Education*, Vol. XXXVII, 2 (March-April 1986).
5. For empirical information on these inequities, see Joshua Cohen and Joel
Rogers, *On Democracy* (New York: Penguin Books, 1983); Martin Carnoy,
Derek Shearer, and Russell Rumberger, *A New Social Contract* (New York:
Harper and Row, 1983); and Apple, *Teachers and Texts, op. cit.*
6. See Michael W. Apple and Lois Weis, eds., *Ideology and Practice in Schooling*
(Philadelphia: Temple University Press, 1983). For some of the complex
debates about this issue, see Apple, *Education and Power, op. cit.*, Michael W.
Apple, ed., *Cultural and Economic Reproduction in Education* (Boston: Routledge
and Kegan Paul, 1982); and Henry Giroux, *Theory and Resistance in Education*
(South Hadley, Mass.: Bergin and Garvey Publishers, Inc., 1983).
7. A representative sampling of these works can be found in the essays of
Huebner, Macdonald, and Greene collected in William F. Pinar, ed.,
Curriculum Theorizing (Berkeley, Calif.: McCutchan Publishing Corporation,
1975). See also Joseph Schwab, "The Practical: A Language for Curriculum" in
Arno Bellack and Herbert M. Kliebard, eds., *Curriculum and Evaluation*
(Berkeley, Calif.: McCutchan Publishing Corporation, 1977); and Elliot Eisner,
The Educational Imagination (New York: Macmillan Company, 1985).
8. Arthur Wise, *Legislated Learning* (Berkeley, Calif.: University of California
Press, 1979).
9. One of the best proposals for this can be found in The Public Education
Information Network, *Education for A Democratic Future: Equity and Excellence*
(St. Louis: Public Education Information Network, 1985). See also Apple,
Teachers and Texts, op. cit., Chapter 8; and Landon E. Beyer, "The Parameters of
Educational Inquiry," *Curriculum Inquiry*, Vol. 16, 1 (Spring 1986).
10. Marcus Raskin, *The Common Good* (New York: Routledge and Kegan Paul,
1986), p. 8.
11. *Ibid.*

12. See Apple, *Teachers and Texts, op. cit.*, and Carol Gilligan, *In a Different Voice* (Cambridge, Mass.: Harvard University Press, 1982). See also the work of Madeleine Grumet, Nell Noddings, and Jo Anne Pagano in education, which has been very insightful in bringing a more feminist approach to questions of curriculum and teaching.

13. The best single source for some of this history is Herbert M. Kliebard, *The Struggle for the American Curriculum* (New York: Routledge and Kegan Paul, 1986).

14. Raymond Williams, *The Long Revolution* (London: Chatto and Windus, 1961). Compare this to the nicely articulated distinction between the "language of critique" and the "language of possibility" made in Stanley Aronowitz and Henry Giroux, *Education Under Seige* (South Hadley, Mass.: Bergin and Garvey Publishers, Inc., 1985), pp. 6–7.

15. Apple, *Ideology and Curriculum, op. cit.*

16. Schwab, "The Practical: A Language for Curriculum," *op. cit.*

17. See Ira Shor, *Culture Wars* (New York: Routledge and Kegan Paul, 1986).

18. See, for example, Apple and Weis, ed., *Ideology and Practice in Schooling, op. cit.*; Landon E. Beyer, "Educational Reform: The Political Roots of National Risk," *Curriculum Inquiry*, Vol. 15, 1 (Spring 1985); and Clarence J. Karier, "The Image and the Reality: Review of *High School* by Ernest L. Boyer," *Curriculum Inquiry*, Vol. 15, 4 (Winter 1985).

19. Dwayne Huebner, "Curriculum as the Accessibility of Knowledge," paper presented at the Curriculum Theory Study Group, Minneapolis, Minn., March 2, 1970.

I

*Curriculum: Its Past
And Present*

TWO

The Effort to Reconstruct
the Modern American Curriculum

Herbert M. Kliebard

In any time and place, what we call *the* American curriculum is actually an assemblage of competing doctrines and practices. Even in ancient Athens, Aristotle noted that a wide disagreement existed as to what was an appropriate course of study:

> At present opinion is divided about the subjects of education. All do not take the same view about what should be learned by the young, either with a view to plain goodness or with a view to the best life possible; nor is opinion clear whether education should be directed mainly to the understanding, or mainly to moral character. If we look at actual practice, the result is sadly confusing; it throws no light on the problem whether the proper studies to be followed are those which are useful in life, or those which make for goodness, or those which advance the bounds of knowledge. Each sort of study receives some votes in its favor.[1]

Many of the same differences regarding the purposes of education and what studies are most conducive to achieving those purposes have extended from Aristotle's time to the present.

It has become almost trite to say that these differences become more acute in periods of significant social change. It is in these periods that the sharpest conflicts develop between what are regarded as the tried-and-true studies and those that represent or symbolize new social forces and directions. Analysis of these trends and conflicts becomes more difficult when we realize, first of all, that a lag may occur between a significant social change and its recognition on a widespread scale. For example, industrialization is widely regarded as having one of the most far-reaching effects on the fabric of American social life. It was accompanied by the dislocation of many people from farm and rural communities to large urban centers, a consequent redefinition of family life, and a transformation of what we mean by *community*. But, for many American citizens, life went on very much as before. It was not until such related events as the tremendous growth in mass journalism in the 1880s, which brought news to small towns and hamlets of such things as urban blight and vice and corruption in the cities, that most Americans sensed the coming of a new kind of society. Likewise, enormous growth in rail transportation in the same period made it possible to break down the isolation that had been largely the case in the towns and villages where most Americans lived.

Second, the response to change, even when widely recognized, is anything but uniform. In many cases, new roles are advocated for social institutions that are perceived as decaying or at least no longer functioning in the way they once did. In the modern era at least, many of the social functions that were once performed by other social agencies such as the family or by religious institutions are seen as the province of the schools, so that even among those who see a need for a radical transformation of social institutions, there may be wide differences as to what directions that transformation should take. To speak, then, of a curricular response to social change as simply a conflict between conservatives on one hand, who envision schools that are consistent with earlier social values, and reformers, on the other, who see a new role for the schools, is really an oversimplification. Reformers as well as conservatives come in various stripes, and the directions they advocate in terms of a curricular response to social change tend to differ as much from one another as from the status quo that they seek to replace.

The Social and Educational Impact of Evolutionary Theory

In the nineteenth century, the status quo in curricular matters, at least in most western societies, tended to be associated with a form of the liberal arts which was dominated by classical languages, masterpieces of literature, and elegance of linguistic expression. In England, to take one example, the standard form of education was associated with building character, a sense of duty, and, especially as expressed by someone like Thomas Arnold of Rugby, with a spirit of service to the empire. Nevertheless, that standard built around classical languages and literary and other humanistic studies came under intense criticism by educational reformers such as Herbert Spencer and Thomas Henry Huxley just after the nineteenth century was half over. Both had been strongly influenced by the rise of science in general and by Darwin's theory of evolution in particular. Spencer tried to carry forward evolutionary theory into the social realm arguing basically that the laws that Darwin had enunciated in terms of the descent of the species could be applied to ethics, economics, sociology, and education. His 1859 essay, "What Knowledge Is of Most Worth?", is widely regarded as a classic of educational reform and contains within it significant indications of certain directions that curriculum reform did in fact take in the late nineteenth and twentieth centuries. For one thing, Spencer sought to replace humanistic studies in the curriculum with scientific ones. His answer to the question he posed in his title was unambiguous:

> What knowledge is of most worth? — the uniform reply is — Science. This is the verdict on all the counts. For direct self-preservation, or the maintenance of life and health, the all-important knowledge is — Science. For that indirect self-preservation which we call gaining a livelihood, the knowledge of greatest value is — Science. For the due discharge of parental functions, the proper guidance is to be found only in — Science. For that interpretation of national life, past and present, without which the citizen cannot rightly regulate his conduct, the indispensible key is — Science. Alike for the most pefect production and highest enjoyment of art in all its forms, the needful preparation is still — Science. And for the purposes of discipline — intellectual, moral, religious — the most efficient study is, once more — Science.[2]

Spencer thus sought to assert the primacy of scientific studies over the more traditional humanistic ones.

In making this claim, Spencer was appealing to a criterion that he tried to establish in judging the worth of school subjects. To him, the supreme criterion by which a program of studies was to be judged was its contribution to self-preservation. Just as survival was the key to evolution, so it became the supreme criterion by which the value of school subjects would be judged. Poetry, although its study could conceivably contribute to the development of taste, was not nearly as valuable a subject as science, which could contribute to such vital areas as health, successful childrearing, and even proper social relations. In making such claims, Spencer was appealing, consciously or unconsciously, to a rising middle class that saw the traditional curriculum not only as exclusionary but as remote from practical affairs and the interests of a modern industrial society.

Spencer's program for reform of the curriculum was also revolutionary in another sense. He saw the curriculum not merely as including a large measure of science but curriculum development as itself scientific. He appealed to the idea that curriculum development involved not simply making considered judgments about what should or should not be included in the course of study, but that scientific laws, when discovered, could dictate the correct content for the curriculum. In particular, Spencer was an exponent of the proposition (widely held in the nineteenth century) that, "The genesis of knowledge in the individual must follow the same course as the genesis of knowledge in the race."[3] In other words, Spencer was appealing to a universal law, which asserted that the course of human history was somehow recapitulated in individual development, and thus the curriculum could be determined through a scientific study of the interrelationship between these two factors. In asserting that a truly scientific curriculum was possible, Spencer was proposing what amounted to the most revolutionary of his reforms.

While there are obvious differences in terms of both social and educational traditions as between England and the United States, a parallel movement for curricular reform developed in America during the late nineteenth century. Actually, Spencer himself enjoyed even greater popularity in America than in England, with such social Darwinists as William Graham Sumner of Yale University spreading and popularizing his message. In general, Sumner preached a doctrine of economic and social *laissez faire* under the assumption that the best social policy was to give natural forces free rein just as they do in the biological sphere. Sumner maintained, for example, "that it is at the present time a matter of patriotism and civic duty to resist the extension of State interference. It is one of the proudest results of political growth that we have reached the point where individualism is possible."[4] The question for Sumner and other social Darwinists was essentially, "Which may we better trust, the play of free social forces or legislative and administrative interference?[5] By implication at least, education was merely an impediment to the doctrine of the survival of the fittest because it represented an obstacle to the free flow of natural laws. (Spencer, for example, actively opposed compulsory state education.)

The major alternative to the social Darwinist view on education was represented by the work of another American sociologist, Lester Frank Ward. Ward, like Spencer and Sumner, was strongly influenced by Darwinian theory, but his interpretation of that theory led him to take almost the opposite social policy direction. Rather than advocating a policy of permitting natural social forces to have free play, Ward in practically all his sociological works emphasized psychic control of the evolutionary process and state intervention in social and economic affairs. He believed that human beings, unlike the

Word

lower animals, have evolved the means to master the forces of nature. They had the power to intervene in the forces of nature and redirect those forces in the interest of human welfare. As the human species evolved the power of intelligence, redirecting the evolutionary process became possible. In fact, intelligent intervention itself became part of the evolutionary process. Like Huxley, Ward believed that survival of the fittest was no iron law in the arena of civic, economic, and social relations. The job of advanced societies was to eliminate insofar as possible the mere struggle for survival. Modern medicine, for example, represented a massive intervention into blind evolutionary forces. It should not be surprising, therefore, that Ward saw education as a vital weapon in the arsenal of society. Through a carefully designed and universal system of education, knowledge could be distributed more widely and thus increase the influence of intelligence in human affairs. In emphasizing the power of intelligence and its potential for social melioration, Ward anticipated, if not influenced, the work of John Dewey. The competing interpretations of the implications of evolution for an industrial society by Spencer and Sumner on one hand and Ward and Dewey on the other indicate that significant social change may give rise not to a single but to multiple interpretations of social and educational policy.

The Social and Educational Climate in the 1890s

Competing interpretations of how the twentieth century curriculum should be reformed emerged immediately out of a period of unrest in the 1890s. The combination of a heightened perception of a transformation in certain social institutions, such as the family and the church, and the psychological force of the pending end to a millennium led social leaders and lay public alike to reexamine the kind of world in which they were living. Crises such as the 1893 economic panic lent further credence to the already widespread idea that a new world was in the making. To some extent, this reexamination amounted to a feeling of alarm in the sense that, with old institutions decaying, society itself seemed in danger of collapsing. With news of crime and corruption in cities reaching large audiences through the popular press and with face-to-face communities giving way to an increasingly depersonalized urban society, it should not be surprising that a new role should be sought for the schools with a revitalized curriculum at the core.

Perhaps the most modest of these efforts followed the lines of Huxley's attempt to create a more equitable balance between the sciences and the humanities in what passed for a liberal education. But, the influence of the new science, particularly as enunciated by Darwin, did not simply raise ques-

Sounds like today

Huxley's attempts to Bal. Sci & humanities

23

tions about the reigning theology of the day; more important, as Dewey once pointed out, it transformed our way of thinking about science itself in areas such as society, morals, and education.[6] Harvard University's powerful president, Charles W. Eliot, for example, sought to establish the doctrine of the equivalence of school subjects, putting science and modern foreign languages on an equal footing with the classical subjects of Latin, Greek, and mathematics.[1] Eliot's reforms were largely contained within the general context of the liberal arts, attempting to modify some of its standard conventions but retaining the ideal of a curriculum whose main function was to liberate the human spirit, inspire an appreciation of beauty, and give one the intellectual mastery that was needed to make independent and sound judgments under a variety of circumstances.

Under the press of the perception that a new world was in the making, however, moderate reformers of the sort that Eliot represented began to seem quite tame, and, in the context of what became a massive drive to reconstruct the American curriculum even came to be regarded as a kind of old guard seeking to forestall the massive changes in the program of studies that was demanded by a modern world. Like Eliot, William Torrey Harris, for example, the influential Commissioner of Education at the time, did not see in the social transformation the necessity to institute a reform of the curriculum that went beyond a selection of the great resources of Western civilization. His opposition to such late nineteenth curricular innovations as manual training earned him the reputation of the "the great conservator." But as the turn of the century approached, center stage in the educational world was turned over to reformers with a much more radical agenda. Three streams of curricular reform emerged around the turn of the century, each challenging in quite different ways the time-honored ideals represented by the liberal arts, even in the modified forms expressed by leaders such as Eliot and Harris.

Social Efficiency as a Response to Social Change

The two major ingredients that made up social efficiency both as a response to social change and a particular way to reform the American curriculum were, first, an effort to inject into the curriculum a stronger element of direct social control than had ever existed before;[8] and, second, an extraordinarily dedicated effort to trim waste in the curriculum by excising studies that had no demonstrated usefulness. In most cases, those subjects were the traditional subjects deemed to be of no practical value. The appeal of an orderly society more self-consciously regulated by social control along with the promise of reform effected not by massive social change but by cutting waste proved to be a potent combination. One of the early manifestations of the appeal of efficiency lay in the scientific management movement led by Frederick Winslow Taylor, who sought to reduce complex processes of manufacture to their most elemental steps and then train workers in the efficient performance of those simple steps. Thus, waste would be reduced sharply by setting precise standards for each unit of work and holding workers to that standard. The appeal to science in this sense lay primarily in an appeal to a kind of objective standard, precision in measuring outcomes, and predictability as to how things will turn out.

It was not long before the budding curriculum field adopted in large measure this version of science and tried to apply it to the job of creating a curriculum. *Scientific curriculum-making*, as it was most frequently called, represents a very direct parallel to scientific management in almost all of its main dimensions. Major national figures in the curriculum world, such as Franklin Bobbitt and W. W. Charters, articulated a position in which minute particulars of the curriculm would be identified through a scientific process of activity analysis. This involved categorizing adult activities into several major categories such as leisure, citizenship, and family living, and then setting detailed objectives in each of the categories. These were direct parallels to the scientific standards that Taylor had prescribed for the process of manufacture. Achieving these objectives was governed by the simple criterion of efficiency. Whatever accomplished those objectives with the least amount of waste was the route to take in developing a curriculum.

But the elimination of waste also had a social dimension. It was also wasteful to teach anything to those who would have no use for it. Why, for example, should we teach algebra or foreign languages to those who, in their adult lives, have no use for mathematics beyond simple calculation or for expressing themselves in other than their native tongues? Therefore, an important concomitant of scientific curriculum-making became curriculum differentiation in which different curricula were prescribed for different groups depending on certain characteristics. These criteria included some measure of native intelligence, probable destination (particularly whether one was destined to go to college or not), and even social class. In this way, the curriculum could be geared directly to the activities one needed to perform in one's adult life. Future engineers would get one kind of education and future truck drivers another. Needless to say, although the practice undoubtedly has a certain utilitarian appeal, it raises in very vivid terms the whole issue of education as social predestination. Although the motivations of the scientific curriculum-makers were most likely humanitarian (e.g., adapting the curriculum to meet the real needs of the school clientele), the question remains as to whether education under these circumstances advanced or stunted social mobility.

25

Child Study and the Curriculum

At the same time that leaders of the scientific curriculum movement were making their voices heard in the educational world, a different reform movement, based on quite different premises, was rising to prominence. The direct utility of social efficiency may have been especially inviting to the curriculum-makers in the early decades of the twentieth century, but its influence was not supreme. At the same time that hard efficiency promised a new era in curriculum reform, the appeal of a natural order of development in the child found strong supporters as well. In a sense, the idea of a child-centered curriculum as well as social efficiency drew on the new status that science enjoyed in the modern world. In the case of child study, science was represented by the idea that the vital question of what should be taught need not remain merely the subject of speculation and vague philosophical argument, but could be derived from natural laws in the same way that Darwin had discovered the laws of natural selection. In particular, the study of the child's own instincts, thought processes, and interests would become the source of the curriculum. Once data on the child's and the adolescent's stages of development could be processed, a scientifically attuned curriculum could be derived.

Leading the way in this direction was one of America's most eminent psychologists, G. Stanley Hall. As leader of the child-study movement in the late nineteenth century, Hall most clearly represented the position that the issue of what should be taught could be derived from careful collection of data on the child's natural interests as well as the modes of thought most characteristic of children and adolescents at various stages in their development. Like Spencer, Hall felt (along with his allies in the American Herbartian movement) that the stages through which a child passed were parallel to the stages of human history. Thus, if there was a historical epoch which might be called savagery, then there would be a stage in the development of children that corresponded to that epoch and in which certain characteristics of the savage were evident. In a curriculum sense, this meant that the materials appropriate for study during that period should reflect that scientifically determined parallel. Thus, it was common in Herbartian schools to teach Longfellow's "Hiawatha" around the second grade because of its special appeal to children going through their savage state of development.

Culture-epochs theory as a specific curriculum theory was rather short-lived, but the idea persisted far into the twentieth century that somehow the child, himself or herself, was the real key to the curriculum riddle. One of the most successful efforts in that direction was launched by William Heard Kilpatrick through his fervent advocacy of the project method.[9] As the basic idea developed, it became clear that the curriculum that was being advocated under that name and later under such labels as the "activity curriculum" and "the experience curriculum" really sought to reverse the standard approach to curriculum-making. For most people, creating a curriculum means deciding what you want to teach and then finding a way to interest students in that subject matter. Kilpatrick and his followers proposed starting with student interests and then bringing in subject matter instrumentally as it bore on pursuing those interests. Therefore, in a typical project, students would decide among themselves what they wanted to do (e.g., staging a play, discovering more about their community) and then the traditional subjects of reading, arithmetic, social studies, and so on would be studied in the context of accomplishing that purpose. For Kilpatrick, "purposing," the expression of the child's own interest in pursuing some activity, remained the essential first step in the curriculum-making process.

According to this approach, the actual learning of subject matter was distinctly secondary to the process of learning (although leaders of the movement like Kilpatrick would also claim that subject matter actually was better mastered under these circumstances than under the traditional ones). The idea of "learning how to learn" with its emphasis on student initiative and active involvement in decisionmaking remained a controlling purpose. To some extent, this emphasis depended on the notion of a problem-solving method which bore some resemblance to what is frequently thought of even today as the scientific method. Advocates of this form of curriculum continued to claim that when children have the opportunity to engage in real (not artificial) problem solving within the school setting, they would form habits of thought that would stand them in good stead in their later lives: They would learn to deal systematically with problems as yet unforseen. However, although some practical benefit would derive from a curriculum organized according to these principles, it would not be nearly as directly functional or as adult oriented as in the case of scientific curriculum-making. The principal focus was on the immediate lives of the students rather than on their future adult roles.

It was natural, therefore, that an antagonism should develop between these contemporaneous movements. Social efficiency oriented educators charged that the activity curriculum did not ensure that children and adolescents would really learn what they need to know because the curriculum was dictated by the sometimes fleeting and sometimes trivial interests of children. In this sense, child-centered curricula acquired an association with "soft" education in which the knowledge and skills that one really needed in the modern world were not really addressed. Although social efficiency education contained within it a strong anti-academic bias, it was serious business. It prepared one directly and efficiently for what life held in store. By contrast, child-centered education seemed to a great many hard-headed school people to be largely frivolous.

The Era of Social Reconstructionism

As already indicated, early portents of a desire to use the schools as an instrument of social change can be found in the late nineteenth century writing of Lester Frank Ward, whose sociological studies led him to believe that the equitable distribution of the world's store of knowledge could reduce invidious class distinctions as well as differences in the status and condition of men and women. For about the first three decades of this century, that impulse to use the curriculum as a force for social change remained something of a subterranean force erupting occasionally in the work of social theorists such as Albion Small.[10] Social reconstructionism's most enduring appeal was to a small coterie of left-wing intellectuals who, beneath the glitter of the "roaring twenties," saw a need to reconstruct social conditions on a major scale. By instilling a critical intelligence in the youth of America as well as an understanding of the dark side of industrialization and its impact on social institutions, a new generation could bring about the needed social change.

Once the stock market crashed in October 1929 and worldwide economic depression was beginning to become visible, the current of social reconstructionism began to flow with vastly increased force. Social reconstructionism's new visibility was probably most dramatically epitomized by the speech that George S. Counts delivered at the 1932 annual meeting of the Progressive Education Association (PEA).[11] The PEA had been formed in 1919 under the leadership of such child-oriented educators as Marietta Johnson and Stanwood Cobb. During the 1920s, the organization grew from a relative handful of members, largely associated with private schools, to a major platform for expressing experimental ideas about education. Over the course of that development, however, the character of the organization also began to change. In particular, professors in major colleges of education (notably Teachers College, Columbia University) such as Harold Rugg and Counts began to assume positions of leadership in the PEA, and the direction of the organization began to change as well. Even Dewey, upon accepting the position of Honorary President, was gently critical of the overwhelmingly child-oriented stand that the organization had followed.[12]

This change in the organization's membership and direction as well as the impact of the Great Depression set the stage for Counts's dramatic challenge to the organization at its 1932 meeting. Accusing the organization of following a program of "anarchy or extreme individualism,"[13] he called for a program much more directly attuned to social welfare and to ameliorating the social conditions of the poor and racial minorities. He alluded to the deficiencies of capitalism that had been responsible for these conditions and called on the schools to confront the social issues of the day directly. Once *social recon that un (lacking social concern)* · · ·)

struc. beh. child-dir = too soft

more, the antagonism between rival reform movements became the subject of
open debate and controversy. From the point of view of the social reconstructionist, a child-centered curriculum was too romantic, too much concerned
with the child as an individual and lacking in the social concern that would
lead to a curriculum directly tied to the social, political, and economic conditions that the country faced. Counts advised the PEA membership not to be
unduly cautious in their policies and to put forward a program of social
reform through the curriculum not even stopping short of what he called "the
bogeys of *imposition* and *indoctrination*" in order to advance it.[14] Although
social reconstructionism excited much attention in the curriculum world of
the 1930s, there is little evidence as to the success of the movement in terms
of actual practice. There is some reason to believe that curriculum reforms
tied to a critical appraisal of American society were not well received in
schools across the country. To a large extent, for example, those reforms were
perceived as being promulgated by a small group of eastern intellectuals.

The most notable exception to the relative lack of success of social
reconstructionism in terms of school practice was the series of social studies
textbooks written by Counts's colleague at Teachers College, Harold Rugg.
Based on generalizations culled from the works of what he called "frontier
thinkers," Rugg sought to infuse in his series what he considered to be
advanced social ideas. He touched on the issue of changing gender roles,
discrepancies of wealth and power in the United States, and militaristic tendencies. In his treatment of World War I, for example, he minimized discussion of battles and individual events and included discussion of secret alli-
ances and economic factors leading to the outbreak of the war such as
competition for trade. At one point, he even suggested that "the American
people, accustomed to peace, were educated to support war."[15] In terms of
sales and readership, the Rugg series was a huge success, but as World War II
approached, demand that school boards abandon the series mounted, and, by
1941, its sales began to decline sharply. Criticism of the American social
system lost most of whatever popularity it enjoyed in the context of imminent
American participation in a great world conflict. The decade of popularity
that the Rugg series enjoyed as well as its rather precipitous decline are
actually interesting examples of how ideas on curriculum interact with general
social, political, and economic conditions.

The Impact of Curriculum Reform in the Twentieth Century

In any society, whether Aristotle's or ours, there can be no unanimity of
opinion at any given time on what is most worthwhile in the culture. There-

fore, that each of the main currents of curriculum reform that found its way into the twentieth century attracted powerful adherents should not be surprising. The curriculum, after all, is a selection of elements from the culture and reflects to some extent the diversity that exists within the culture. Great value is accorded at one and the same time to intellectual mastery, safe driving, and occupational proficiency as components in the curriculum. Moreover, social conditions, such as the Great Depression and the Cold War, created climates that were at least temporarily conducive to different positions at different times. What emerges as a dominant strain in the curriculum is not a function of the force of a particular proposal alone but the due interaction of curriculum ideas and sympathetic or antagonistic social conditions. Therefore, over the course of time, one would expect that first one current then another should assume prominence and that, to some extent, they should all exist side by side.

The three currents of curriculum reform must also be seen against the backdrop of a traditional humanist curriculum that consisted of conventional subjects such as English, history, and mathematics. That curriculum proved more resilient than many reformers expected. The substitution of the project for the subject as the basic building block of the curriculum, as the followers of Kilpatrick advocated, was too fundamental a change for most to accept, as was the substitution of "areas of living" as the social efficiency educators proposed. Even John Dewey, the quintessential American educational reformer, was, more often than not, interested in reconstructing the existing subjects than in replacing them with something else.

Finally, in periods when curriculum reform had charged the atmosphere, it was probably more important for school systems simply to change than to change in a particular ideological direction. While there have always been particular trends favoring one approach to curriculum rather than another, the major currents of curriculum reform actually tend to exist side by side. At the same time that some proponents of curriculum reform were proclaiming that the curriculum should be derived from the spontaneous interests of children, others were proposing that the curriculum should be a direct and specific preparation for adulthood. Still others saw an urgent need to infuse into the curriculum a strong element of social criticism. Each doctrine had an appeal and a constituency. And, rather than make a particular ideological choice among apparently contradictory curriculum directions, it was perhaps more politically expedient on the part of practical school administrators to make a potpourri of all of them. This, in fact, is what the American curriculum has become.

Notes

1. Aristotle, *Politics* (New York: Oxford University Press, 1945), p. 244.

2. Herbert Spencer, *Education: Intellectual Moral and Physical* (New York: D. Appleton and Company, 1860), pp. 84–85.

3. *Ibid.*, p. 117.

4. William Graham Sumner, "State Interference," in *Social Darwinism*, Stow Parsons, ed. (Englewood Cliffs, N. J.: Prentice-Hall, 1963), p. 108.

5. *Ibid.*, p. 109.

6. John Dewey, "Darwin's Influence upon Philosophy," *Popular Science Monthly* 75(July 1909):90–8.

7. National Education Association, *Report of the Committee on Secondary School Studies* (Washington, D. C.: Government Printing Office, 1893).

8. See, for example, Barry Franklin, *Building the American Community: The School Curriculum and the Search for Social Control* (London: Falmer Press, 1986).

9. William Heard Kilpatrick, "The Project Method," *Teachers College Record* 19 (September 1918):319–35.

10. See, for example, Albion Small, "Demands of Sociology upon Pedagogy," *Journal of Proceedings and Addresses of the Thirty-fifty Annual Meeting of the National Education Association*:174–84.

11. George S. Counts, "Dare Progressive Education Be Progressive?" *Progressive Education* 9:257–63.

12. John Dewey, "Progressive Education and the Science of Education," *Progressive Education* 5(July–August–September 1928):197–204.

13. Counts, *op. cit.*, p. 258.

14. *Ibid.*, p. 259.

15. Harold O. Rugg, *A History of American Government and Culture* (New York: Ginn and Company, 1931):559.

THREE

Contestation and Curriculum:
The Efforts of American Socialists, 1900–1920

Kenneth N. Teitelbaum

American public schooling is marked by a dual tension that emanates from its being enmeshed in a capitalist democratic state. At the same time that it strives to serve industrial needs, it is also expected to promote democratic purposes.[1] While the former has dominated throughout this century, at various historical moments one or the other imperative may hold sway. In the 1960s, for example, social movements that promoted egalitarian principles and policies seemed to make headway over the forces that sought more direct linkages between schools and the needs of capital production and accumulation. The more recent period has witnessed the ascendency of conservative, business-oriented interests in educational debates about organization, policy, and the curriculum.

During the past century, this tension has resulted in public schooling in effect functioning as a "contested terrain." Conflicts over goals and practices have taken place not just within the corridors, meeting rooms, and classrooms of schools but outside of them as well. The history of educational debates in the United States has included the direct involvement not only of federal and state education officials, community school board members, teacher educators, school administrators, teachers, and parents, but also political and business leaders, conservative and liberal social reformers, and working-class, women, racial, and ethnic interest groups.[2] In varying ways, to differing extents, and with unequal results, all have sought to influence educational goals, school organization, and everyday teaching and curriculum.

The focus of this historical essay is between 1900 and 1920, a period when American society experienced a marked intensification of industrialization, immigration, urbanization, and bureaucratization. Widespread and rapid changes occurred in material conditions, ideologies, and culture. These were particularly critical years in the evolution of American education, a time when public schooling greatly expanded and commanded heightened attention from many segments of society. While elite groups sought to link the public school system more closely to an ideology based on social control and efficiency, others viewed it primarily as a viable and, in fact, crucial vehicle for social and economic reform. With the closing of the frontier and the growth of corporate business, schooling seemed to play an increasingly key role in American life, with regard not only to individual success but also to what American society was going to look like in the years ahead.[3]

The social ferment of the period in general also created the impetus and the opportunities for radical agitation. Socialist activists were generally optimistic that they could play a decisive role in the reconstruction of American life. As one former Socialist Party member later recollected, in 1912 "we all thought that socialism was around the corner."[4] Evidence at the time supported a somewhat optimistic perspective, as hundreds of radical activists won election to political office, thousands of skilled and unskilled laborers were recruited to allied political parties, unions and fraternal groups, and public questioning of traditional political and economic relations was widespread.[5]

Socialist contestation of dominant social relations took many forms during this time. Not only were there efforts to oppose existent practice but also attempts to construct an emergent culture that stressed new meanings and values.[6] Particularly noteworthy were the publication of several hundred radical newspapers and periodicals, in English and more than a dozen other languages, and the sponsorship of numerous debating, literary and dramatic clubs, choruses, libraries, street corner speeches, rallies, and parades. American Socialists also developed their own formal educational activities for adults, such as correspondence courses, lyceum lectures, local study classes, and schools such as the Rand School of Social Science in New York City and the Finnish Working People's College in Smithville, Minnesota. These educational ventures provided instruction in the nature of industrial capitalism, the class struggle, radical economics and philosophy, and subjects of more practical or cultural interest to workers (e.g., union organizing, public speaking, bookkeeping, shorthand, composition, English literature, and popular music).[7]

In an attempt to promote significant changes from within the democratic capitalist state, radicals also sought to become public school board members and school administrators and teachers. Between 1909 and 1911, for instance, more than 100 Socialist school officials were elected in small towns such as Muscatine, Iowa and Basin, Montana; in small cities such as Flint, Michigan and Berkeley, California; and in large cities such as Cincinnati, Ohio and Milwaukee, Wisconsin. At the same time, the Party established its own Socialist Teachers Bureau to help match radical teachers with sympathetic school administrators.[8] And in numerous articles, pamphlets, books, and speeches, Socialists and other radicals directly challenged the content and processes of the formal education provided by the state, which they increasingly viewed as in large part functioning to advance the interests of dominant (i.e., nonworking-class) groups in society. Finally, grass-roots radicals also organized their own educational and recreational activities for the children of working-class families, such as clubs, choruses, camps, picnics, parades, and the like. In the more formal and structured of these endeavors, Sunday schools, they created a body of curricula that opposed the dominant messages being transmitted in the public schools and by other social institutions.

This chapter focuses on two kinds of attempts by American Socialists during 1900 and 1920 to contest overtly mainstream school curriculum: their oral and written critiques of public schooling and, in more detail, their creation of alternative Sunday schools for children. This discussion is intended to address two general points. First, while school curriculum selection tends to be viewed as neutral and consensual, a close examination of our past reveals that serious challenges have been levied not only against that perspective of curriculum work but also against the particular arrangement of materials, values, and ideas that have dominated our public school practice. Second, a consideration of a specific body of knowledge that by and large has *not* found its way into mainstream curriculum-making might be helpful to those today who attempt to develop an emancipatory vision in the curriculum field, or what others have referred to as a "language of possibility."[9]

Socialist Critiques of Public School Curriculum

While support for the institution of public schooling remained strong among American Socialists at the turn of the century, a more critical perspective of the internal dynamics of public school classrooms also began to emerge. Many radical educational critics were clearly influenced by the critiques of schooling by proponents of progressive education. However, unlike child-centered advocates, Socialists linked the public schools more directly to their capitalistic character and maintained a primary focus on what they thought would be of most benefit to the country's millions of skilled and unskilled laborers. Moreover, classrooms were portrayed as not just teaching academic and social skills to individual children but preparing (or not preparing) groups of children for their role in the struggle to eliminate economic inequities and to establish a more democratic form of citizenship. Socialist critics thus outlined ways in which the public school curriculum was fostering not just passivity and uncritical thinking in general, but also a hierarchial division of mental and manual labor, a glorification of the profit motive, and the acceptance of such social conditions as poverty, unemployment, and union busting. In essence, schools were viewed not just in relation to the wider society but more specifically to the revolutionized society which Socialists sought to bring about.[10]

Radical educational critics of the time were becoming more aware that working-class viewpoints were being systematically eliminated from public schools when they stood in opposition to dominant capitalist interests. The political slant of school curriculum was hardly sympathetic to the forces of reform, let alone radical change, in American society.[11] This was especially the case in the emerging social studies field. For example, Socialist garment unions, such as the International Ladies' Garment Workers' Union (ILGWU) and the Amalgamated Clothing Workers of America (ACWA), complained that the public schools had "serious gaps," in particular with regard to an ignorance of the economic foundations of American life and of the existence and historical importance of such figures as Nat Turner, Mother Jones, and Eugene Debs. The valuable contributions of organized labor were ignored; schools seemed to be generally hostile to labor, often using it as a scapegoat for social problems. Terms such as *free enterprise* went unchallenged and unanalyzed despite the realities of the corporate structure.[12]

Socialist activists interested in educational issues urged fellow radicals to become more concerned about the school's role in educating future wage workers in "a habit of slavish obedience to the capitalist rule and of prejudice against the working-class movement." They argued that, "Socialists have need to watch schools where the minds of their children are in danger of being perverted to capitalist purposes."[13] Specific examples of public school teaching and administration drew the ire of local radical activists in many areas of the country. In 1902, the inculcation of militarism in public schools was condemned by the Social Democratic Party in Yonkers, New York. They protested the procurement of $1,100 by the local board of education to buy guns for the high school cadet corps, suggesting that the measure was a ploy to train students in the military spirit, in particular so that later they would be able and willing to help the state militia when called on to suppress strikes.[14] Similarly, a 1919 pageant at North Division High School in Milwaukee, Wisconsin, entitled "The Land of Opportunity," was severely criticized by local Socialists as "a vicious slam at organized labor . . . [that] holds up to the approval of the children the ideal of militarism." One father commented in amazement that "they would dare to attempt such a thing in a district of the city populated by the very working class they are seeking to insult."[15] Elizabeth Thomas, a Socialist school board member in Milwaukee, called for an official inquiry of the incident.[16] The Socialist-dominated Federated Trades Council (FTC) conducted its own investigation and found that the pageant represented "a disgraceful attempt to blacken the local labor movement in the eyes of the school children, many of them from working-class homes."[17] At issue in particular was the last of six scenes of the pageant. The previous five scenes depicted why people from other countries had emigrated to the United States; for example, because of religious persecution, military oppression, and heavy taxation. The FTC described the action of the sixth scene as follows:

> The last episode was devoted to the United States, but instead of presenting a land of opportunity, it was devoted to the labor question. As a prelude, several girls, dressed in black, called Frenzies and meant to represent discontent, came upon the stage and danced about, led by another figure dressed entirely in red, who was called License. Then Peace, all dressed in white and bearing an American flag, appeared and drove the Frenzies and License away. At this point labor came on the scene, labor being represented by a crowd of ill-dressed and hungry-looking workmen in the land of opportunity. A labor speaker stood upon a box and urged the men to commit violence, and another, called a loyal workman, answered him. The workmen became riotous, one of them shot another, and down the aisle from the front of the hall came a company of regulars, carrying guns. They rushed the stage, charged the workingmen at the point of bayonets, and the workmen crouched down at the back of the stage. A judge-like individual, who was called Law and Order, appeared and made a long speech over the body of the dead workmen, telling the workmen to be good and 'not to bite the hand that feeds them.' This ended the pageant.[18]

The public protests of Thomas, the FTC, and other local Socialists apparently "fell on deaf ears."[19]

Another dispute in Milwaukee centered around the schools' use of the *Current Events* newspaper. Socialist activists in New York City had earlier criticized the paper's "propagandistic" depiction of Bolshevik rule in Russia.[20] Editors of the socialist *Milwaukee Leader* complained that it was nothing more than "a staunch defender of the capitalist system [that] is systematically poisoning the minds of our children."[21] In the spring of 1920, the Rules Committee of the Milwaukee School Board, with two socialist members, voted 3-to-1 to ban *Current Events* from the local public schools, asserting that its articles were too partisan and antagonistic toward labor.[22] However, at a stormy monthly meeting of the entire school board, the committee's minority report, which claimed that the newspaper's perspective was simply "patriotic," was accepted by a 10-to-4 vote. Elizabeth Thomas commented: "It is quite amusing to talk of a free press when *Current Events*, with only one side of the story, is allowed to circulate in the schools. If the papers which give the other side were allowed in the schools, we could begin to talk of free speech."[23]

While radicals were clearly not hesitant to criticize individual teachers and administrators for activities with which they had serious disagreement, in general they did not portray individual school participants as primarily to blame. Just as it was not the fault of the individual worker when he or she failed to embrace the socialist cause, here too it was somehow "the system" that was to blame, that worked against the individual teacher (or worker) seeing the folly or evil of his or her ways. This reliance on "the system" and the "false consciousness" of individual participants to explain nonprogressive actions was summed up rather hyperbolically by Bruce Calvert:

> Most of them [teachers] know no better. They are themselves the ripe products of the system. They but do as they have been taught. They have never been asked or permitted to think. They have just blindly accepted what was fed to them and asked no questions for God's sake. Some, a very few, do know better. But they are about as potent as a grasshopper in the maw of an elephant to make any changes. They have to teach what they are told, at the cost of their jobs if they refuse. . . . All is cut and dried for them. They get their orders from the man higher up.[24]

Along with their criticisms of public schools, radical critics also suggested ways in which education might look different in a Socialist America. Scott Nearing, for instance, stressed the need to inculcate more of a sense of social morality along with individual morality, of social responsibility and cooperation rather than intense individualism and competition. William English Walling arqued for a curriculum informed by the need for fundamental social change.[25] Similarly, a 1917 editorial in the socialist *Milwaukee Leader* stressed the need

> to educate the child to make him a useful member of society. It is their [the Socialists'] purpose that the schools shall equip the children to cope with their environment and to bring out the best that is in them — not by grinding them through an educational mill as sausages are ground from a machine, but by giving the individual opportunity to develop to his fullest capacity in the direction that his talents are most promising. But in giving the individual opportunity, at the same time they recognize the need for cultivating the social consciousness and community spirit.[26]

37

Charles P. Steinmetz of Schenectady, New York, perhaps cut to the core of the socialist difference when he suggested that "under capitalism our children are taught that their main mission in life is to make a living," while "under Socialism they will be taught that the only thing worth working for or worth living for is to make this a better world to live in."[27] All children were capable of benefitting from an education guided by such a perspective. Thus, with implications for the emerging support for curriculum differentiation in the public schools, Nearing emphasized that although "the people cannot all be scholars," that in fact there was no necessity for that to be the case, "they can all be intelligent upon the great issues of life."[28] Another *Milwaukee Leader* editorial criticized the public school curriculum for being "dominated by the forces of standpattism and reaction[,] . . . by men and women who have the stocks-and-bonds outlook upon life." In contrast, "Socialists do not want to teach the children Socialism. They only want to teach them to think for themselves — to lead their minds out, which is the true meaning of education — and protect them from the deadening effects of prejudice and falsehood."[29]

This dilemma, perhaps a common one in radical educational theory, of teaching children to think for themselves at the same time as guarding against their learning of "prejudice and falsehood," was commonly left unexplored and sometimes even unrecognized. Moreover, Socialist educational critics appear to have embraced a rather mechanistic view of the relationship between capitalist economic relations and public educational practice. At the same time, however, they did adopt a less myopic and more democratic perspective of the social and political character of school curriculum than was the case for most other contemporary observers.

A Socialist Alternative: Sunday Schools for Working-Class Children

Although relatively few in number, some grass-roots radical activists sought to go beyond critiques of public schooling and general suggestions of what a socialist education might look like. With very little or no financial remuneration and with little tangible support from the national and state leaderships of the Socialist Party of America, they organized alternative educational experiences for working-class children. The most formal of these were two-hour weekend schools, most commonly referred to as Socialist Sunday Schools.[30] In these settings, children from radical working-class families, ages six to 14, were offered a curriculum intended to counter the overly competitive, individualistic, antiworking-class, nationalistic, and militaristic themes that seemed to prevail in contemporary public schools and other social institutions. These Sunday Schools represent another component of socialist contestation of mainstream American culture and curriculum.

Between 1900 and 1920, local Socialist activists established at least 100 English-speaking[31] Sunday Schools for children in 64 cities and towns in 20 states. The schools most prominently mentioned in newspaper and personal accounts were located in Boston, Haverhill, Brockton, Providence, Hartford, New York City, Newark, Rochester, Buffalo, Philadelphia, Pittsburgh, the District of Columbia, Cleveland, Chicago, Milwaukee, and Los Angeles. New York City had at least 14 different schools in operation during this 20-year period, Chicago had ten, and Milwaukee, Boston, Cleveland, Pittsburgh, and Providence each had at least three different schools.[32] Like the political movement from which they sprang, the Socialist Sunday Schools lacked uniformity, especially with regard to the facilities and materials they enjoyed. School enrollments also varied a great deal, no doubt reflecting differences in the size of communities, the strength of local radical movements, and the commitment of local socialists to educational as opposed to strictly political and economic ventures. Some "schools" really consisted of one or two classes, with fewer than ten children in each class. Such was the case initially for the school in Newport, Kentucky, which was organized in March 1909 with only five children but had 35 students and two teachers by the summer.[33] On the other end of the scale were schools in the Brownsville section of Brooklyn, with more than 600 children attending in 1917–18, and in Rochester, New York, with about 400 students in 1913–14.[34] The majority of schools had an enrollment of about 70 to 100 students. While some schools lasted for only one school year, most others lasted for several years. A few schools, particularly ones in New York City, remained in operation for a decade or more.

While such differences did exist, certain general patterns within the movement did emerge. Of course, all of the schools shared a profound sense of the ills of the capitalist system and of the need for Socialist transformation of American society, as well as the belief that such a perspective needed to be transmitted to youngsters in a formal educational setting. The schools were usually organized by members of the Socialist Party, both men and women (though predominantly the latter). They were secular in nature, meeting on Sundays because it was the only day off for many American workers at the time. (This made it more likely that parents could take young children to school and remain for adult classes, socialize, and participate in Sunday School activities). They also generally eschewed any ethnic identification, adopting the Socialist Party's approach in downplaying such differences for the sake of class solidarity.[35]

Participants cited three rationales in particular for the establishment of the Sunday schools. One was that the schools, albeit meeting only two hours each week, could play a key role in helping to counteract the growing influence of capitalist social institutions on working-class youth. Virtually all aspects of dominant culture were included in such arguments. For instance, Kendrick Shedd of the Rochester and Milwaukee schools lamented the extent to which "the young are being systematically 'doped' into a condition of insensibility toward the vital things of life. They are being base-ballized and funny-paperized and tangoized and pleasurized and motion-picturized until they have no thought of anything worth while [sic] in life."[36] Frances Gill of New York City referred to the public schools when she argued that, "It is inconceivable that the children of the workingmen should receive their only education and preparation for life from schools whose every interest is bound up in the maintenance and perpetuation of the instruments of their own oppression." It followed, then, that because "the educational system of the elementary schools is not adapted to the needs of the workingman's child, it should be supplemented by an organized effort to correct its faults of omission and commission."[37] Similarly, Helen Lowy of Chicago, Illinois, recounted how a principal spoke to night school students on the benefits of the Republican Party and, according to Lowy, closed with the hope that "you will all pray that Theodore Roosevelt will be elected." She concluded, "Thus it is that they teach our children in our public schools, and this influence we must counteract in our Socialist Sunday Schools."[38] The argument of another advocate illustrated the dialectical relationship between hegemonic culture and the forces of counterhegemony: she suggested that, "if the Public School system were what it should be there would be no need for Socialist [Sunday] Schools."[39]

A second, related rationale involved the role that the schools could play in helping to establish a sense of community and continuity within the radical movement at a time when generational differences in life experiences appeared to be growing. In the face of a multitude of influences geared to the contrary, the Sunday Schools could help to socialize the children of radical working-class families to form a lifelong commitment to Socialist principles and culture. While many informal ways existed to encourage an attachment to the radical community, for instance familial influences, Party local affairs, parades, clubs, and the like, proponents stressed the more systematic role that a formal weekend education for children could provide. The staff of the West Hoboken, New Jersey school, for example, expressed the concern that "a large percentage of children of Socialists and sympathizers are lost to the movement every year. The parents, either through inability to render the subject interesting or from some other cause, allow the children to go astray as a result of the patriotic teachings of the public schools or the influence of the capitalist press."[40] The Socialist Sunday Schools could be a first step in helping to prevent this kind of loss to the radical community. In turn, as Kendrick Shedd suggested, working in the Socialist school also had a salutary effect on the older comrades. He wrote: "They [the adults] grow in the process. They themselves become innoculated. They grow enthusiastic. They grow in spirit and in purpose. They renew their youth and light anew the slumbering fire. . . . They grow less crusty. Their heart beats a little faster. They are helping."[41] In dual ways, then, for the present and for the future, for adults and for children, the schools could help to foster a stronger Socialist community.

The third rationale was that the schools could help the children of radical, working-class families to attain a more intelligent understanding and appreciation of specific Socialist tenets and Socialist Party positions. Exactly what would constitute an appropriate education was not always made clear nor agreed upon. But the children would at least be exposed to a body of knowledge and a way of thinking that they would not receive formally elsewhere. As one observer put it, the children could at least be given "some elementary understanding of what the working class was fighting for."[42] The staff of the Los Angeles, California school announced their intention to provide the children with "a correct knowledge of history and economics."[43] And Esther F. Sussman of Hartford, Connecticut, reported that the children there were being taught "the fundamentals of scientific Socialism so that when they grow up they may be able to face and overcome the social problems of the day with intelligence and broadmindedness."[44]

Of course, the schools were never expected to offer a *complete* socialist education for youth, only a more formal and systematic one than could be provided at home and at other Party-sponsored activities. Yet despite the limitations of time, funding and staffing inherent in this alternative schooling movement, it did put together a perhaps surprisingly extensive body of curriculum materials. While considerable disagreement was evident among participants about the specific form that radical teaching should take and different methods did predominate in different schools, the curriculum as a whole consisted of lecture outlines; discussion questions; readers and magazines; poems, essays, and sayings for recitations; games and role-playing activities; field trips and nature hikes; guest speakers; flag drills; songs; and plays and pageants. The more successful schools made use of lesson topics, questions, recitations, song cards, and dramatic scripts that were locally developed and professionally printed. Other schools depended more heavily on other socialist and nonsocialist sources, such as the *Young Socialists' Magazine* and the anthropological books of Katherine Dopp, or had to adapt lessons from more adult-oriented materials, such as Walter Thomas Mills' *The Struggle For Existence*.[45] But in all schools, it was hoped that the children could receive a systematic education guided by a social vision that seemed to be sorely missing from the public schools.

Alternative Curriculum Themes from the Socialist Perspective

These schools were closely allied with a political movement that in large part defined issues affecting the quality of life and the possibilities of change in terms of the processes and structures of the social system. It is hardly surprising, then, that much of the curriculum of the Socialist Sunday Schools was what would be thought of today as "social studies." As Kendrick Shedd stressed, "Anything that concerns the conditions under which human beings live is of interest to us."[46] In a general sense, the schools focused on the development of "social awareness" and, as William F. Kruse of the Party's Young People's Office noted, on the will and desire of students to "work as well as talk for their ideal."[47] More specific themes were also present and provide a more concrete indication of the contested messages of these Socialist schools. While some were emphasized more and taught more directly than others, they each represented a significant element of Socialist teaching. Although not easily separated from each other, 12 major themes can be highlighted.

The first curricular theme involved the concept of "the abstract individual." Michael Apple recently described this individualism as related to the fact that "our sense of community is withered at its roots. We find ways of making the concrete individual into an abstraction and, at the same time, we divorce the individual from larger social movements which might give meaning to 'individual' wants, needs, and visions of justice."[48] Socialist curriculum materials were infused with a perspective emphasizing the place of the individual in the social world, and the interdependence of the individual with countless others, especially workers. Such was the case, for instance, when teachers and students from the Omaha, Nebraska school took trips to local manufacturing plants in 1904. Bertha Mailly, then a teacher at the school (and who later helped initiate schools in Boston, Massachusetts and New York City), discussed with the children how one guide at a shoe factory told the children proudly about the work of the machines without any reference to the laborers in the plant. Mailly made a point of stressing the children's debt to such unknown workers for the shoes that they wore.[49]

A second theme integrated into the Socialist Sunday School curriculum involved an emphasis on the students being conscious and proud of being a part of the working-class community. The dignity of labor (if not all laborers) was often stressed and virtually every social problem was viewed primarily from the perspective of its effect on workers. Moreover, class struggle, rather than class compromise, was suggested as the effective strategy for workers to follow. This theme was imparted, for instance, in a series of lessons developed by Bertha Fraser of Brooklyn.[50] Her course of study included three lessons devoted "to a comparison between the working class and the idle class: first, in connection with food; second, clothing; and last the homes." A follow-up lesson focused on "the cause of the contrast — the unequal distribution of the products due to the exploitation of labor, and the consequent suffering of the working class." The last two lessons dealt "with the remedy and how it is to be applied."

Cooperative and collectivist rather than competitive and privatized economic relations was a third theme of this curriculum. Lesson materials focused on the nature and advantages of public ownership and management of industry at a time when public ownership of utilities was considered a radical demand. This sense of cooperation and collectivism was in fact broadly applied, so that "working together" in a variety of ways was viewed not only as a key to working-class success in contesting the capitalist system but also to more equitable and congenial social relations. Thus, an entire year's curriculum for a Milwaukee school was guided by the general theme of "cooperation in everyday life."[51] Thirty-one lessons comprised this course of study, including the following lesson topics: Playing Together; Keeping Well Together; Learning Together; Owning Together; Being World Citizens Together; Governing Together; Judging Together; Investing Together; Owning Books Together; Rejoicing Together; Running a Newspaper Together; Building Together; and Running Industry Together. Role-playing activities (although they were not referred to as such), accompanied by discussion questions, played a prominent part in the lessons. Plans for the initial lesson on "Singing Together," for example, looked like this:

1. Let a number of children try to sing different songs at the same time. Then the same song starting at different times. Then the same song starting together but at different pitches. Then end with utter confusion and shouting and disorder.
2. Dismiss children to go to the classes. Class hints: What was the trouble? Shall we stop singing altogether? Why not? How shall we have good singing? What is needed to sing together? Why not have each sing alone?
3. School reassembles. Superintendent reminds school of disorder at beginning of lesson. Any suggestions for better way of doing things? Children will volunteer results of class period. A number of children will then try to sing together in orderly manner. More are added. Finally the whole school together gives everyone a chance to take part, each helping the other, and results in harmony and good feeling. Singing separately in competition gives only one or two a chance, while the majority must remain silent, or results in disorder and confusion and noise. Let us sing together.[52]

The fourth theme was internationalism, the sense of viewing oneself as inextricably linked to the interests of others (i.e., workers) in other nations. Correspondence with schools and youth clubs in other countries was carried out not just to gather information but also to encourage a linkage with radical political movements abroad. International songs and flags were a part of the lessons at most schools. In 1913, for example, a flag drill at the Rochester Socialist Sunday School included the following recitation by a group of students: "To the Cause of the World-Workers, and of International Solidarity and Brotherhood, Symbolized by this Crimson Banner, We Hereby Dedicate Our Strength, Our Hopes, and Our Lives!" A "parade of nations" followed, with Socialist vote tallies from different nations written on the front of cards that the children carried.[53] Rather than discouraging this emphasis, World War I intensified the schools' focus on the international character of a successful Socialist movement. Future workers in the United States needed to realize that workers in other countries shared a common enemy, the capitalist system, and a common aim, its overthrow.

The related fifth theme was antimilitarism, especially during the middle years of the second decade when the European conflict started and the United States massed troops along the Mexican border. This was associated with what David S. Greenberg of New York City referred to as "anti-sham patriotism."[54] Militarist adventures were viewed as primarily hurting the lives of workers (who had to fight in such endeavors), breaking down a feeling of internationalism, and taking attention and funds away from domestic needs. Illustrating this perspective are the first and last verses of a song written by Kendrick Shedd and used in Rochester and Milwaukee schools and no doubt in others as well. It is entitled "War What For?":

In this here song we sing of war, war, war, war,
We know too well what it is for, for, for, for
In war the working men they kill, kill, kill, kill
So that the rich their coffers fill, fill, fill, fill.

I never would a soldier be, be, be, be
Unless it were to make men free, free, free, free
If they will call me a traitor, if I won't be shot,
I'd rather be a traitor than a patriot![55]

The sixth theme involved a revisionist interpretation of history, economics, and sociology. Socialist Sunday School children were exposed to lessons that transformed traditional social studies content so that the laboring class was perceived as an instrumental motor for social progress. Heroes and heroines whose birthdays were celebrated in the pages of the *Young Socialists'*

Magazine included William Lloyd Garrison, Susan B. Anthony, William Morris, Karl Marx, Mother Jones, Eugene Debs, and other national and international social critics and activists. Socialist agitators were portrayed not as a lunatic fringe of bombthrowers but rather as the only hope for workers to significantly improve their lot. The plight of the poor was viewed not as the result of defective skills or character on the part of the individual but rather primarily caused by capitalist economics. This latter aspect was expressed in an essay entitled "Why Men Are As They Are," written by Abraham Jacobson, an 11-year-old student at a New York City school:

> In the capitalist system it cannot be different, because most children, instead of educating themselves, go to work and work all their lives from early morning till late at night. When they are married and have children they hardly have time to see their children, because they go to work while their children sleep, and when they come home it is the same. Some men work seven days out of a week to make some kind of a poor living. When these men meet by some chance, with their friend, they are afraid to tell him the truth about their work, because their friend might go up to the boss and work for cheaper wages than his friend did. In this way people cannot be kind, true, or honest.[56]

The seventh theme involved the study of anthropology and in particular the evolution of the human race, with an emphasis on the progress of people from the Stone Age to the Iron Age to feudalism to capitalism, with the logical next step in "the struggle for existence" being socialism. It was an optimistic message, and one that embraced a liberal notion of progress, but it subverted conventional teaching by positing the necessity and inevitability of a next, socialistic stage of human civilization. Anthropological accounts were further guided not so much by a sense of how "primitive" early people were but by the cooperative and collective spirit that had stood them well, a spirit that was portrayed as "natural" to humankind but suppressed by capitalist social relations. According to one school participant, the goals of such lessons were also "to show the child that change and adaptation are ever universal," and to foster "the general principle to go from old to new, from simple to complex, from concrete to abstract, to appeal to the imagination."[57]

Social equity was the eighth theme of the Socialist Sunday School curriculum. The materials generally adopted the political vision of most Socialist Party members that class struggle was preeminent, that is, that racial and sexual inequities could not be fully addressed until the capitalist organization of society was eradicated. Economic interests were viewed as decisive throughout history and "wage slavery" was the condition that in particular needed to be the focus. True equality of opportunity meant that workers had to have the same advantages in life as managers and owners, that, in essence, wage slavery had to be eliminated. Adequate levels of food, clothing, and shelter were viewed as the most basic concerns of human life, from the beginning of civilization to the present, with only a socialistic society being able to guarantee that all individuals would not suffer from the want of them.

The ninth theme focused on specific social problems. In fact, many of the lesson outlines represent a kind of social problems approach more than they do the direct teaching of socialist principles. What differentiated the social problems approach of these socialist teachers from other educators was their consistent emphasis on poverty, unemployment, unhealthy and unsafe work conditions, child labor, alcoholism, poor housing and sanitary facilities, the despoliation of nature, disease, and the like being endemic to industrial capitalism. Social problems were not viewed as isolated phenomena that could be individually attacked and resolved by well-meaning reformers but rather as integral features of capitalist America. For instance, in the "Slums, Sweatshops, Sickness and Disease" lesson from the "Home Destroyers" series that was used by the Rochester school, students learned that there could be "no true homes for workers while Capitalism robs them of health, time, comforts, life." In another lesson that focused on "Divorce," attention was placed on the economic pressures that made it difficult for spouses to stay together (e.g., "What drives people to divorce? If homes were 'sweet' would there be so many divorces? Is divorce a matter of religion or economics?")[58] Aiming "to develop the children into useful citizens" at the Third Assembly District Socialist Sunday School in the Bronx thus did not refer merely to voting and participating in uncontroversial social service activities. It meant helping to bring about the eradication of serious social problems in the only way that could be effective, by agitating for the end of capitalism.[59]

The tenth theme of the socialist curriculum also placed considerable emphasis on the everyday conditions of workers' lives and sought to expand the children's awareness and appreciation for the need for good hygiene, healthy diets, proper exercise, safety, nature outings, and so forth. The emphasis here was on public health: concern for these aspects of everyday life was not just for the benefit of the individual but also for the community. After all, sickness can spread to others, nature can be enjoyed by others, and it is the responsibility of everyone not just for themselves but for others to learn to take care of these matters. Such aspects would frequently be linked to other, more political concerns. This can be seen in a recitation performed by students in Rochester and Buffalo (and probably elsewhere as well), entitled "We Want":

We want more of sunshine and air;
We want less of worry and care.
We want every joy for each girl and boy,
And we want for each mortal his share.

We want all the best of the Earth;
We want more of pleasure and mirth.
We want all the best and we want the rest,
And we want all the value we're worth.

We want to be well and to know,
We want for good health a fair show,
We want to be bright and we long for light,
And we all want to live and to grow.

We want of the world full control,
We'll have nothing less than the whole,
All value we make the whole we'll take,
And the time to develop the soul.

The eleventh theme involved the presentation of the Cooperative Commonwealth as potentially embracing the ideal conditions of human life. Such a socialist society would feature public ownership and management of industry and social property, economic equality, the elimination of prejudice, and more healthy and equitable living conditions and personal relations. Associated with this focus was the notion that Socialism should in fact be identified with "happiness." This was used as an argument for augmenting the curriculum, so that in many schools lectures and recitations were accompanied by games, trips, concerts, pageants, picnics, and the like. If the children had fun, they would think of being part of a socialist community as an enjoyable experience. Of course, even children's games could be instilled with a radical message. For instance, a former student of the Los Angeles school remembers that games such as "Tag" and "Tug of War" were given "worker versus boss" interpretations.[61]

Finally, the Socialist Sunday School curriculum sought to instill a generally critical approach to everyday life, dominated as it was by capitalist social institutions. Public schools, for example, were not portrayed as politically neutral and the children were taught not to accept at face value what was being taught in them. While no one recommended that the children outrightly reject the messages and practices of the public schools while they were there, the entire content of this alternative curriculum was intended to reveal that if "truths" existed, and they certainly did for these Socialists, they would not necessarily be found in mainstream social institutions.

It was not just a matter of focusing on different heroes and different interpretations of important events. In some lessons, alternative notions of everyday concepts were also considered. At the Rochester school, discussion questions about "justice," for example, were developed by Kendrick Shedd and comprised part of the 1912–13 curriculum:

47

Is competition just?
Do the workers get justice?
Have we political justice?
Name some instances of political injustice.
Are these things just:
    Child wage workers?
    Mothers employed outside of their homes?
    Use of militia to settle strikes?
    War? Capitalist courts? Capitalist press?
    Suppression of Free Speech and Assemblage?
What is justice?[62]

Shedd's lessons were thus intended to begin with a discussion that related the general topic to contemporary social conditions and to then conclude with a definitional question. Children were encouraged to view commonsensical everyday notions critically and then, in the light of the unsatisfactory nature of prevailing views, to adopt alternative perspectives of them. What might be considered abstract philosophical constructs were linked to the unequal relations of social life, in particular as they are experienced by the working class.

While this has not been an exhaustive discussion of Socialist children's schools, it should serve to highlight their major organizational features and their specific curricular themes. Of course, this oppositional educational movement never really had much of an opportunity to develop its principles and practices beyond a limited amount of time and a limited school setting. The momentum for organizing Sunday Schools essentially disappeared during the split in the radical movement and repressive political climate from 1918 to 1921. Still, the character of this educational movement was noteworthy for its overt challenge to the values and ideas that predominated in the public schools. Perhaps the central difference of this Socialist curriculum was summarized in 1910 by Sadie Lindenberg, a student at a Socialist Sunday School in Brooklyn. She described what she was learning this way:

> Not alone has it broadened my outlook on all questions connected with life in general, but it has also caused me to view with kindred feeling the sufferings of all less fortunate than myself.
>
> The Social [sic] school has taught me to distinguish more clearly the difference between government as it is and as it should be. It has taught me to be useful to all people, to be a useful member of the community, taking an absorbing interest in all things that concern the welfare of all its members. Thus you see that the Social school has taken me from the drift, as it were, and educated me to feel the impulses of affectionate interest in all things pertaining to the welfare and good of all people.[63]

Conclusion

The primary intent of this historical essay has been to illuminate the very existence of past contestation, not so much the reasons why the groups and individuals discussed are among the "losers" in the struggle for the American curriculum. That Socialist Sunday School advocates were not the victors can be explained in large part with reference to the demise of the political movement with which they strongly attached themselves. But maybe we should not be too certain of their defeat. While we cannot reasonably posit some future triumph of their educational ideas and practices, perhaps things might have looked quite different if their efforts had never taken place.

The question naturally arises of whether this examination of past contestation matters at all for current curriculum theory and practice. Clearly, the Socialists developed a critical perspective and a body of lesson materials and activities that should not be adopted directly as a critical pedagogy today. It would be somewhat ridiculous to expect otherwise, considering that this work took place more than 65 years ago, when public ownership of utilities and unemployment insurance were considered radical demands and when progressive educational ideas were first being widely discussed. Moreover, the character of the Socialist curriculum itself is perhaps deficient. For example, there is a serious devaluing of other social categories of domination besides class, most notably gender and race; although the social vision embedded in the materials stresses critique, cooperation, and collectivism, the activities planned for the children are lacking in opportunities for creative self-expression, self-criticism, and collaboration; and while to be congratulated for emphasizing the significance of material relations in our everyday lives, the focus is overly economistic. Moreover, it perhaps represents more of a curriculum for Socialist children than a Socialist curriculum for children. That is, while the children did not all come from Socialist families, their backgrounds were predominantly working class and politically radical. There was never the necessity to develop a full-blown educational theory that was fully cognizant of the nature of childhood learning and that could accommodate the diversity and lack of progressive politics that mark the general community of school children.

But there are two related claims to consider here. First, Socialist contestation of mainstream curriculum, as represented in their critiques of public schooling and their Sunday School curriculum, perhaps do offer hints of "really [or critically] useful knowledge" for children from which to draw upon. This idea of "really useful knowledge" has a long history in radical circles, dating back to the efforts of radical working-class educational associations in early nineteenth century England. Drawing on the work of Richard

Johnson, the American Socialist Sunday School curriculum can be viewed as having addressed three aspects of this conception of educational knowledge.[64] First, it encouraged the children to have pride in their working-class backgrounds and to view their subordinate status as shared and systematic, thus creating a sense of solidarity with others from the same social class. Second, it utilized the everyday concerns of workers' lives to elaborate on the social problems that many people face and the relationship between these problems and the character of contemporary society. Third, it focused on the need for fundamental social change and, more specifically, comprehensive strategies to overcome effectively the hardships and sense of powerlessness that oppressed groups experience.

While the Socialist Sunday School curriculum is seriously outdated and even wrongheaded in some ways, even for those sympathetic to its central focuses on equality and justice, it did attempt to include these three features of really (or critically) useful knowledge. Perhaps a modified version of this curriculum can help to guide current attempts to construct lesson ideas and activities that emphasize more equitable social and economic relations. The Socialist alternative certainly provides new meaning to the commonplace overall goal of social studies instruction, that is, the promotion of "good citizenship."

More generally, a serious consideration of past contestation can perhaps help to clarify the political nature of school curriculum development. The fundamentally political character of curriculum refers not only to the fact that some involved in the curriculum selection process have more power to decide matters than others; but also to the realization that school knowledge is tied to issues of cultural and economic reproduction. Indeed, if the messages of the Socialists seem overly propagandistic or political in tone, it may only be because they are not the usual ones we have come to expect in schools. For instance, learning in a public school to invest in the stock market is as much an act of advocacy as learning in a Socialist school to pool one's resources in cooperative ventures. And while our public schools do not sing about "The Red Flag" or portray corporate capitalists as inhumane individuals motivated primarily by greed, they do have ultra-patriotic essay contests sponsored by the Daughters of the American Revolution (DAR), the singing of the militarist "Star Spangled Banner," the staging of playlets about the first Thanksgiving that offer little mention of how the colonists treated Native Americans, and many other instances of lessons that are steeped in "propagandistic" overtones. Recently, there has also emerged an "Adopt-A-School" program that encourages local businesses (e.g., banks, real estate firms, energy companies) to supply supplementary materials and support for local public schools. While it is clear that the current fiscal crisis in school funding is the immediate impetus for such a program, what may be less clear to school participants are the ideological nature and possible pedagogical ramifications of such a venture. To what extent, for example, might product advertising be taught as nutrition education, the benefits of nuclear energy as energy education, industry public relations as environmental education, and corporate promotion as economics education?[65] And whose interests would be primarily served by such instruction?

The Socialists discussed in this chapter were not the elite theorists and organizers of the Socialist Party. But they knew full well, more than 60 years ago, that schooling is in part a decidedly political enterprise, that school reform is not just an educational process but a political one as well. In essence, the question in teaching is not whether to advocate or not, but the nature and extent of one's advocacy. The question is not whether to encourage a particular social vision in the classroom but what kind of social vision it will be. The efforts of American Socialists during the Progressive Era help to underscore the political nature of schooling, reminding people then and now that what is taught is not necessarily reality but a *particular* version of it.

Herbert Kliebard observed almost two decades ago that to many curriculum developers and researchers there seems to be "something anomalous and perhaps even subversive about attempting to see the field of curriculum in some kind of historical perspective."[66] In a way, perhaps a reason for this is because in the historical perspective, alternatives to current practice become known and clarified. This can only muddy the waters of fortifying the present arrangements of economic and cultural power. An awareness of past contestation of American curriculum work can thus reveal not only the inherently political nature of dominant educational practice but also concrete alternatives to it. It may further help us to better understand the possibilities of transformation and, perhaps most importantly, the possibilities within people.[67] In an age wrought with pessimism and cynicism, this may indeed be a considerable achievement for which to strive.

Notes

1. Martin Carnoy and Henry M. Levin, *Schooling and Work in the Democratic State* (Stanford, Calif.: Stanford University Press, 1985).

2. See, for example, William J. Reese, *Power and the Promise of School Reform: Grass-Roots Movements During the Progressive Era* (Boston: Routledge and Kegan Paul, 1986).

3. See, for example, Howard Zinn, *A People's History of the United States* (New York: Harper and Row, 1980); David F. Noble, *America By Design* (New York: Alfred A. Knopf, 1977); Richard L. Ehrlich, ed., *Immigrants in Industrial America, 1850–1920* (Charlottesville: University Press of Virginia, 1977); David

B. Tyack, *The One Best System* (Cambridge, Mass.: Harvard University Press, 1976); Joel H. Spring, *Education and the Corporate State* (Boston: Beacon Press, 1972); James Weinstein, *The Corporate Ideal in the Liberal State, 1900–1918* (Boston: Beacon Press, 1968); and Robert Wiebe, *The Search For Order, 1877–1920* (New York: Hill and Wang, 1967).

4. Quoted in Betty Yorburg, *Utopia and Reality: A Collective Portrait of American Socialists* (New York: Columbia University Press, 1969), p. 11.

5. See, for example, Mari Jo Buhle, *Women and American Socialism, 1870–1920* (Urbana: University of Illinois Press, 1981); James R. Green, *Grass-Roots Socialism: Radical Movements in the Southwest, 1895–1943* (Baton Rouge: Louisiana State University Press, 1978); Bruce M. Stave, ed., *Socialism and the Cities* (Port Washington, N. Y.: Kenikat Press, 1975); James Weinstein, *The Decline of Socialism in America, 1912–1925* (New York: Vintage Books, 1969); David A. Shannon, *The Socialist Party of America* (Chicago: Quadrangle Books, 1955); and Lillian Symes and Travers Clement, *Rebel America* (New York: Harper and Bros., 1934).

6. The notion of "emergent culture" is discussed in Raymond Williams, *Marxism and Literature* (Oxford: Oxford University Press, 1977).

7. An examination of socialist educational activities for adults is contained in Kenneth Teitelbaum, "Schooling for 'Good Rebels': Socialist Education for Children in the United States, 1900–1920" (unpublished Ph.D. dissertation, University of Wisconsin–Madison, 1985), pp. 120–139.

8. "Socialist Elective Officials — United States," in the *Socialist Party of America Papers*, microfilm edition (Glen Rock, N. J.: Microfilming Corporation of America, 1975), reel 6; and miscellaneous reports, in *ibid.*, reel 76.

9. Stanley Aronowitz and Henry A. Giroux, *Education Under Siege: The Conservative, Liberal, and Radical Debate Over Schooling* (South Hadley, Mass.: Bergin and Garvey Publishers, Inc., 1985).

10. See, for example, Joseleyne Slade Tien, "The Educational Theories of American Socialists, 1900–1920" (unpublished Ph.D. dissertation, Michigan State University, 1972), p. 92.

11. For documentation of antireform sentiments in nineteenth century school textbooks, see Ruth M. Elson, *Guardians of Tradition: American Schoolbooks in the Nineteenth Century* (Lincoln: University of Nebraska Press, 1964).

12. Robert Joseph Schaefer, "Educational Activities of the Garment Unions, 1890–1948" (unpublished Ph.D. dissertation, Columbia University, 1951), pp. 5–9.

13. *The Worker*, October 6, 1901.

14. *The Worker*, January 12, 1902.

15. *Milwaukee Leader*, November 19, 1919.

16. *Milwaukee Leader*, December 27, 1919.

17. *Milwaukee Leader*, January 23, 1920.

18. *Ibid.*

19. *Ibid.*

20. *New York Call,* October 28, 1919.

21. *Milwaukee Leader,* March 7, 1921.

22. *Milwaukee Leader,* May 27, 1920.

23. *Milwaukee Leader,* June 2, 1920.

24. *New York Call,* August 19, 1917. For a critical (and, I think, somewhat distorted) interpretation of the Socialists' tendency to take a condescending view of workers, see Aileen S. Kraditor, *The Radical Persuasion: Aspects of the Intellectual History and the Historiography of Three American Radical Organizations* (Baton Rouge: Louisiana State University Press, 1981).

25. Joselyne Slade Tien, *op. cit.,* pp. 131–32.

26. *Milwaukee Leader,* March 5, 1917.

27. *Appeal to Reason,* August 8, 1914.

28. Scott Nearing, *A Nation Divided (or Plutocracy Versus Democracy)* (Chicago: Socialist Party of the United States, 1920).

29. *Milwaukee Leader,* March 19, 1923.

30. Although most of the schools were called *Sunday Schools,* several of them were actually known by other names, such as the Children's Socialist Lyceum in Los Angeles and the Arm and Torch League in Cincinnati. No doubt local factors at particular times encouraged the adoption of different names. But all the schools referred to as *Socialist Sunday Schools* in this chapter were basically considered as such at the time.

31. There were at least as many non-English speaking radical (usually socialist) weekend children's schools established by radical groups from the German, Jewish, Finnish, and other ethnic communities. Schools which used a language other than English are not included in this analysis. Their characters (e.g., curriculum) were slightly different with regard to their ethnic identification. For more on these other schools, see Kenneth Teitelbaum, *op. cit.,* pp. 305–37. For a detailed discussion of anarchist schools for children in the United States, see Paul Avrich, *The Modern School Movement: Anarchism and Education in the United States* (Princeton, N. J.: Princeton University Press, 1980).

32. For a listing of the locations of most of the Socialist Sunday Schools, see Kenneth Teitelbaum and William J. Reese, "American Socialist Pedagogy and Experimentation in the Progressive Era: The Socialist Sunday School" *History of Education Quarterly,* 23 (Winter 1983), p. 439.

33. *Socialist Woman,* 2 (September 1909), p. 9; and *Progressive Woman,* 3(October 1909)14.

34. *New York Call,* November 17, 1917 and March 7, 1918; and "Rochester Socialist Sunday School Scrapbooks, Vols. II and III," in the *Kendrick Philander Shedd Papers,* located at the University of Rochester, Rush Rhees Library, Rochester, N. Y. (Henceforth, this collection will be referred to as *Shedd Papers.*)

35. The nature of the Socialist Sunday Schools is discussed at greater length in Kenneth Teitelbaum, *op. cit.*

36. *Milwaukee Leader*, January 19, 1915.

37. *The Worker*, January 26, 1907.

38. Helen Lowy, "The Importance of Socialist Sunday Schools," *Progressive Woman*, 4(December 1910)15.

39. *New York Call*, April 7, 1912.

40. *New York Call*, October 2, 1910. Socialist youth activists rarely considered the possibility that some children, especially those who were able to attain a more middle-class lifestyle as they grew older, "went astray" simply because they found the socialist message presented to them to be unpersuasive.

41. *New York Call*, July 25, 1915.

42. Oakley C. Johnson, *The Day Is Coming: Life and Work of Charles E. Ruthenberg* (New York: International Publishers, 1957), p. 47.

43. *Progressive Woman*, 3(December 1909)14.

44. *Young Socialists' Magazine*, 4(September 1911)15.

45. For a discussion of Dopp (who had been a student of John Dewey's at the University of Chicago) and her books (which were published by Rand McNally and Company), see Kenneth Teitelbaum, "The Construction of Alternative School Text: Teaching the ABCs of Socialism to Children, 1900–1920," unpublished paper presented at the annual meeting of the American Educational Research Association, Washington, D. C., April 1987. See also Walter Thomas Mills, *The Struggle For Existence* (Chicago: International School of Social Economy, 1904).

46. *New York Call*, June 20, 1915.

47. William F. Kruse, "Socialist Education For Children," *Young Socialists' Magazine*, 11(March 1917)9–10.

48. Michael W. Apple, *Ideology and Curriculum* (London: Routledge & Kegan Paul, 1979), p. 9.

49. *The Worker*, January 24, 1904.

50. Bertha Matthews Fraser, *Outlines of Lessons for Socialist Schools for Children* (New York: Children's Socialist Schools Committee of Local Kings County, Socialist Party, 1910).

51. Lesson outlines for this course of study were published throughout the 1917–18 school year in the *Milwaukee Leader*.

52. *Milwaukee Leader*, September 29, 1917.

53. "Rochester Socialist Sunday School Scrapbooks, Vol. IV," *Shedd Papers*.

54. David S. Greenberg, *Socialist Sunday School Curriculum* (New York: The Socialist Schools Publishing Association, 1913).

55. *New York Call*, May 13, 1913.

56. *The Worker*, July 20, 1907.

57. *New York Call*, March 21, 1913. See also Bertha H. Mailly, "Socialist Schools," *Unity of Labor*, 1 (April 1911?), pp.10–1. Katherine Dopp's books were used for just such purposes.

58. "Rochester Socialist Sunday School Scrapbooks, Vol. II," *Shedd Papers*.

59. *New York Call*, December 6, 1918.

60. "Rochester Socialist Sunday School Scrapbooks, Vol. II," *Shedd Papers*.

61. Peggy Dennis, "The Twenties," *Cultural Correspondence*, 6–7(Spring 1978)84.

62. "Rochester Socialist Sunday School Scrapbooks, Vol. II," *Shedd Papers*.

63. *New York Call*, May 8, 1910.

64. Richard Johnson, "'Really useful knowledge': radical education and working-class culture, 1790–1848," in John Clarke, Chas Critcher, and Richard Johnson, eds., *Working Class Culture: Studies in History and Theory* (London: Hutchinson, 1979), pp. 75–102. Also see Stanley Aronowitz and Henry A. Giroux, *op. cit.*, pp. 157–58.

65. Sheila Harty, *Hucksters in the Classroom: A Review of Industry Propaganda in Schools* Washington D. C.: Center for Study of Responsive Law, 1979).

66. Herbert M. Kliebard, "The Curriculum Field in Retrospect," in Paul W. F. Witt, ed., *Technology and the Curriculum* (New York: Teachers College Press, 1968), pp. 69–70.

67. See interview with E. P. Thompson, in Henry Abelove, Betsy Blackmar, Peter Dimock, and Jonathan Schneer, eds., *Visions of History* (New York: Pantheon Books, 1984), p. 16.

FOUR

What Goes On in Classrooms?
Is This the Way We Want It?

Kenneth A. Sirotnik

Considerable time and energy have been expended on developing the formal curriculum of American schooling as though this curriculum would have some impact on or connection with what goes on in public school classrooms. Reams of paper and countless hours of staff time at state and district levels, for example, go into the development and dissemination of curriculum guides that set forth educational philosophy statements and general goals and, to varying degrees, the specific objectives, learning activities, teaching strategies, and assessment procedures, which, taken as a whole, comprise a general definition of *curriculum*.[1] Periodically, chunks of time are also spent by national commissions reviewing the current state of education and developing similar agendas of expectations for schools. Other segments of the community (business groups, social agencies, parents, etc.) also contribute, directly or indirectly, to the formal curriculum through school boards, task forces, surveys, and so forth.

Much in the way of human and material resources, then, underlie the architecture of curriculum and, therefore, underlie what I refer to as *curricular expectations*. For example, the goal statement, "To develop students' capacities to be critical and creative thinkers," establishes several curricular expectations for the ways in which teachers might interact with students, students might interact with each other, content and activities might be organized, student learning might be evaluated, and so forth. The goal statement, "To develop students' mental capabilities to store and retrieve information and follow instructions for the use of information," establishes several curricular expectations that probably overlap very little with those for the previous goal statement. This chapter focuses on the juxtaposition of our expectations for schooling with what, in fact, appears to be happening in classrooms across the United States.

The authors of Chapters 2 and 3 of this volume have made it clear that curriculum proposals have not been entirely uniform over the history of public schooling. Indeed, perhaps the only uniform trend in these expectations has been the swinging back and forth of the curriculum pendulum between the "hard" and "soft," between "back-to-the-basics education" and "progressive education," between "meritocratic" and "democratic" notions of educational "excellence" and "equity." Notwithstanding the more specific, substantive concerns of these competing curricular visions, the pendulum appears to be driven largely by political/ideological constellations of values, beliefs, and human interests.[2] On the one hand are those who see schools as benign agents of socialization, as places where the Mannian and Jeffersonian notions of preparing all the nation's youth both to serve and reap the benefits of their society are played out. On the other hand are those who see schools as malignant agents of social control, as convenient places where society can reproduce racist, classist, and sexist attitudes and socioeconomic stratifications. To be sure, characterizing schooling (and the implied curriculum) in such polarized terms tends to overlook other important sources of disagreement. Kliebard, for example, notes at least three "currents of curriculum reform" counter to the liberal arts/humanist tradition of curriculum in the nineteenth century: the social efficiency emphasis on training students for their future; the child study emphasis on development and growth; and the social reconstructionist emphasis on building a new and better social order.[3]

My point here, however, is not to develop a definitive taxonomy of curricular tensions, but simply to emphasize their existence both historically and currently. These tensions, however categorized, comprise what Goodlad, Klein, and Tye call the *ideological* domain of curriculum.[4] But, as these authors point out, additional domains must be described and interpreted if one wishes to engage in a thorough curriculum inquiry.[5] For example, what curriculum does one see upon inspecting the written curriculum guides at state and district levels referred to above? What one sees in this *formal* curriculum is not surprising considering the history of crosscurrents in the ideological curriculum. As Boyer and Goodlad both noted in their recent reports on schooling, "we want it all"—the academic/intellectual, career/vocational, social, and personal functions of schooling.[6]

Consider the way these functions have been manifested in general goal statements for schooling. In *A Study of Schooling*, for example, we found that teachers, parents, and students from elementary through secondary levels rated all four goal areas above an average 3.5 rating on a 4-point scale of importance.[7] Even when these respondents were forced to choose between the four goal areas, consensus was not obtained on any one of them. In Table 1, we can see that although "intellectual development" is usually the most-emphasized apparent (what seems to go on) or ideal (what ought to go on) function, a substantial number of persons viewed other functions to be of primary importance. Note, for example, the shift in primary importance from intellectual development to the other functions as the respondents shift from the apparent to the ideal perspectives. These data—part of the *perceived* curriculum domain— anticipate the main theme to follow—*viz.*, what people want is considerably more broad than what goes on (and what is perceived to go on or experienced) in schools and classrooms.

TABLE 1
Teacher, Parent and Student Views of the Single Most Emphasized Apparent and Ideal Functions of Schooling[a]

| | | Function | | | | | | | |
| | | Intellectual | | Social | | Personal | | Vocational | |
Level & Data Source	N[b]	Apparent	Ideal	Apparent	Ideal	Apparent	Ideal	Apparent	Ideal
Elementary									
Teachers	278	78.5	48.9	12.2	14.0	6.1	33.5	3.2	3.5
Parents	1653	68.9	57.6	13.6	9.3	11.4	24.5	6.0	8.6
Students	1565	61.4	47.1	11.1	13.8	11.9	17.3	15.5	21.8
Junior High									
Teachers	392	64.4	46.7	16.3	13.9	8.7	29.3	10.7	10.1
Parents	5099	56.3	51.1	19.5	9.5	11.2	21.1	13.0	18.2
Students	4655	64.1	38.0	11.7	13.4	11.2	18.3	13.1	30.3
Senior High									
Teachers	653	52.2	45.6	18.0	9.9	6.8	29.7	23.0	14.8
Parents	3961	43.1	46.5	19.0	8.7	10.2	19.3	27.8	25.5
Students	6727	61.6	27.3	10.2	15.9	13.2	25.6	14.9	31.1

[a]Table entries are percentages.
[b]Average number of respondents.

These expectations are manifest in one form or another in virtually all formal curriculum documents at the state level. In analyzing the content of these documents, Goodlad and his associates synthesized a short but impressive array of the most commonly appearing goals for schooling in the United States.[8] (See the Appendix to this chapter.) Again, the list as specified is not to be found in any one formal curriculum document, yet the essential features of the list are found in all of them.[9] As Goodlad summarized, "We are not without goals for schooling. But we are lacking an articulation of them and commitment to them."[10]

I emphasize the diverse array of curricular expectations for schooling held by significant constituencies and the often conflicting ideological commitments running through them because they serve in striking contrast to what appears to happen in American classrooms.[11] They serve to illuminate what I must infer to be a chronic case of educational doublespeak — what we say we want and what, in effect, we promote in the name of public school education.

What, Then, Goes on in Classrooms?

In reviewing the information upon which much of what follows is based, I realized that these data were a decade old.[12] This posed a considerable problem as to what tense to use in recounting the results. I recalled a conversation that I had more than 12 years ago with some public school teachers as I explained to them what we planned to do in *A Study of Schooling* — go in and observe in excess of 1,000 elementary and secondary classrooms, on three different occasions (days or periods) each, looking for the kinds of teacher-student interactions and classroom configurations that appear to characterize the process of teaching and learning. Their response was similar to this: "Typical educational researchers . . . they go and spend a lot of money to find out what we already know — teachers spend most of their time talking to the class or monitoring students as they work on a written assignment; students, of course, spend most of their time presumably listening to the teacher or doing in-class assignments."

I then recalled a conversation several years later with some educational researchers as I explained some of our study's observational findings: teachers spend most of their time talking to the class or monitoring students as they work on a written assignment; students, thus, spend most of their time presumably listening to the teacher or doing in-class assignments. Their response was, "So, what else is new?"

No one ever said being an empiricist was going to be easy. I have decided to use the present tense and leave it to interested researchers to demonstrate that things have suddenly changed in the last decade in contrast to 90 years of previous classroom life.

The 90-year mark comes from Cuban's analysis of "constancy and change" in American classrooms from 1890 to 1980.[13] What he found was a lot of constancy and little change. In describing and interpreting nearly 7,000 quantitative, qualitative, and even pictorial accounts of classroom life — including the observational data collected on the 1,016 classes in *A Study of Schooling* — Cuban concludes that ". . . the data show striking convergence in outlining a stable core of teacher-centered instructional activities in the elementary school and, in high school classrooms, a remarkably pure and durable version of the same set of activities."[14]

This is not to say that Cuban did not find any evidence of change over 90 years. He notes, for example, several historians (e.g., Cremin and Spring) who claim that fundamental changes occurred in American classrooms in the 1920s and 1930s under the influence of the progressive education movement. He goes on, however, to note some fairly convincing counterarguments by others (e.g., Bowles and Gintis; Katz; Tyack; and Zilversmit).[15] Finally, Cuban quotes Dewey himself who, around 1950, notes that the progressive movement ". . . is largely atmospheric; it hasn't yet really penetrated and permeated the foundations of the educational institution."[16]

Regardless of the historical verdict, it seems fair to speculate that classrooms have, to some extent, become a bit more open, loosely structured, less formal places, probably due to child-centered reforms, particularly at the elementary levels of schooling. Nonetheless, descriptions of classrooms based upon the earliest observational studies at the turn of the century are remarkably consistent with those based on subsequent and substantial observational studies on up through the late 1970s.[17] In 1912, for example, Stevens interpreted her observational data thusly: "The fact that one history teacher attempts to realize his educational aims through the process of 'hearing' the textbook, day after day, is unfortunate, but pardonable; that history, science, mathematics, foreign language, and English teachers, collectively are following in the same groove, is a matter for theorists and practitioners to reckon with."[18] Let us see what our data in *A Study of Schooling* portray.[19]

Focusing on average teacher-student interactions at both elementary and secondary levels, about 75 percent of class time is instructional, 20 percent is spent on routines (roll-taking, preparation, clean-up, etc.), and the remaining 5 percent is almost evenly divided between discipline/behavioral control and miscellaneous social, noninstructional interactions. Nearly 70 percent of the total class time involves verbal interaction or "talk," mostly in the instructional context. Teachers talk about one-half of the total time in class while students talk less than one-fifth of the time; in effect, teachers out-talk students by a ratio of nearly 3-to-1. The rest of the teachers' time is approximately divided into 10 percent chunks devoted to working alone (usually at their desks), monitoring/observing students, and moving around the classroom.

The modal teacher-initiated, instructional activity — ranging from 18 percent of the time in elementary classes to 28 percent in high school classes — is instructing or explaining, usually *vis-à-vis* the total class. Only 6 percent of the instructional time is spent asking questions; 5 percent of this time involves direct questioning calling mainly for factual recall and comprehension, while 1 percent is devoted to "higher" cognitive and affective learning. Providing corrective feedback is rarely noticed (less than 3 percent at elementary and secondary levels); providing guidance, encouragement, or praise is also rare, totalling barely in excess of 3 percent at the elementary level and less than 2 percent at the secondary levels.

Student-initiated interactions with teachers, of any type in any context, occupy one-third of the time in elementary classes and only one-fifth of the time in secondary classes. Much of this time is spent in the instructional context, responding to the teacher (about 15 percent and 10 percent, respectively, at elementary and secondary levels). Interestingly, only 5 percent of the teachers' time is spent responding to student-initiated interactions. All interactions appear to take place in a relatively neutral affective environment; less than 3 percent of classroom time can be characterized as really positive or negative in tone.

Our observation instrument also permitted us to focus away from specific teacher-student interactions and focus on more general classroom configurations of people and activities. These results simply reinforced the above findings. The modal categories of activities involving the most students at any point in time at either elementary or secondary levels are explaining/lecturing by the teacher or working on written assignments. Among the rarest categories of activities involving the fewest numbers of students are demonstration, discussion, reading, role play, and simulation. Whatever the activities in progress, more than a 50 percent likelihood exists that students will be directed by the teacher (usually as a total class group); nearly a 40 percent likelihood of working independently (usually on a class assignment); and less than a 10 pecent likelihood of working together in smaller groups on some common task.

Finally, although some differences between classes due to subject matter did occur, these did not mitigate against the general patterns noted already. The elementary data, however, afforded us the opportunity to estimate the amount of time allocated to the various subject areas commonly taught at this level.[20] These estimates are as follows: English/reading/language arts, 64.0 percent; mathematics, 17.5 percent; science, 8.7 percent; the arts, 5.0 percent; and social studies, 4.9 percent. It is hard to imagine getting any closer to the 3 R's than this.

Is This The Way We Want It?

If the perennial call to get back to the basics is really a widely shared view of public schooling, then I suppose the answer is more a qualified "Yes" than "No." By inference, it might be concluded that significant numbers of people in influential positions appear satisfied with a narrowly conceived curriculum and merely exhort educators, periodically, to do it better (e.g., raise standardized test scores). Perhaps these people, along with many others, actually perceive that what goes on in classrooms (or what they recollect went on when they were students) corresponds with their images of a comprehensive curriculum such as suggested by the goal outline in the Appendix. This is contraindicated, however, by the teacher, parent, and student perceptions reported in Table 1. But then teacher, parent, and student constituencies may not really have all that much influence – and/or are not generally inclined to exert their influence under current conditions and circumstances – on actual decisions about, and resource allocations for, what goes on in schools. And perhaps the writers of curriculum documents labor less under the realities of schooling and more under ideal visions of schools as places where multiple functions should be served and multiple goals should be met – places that should seek their purposes from studies of the disciplines, of children and youth, of contemporary society, of psychology, and of philosophy.[21]

For whatever reasons, it seems clear that many curricular expectations established by typical arrays of common goals for American public schools enjoy little in the way of empirical support based upon what goes on in classrooms. In fact, if these expectations were aligned with typical classroom life, goal statements in the formal curriculum would read more like this: to develop in students the abilities to think linearly, depend upon authority, speak when spoken to, work alone, become socially apathetic, learn passively and nonexperientially, recall information, follow instructions, compartmentalize knowledge, and so on.

Many others have critiqued the operational curriculum in light of the formal curriculum and the ideologies at the base of this curriculum.[22] I note only two examples to help illustrate the disjuncture between curricular expectations set in motion by espoused goals and the curricular realities of most classrooms: First, consider the often-stated goal, "To develop critical and independent thinking that enables students to make judgments and decisions in a wide variety of life roles and intellectual activities." Then examine critically the "critical thinking" curriculum that has received growing attention over the last several years.[23] I conclude that much of this curriculum, although certainly a cut above ordinary classroom fare, mostly equates "critical thinking" with Bloom's Taxonomy and/or problem solving of the deductive and inductive variety. Rarely does the curriculum treat critical thinking as a dialectical process of reflective thought and communication, of competent discourse between people having both common and conflicting values, needs, and human interests.[24]

The typical classroom interactions, activities, and climates observed in *A Study of Schooling* were, of course, anything but "critical" – students speaking less than 20 percent of the time in class (and this is usually in response); students rarely conversing with one another or engaging in discussion, role play, simulations, or demonstrations; questions being addressed to students that are preponderantly those demanding only basic recall and comprehension skills; and little affect being generated other than what can be described as "neutral."

A second example, and one intimately related to the acritical nature of classroom life, is the ubiquitous way in which we evaluate the outcomes of teaching and learning. We see how well students can pick the "most correct" answer out of four or five possible answers to relatively artificial, well-structured, mini-problems. Then we standardize all this so that we can compare students to one another more than to what we tried to teach them. We assess student achievement in this fashion in an ambiguous world where most questions are complex, interdependent, and ill-structured, and where there are likely to be more "solutions" floating about in search of problems rather than the other way around.[25]

Space does not permit outlining similar critiques of what we do (or do not do) in relation to some of our other cherished educational goals for children (self-confidence, citizen participation, career decisionmaking, and the like). Nonetheless, is this the way we want it? Obviously, the question is meant to be rhetorical. But the conditions and circumstances seem clear — this is the way we've got it.

Educational Rhetoric and Critical Inquiry in Schools

In light of the above data and historical evidence, I find the continual displays of lists of lofty educational goals a curious phenomenon. What is the purpose of such lists? What roles are these goals — and the formal curriculum surrounding them — really intended to play? What interests are being served by curriculum documents that essentially gather dust in state and district offices?[26] For example, do the goals serve to remind us of what we wish we could do and what we ought to be doing in schools, if only we could? Are they beacons of hope in generally difficult educational conditions and circumstances?[27] Or perhaps, as Meyer and Rowan might suggest, the formal curriculum is merely a symbolic device whereby, through ceremony and ritual, the revered, multiple functions of schooling are confirmed and, *a priori*, believed to actually occur.[28] More insidious, perhaps, is the smokescreen provided by this mythology of lofty purpose relative to the supplies and demands — met rather well by schools — of a socially, economically, and politically stratified society.[29]

I leave it to others more situated in curriculum theory and practice than I to question more thoroughly the function of educational rhetoric *vis-à-vis* educational practice. It seems clear to me, however, that the issues raised herein, problematic as they are specifically for schools, are more fundamentally problems of a political society—a society that uses schools as basic skills training sites for youth, child-care facilities for the community, workplaces for adults, and political footballs for local, state, and federal governments. How, for example, can schools behave constructively and proactively in a society governed by those who would, on the one hand, issue commission reports (like *A Nation at Risk*) suggesting that we are caught in a web of educational mediocrity while, on the other, decrease funded support for public school improvement and advocate subsidies for private schooling?

I am not particularly sanguine about the likelihood of profound societal changes, however. The reporting of data such as those in this chapter, therefore, is done in the effort to promote a kind of "truth in advertising" for those of us committed to the ideals of equity and excellence in *public* schooling. It is done with the hope that a more honest alignment of the formal and operational curriculum may provide a more authentic point of departure for a critical dialogue on what schooling ought to be about.

My hope resides mostly in the vast and latent reservoirs of power and caring represented in the millions of teachers, administrators, district staff members, and college- and university-based educators who can be empowered to engage in school improvement practices through *critical inquiry*. In other work, my colleagues and I have attempted to explore the potential of critical inquiry and outline the process.[30] Essentially, critical inquiry is a rigorous, time-consuming, collaborative, informed, school-based dialectic around generic questions such as: What is going on in the name of X? (X is a place-holder for things like educational goals and schooling functions; instructional practices like the use of time, tracking students, and achievement testing; organizational practices like leadership, decisionmaking, and communication; etc.). How did it come to be that way? Whose interests are being (and are not being) served by the way things are? What information and knowledge do we have—and need to get—that bear upon the issues? (Get it and continue the dialogue.) Is this the way we want it? What are we going to *do* about all this? (Get on with it.)

These six questions are not just another Organizational Development-type exercise in "needs assessment," "prioritizing," and the like. They are not capable of being "boxed and arrowed" in a linear flowchart. All of these questions can be relevant (and usually are) at any time during critical inquiry. The questions must be thought of as heuristics—much like probes are used in structured interviews—designed to keep the inquiry alive and productive. The first two questions are intended to remind participants that problems have a present and historical context, and that they must be situated in these

64

contexts in order to be understood. The third question demands of participants that they confront (constructively) the political reality of significant educational issues; that they recognize and contend with embedded values and human interests. The fourth question demands of participants that the inquiry be informed — that knowledge of all types be brought to bear upon the issues. Finally, the last two questions are intended to remind participants that all is not talk; that, notwithstanding the omnipresent ambiguity in educational organizations, action can and must be taken, reviewed, revised, retaken, and so forth.

At the heart of critical inquiry, therefore, is the willingness and ability of people to engage in competent discourse and communication.[31] This is no mean undertaking, especially within and between places called schools and school districts, and potential collaborators in universities. Strong leadership that empowers rather than disenfranchises participants is required, as is leadership that can effectively facilitate group processes. Much work has been done in the area of group facilitation, and it will not be reviewed here. But I emphasize again that we are not talking about OD-type games that can be packaged and played out by organizational consultants. We are talking about rigorous and sustained discourse wherein people have a good chance of being understood and trust one another as being sincere in their intentions, the discussion is infused with knowledge of all types, and values and human interests are legitimate issues in the dialogue. To come close to this kind of conversation, people must have real opportunities to enter into the discourse and challenge constructively what others have to say and the basis on which they say it; say how they feel and what their own beliefs, values, and interests are; and participate equally in controlling the discussion.

Clearly, the methodology being advocated consists of informed discourse, a language of empowerment, and experimental action, with the full recognition that education and schooling is a political activity. The human interests being served through the euphemisms of educational rhetoric, therefore, must be called into question continually as part of the inquiry process. As Orwell noted keenly 40 years ago, "The great enemy of clear language is insincerity. When there is a gap between one's real and one's declared aims, one turns as it were instinctively to long words and exhausted idioms, like cuttlefish squirting out ink. In our age, there is no such thing as 'keeping out of politics'."[32]

As educators, we need to be critically (and perhaps painfully) aware of what we say we do, what we actually do, and the political and ethical contexts in which we do it. Public education is fundamentally a *normative* enterprise out of which flow major implications for what schools are for, how curriculum is conceptualized and practiced, what constitutes a profession of teaching, how the preparation of educators is conceptualized and practiced, and so on.

65

It is my view, for example, that the answer to the question, "Is this the way we want it?" *should be* "No." And to the extent that we continue to make impossible—by action or inaction—the conditions and circumstances for critical inquiry in schools, we will never get beyond descriptive questions of "what is" and to the more crucial imperative, "This is the way it *ought* to be!"

With no intent to develop the argument further, I will suggest that an appropriate normative position must begin with our nation's commitment to a democratic conception of the common public school and the guarantee of an excellent and equitable education for all children and youth. Kerr,[33] for example, argues that fairly clear moral imperatives are found for the practice of education that flow directly from conceptions of justice and culture—not only in terms of individual and social responsibilities, but in terms of the way culture is experienced; the way knowledge is generated, understood, and acted upon. Her argument suggests that:

> While various kinds of training . . . and specific content emphases . . . might be defensible for particular purposes, by themselves they cannot and should not be expected to substitute for the central task of schooling: education as an initiation into the ways of understanding and inquiring. Education so conceived cannot be improved by courses in critical thinking, for it is itself an initiation into the disciplines of critical thinking. It cannot be passed over in favor of "basic education," for there is no education that is more basic.[34]

I believe that as educators committed to public schooling, we can do no less than attempt to realize such images of educational excellence in future observations of actual classroom life.

Notes

1. In John I. Goodlad, M. Frances Klein, and Kenneth A. Tye, "The Domains of Curriculum and Their Study," in *Curriculum Inquiry: The Study of Curriculum Practice*, John I. Goodlad and Associates, eds. (New York: McGraw Hill, 1979), the following commonplaces broadly define curriculum: goals and objectives, materials, content, learning activities, teaching strategies, evaluation, grouping practices, and time and space usages.
2. Alex Molnar, "Schools and Their Curriculum: A Continuing Controversy," in *Current Thought on Curriculum*, Alex Molnar, ed. (Alexandria, Va.: Association for Supervision and Curriculum Development, 1985).
3. Herbert M. Kliebard, "Three Currents of American Curriculum Thought," in Molnar, *Current Thought on Curriculum, op. cit.*, and Chapter 2 herein.

4. John I. Goodlad, M. Frances Klein, and Kenneth A. Tye, "The Domains of Curriculum and Their Study," in *Curriculum Inquiry: The Study of Curriculum Practice*, John I. Goodlad and Associates, eds. (New York: McGraw Hill, 1979).

5. Briefly, these are the formal, perceived, operational, and experiential domains — what is written down in state and local curriculum documents, what is thought to be the curriculum by interested persons (particularly teachers), what is observed to happen in classrooms, and what is experienced by students, respectively. The perceived and experiential domains are probably the hardest to deal with empirically, and I treat them only in passing in this chapter. For more extensive treatments, see: Barbara Benham Tye, *Multiple Realities: A Study of 13 American High Schools* (Lanham, Md.: University Press of America, 1985); John I. Goodlad, *A Place Called School: Prospects for the Future* (New York: McGraw Hill, 1984); Jeannie Oakes, *Keeping Track: How Schools Structure Inequality* (New Haven, Conn.: Yale University Press, 1985); and Kenneth A. Tye, *The Junior High: School in Search of a Mission* (Lanham, Md.: University Press of America, 1985).

6. Ernest L. Boyer, *High School: A Report on Secondary Education in America* (New York: Harper and Row, 1983); Goodlad, *A Place Called School.*

7. The only exceptions were parent and teacher ratings of the importance of the career/vocation function for *elementary* schools; yet these were still above 3.0 on the average. See Betty C. Overman, *Functions of Schooling: Perceptions and Preferences of Teachers, Parents and Students* (A Study of Schooling Technical Report No. 10, 1980, ERIC No. ED 214 880).

8. Goodlad, *A Place Called School, op. cit.*, pp. 51–6. See also, Patricia A. Bauch, *States' Goals for Schooling* (A Study of Schooling Technical Report No. 35, 1982); and M. Frances Klein, *State and District Curriculum Guides: One Aspect of the Formal Curriculum* (A Study of Schooling Technical Report No. 9, 1980, ERIC No. ED 214 879).

9. The same observation was made by Theodore R. Sizer, *Horace's Compromise: The Dilemma of the American High School* (Boston: Houghton Mifflin, 1984), p. 77.

10. Goodlad, *A Place Called School, op. cit.*, p. 56.

11. Take as an illustration the cluster of "vocational goals" and the "enculturation goals" (particularly III.C.4 in the Appendix). One can easily infer the impending ideological conflicts between those seeing schools as benevolent agents for socializing future citizens and those advocating radical social reconstruction as the only viable means for countering the hegemonic agency of schooling. (See Stanley Aronowitz and Henry A. Giroux, *Education Under Siege: The Conservative, Liberal, and Radical Debate Over Schooling* (South Hadley, Mass.: Bergin and Garvey Publishers, Inc., 1985.) For example, if I were constructing "vocational/career" goals, I would probably end up using language suggesting the emancipation and empowerment of young people through a curriculum of reflection and critique of historical and current social, economic, and political conditions and circumstances. In any case, the array of goals in the Appendix is *not* being suggested as *the* list of "oughts" for American schooling; rather, the list is a convenient means for highlighting discrepancies between the

existing formal and operational curriculum and, it is hoped, provoking a more critical inquiry into both.

12. Data collection took place in the spring and fall of 1977. I first reported the observation summary analyses in "A Study of Schooling Technical Report No. 29," 1981, ERIC No. 214 897; subsequently, they were reported in Kenneth A. Sirotnik, "What You See Is What You Get: Consistency, Persistency, and Mediocrity in Classrooms," *Harvard Educational Review* 53 (1983):16–31.

13. Larry Cuban, *How Teachers Taught: Constancy and Change in American Classrooms 1890–1980* (New York: Longman, 1984).

14. *Ibid.*, p. 238.

15. *Ibid.*, pp. 104–6. See Samuel Bowles and Herbert Gintis, *Schooling in Capitalist America* (New York: Basic Books, 1976); Lawrence Cremin, *Transformation of the Schools* (New York: Vintage, 1961); Michael Katz, *Class, Bureaucracy and School* (New York: Praeger, 1971); Joel Spring, *Education and the Rise of the Corporate State* (Boston: Beacon Press, 1972); David Tyack, *The One Best System* (Cambridge, Mass.: Harvard University Press, 1974); and Arthur Zilversmit, "The Failure of Progressive Education, 1920–1940," in *Schooling in Society*, edited by Lawrence Stone (Baltimore, Md.: Johns Hopkins Press, 1976).

16. Cuban, *How Heachers Taught, op. cit.*, p. 113; quote is from *Dewey on Education*, Martin Dworkin, ed. (New York: Teachers College Press, 1959), pp. 129–30.

17. Compare, for example Romiett Stevens, *The Question as a Measure of Efficiency in Instruction: A Critical Study of Classroom Practice* (New York: Teachers College Press, Contributions to Education No. 48, 1912) to reports such as E. J. Amidon and J. B. Hough, eds., *Interaction Analysis: Theory, Research and Application* (Reading, Mass.: Addison-Wesley, 1967); Michael Dunkin and Bruce J. Biddle, *The Study of Teaching* (New York: Holt, Rinehart & Winston, 1974); John I. Goodlad, M. Frances Klein, and Associates, *Behind the Classroom Door* (Worthington, Ohio: Jones, 1970); James Hoetker and William P. Ahlbrand, "The Persistence of the Recitation," *American Educational Research Journal* 6 (1969):145–67; and Philip W. Jackson, *Life in Classrooms* (New York: Holt, Rinehart & Winston, 1968).

18. Stevens, "The Question as a Measure of Efficiency," p. 16.

19. Observational data on 129 elementary and 887 secondary classes were collected from a purposive sample of schools from across the nation which varied considerably in terms of school size, economic status of the community, race/ethnicity of the student body, and regional location and characteristics. Each class was observed over a two-week period on three different occasions (full days at the elementary level and full periods at the secondary level). Primary data were collected through the "five-minute interaction" and "classroom snapshot" portions of the observational system. The former feature provided a fairly continuous accounting of how time was spent in the classroom, focusing upon the teacher and the interactive process between teacher and students. The latter feature provided an accounting of all people in the classroom in terms of activities in progress and grouping configurations. More details of the observational system can be found in Sirotnik, "What You See Is What You Get."

20. Each elementary class was observed for approximately four hours on each of three days. The four hours were chosen so as to maximize the opportunity to observe instructional activity.

21. Ralph W. Tyler, *Basic Principles of Curriculum and Instruction* (Chicago: University of Chicago Press, 1949).

22. Discussions such as those of Michael W. Apple, *Ideology and Curriculum* (Boston: Routledge & Kegan Paul, 1979), and Michael W. Apple and Nancy R. King, "What Do Schools Teach?" *Curriculum Inquiry* 6(1977):341–58 are useful to insert at this point.

23. Much of this has been chronicled in the issues of *Educational Leadership* 42(September 1984); 42(November 1984); 42(May 1985); and 43(May 1986).

24. See, for example, the critiques by Richard W. Paul, "Critical Thinking: Fundamental to Education for a Free Society," *Educational Leadership* 42(September 1984):4–14; and "Bloom's Taxonomy and Critical Thinking Instruction," *Educational Leadership* 42(May 1985):36–39. For an analysis of what critical teaching and learning can be about in a specific subject area, see Walter C. Parker, "Teachers' Mediation in Social Studies," *Theory and Research in Social Education*, forthcoming.

25. See Norman Frederiksen, "The Real Test Bias: Influences of Testing on Teaching and Learning," *American Psychologist* 39 (1984): 193–202; and James G. March, "Model Bias in Social Action," *Review of Educational Research* 42 (1972):413–29.

26. In *A Study of Schooling*, teachers were asked how much influence each of 11 different sources had on what they taught in various subjects. Although some variation was obtained across subjects, percentages of teachers responding "a lot" (versus "some," "little," or "none") to the influence of state and district curriculum guides were in the neighborhoods of 10 percent and 20 percent, respectively. These were in contrast to "a lot" responses generally in the 70 percent to 90 percent range for the source "your own background, interests, and experiences." See M. Frances Klein, *Teacher Perceived Sources of Influence on What is Taught in Subject Areas* (A Study of Schooling Technical Report No. 15, 1980, ERIC No. ED 214 885).

27. I am thinking here of such things as the growing incidences of student drug and alcohol abuse, increasing student demographic heterogeneity and diversity in cultural values, increasing student dropout and transiency, decreasing educational budgets, relatively low teacher salaries, poor quality of beginning teachers, low morale of experienced teachers, high rate of teacher burnout, impending teacher shortages, little or no quality time in the work setting for practicing educators to reflect constructively upon their practice, and so on. Documentation of the demographics of schooling can be found in the May 14, 1986 issue of *Education Week* Vol. 5, No. 34, pp. 14–37. Reports on the state of teaching include: L. Darling-Hammond, *Beyond the Commission Reports: The Coming Crisis in Teaching* (Los Angeles: Rand Corporation 1984); C. E. Feistritzer, *The Making of a Teacher: A Report on Teacher Education and Certification* (Washington, D. C.: National Center for Education Information, 1984); D. H. Kerr, "Teaching Competence and Teacher Education in the

United States," *Teachers College Record* 84(1983):525–52; T. R. Sizer, "High School Reform and the Reform of Teacher Education," the 1984 De Garmo Lecture, Society of Professors of Education, February 1984; G. Sykes, "Contradictions, Ironies, and Promises Unfulfilled: A Contemporary Account of the Status of Teaching," *Phi Delta Kappan* 65(1983):87–93.

28. John W. Meyer and Brian Rowan, "Institutionalized Organizations: Formal Structure as Myth and Ceremony," *American Journal of Sociology* 83(1977):340–63.

29. See, for example, the arguments in Oakes, *Keeping Track, op. cit.*; Clarence Karier, *Shaping the American Educational State, 1900 to Present* (New York: Free Press, 1975); Arthur G. Powell, Eleanor Farrar, and David K. Cohen, *The Shopping Mall High School: Winners and Losers in the Educational Marketplace* (Boston: Houghton Mifflin, 1985); and Joel Spring, *The Sorting Machine: National Educational Policy Since 1945* (New York: McKay, 1976).

30. Much of this work can be found in Kenneth A. Sirotnik and Jeannie Oakes, "Critical Inquiry for School Renewal: Liberating Theory and Practice," in *Critical Perspectives on the Organization and Improvement of Schooling*, Kenneth A. Sirotnik and Jeannie Oakes, eds. (Boston: Kluwer-Nijhoff, 1986); Kenneth A. Sirotnik, "Evaluation in the Ecology of Schooling: The Process of School Renewal," in the 1987 Yearbook, Part I, of the National Society for the Study of Education, *The Ecology of School Improvement*, John I. Goodlad, ed. (Chicago: University of Chicago Press, 1987); and Kenneth A. Sirotnik, "The School as the Center of Change," in *Schooling for Tomorrow: Directing Reforms to Issues that Count*, Thomas J. Sergiovanni and John H. Moore, eds. (Boston: Allyn & Bacon, forthcoming).

31. The conceptual and practical work of philosophers and activists such as Jurgen Habermas and Paulo Freire is particularly relevant here as it might be applied to the work settings of educators. See Jurgen Habermas, *Communication and the Evolution of Society* (Boston: Beacon Press, 1979) and Paulo Freire, *Education for Critical Consciousness* (New York: Continuum, 1973). See also, Sirotnik and Oakes, "Critical Inquiry for School Renewal," *op cit.*

32. George Orwell, "Politics and the English Language," in *In Front of Your Nose 1945–1950, the Collected Essays, Journalism, and Letters of George Orwell*, vol. 4 (p. 137), Sonia Orwell and Jan Angus, eds. (New York: Harcourt Brace Jovanovich, 1968). Thanks to my colleague Roger Soder for bringing Orwell's essay to my attention.

33. Donna H. Kerr, "Authority and Responsibility," in *The Ecology of School Renewal*, 86th Yearbook of the National Society for the Study of Education, Part I, John I. Goodlad, ed. (Chicago: University of Chicago Press).

34. *Ibid.*, p., 25.

Appendix

A Summary of Typical Educational Goals Espoused for Public Schooling in America

I. Academic Goals

A. Mastery of Basic Skills and Fundamental Processes

1. Learn to read, write, and handle basic arithmetical operations.
2. Learn to acquire ideas through reading and listening.
3. Learn to communicate ideas through writing and speaking.
4. Learn to utilize mathematical concepts.
5. Develop the ability to utilize available sources of information.

B. Intellectual Development

1. Develop the ability to think rationally, including problem-solving skills, application of principles of logic, and skill in using different modes of inquiry.
2. Develop the ability to use and evaluate knowledge, i.e., critical and independent thinking that enables one to make judgments and decisions in a wide variety of life roles — citizen, consumer, worker, etc. — as well as in intellectual activities.
3. Accumulate a general fund of knowledge, including information and concepts in mathematics, literature, natural science, and social science.
4. Develop positive attitudes toward intellectual activity, including curiosity and a desire for further learning.
5. Develop an understanding of change in society.

II. Vocational Goals

A. Career Education–Vocational Education

1. Learn how to select an occupation that will be personally satisfying and suitable to one's skills and interests.
2. Learn to make decisions based on an awareness and knowledge of career options.

3. Develop salable skills and specialized knowledge that will prepare one to become economically independent.
4. Develop habits and attitudes, such as pride in good workmanship, that will make one a productive participant in economic life.
5. Develop positive attitudes toward work, including acceptance of the necessity of making a living and an appreciation of the social value and dignity of work.

III. Social, Civic, and Cultural Goals

A. Interpersonal Understandings

1. Develop a knowledge of opposing value systems and their influence on the individual and society.
2. Develop an understanding of how members of a family function under different family patterns as well as within one's own family.
3. Develop skill in communicating effectively in groups.
4. Develop the ability to identify with and advance the goals and concerns of others.
5. Learn to form productive and satisfying relations with others based on respect, trust, cooperation, consideration, and caring.
6. Develop a concern for humanity and an understanding of international relations.
7. Develop an understanding and appreciation of cultures different from one's own.

B. Citizenship Participation

1. Develop a historical perspective.
2. Develop knowledge of the basic workings of the government.
3. Develop a willingness to participate in the political life of the nation and the community.
4. Develop a commitment to the values of liberty, government by consent of the governed, representative government, and one's responsibility for the welfare of all.
5. Develop an understanding of the interrelationships among complex organizations and agencies in a modern society, and learn to act in accordance with it.
6. Exercise the democratic right to dissent in accordance with personal conscience.
7. Develop economic and consumer skills necessary for making informed choices that enhance one's quality of life.
8. Develop an understanding of the basic interdependence of the biological and physical resources of the environment.

9. Develop the ability to act in light of this understanding of the interdependence.

C. *Enculturation*

1. Develop insight into the values and characteristics, including language, of the civilization of which one is a member.
2. Develop an awareness and understanding of one's cultural heritage and become familiar with the achievements of the past that have inspired and influenced humanity.
3. Develop understanding of the manner in which traditions from the past are operative today and influence the direction and values of society.
4. Understand and adopt the norms, values, and traditions of the groups of which one is a member.
5. Learn how to apply the basic principles and concepts of the fine arts and humanities to the appreciation of the aesthetic contributions of other cultures.

D. *Moral and Ethical Character*

1. Develop the judgment to evaluate events and phenomena as good or evil.
2. Develop a commitment to truth and values.
3. Learn to utilize values in making choices.
4. Develop moral integrity.
5. Develop an understanding of the necessity for moral conduct.

IV. *Personal Goals*

A. *Emotional and Physical Well-Being*

1. Develop the willingness to receive emotional impressions and to expand one's affective sensitivity.
2. Develop the competence and skills for continuous adjustment and emotional stability, including coping with social change.
3. Develop a knowledge of one's own body and adopt health practices that support and sustain it, including avoiding the consumption of harmful or addictive substances.
4. Learn to use leisure time effectively.
5. Develop physical fitness and recreational skills.
6. Develop the ability to engage in constructive self-criticism.

B. *Creativity and Aesthetic Expression*

1. Develop the ability to deal with problems in original ways.
2. Develop the ability to be tolerant of new ideas.

3. Develop the ability to be flexible and to consider different points of view.
4. Develop the ability to experience and enjoy different forms of creative expression.
5. Develop the ability to evaluate various forms of aesthetic expression.
6. Develop the willingness and ability to communicate through creative work in an active way.
7. Seek to contribute to cultural and social life through one's artistic, vocational, and avocational interests.

C. *Self-Realization*

1. Learn to search for meaning in one's activities, and develop a philosophy of life.
2. Develop the self-confidence necessary for knowing and confronting one's self.
3. Learn to assess realistically and live with one's limitations and strengths.
4. Recognize that one's self-concept is developed in interaction with other people.
5. Develop skill in making decisions with purpose.
6. Learn to plan and organize the environment in order to realize one's goals.
7. Develop willingness to accept responsibility for one's own decisions and their consequences.
8. Develop skill in selecting some personal, lifelong learning goals and the means to attain them.

II

Curriculum and Planning

FIVE

Models of Curriculum Planning

George J. Posner

How does one plan a curriculum? For many students of curriculum, the answer to this question constitutes a major goal of their studies. In this chapter, we will attempt to determine the ways educators have addressed this question.

Many students find answers to this question in the curriculum literature to be somewhat confusing. The so-called Tyler Rationale prescribes four "questions" that any curriculum planner must address;[1] Taba provides seven "steps" to follow;[2] Walker's "naturalistic model" describes three "elements" of curriculum planning;[3] Johnson's "model" represents the curriculum as an "output of one system and an input of another";[4] and Goodlad's "conceptual system" describes three different "levels" of curriculum decisionmaking.[5] What accounts for this wide array of answers to the question of curriculum planning? Or, alternatively, are they answers to different questions?

In this chapter, I argue that this wide variety of approaches to curriculum planning can be partially understood as a set of responses to different curriculum planning questions. We will examine answers to three different questions related to curriculum planning:

1. The procedural question: What steps should one follow in planning a curriculum?

2. The descriptive question: How do people actually plan curricula; i.e., what do they do?
3. The conceptual question: What are the elements of curriculum planning and how do they relate to one another conceptually?

In order to understand curriculum planning more fully, we must examine not only different curriculum planning questions, but also different curriculum planning perspectives. I maintain[6] that one perspective on curriculum planning has dominated curriculum thought and, thus, influenced not only the answers to the three questions outlined above, but even the formulation of these questions. I then examine briefly another perspective that not only answers the three questions in radically different ways but also argues for the priority of other questions and, in particular, underlying ideological questions.

The Technical Production Perspective

The dominant perspective is best represented in Ralph Tyler's work. Tyler's rationale for curriculum planning has been a major influence on curriculum thought since its publication in 1949.[7] It has been interpreted by most educators as a procedure to follow when planning a curriculum; that is, as an answer to the *procedural* question, what steps does one follow in planning a curriculum?[8] Because of its importance, I examine its features.

Tyler suggests that when planning a curriculum, four questions must be answered. First, planners must decide what educational purposes the school should seek to attain. These "objectives" should be derived from systematic studies of the *learners*, from studies of contemporary life in *society*, and from analyses of the *subject matter* by specialists. These three sources of objectives are then screened through the school's *philosophy* and through knowledge available about the *psychology of learning*. The objectives derived in this way should be specified as precisely and unambiguously as possible, so that evaluation efforts can be undertaken to determine the extent to which the objectives have been attained.

Second, planners must determine what educational experiences can be provided that are most likely to attain these purposes. Possible experiences are checked for consistency with objectives and for economy.

Third, the planner must find ways that these educational experiences can be organized effectively. The planner attempts to provide experiences that have a cumulative effect on students. Tyler recommends that experiences build on one another and enable learners to understand the relation among their learning activities in various fields. In so doing, attention should be given to the *sequence* of experiences within each field (e.g., mathematics) and to *integration* of knowledge across fields. Certain concepts, skills, and values are sufficiently complex to require repeated study in increasing degrees of sophistication and breadth of application, and sufficiently pervasive to help the student relate one field to another. The planner uses these *organizing elements* to provide the sequence and integration the curriculum requires.

Finally, the planner must determine whether the educational purposes are being attained. Objective evaluation instruments (e.g., tests, work samples, questionnaires, and records) are developed to check the curriculum's effectiveness. The criterion for success is behavioral evidence that the objectives of the curriculum have been attained.

The Tyler Rationale and, in particular, his four questions regarding the selection of educational purposes, the determination of experiences, the organization of experiences, and the provision for evaluation, have dominated thought on curriculum planning for nearly 40 years. Moreover, the publication of Tyler's syllabus represents not the beginning of its influence but, instead, a distillation of ideas derived from the founders of the curriculum field in the first quarter of this century.[9] In fact, Bobbitt's seminal books on curriculum[10] and, in particular, their focus on the development of specific objectives based on scientific methods, established the basic approach to curriculum planning continued by Tyler in his syllabus.

Since its publication in 1949, educators representing a wide range of orientations have turned to the Tyler Rationale for an analysis of the procedural questions of curriculum. Test-oriented behaviorists such as James Popham use it explicitly for the selection of objectives.[11] Course planning guides, such as those by Posner and Rudnitsky[12] and by Barnes,[13] use elaborations of the Tyler Rationale as the basis for their handbooks. Even humanistic educators such as Elliot Eisner, who have spent considerable effort criticizing Tyleresque objectives and evaluation approaches, when it comes time to discuss procedure, revert (perhaps unknowingly) to a step-by-step approach that differs only slightly from the Tyler Rationale.[14]

Perhaps the major reason for the domination of curriculum planning by the Tyler Rationale is its congruence with our assumptions about both schooling and curriculum planning. Unquestioned acceptance of these assumptions even makes conceiving of an alternative to this basic approach impossible.

Schooling is assumed to be a process whose main purpose is to promote or produce learning. Students are termed *learners;* objectives are conceived in terms of desirable learning; evaluation of the school's success is targeted almost exclusively on achievement test scores; "educational" goals are distinguished from "noneducational" goals by determining if they can be attributed to learning;[15] "curriculum" is defined (not by Tyler but by his followers, such as Goodlad) in terms of "intended learning outcomes."[16] Thus, schooling is conceived as a *production system*, in which individual learning outcomes are the primary product. After all, if learning is not what schooling is for, then what could be its purpose?

Further, curriculum planning is assumed to be an enterprise in which the planner objectively and, if possible, scientifically develops the means necessary to produce the desired learning outcomes. There is no place for personal biases and values in selecting the means; effectiveness and efficiency in accomplishing the ends are primary. This *means-end reasoning* process serves as the logic underlying all rational decisionmaking. Educational experiences are justified by the objectives that they serve.

This means-ends rationality is taken a step further when ends not only serve as the primary justification for means but also as the starting point in planning. After all, as this perspective rhetorically asks, how can one decide on educational means except by referring to educational ends? The use of a travel metaphor convinces planners that they must determine the destination before deciding on the route they should take and thus assume a *linear* view of means and ends.

The means-ends rationality leads to the assumption that it is a *technical* matter to decide such issues as instructional method and content, a matter best reserved for people with technical expertise about the methods and content optimally suited for particular objectives. As technical experts, they have the responsibility of disallowing their own values from clouding the objectivity of their work; that is, they try to keep their work value free. Even decisions about purpose are conceived as a technical matter based on specialized knowledge which experts develop, either from studies of learners and contemporary society or by virtue of their subject matter expertise. After all, who is better equipped to make these decisions than the people with the most knowledge relevant to the decisions?

I refer to views on curriculum planning that uncritically accept these assumptions as based on a *technical production* perspective. They are *technical* if they consider educational decisions to be made objectively, primarily by experts with specialized knowledge; they are *production-oriented* if they view schooling as a process whose main purpose is to produce learning, in which the logic of educational decisonmaking is based on means-ends reasoning. Furthermore, they are *linear* technical production models if they require the determination of ends before deciding on means.

The technical production perspective has served as a basis for a variety of models intended to guide curriculum thought (particularly when complemented with the assumption of linearity). I examine some major analyses of curriculum planning that accept the central assumptions of this perspective but differ in important ways. They can be interpreted as answers to the basic procedural, descriptive, and conceptual questions of curriculum planning.

The Procedural Question

As a basic approach to curriculum development, the Tyler Rationale was used as a point of departure by many writers sympathetic to its general orientation. Some of these writers, most notably Hilda Taba, attempted to refine it by adding steps and by further subdividing each of Tyler's four planning steps.[17]

Taba

Taba's work represents the most detailed elaboration of the Tyler Rationale. Like Tyler, she explicitly accepts the assumption that curriculum planning is a technical (or "scientific") rather than a political matter.

> *Scientific* curriculum development needs to draw upon analysis of society and culture, studies of the learner and the learning process, and analyses of the nature of knowledge in order to determine the purposes of the school and the nature of its curriculum.[18] (Emphasis added.)

She argues for a "systematic," "objective," "scientific," and "research-oriented" approach to curriculum development, requiring "objectivity."[19] She laments that

> the tradition of rigorous scientific thinking about curricula is not as yet well established. . . . Curriculum designs are espoused on the basis of their concurrence with a set of beliefs and feelings, rather than by their verifiable consequence on learning or their contribution to educational objectives.[20]

Her view of curriculum development "requires expertness of many varieties,"[21] including

> technical skills in curriculum-making, mastery of intellectual discipline, the knowledge of social and educational values which underlie educational decisions, and the understanding of the processes of educational decisions and human engineering.[22]

Like Tyler, Taba also accepts the assumption that learning is the ultimate purpose of schooling. Her focus on the selection and organization of "learning experiences," her preoccupation with learning outcomes and learning objectives in her evaluation approach, her emphasis on learning theory in the selection of objectives, and the centrality of learning objectives in her curriculum development model all imply a learning-oriented view of schooling. As Taba succinctly states: "curricula are designed so that students may learn."[23]

Her approach is more prescriptive than Tyler's regarding the procedure of curriculum planning. Whereas Tyler offers four questions that must be addressed, Taba forcefully argues for the *order* of her seven steps.

> If one conceives of curriculum development as a task requiring orderly thinking, one needs to examine both the order in which decisions are made and the way in which they are made to make sure that all relevant considerations are brought to bear on these decisions. This book is based on an assumption that there is such an order and that pursuing it will result in a more thoughtfully planned and a more dynamically conceived curriculum. This order might be as follows:
>
> Step 1: Diagnosis of needs;
> Step 2: Formulation of objectives;
> Step 3: Selection of content;
> Step 4: Organization of content;
> Step 5: Selection of learning experiences;
> Step 6: Organization of learning experiences; and
> Step 7: Determination of what to evaluate and of ways and means of doing it.[24]

Thus, Taba's model is not only a technical-production model but also linear.

Schwab

Joseph Schwab takes issue with several of Tyler's and Taba's views, including the focus on objectives, the clear separation of ends and means, and the insistence on an orderly planning procedure.[25] In order to characterize planning more appropriately, he offers curriculum planners the concept of "deliberation."

> Deliberation is complex and arduous. It treats both ends and means and must treat them as mutually determining one another. It must try to identify, with respect to both, what facts may be relevant. It must try to ascertain the relevant facts in the concrete case. It must try to identify the desiderata in the case. It must generate alternative solutions. It must make every effort to trace the branching pathways of consequences which may flow from each alternative and affect desiderata. It must then weigh alternatives and their costs and consequences against one another, and choose, not the *right* alternative, for there is no such thing, but the *best* one.[26]

Schwab's concept of deliberation is the centerpiece of this "practical" language for developing curricula. For Schwab, this practical language is preferable to the single-theory approaches that have dominated curriculum development. Single-theory curricula, such as a science curriculum based on Piagetian theory, a course on the novel as a source of vicarious experience, or a math curriculum based on set theory, are fundamentally flawed, according to Schwab. They are flawed in three ways in their reliance on a single principle or theory for curriculum planning.

1. *The Failure of Scope* . . . One curriculum effort is grounded in concern only for the individual, another in concern only for groups, others in concern only for cultures, or communities, or societies, or minds, or the extant bodies of knowledge. . . . No curriculum, grounded in but one of these subjects, can possibly be adequate or defensible.[27]

2. *The Vice of Abstraction* . . . All theories, even the best of them . . . , necessarily neglect some aspects and facets of the facts of the case. A theory (and the principle derived from it) covers and formulates the *regularities* among the things and events it subsumes. It abstracts a general or ideal case. It leaves behind the nonuniformities, the particularities, which characterize each concrete instance of the facts subsumed. . . . Yet curriculum is brought to bear, not on ideal or abstract representations, but on the real thing, on the concrete case, in all its completeness and with all its differences from all other concrete cases on a large body of fact concerning which the theoretic abstraction is silent.[28]

3. *Radical Plurality* . . . Nearly all theories in all the behavioral sciences are marked by the coexistence of competing theories. . . . All the social and behavioral sciences are marked by the "schools," each distinguished by a different choice of principle of enquiry, each of which selects from the intimidating complexities of the subject matter the small fraction of the whole with which it can deal. . . . The theories which arise from enquiries so directed are, then, radically incomplete, each of them incomplete to the extent that competing theories take hold of different aspects of the subject of enquiry and treat it in a different way. . . . In short, there is every reason to suppose that any one of the extant theories of behavior is a pale and incomplete representation of actual behavior. . . . It follows that such theories are not, and will not be, adequate by themselves to tell us what to do with actual human beings or how to do it. What they variously suggest and the contrary guidances they afford to choice and action must be mediated and combined by eclectic arts and must be massively supplemented, as well as mediated, by knowledge of some other kind derived from another source. . . . It is this recourse to accumulated lore, to experience of actions and their consequences, to action and reaction at the level of the concrete case, which constitutes the heart of the practical. It is high time that curriculum do likewise.[29]

Curriculum planning can be no more based on single theory than can other complex decisions such as choosing a spouse, buying a car, or selecting a president.

In order to repair these deficiencies of theory as a basis for curriculum planning, Schwab offers the "eclectic" as an approach to curriculum planning. Theory brings certain features of a phenomenon into focus, helping the curriculum planner to understand better that aspect of the situation. For example, Piagetian theory helps the planner understand the student's cognitive development. Curriculum planners trained in the "eclectic arts" not only can use theory to view phenomena, they also know which aspects of the phenomenon each theory obscures or blurs. For example, Piagetian theory obscures the social psychology and sociology of classrooms. Finally, the eclectic arts allow the curriculum planner to use various theories in combination "without paying the full price of their incompleteness and partiality."[30]

In order to avoid the "tunnel vision" associated with any theory, Schwab recommends not only a deliberative method for curriculum planning but also suggests the participants in this process. According to Schwab, at least one representative of each of the four "commonplaces" of education must be included, i.e., the learner, the teacher, the subject matter, and the milieu. (Note the similarity with Tyler's three "sources.") In addition to representation of each of these four commonplaces, a fifth perspective, that of the curriculum specialist (trained in the practical and eclectic arts), must be present.[31]

Schwab's approach to curriculum planning accepts some assumptions of the Tyler Rationale and rejects others. Curriculum planning for both Schwab and for Tyler is a technical matter requiring expert knowledge. The representatives of each of the four commonplaces are to be experts in each commonplace. For example, the representative of "the learner" is to be a psychologist, not a student. Furthermore, the curriculum specialist is to be a trained expert in the arts of the practical and of the eclectic (as Schwab defines them).

Furthermore, Schwab's indictment of theory-driven curriculum development would lead to a general condemnation of any predetermined framework to be used as a starting point. Because theories and ideologies are both belief systems that reduce the educational planner's ability to discern the complexities of a particular situation and to consider alternatives, they must be avoided. Thus, Schwab, too, requires a nonideological posture for curriculum development.

Although technical in its reliance on experts, Schwab's approach rejects the constraints inherent in the clear separation of means and ends, insisting instead on a more flexible, varied, and iterative planning process. Deliberation is not characterized by specified procedural steps carried out in prescribed order.

The Descriptive Question

The problem with the Tyler Rationale, according to some writers, is that it does not describe what curriculum developers actually do when they plan a curriculum. Of course, none of the procedural models were intended to describe the actual work of practitioners. Nevertheless, the difficulties in implementing the Tyler Rationale suggest possible inherent weaknesses in its basic approach. Perhaps a more useable approach to curriculum planning can derive from an empirical investigation of curriculum development projects, particularly studies of notably successful ones.

Walker

Decker Walker's naturalistic model is based on this premise.[32] This model consists of three elements: "the curriculum's *platform*, its *design*, and the *deliberation* associated with it."[33]

The *platform* is "the system of beliefs and values that the curriculum developer brings to his task and . . . guides the development of the curriculum. . . . The word *platform* is meant to suggest both a political platform and something to stand on."[34]

Platforms consist of "conceptions," "theories," and "aims." Beliefs about what is learnable and teachable (such as "creativity can be taught") and, more generally, about what is possible, are conceptions. Beliefs about what is true are theories; for example, a belief that "motivation to learn is primarily based on the individual's history of successes and failures." Beliefs about "what is educationally desirable" are "aims"; for example, "we should teach children to learn how to learn." In addition to these three carefully conceptualized and explicit types of planks in a curriculum's platform, two others are significant. "Images" of good teaching, of good examples, and of good procedures to follow, though not explicit, often are influential in curriculum decisions. For example, exemplary literary works, physics problems, and teaching techniques often underlie curricular choices.[35]

In contrast with Tyler and Taba, Walker, like Schwab, prefers to view a curriculum not as an object or as materials but as the events made possible by the use of materials. It follows, then, that a curriculum's design can be specified by "the series of *decisions* that produce it . . . [that is] by the choices that enter into its creation."[36]

The process by which design decisions are made is "deliberation," a concept borrowed directly from Schwab. Deliberation, for Walker, consists of "*formulating decision points, devising alternative choices* at these decision points, *considering arguments* for and against suggested decision points and . . . alternatives, and finally, *choosing* the most defensible alternative. . . ."[37] Alternatives are compared in terms of their consistency with the curriculum's platform, and, when necessary, additional sources of information (or "data") are sought.

When planners resolve difficult decisions stemming from contradictions in the platform, they may preserve and accumulate these "precedents" for later situations, much as the courts use prior decisions as a basis for present decisions by simply citing precedent. Walker refers to "the body of precedents evolved from the platform" as "policy."[38] He thus distinguishes the principles accepted from the start (i.e., the platform) from those that evolve from the application of the platform to design decisions.

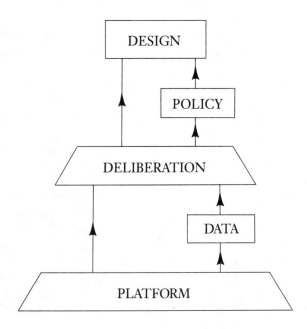

Figure 1. A schematic diagram of the main components of the naturalistic model.[39]

Walker's model, like Schwab's, is less linear than Tyler's or Taba's and relegates objectives to a less central position in the curriculum development process. Objectives constitute only one type of one component (i.e., aims) of Walker's platform. There is, thus, no clear separation of ends and means. Walker's platform includes beliefs about both. Although he does not specifically mention ideological beliefs as possible planks in a platform, he does not preclude them. But, like Schwab, Walker's model leaves unquestioned the assumption regarding the primary role of experts. Surprisingly, Walker never raises the issue of the discrepancy between the platforms of the project director, on the one hand, and of the teachers or students who ultimately must negotiate the meaning of the curriculum, on the other hand.

As Walker himself points out:

> While Schwab's view of curriculum-making [and Walker's model which is based on it] is less linear and comprehensive and more flexible and dialectical than the Tyler rationale, the same kinds of questions that Tyler asks need to be addressed at some point in deliberation. We still need to ask what our purposes are and how we might achieve them; we still need to find out if we have done so in our particular setting. Schwab himself recognizes this, and so the dominance of the Tyler Rationale in thinking about curriculum making seems to be unshaken.[40]

The Conceptual Question

Tyler begins his book by denying that his Rationale is "a manual for curriculum construction"; it does not describe "the steps to be taken . . . to build a curriculum."[41] Instead, he regards his Rationale as one "conception of the elements and relationships involved in an effective curriculum."[42] In fact, he concludes his book with an often overlooked statement:

> The purpose of the rationale is to give a view of the elements that are involved in a program of instruction and their necessary interrelations. The program may be improved by attacks beginning at any point, providing the resulting modifications are followed through the related elements until eventually all aspects of the curriculum have been studied and revised.[43]

Therefore, although often regarded as a linear procedural model, the Tyler Rationale is most appropriately viewed as a conceptual model. Just as Taba elaborated the Tyler Rationale into a detailed procedural model, Goodlad and Johnson have used Tyler's work as a point of departure for their own conceptual models.

Goodlad

John Goodlad, one of Tyler's students in a course using the Rationale as a syllabus, adopts virtually every aspect of Tyler's model in his own conceptual model.[44] He shares Tyler's concern with providing an account of rationality in curriculum planning, attributing "human frailty" to any departures from the strict means-ends logic.

However, Goodlad's major contribution to curriculum models is his elaboration of the Tyler Rationale, describing three levels of curriculum planning. The *instructional level* is closest to the learner. Curriculum planning at this level involves selecting the "organizing centers for learning"[45] (the stimuli to which the student responds), and deriving the precise educational objectives from the institution's educational aims.

The level above the instructional level Goodlad terms *institutional.* Curriculum planning here involves formulating general educational objectives and selecting illustrative learning opportunities.

The highest level Goodlad terms *societal.* Curriculum planning at this level is done by the "institution's sanctioning body,"[46] such as a school board. This body is responsible for formulating educational aims in order to attain a set of selected values.

Since Goodlad first proposed the three levels, his model has been substantially elaborated by extending them to include the state and federal levels.[47] The notion of levels contributes significantly to curriculum planning models by providing a technical production perspective on the question: Who should decide what in curriculum planning? This seemingly political and ethical question is thus answered as a technical question, that is, Who has access to the appropriate "data sources"?[48]

Johnson

Mauritz Johnson's conceptual model evolved over a ten-year period from 1967 to 1977. His early (and most often cited) version in 1967 stipulated a definition of curriculum as "a structured series of intended learning outcomes," and carefully distinguished between often confused concepts, including curriculum development and instructional systems, platforms and theories, sources of curriculum and criteria for curriculum selection, curricular and instrumental content, curriculum evaluation and instructional evaluation, and education and training.[49] But he recognized that his 1967 model was incomplete: It did not provide for goal setting, instructional planning, evaluation, situational (or frame) factors, or managerial aspects. Johnson's 1977 P-I-E model (i.e., planning, implementation, and evaluation) provided this needed elaboration.[50] Although highly complex, it can be reduced to the basic claim that rational planning involves a planning, an implementation, and an evaluation aspect (the "linear technical" dimension), each of which can, in turn, be planned, implemented and evaluated (the managerial dimension). Thus, one can plan, implement, and evaluate a given planning process, a given approach to implementation, and a given evaluation strategy. Furthermore, all of these activities are governed by a set of natural, temporal, physical, economic, cultural, organizational, and personal "frame factors" that act as resources and restrictions on both curriculum and instruction.[51]

The basic P-I-E model, when applied to curriculum and instruction, results in five elements: goal setting, curriculum selection, curriculum structuring, instructional planning, and technical evaluation. The comparability of Johnson, Goodlad, Tyler, and Taba is clear.

Elements Johnson (1977)	Questions Tyler (1950)	Steps Taba (1962)
Goal setting	What educational purposes?	Diagnosing needs
Curriculum selection		Formulating specific objectives Selecting content
Curriculum structuring		Organizing content Checking balance and sequence
Instructional planning	What educational experiences? How to organize educational experiences?	Selecting learning experiences Organizing learning experiences
Technical evaluation	How to determine whether purposes are attained?	Determining what and how to evaluate

Table 2: Johnson's model compared with two other analyses of curriculum and curriculum development.[52]

Not only do Johnson's concepts correlate closely with Tyler's questions, Goodlad's data sources, and Taba's steps, but at a deeper level Johnson shares all the major assumptions of the technical production models. Johnson argues that the theoretical (i.e., understanding) and the ideological (i.e., advocacy) "exist in . . . conceptually distinct worlds."[53] Further, he claims that technology may be influenced by theory and research, but not by ideology. Like Tyler, Johnson disavows Taba's linear planning approach, but assumes a means-end logic underlying rational planning. Furthermore, like Goodlad, Johnson's concept of curriculum as "intended learning outcomes" makes clear his assumption of learning as the primary purpose of schooling.

A Critical Perspective

The works of Tyler, Taba, Walker, Schwab, Johnson, and Goodlad represent the dominant thinking in the curriculum field regarding curriculum planning. Although dissent is found among these works regarding specific aspects of the technical productive perspective, I have argued that they share many assumptions. The same point regarding family resemblances and family squabbles might be made for another perspective that has emerged as a response to the dominant viewpoint. As might be expected, this perspective, termed *critical*, takes issue with each of the basic assumptions of the dominant view. This perspective is best understood by examining how it responds to each of the three questions posed by the dominant viewpoint. For this analysis, I focus on Paulo Freire's work.

Freire

Paulo Freire's criticism of schooling practices is captured by his analysis of the banking metaphor.

> Education . . . becomes an act of depositing, in which the students are the depositories and the teacher is the depositor. Instead of communicating, the teacher issues communiques and makes deposits which the students patiently receive, memorize, and repeat. This is the "banking" concept of education, in which the scope of action allowed to the students extends only as far as receiving, filing, and storing the deposits.[54]

The view of curriculum planning that follows from the banking concept of schooling is "that the educator's role is to regulate the way the world 'enters into' the students."[55] The curriculum planner's task is "to organize a process . . . to 'fill' the students by making deposits of information which *he* considers to constitute true knowledge."[56] (Emphasis added.) Thus, Freire is drawing attention to the dominant perspectives's assumption that those with special knowledge make decisions for and about those without that knowledge. This criticism echoes the view of Tyler's critics who claim that his Rationale embodies a "factory" metaphor in which the student is merely the raw material to be fashioned by the "school-factory" into a "product drawn to the specifications of social convention."[57] The critical perspective then, asks us to question the authority of experts in curriculum planning and urges a more democratic relationship between teacher and student.

As an alternative to the curriculum-planning models associated with the technical-production perspective, Freire describes the "emancipatory" approach. Briefly stated, the approach emphasizes "critical reflection" on one's own "concrete situation."[58] In contrast with the banking method, Freire's "problem-posing"[59] method requires "dialogue"[60] in which teacher and student are "critical coinvestigators."[61] They both

> . . . develop their power to perceive critically the way they exist in the world with which and in which they find themselves; they come to see the world not as a static reality, but as a reality in process, in transformation.[62]

This "critical consciousness"[63] is developed in a series of steps. First, a team of educators helps the people in a particular place to develop "generative themes"[64] (e.g., culture, underdevelopment, alcoholism) that represent their view of reality. From this set of themes, a group of professional educators and nonprofessional local volunteers, through "dialogue," cooperatively identify themes to be used for the curriculum and develop instructional materials for each of them. Then the materials are used in "culture circles"[65] as the focus of discussions. The materials, including readings, tape recorded interviews, photographs, and role plays, are designed to reflect characteristics of people's lives and, thus, to stimulate critical reflection about their lives. Ultimately this process leads to "praxis," action based on "critical reflection,"[66] the goal of Freire's pedagogy.

Although Freire's approach does, in fact, answer the procedural question with a step-by-step approach to curriculum planning, it conflicts with most of the basic assumptions of the technical production model. This approach takes issue with the authority of "experts" in curriculum planning decisions. "Dialogue" requires "critical reflection" by both teacher and student as "coinvestigators."[67] The problem-posing approach also requires dialogue with the "students" for the formulation of the generative themes to be used in the curriculum; ". . . [t]his view of education starts with the conviction that it cannot present its own program but must search for this program dialogically with the people. . . ."[68]

The "ideological pretense of the value-free curriculum decision"[69] is abandoned. Abandoning this pretense also undermines the assumption that curriculum development involves purely technical decisions. Thus, curriculum planning is not viewed as a technical matter, but instead as a political and ideological matter. The purpose of the process is for the people "to come to feel like masters of their thinking by discussing the thinking and views of the world explicitly and implicitly manifest in their own suggestions and those of their comrades."[70] Similarly, the end product is not a learning outcome but critical reflection and action upon reality. Of course, learning outcomes, such as ability to reflect critically, are desirable. But political action by the oppressed aimed at their own liberation is the ultimate purpose. To reduce this approach to a set of intended learning outcomes would be to miss its point of political activism.

It is important to note that Freire is at once providing (1) a *descriptive* account of the way teaching and, by implication, curriculum planning is conducted, through the use of the banking metaphor; (2) a *procedural* model by which curriculum should be planned, that is, through the use of generative themes; and (3) a *conceptual* analysis of the fundamental elements of education and their relationships, through an analysis of key concepts including oppression, liberation, critical reflection, dialogue, problem-posing, praxis, human-ization, the theme, codification, object/subject, among others.

Many other scholars approach curriculum planning from a critical per-spective. They ask descriptive and conceptual questions which implicitly attempt to undermine the assumptions on which the technical production perspective rests:

1. What knowledge does the curriculum count as legitimate, and what does it not count?[71]
2. To what extent does the curriculum organization presuppose and serve to "legitimate a rigid hierarchy between teacher and taught?"[72]
3. How does the curriculum enable the school to achieve its primary purposes of social reproduction and hegemony?[73]
4. Who has the greatest access to high-status and high-prestige knowl-edge?
5. Who defines what counts as legitimate knowledge?[74]
6. Whose interests does this definition serve?[75]
7. How do the dominant forms of evaluation serve to legitimize curricu-lum knowledge?[76]
8. To what extent is the schools' sorting function more significant than its educative function?
9. What are the features of the schools' hidden or implicit curriculum, and to what extent does this aspect of schooling mediate teaching the official curriculum?

Underlying these questions is a view that "power, knowledge, ideology, and schooling are linked in ever-changing patterns of complexity."[77] These questions implicitly criticize the view that schools and their curricula can, should, or do provide students with experiences objectively derived from or even primarily justified by a set of learning objectives and that the primary purpose of schooling is to facilitate learning in individuals. For those critical theorists concerned primarily with the hidden curriculum, the official cur-riculum is largely trivial in its significance when compared with implicit messages in the schools' rules and norms of behavior. To other critical theo-rists, the official curriculum is significant not because of its explicit learning objectives, but because of the knowledge it legitimizes and delegitimizes, the effects of this process, and the manner in which it distributes this knowledge differently to different classes of students.

Thus, a critical perspective, although it attempts to provide answers to the procedural, descriptive, and conceptual questions, focuses on another question, a quesiton that takes issue with a fundamental assumption of the technical production perspective: If all curriculum decisions are inherently ideological and political, and therefore an objectively based means-end rationality is itself an ideological pretense, then what is the mode of curriculum rationality?

Ideological Questions

Writers taking the strict technical production perspective attempt to produce ideologically neutral models. Johnson, for example, using ideas from Scheffler, draws a sharp distinction between definitions of curriculum (together with the models on which they are based) which are "programmatic (doctrinal)" and those which are "analytic" or explanatory.[78] He is clearly impatient with confusions of this sort that have plagued the curriculum field. Unfortunately, according to Johnson, various curriculum writers use their curriculum planning models as ideological "platforms" rather than as descriptions or explanations.[79] These platforms have exhorted educators to offer experiences "having a maximum of lifelikeness for the learner,"[80] "to develop individuals along lines consonant with our ideal of the authentic human being,"[81] and to discipline "children and youth in group ways of thinking and acting,"[82] to mention just three notable examples.

These ideological positions are to be avoided and even condemned, according to writers from the technical production perspective. They claim that it is up to the school, not curriculum theorists, to decide what purposes the school curriculum should adopt. Recall that Tyler's first question is followed by a set of technical procedures that any school can use to decide on its purposes. Thus, the rationality of curriculum planning from the technical production perspective is not based on a particular purpose, ideology, or doctrine, but on deciding that purpose objectively and systematically and then by using effective and efficient means for accomplishing it. Therefore, this perspective considers ideological questions to be a procedural step in curriculum planning, not questions to be answered definitively for all curriculum planning.

Critical theorists, however, disagree. Freire regards the development of a critical consciousness to be the only defensible pedagogical purpose. Giroux agrees with Herbert Marcuse that curriculum planning must be committed to "the emancipation of sensibility, reason and imagination, in all spheres of subjectivity and objectivity."[83] Each critical theorist has his or her own ideology. Each agrees that the dominant perspective's pretense of neutrality serves to divert criticism of the dominant ideology.

Conclusion

The problem with studying a topic by answering a series of questions should now be apparent. The questions one asks and what one accepts as a legitimate answer channel the investigation. We have seen how this happens in curriculum models. Different models can be seen as answers to different questions or as different notions of legitimate answers.

Each of the two perspectives examined has made a contribution. The technical production perspective has provided a view of rationality in curriculum planning and has outlined what techniques a curriculum planner needs to master. The critical perspective raises our consciousness regarding the assumptions underlying our work in curriculum. By giving us ground to stand on outside the dominant approach, it has enabled us to examine critically the technical production perspective, to identify its blind spots, and to understand its political and social implications.

Study of curriculum models thus provides two necessary and complementary elements: curriculum development technique and a curriculum conscience. Knowing how to develop a curriculum is what I term *technique*. Being able to identify the assumptions underlying curriculum discussion, that is, understanding what is being taken for granted, is what I term a *curriculum conscience*. A curriculum planner without the former is incompetent ("but what can you do?") and without the latter is ungrounded ("merely a technician"). A "complete" curriculum planning model is not what the field needs. The field needs curriculum planners not only able to use various models but also aware of the implications of their use.

Notes

1. Ralph W. Tyler, *Basic Principle sof Curriculum and Instruction* (Chicago: University of Chicago Press, 1949).

2. Hilda Taba, *Curriculum Development: Theory and Practice* (New York: Harcourt, Brace & World, 1962).

3. Decker Walker, "A Naturalistic Model for Curriculum Development," *School Review* (November 1971)51–65.

4. Mauritz Johnson, "Definitions and Models in Curriculum Theory," *Educational Theory*, 17, 1(April 1967):127–40. Also reprinted in Bellack and Kliebard, 3–19.

5. John I. Goodlad and Maurice N. Richter, Jr., "Decisions and Levels of Decision-Making: Process and Data-Sources," in Arno A. Bellack & Herbert M. Kliebard, eds., *Curriculum and Evaluation* (Berkeley, Calif.: McCutchan Publishing Corporation, 1977), 506–16.

6. See similar arguments by Daniel Tanner and Laurel N. Tanner, *Curriculum Development: Theory Into Practice*, second edition (New York: Macmillan, 1980); William H. Schubert, *Curriculum: Perspective, Perdigm, and Possibility* (New York: Macmillan, 1986); and Decker F. Walker and Jonas F. Soltis, *Curriculum and Aims* (New York: Teachers College Press, 1986).

7. Tyler, *op. cit.*

8. Note, however, that Tyler himself disagrees with this interpretation. I discuss this matter further in a subsequent section.

9. See Kliebard's Chapter 2 herein for a thorough treatment of recent curriculum history.

10. Franklin Bobbitt, *The Curriculum* (Boston: Houghton Mifflin, 1918); and Franklin Bobbitt, *How To Make a Curriculum* (Boston: Houghton Mifflin Co., 1924).

11. W. James Popham and Eva L. Baker, *Systematic Instructing* (Englewood Cliffs, N. J.: Prentice-Hall, 1970).

12. George J. Posner and Alan N. Rudnizsky, *Course Design: A Guide to Curriculum Development For Teachers*, third edition (New York: Longmen, 1987).

13. Douglas Barnes, *Practical Curriculum Study* (London: Routledge & Kegan Paul, 1982).

14. Elliot W. Eisner, *The Educational Imagination* (New York: Macmillan, 1985).

15. This distinction is attributable to Mauritz Johnson, not Tyler, who avoided definitions in his book. See Mauritz Johnson, *Intentionality in Education: A Conceptual Model of Curricular and Instructional Planning and Evaluation* (Albany, N. Y.: Center for Curriculum Research and Services, 1977), pp. 47–8.

16. Goodlad, *op. cit.*

17. Taba, *op. cit.*

18. *Ibid.*, p. 10.

19. *Ibid.*, pp. 462–66.

20. *Ibid.*, p. 463.

21. *Ibid.*, p. 479.

22. *Ibid.*, p. 480.

23. *Ibid.*, p. 12.

24. *Ibid.*, pp. 11–2.

25. Joseph J. Schwab, *The Practical: A Language For Curriculum* (Washington, D. C.: Naitonal Education Association, 1970). A shorter version was published in *School Review*, 78(November 1969):1–24, and reprinted in several anthologies, including Bellack and Kliebard, *op. cit.*, pp. 26–44.

26. *Ibid.*, p. 36.

27. *Ibid.*, pp. 21-3.

28. *Ibid.*, pp. 25–6.

29. *Ibid.*, p. 28.

30. *Ibid.*, p. 12. Joseph J. Schwab, "The Practical 3: Translation Into Curriculum," *School Review*, 79(1973):501–22.

31. *Ibid.*

32. Walker, *op. cit.*

33. *Ibid.*, p. 22.
34. *Ibid.*, p. 52.
35. *Ibid.*
36. *Ibid.*, p. 53.
37. *Ibid.*, p. 54.
38. *Ibid.*, pp. 57–8.
39. *Ibid.*, p. 58.
40. Walker and Soltis, *op. cit.*, p. 51.
41. Tyler, *op. cit.*, p. 1.
42. *Ibid.*, p. 1.
43. *Ibid.*, p. 128.
44. Goodlad and Richter, *op. cit.*
45. *Ibid.*, p. 510.
46. *Ibid.*, p. 510.
47. See, for example, Michael W. Kirst and Decker F. Walker, "An Analysis of Curriculum Policy-Making," *Review of Educational Research*, 41, 5(1971):479–509. Also reprinted in Bellack and Kliebard, *op. cit.*, pp. 538–68.
48. Goodlad and Richter, *op. cit.*, p. 506.
49. Johnson, 1967, *op. cit.*
50. Johnson, 1977, *op. cit.*
51. *Ibid.*
52. *Ibid.*, p. 34.
53. *Ibid.*, p. 9. Paulo Freire, *Pedagogy of the Oppressed* (New York: Seabury Press, 1970).
54. *Ibid.*, p. 58.
55. *Ibid.*, p. 62.
56. *Ibid.*, pp. 62–3.
57. Herbert M. Kliebard, "Bureaucracy and Curriculum Theory," in Bellack and Kliebard, *op. cit.*, p. 613.
58. Freire, *op. cit.*, p. 52.
59. *Ibid.*, p. 66.
60. *Ibid.*, p.76.
61. *Ibid.*, p. 97.
62. *Ibid.*, p. 7.
63. *Ibid.*, p. 54.
64. *Ibid.*, p. 86.
65. *Ibid.*, p. 113.

66. *Ibid.*, pp. 52–3.

67. *Ibid.*, p. 68.

68. *Ibid.*, p. 118.

69. Henry A. Giroux, "Toward a New Sociology of Curriculum," in Henry A. Giroux, Anthony N. Penna, and William F. Pinar, eds., *Curriculum and Instruction* (Berkeley, Calif.: McCutchan Publishing Corporation, 1981), p. 106.

70. Freire, *op. cit.*, p. 118.

71. Michael F. D. Young, "An Approach to the Study of Curricula as Socially Organized Knowledge," in Michael F. D. Young, ed., *Knowledge and Control* (London: Collier-Macmillan, 1971). Also in Bellack and Kliebard, *op. cit.*, pp. 254–85; Giroux, *op. cit.*, p. 104.

72. Young, *op. cit.*, p. 36.

73. *Ibid.*; Giroux, *op. cit.*

74. Young, *op. cit.*

75. Giroux, *op. cit.*

76. *Ibid.*

77. *Ibid.*, p. 194.

78. Johnson, 1967, *op. cit.*, pp. 4–5.

79. *Ibid.*, p. 5.

80. Harold O. Rugg, ed., *The Foundations of Curriculum-Making*, 26th Yearbook of the National Society for the Study of Education (Part II) (Bloomington: Public School Publishing Co., 1972), p. 18.

81. Robert S. Zais, *Curriculum: Principles and Foundations* (New York: Harper and Row, 1976), p. 239.

82. B. Othanel Smith, William O. Stanley, and J. Harlan Shores, *Fundamentals of Curriculum Development*, revised edition (Yonkers-on-Hudson, N.Y.: World Book Co., 1957), p. 3.

83. Giroux, *op cit.*, p. 106.

SIX

Curriculum Planning and the State: The Dynamics of Control in Education

Dennis L. Carlson

T his chapter contextualizes the discussion of curriculum planning, first
by examining its character, structure, and educational and social consequences within the existing political and economic system, and second by
providing a conceptual framework for a redefinition of curriculum planning
consistent with democratic rather than capitalist values and organizational
styles.[1] The analysis of the process by which the curriculum is planned, which
at first glance might appear to involve a quite narrow, insulated, and technical
field of inquiry, actually illuminates fundamental questions that are political
in nature. They entail deep conflict over institutional control and direction
among divergent social groups.

   That these highly politicized questions have not generally been raised in
the professional literature on curriculum planning is only indicative of the
pervasiveness of dominant worldviews in the culture generally, and more
particularly in the public schools, that serve to depoliticize issues by treating
them as merely exercises in administrative rationality. The key principle
underlying a critical assessment of curriculum planning, then, is that linkages
exist between abstract planning models and structures of domination in the
sociocultural and political spheres. Dominant curriculum planning models
contribute to shaping what goes on in schools and classrooms in ways that

help ensure that schools participate in the maintenance of existing capitalist structures, relations, and worldviews. And because these curriculum planning models have their origins in business and managerial models of accountability and top-down control, their widespread adoption in the public schools may be understood as part of a broader sociopolitical phenomenon involving the penetration of capitalist ideologies and organizational forms in spheres outside the directly economic.

Aside from describing dominant curriculum planning models and tracing their historical development in the schools, I also explore some of the contradictions inherent in these approaches to planning that ultimately undermine their effectiveness. For within the historical dynamics of capitalist society, top-down models of planning are often undertaken to deal with crises that threaten system stability, but that, in the process, also generate their own problems. The problem of planning within a capitalist context is thus not fully resolved if indeed it is resolvable. In the final section, I address the issue of formulating an alternative, democratic approach to curriculum planning, one that overcomes the contradictions inherent in current state-sponsored models and offers a framework for the realistic pursuit of excellence in the schools. While such an alternative model is not fully realizable under current political and economic conditions, some things can be supported in the immediate future consistent with democratic political agendas and principles.

Curriculum Planning in Sociohistorical Context

A basic premise of the critical study of education that has emerged in America and Great Britain over the past decade or so is that the maintenance and reproduction of capitalist structures depends increasingly upon state intervention — including state control of the schooling process. That is, social and economic reproduction depends not only on certain modes of economic organization and control; it also entails structuring social activity through various public institutions, such as the schools, so they operate in general accord with capitalist priorities.[2] Because the schools prepare future citizens and workers, the effective reproduction of the existing network of social relations and structured inequalities depends on a high level of integration of the schools with the ideology of advanced capitalism, as well as with its organizational styles.

State educational planning, and particularly curriculum planning, may then be defined as that set of mechanisms and procedures through which state power is brought to bear, and state objectives realized, *vis-à-vis* this important reproductive role of schooling. It is one way, then, of overriding the long tradition of local school autonomy in America to ensure that local districts organize the instructional program in ways that do not fundamentally alter the essential structures and processes of capitalism. Whatever the image of local democratic control of the schools, the reality is one of declining local autonomy, with local curricular decisions increasingly made within the guidelines and in accordance with objectives established at higher tiers of government.[3] If curriculum planning represents the cutting edge of state intervention in public education, it is largely because the curriculum is really the primary tool for the production of learning outcomes in individual schools and classrooms far removed from the locus of state power. For a number of reasons, and under conservative as well as liberal administrations, governmental bureaucracies — at both the state and federal levels concurrently — have expanded their sphere of control over the nation's schools and usurped planning responsibilities traditionally delegated to local school officials.

I employ the notion of *the state* and, more particularly, *the advanced capitalist state* as a basic element of my argument thus far; I now want to be more precise about what I mean by this term and how I use it in this essay. Basically, I mean by the capitalist state that constellation of governmental agencies at various tiers (local, state, and federal) that intervene in the society and the economy in ways that tend to support the maintenance of dominant capitalist interests, organizational models, and structured systems of inequalities. In modern western democracies, the state legitimates this role as being in the interests of the society as a whole and as democratically-supported. The state claims to be a neutral party with respect to class conflicts, and state policy-makers and administrators claim to make decisions on a purely rational or technical basis, rather than a political one.[4] The most forceful critique of this liberal democratic model of the disinterested state has been made by the so-called structuralist Marxists in western Europe, including, most notably, Poulantzas and Althusser.[5] Structuralists argue that the state cannot be understood as an autonomous or independent agency within capitalist society but rather reflects the balance of power among classes and therefore serves a primarily reproductive role *vis-à-vis* the maintenance of the existing order. Even though various divisions or apparatuses within the state are recognized as having some relative autonomy, the structuralist model emphasizes the cohesiveness of the state's role.

Because it tends to promote this image of uniformity and common purpose, with the state viewed as acting as a single force and agency, the structuralist model has come under increasing criticism by less deterministic and less politically pessimistic analysts on the Left, whom I will here lump together under the term neo-Marxists. The neo-Marxist model of the state differs from the structuralist one not in its rejection of the notion that the state represents class interests but in its acknowledgement that the state is also a site of struggle. This model emphasizes that there is some limited room within the state for counterhegemonic activity, and that the state is not, therefore, reducible to a mere epiphenomenon of the economic base.[6] The state's operation and role in any given situation is not wholly determinable, and progressive social elements may use the state, or elements of it, to address some of their concerns. These aspects of democratic control, along with democratic social ideals that continue to exist within the context of a capitalist economy, also provide a driving force for transformative change and constantly threaten the long-run stability of the current system. For example, Jurgen Habermas views the state as an input-output system, with the input being "mass loyalty" or consent, democratically (electorally) obtained.[7] State interventions, from this perspective, are forms of crisis avoidance or management. When the state exercises its power to enable some to profit more than others, it constantly risks losing its legitimacy in the eyes of the public. This legitimation crisis is compounded by the fiscal crisis the state faces, with the tendency for essential social services to be cut back to unacceptable levels, so that the social system becomes even more inequitable and public support more uncertain.[8] The state is viewed as attempting to alleviate persistent contradictions and conflicts as the balance of power between the various groups and coalitions shifts and changes. Overall, the neo-Marxist model of the state helps illuminate the complex relationship between the pervasive role of the state in supporting dominant socioeconomic interests, organizational models, and worldviews, and the formal democratic controls and democratic ideals that undergird the legitimacy of the modern democratic capitalist state.

While the neo-Marxist model of the state I sketched above is nondeterministic in important ways, it also accepts the notion that the state overwhelmingly serves the interests of elite socioeconomic groups. Therefore, in discussing state planning, and more specifically state curriculum planning, I begin with an examination of how the state planning process perpetuates and promotes capitalist models of organization and control. Subsequently, I take up the issue of contradictions and crisis tendencies within state planning. This century has witnessed vastly increased intervention by the state into the affairs of the society generally as well as the economy per se, a centralization of state power, and a depoliticization of state control through new forms of rational administration. Publicly-elected governing boards, including school boards, have been encouraged to limit their involvement to the promulgation of broad policy guidelines and to leave the planning and implementation of policy, along with the everyday operation of public institutions, to specially trained administrators. George H. Wood refers to this conception of democratic control of public institutions as "protectionist democracy," in which the public's role is limited to choosing among political elites in general elections who supposedly represent and protect the public interest through the efficient management of institutions.[9]

This is also a state model that is, of course, highly compatible with capitalist ideology in that it presupposes a centralization of power and authority. Key decisions are relegated to top management, which determines the type and level of system production, the particular forms of institutional organization, and the standards for evaluating instructional effectiveness. In education, the historical movements for "clean government," an end to the political control of the schools by ward politicians, and the consolidation of school districts with an increase in educational administrators, have been consistent with this growing centralization of the state and the growing role of state planning.[10]

Related to the growth of centralized state planning in this century has been the widespread adoption by the state of new planning models borrowed from industry. The first of these new planning models was associated with *scientific management*, a form of management that virtually revolutionized American industry in the first few decades of this century.[11] The objective of scientific management, according to its early advocate, Frederick Taylor, was the "*enforced* standardization of methods, *enforced* adoption of the best implements and working conditions, and *enforced* cooperation of all the employees under management's detailed direction."[12] All participants in institutional work processes, it was argued, should be defined in terms of exact responsibilities and assessed on the basis of success in meeting their assigned responsibilities. That is, scientific management proposed a form of institutional accountability based on a clearly delineated chain of command and role formalization. The more one moves up the hierarchy, the more one knows about the activities of those below; and conversely, the more one moves down the hierarchy, the less is known about the activities of those above. This can be called *hierarchical accountability* rather than *democratic accountability* because it facilitates social control over an institution by a powerful elite at the top of a bureaucratic pyramid.[13]

In the schools, scientific management and hierarchical accountability have implied the rigid specification and differentiation of administrative (managerial) and teaching (labor) roles. Top-level administrators *conceive* of plans, teachers and principals *execute* them. Scientific management also implies a heightened concern with quantifying and standardizing measures of school "output" which means increased standardized testing to hold schools more accountable. As with the clean government movement, support for school system accountability has come from both progressive and conservative social groups. Taxpayers, afterall, want to ensure that they get their money's worth out of the schools, so accountability systems have some political appeal. Nevertheless, they too have had the predominant effect of helping to bring the schools into closer alignment with the interests of elite social groups and with the organizational forms typical of advanced capitalism.

By the 1950s, the movements for clean government, scientific management, and accountability had all become incorporated in a new systems theory of society and institutional operation and control. *Systems theory*, as it has been developed in abstract terms in American social science and more pragmatically in state planning agencies, implies that the society is a broadly consensual and cohesive whole — with various institutions, public and private, serving specialized and functional roles that benefit the social system overall. The schools, for example, are presumed to foster socializing and training of the young so that they can make productive contributions to society.[14] Schools process student inputs to generate learning outputs. Questions that systems theory raises about the schools' operation concern how efficiently they perform their assigned roles and what impediments or dysfunctions impede the system from operating more efficiently and effectively. Reform is thus viewed as an adjustment in the steerage of the system designed to improve institutional effectiveness or efficiency and lessen system dysfunctions. In order to facilitate the proper steerage of the schools, cadres of educational planners are presumed to be needed, who constantly monitor the quantitative output of the system and assist local educators in fine-tuning their instructional delivery systems. By focusing on a narrow means-ends rationality, deep-rooted structural problems, along with proposals for transforming rather than merely reforming the system, implicitly are not considered. The result is a shrinking of the overtly political sphere of democratic decisionmaking and a corresponding expansion of the state managerial sphere. By the 1960s, a number of American social theorists heavily influenced by this systems theory even began to talk of the end of ideology in government.[15] From a critical perspective, however, systems theory does not represent an end of ideology as much as a further attempt at depoliticizing ideology; and, as I develop more fully below, systems theory does not appear to resolve the basic underlying contradictions that plague efforts to maintain system stability and legitimacy.

When *systems theory* is translated into practical planning programs and techniques, we may refer to it as *systems management*. Perhaps the most important and comprehensive form of systems management within government is the planning, programming, and budgeting system (PPBS).[16] In most basic terms, PPBS means that the state's budgeting decisions are based on evidence of an explicit plan by local public agencies and institutions receiving state funds. This plan details the specific objectives of institutional programs, the steps involved in realizing these objectives, and the quantitative assessment techniques that will be employed to determine whether objectives have been sufficiently met. Specific informational categories are designated by the state for which "hard" data is required. Each round of budgeting decisions is then made at least partially on the basis of demonstrated performance (or lack of performance) over the previous budgeting period. This means that programs must continue to demonstrate their productivity or face budget cutbacks and possible reorganization. In 1960, the federal Department of Defense under the leadership of Robert McNamara — an enthusiastic supporter of systems management — became the first governmental agency to adopt the new management revolution that had already begun to transform corporate planning. Approximately four years after systems management was instituted in the Department of Defense, in the summer of 1965, President Lyndon Johnson announced that it would be required in all federal agencies and departments. Each agency was mandated to organize a specialized planning staff with analytic capacity to execute a multiyear planning and programming procedure and to collect data to aid agency heads in making policy decisions.

At the U.S. Office of Education, Commissioner Harold Howe II announced that a total reorganization was underway to place all education programs "on a basis comparable to that of the Department of Defense, where the planning, programming, and budgeting operation has been effectively adopted."[17] The vastly expanded federal education budget in the 1960s was then used to pressure local school districts to adopt the new planning guidelines if they wanted to share in the wealth. School districts were expected to generate quantitative data on output goals and assessment procedures if they wanted to be considered for federal program development monies. Leon Lessinger, Associate Commissioner of Education in the Johnson Administration, talked of a new era in the schools, with local curriculum decisions increasingly brought under the control of a comprehensive master plan. Lessinger argued that:

> Such a plan should be based on 'market research,' that is, an investigation of the needs of the students in each particular school. It should also be based on research and development to facilitate constant update of specifications to meet these needs. Through the plan the school district would be able to measure its own output against the way its students actually perform. It would be able to see exactly what results flow from the dollars it has invested. . . . To assure that the plan will provide quality, it should use a mix of measurements that are relevant, reliable, objective, easily assessable, and that produce data in a form that can be processed by modern-day technology.[18]

State legislatures also began to mandate PPBS procedures in evaluating programs; because education typically consumes about one-half of the state budget, local school districts were compelled to reorganize their programs to meet state information needs.

I have suggested that systems management, like earlier forms of rational administration of state agencies and public institutions, has served to centralize state control over the schools and to legitimate this control as apolitical or socially neutral when in fact it has served the interests of social and economic groups differentially. At the same time, this imposition of top-down control has often been supported by wide segments of the voting public as a way of improving school efficiency and ensuring that the schools are held accountable to the public. In the 1960s, for example, the Great Society and War on Poverty legislation of the Johnson Administration was supported for good reason by many disadvantaged groups because it was to some extent aimed at ensuring greater equality of opportunity within the system. Similarly, in the 1970s and 1980s, public concerns for accountability, as I have already indicated, are at least partially progressive in both intent and effect. Nevertheless, in both cases, the primary result of legitimate public concern about making the schools more responsive to the people has been a further centralization of an educational planning role that is undemocratic, promotes the further disempowerment of groups disadvantaged by schooling, and perpetuates the current structured system of inequalities. Michael W. Apple speaks eloquently of this paradox in American education:

> Popular classes and groups have demanded recognition of their rights as persons. The state has had to recognize these rights in ways that were simply not the case before, if only to preserve its own legitimacy. However, the way in which this sought after extension is accomplished by the state apparatus is by first establishing formal and rational procedures and attempting to expand their use throughout all areas under the state's control, and second by then bringing under its control other areas of social life that were not under state control previously.
>
> It is this formalization that is one of the fundamental contradictions of liberal curricular and educational policy. What started out as a struggle within the state to bring about more democratic forms (person rights) ultimately increases centralization and rationalization.[19]

The other side of this picture is that by failing to provide real equality of opportunity (in fact, by continuing to promote *inequalities* of opportunity) and by failing to address the public's concern for democratic controls as well as efficiency in the schools, the state threatens to increase public discontent with the operation of the schools and ultimately undermines the legitimacy of state intervention in education.

Systems Models of Curriculum Planning at the Classroom Point of Production

To be more specific about some of the effects of adopting dominant state-sponsored systems models, look at the actual "point of production" of

105

the learning outcomes. I focus on three specific types of educational changes associated with systems planning models: changes in the *form* of the curriculum consistent with notions of individualization, changes in the *content* of the curriculum consistent with a basic skills orientation, and changes in the role of the teacher consistent with deskilling and the substitutability of labor.

The key to control over the classroom point of production from the systems management perspective is control over curricular form: if the *form* of the curriculum can be sufficiently predetermined and standardized, then its *use* by teachers and students can be strongly influenced. In fact, one might go as far as saying that top-down state planning in education would not work very well without a reconceptualization and technical reorganization of traditional curricular forms. Systems planning forms of curriculum are highly rationalized. Knowledge to be learned and activities to be performed by students are first fragmented into a series of small bits of knowledge (*competencies* or *skills* as they are called in behavioral science), which are then reassembled in a hierarchical sequence. The student approaches the curriculum as a series of small, sequential tasks to be completed and skills to be mastered. No questions need be raised pertaining to what is to be done, how it is to be done, or in what order it is to be completed. The student's task, with the guidance of the teacher, is to execute the curricular plan laid out before him or her. This is referred to as an *individualized curriculum* because materials are designed to be self-guided by individual students, who are placed in the curriculum based on an assessment of their individual skill needs. Rationalization of curriculum form along these lines represents a rather direct application of scientific management principles from industry.[20] Individualization not only facilitates hierarchical accountability to management, it also partly socializes students into forms of work that dominate in large sectors of the economy, where work processes are highly rationalized and where workers are expected to adhere closely to a predetermined sequence of activities and operations.[21]

Although some work had been done on objective-based or individualized curricular systems as early as the 1950s, it was not until the late 1960s, when the federal government began subsidizing research and development of a systems model of the curriculum, that significant advances were made. Under the auspices of the Elementary and Secondary Education Act of 1965, 20 regional educational research and development centers and laboratories were established, most of them on major university campuses, and charged with the formulation, planning, and testing-out of a workable model of individualized curriculum that could be widely adopted in the nation's schools consistent with new PPBS formats.[22] Thus, as with the National Defense Education Act in the 1950s, which led to the development and ultimately the marketing of the so-called new math and science curriculum, the federal government in the

1960s facilitated the development of new individualized curricular programs. In the early 1970s, federal research and development monies were drastically reduced, and the centers and laboratories moved to become more self-supporting by packaging and marketing curricular materials they developed for local school systems. In the 1980s, as the educational research and development portion of the federal budget has continued to decline, textbook publishers have assumed more responsibility, and a larger share of the profits, involved in the further development and marketing of individualized curricular programs. The major selling point of these programs has always been that they provide the kinds of quantitative data on system productivity that the state requires under new budgeting guidelines. School systems that continue to hold out or lag behind in making the transition to systems models of curriculum find it increasingly difficult to satisfy state officials in making budgetary requests.

My concern here is with the interplay between a particular state-sponsored curriculum planning model and the resultant form the curriculum assumes. Of course, curriculum is more than a technology of form; it is also, and more commonsensically, a corpus of knowledge selected by educators to be conveyed to students in the educational process. How, then, do systems models of curriculum planning influence conceptions about what should be learned? Inextricably linked to the movement to individualize the form of the curriculum has been a corresponding movement among professional educators and within elements of the state to emphasize basic skills as the foundation of the public school curriculum. The rationalization of the instructional process, as I have already indicated, involves an extreme reduction and objectification of abstract knowledge into series, or arrays, of discrete skills to be mastered. Based on Basil Bernstein's theoretical framework, in such a curriculum the relationship among the various elements in the corpus of knowledge is closed.[23] In contrast, integrated curricula incorporate elements of knowledge that stand in open relationship to one another, so that their interconnectedness is grasped. Individualized curricular programs cannot be associated with integrative conceptions of knowledge and learning as long as they must rely on processes of fragmentation and rationalization; this means that support for the further individualization of the curriculum (in a technological sense) must also imply support for a basic-skills orientation to student learning. What is required of students under most systems of individualized instruction is not critical thinking, or even a very high level of analytic thinking. Instead, students learn a form of purposive-rational thinking about things that may severely restrict their capacities to understand the linkages between social phenomena or envision alternatives.

A third major impact of dominant state-sponsored models of curriculum planning at the level of practice has to do with the reconceptualization of the teacher's role *vis-à-vis* the selection, organization, and transmission of the curriculum to students. Individualized, output-based curricula are designed to be self-guided by individual students; therefore, they are also teacher proof in a way the traditional textbook is not. The newer curricular materials are designed so that teachers are no longer the primary transmitters or interpreters of curriculum knowledge. Instead, they spend much more time monitoring and supervising ongoing classroom work processes. Apple writes of these changes:

> Skills that teachers used to need, that are deemed essential to the craft of working with children — such as curriculum deliberation and planning, designing teaching and curricular strategies for specific groups and individuals based on intimate knowledge of these people — are no longer as necessary. With the large-scale influx of prepackaged material, planning is separated from execution. The planning is done at the level of production of both the rules for use of the material and the material itself. The execution is carried out by the teacher.[24]

One related impact of systems planning models on the role of the teacher has been a heightened concern for evaluating teachers according to their abilities to increase the level of student time on task in the classroom. Research within education on pupil engagement, pupil time on task, or pupil attention has an extensive history that reflects a continuing concern for gaining greater control over the time element in the classroom productivity calculus.[25] We may view this research as the educational counterpart of time-and-motion studies conducted by efficiency experts in industry. Control of the time element in classroom instruction becomes essential in systems models of the curriculum because system-level output goals for student achievement are tied to a time schedule that corresponds with major rounds of standardized testing. Yearly achievement goals for each class are translated into monthly, weekly, and ultimately daily goals for progress in specified skill areas, which pressures both teachers and students to maintain the pace lest they be ill-prepared for the next round of testing.

Finally, while teacher's work is deskilled through the individualization of the curriculum, it is also, and in a related way, both "cheapened" and made more substitutable. For, as the curriculum is teacher proofed through rationalization, teachers themselves become more interchangeable and substitutable as units of instructional labor. Experience in the craft of teaching becomes less essential and therefore devalued by the system. Thus, in many of our nation's school districts — particularly urban ones — the use of underqualified, inexperienced, and even unlicensed permanent substitutes is on the rise, and it seems likely that the wider adoption of systems models of the curriculum will only encourage this phenomenon.[26] In spite of the concerns voiced by various commission reports on the schools that teachers be treated more professionally, the reality may continue to be the further deskilling of many teachers and the worsening of their working conditions as individualized instructional systems become more pervasive.

In this section, I have focused upon an examination of some of the ways a dominant curriculum planning model has influenced the form and content of the curriculum and the role of the teacher, and has thereby worked to bring the schools into closer accord with economic worldviews and organizational styles in the fulfillment of schools' reproductive role. This, however, is only one side of a complex reality, and a critical appraisal of curriculum planning must also include some discussion of the contradictions and destabilizing tendencies within dominant state planning models that work to undermine top-down control. It is not merely coincidental, after all, that the current malaise of public education and the so-called crisis of excellence arises out of a context in which state models of curriculum planning have become ever more powerful and pervasive. As reaction formations to endemic conflicts and contradictions within state sponsored schooling, systems models may help overcome some problems at the same time that they promote others. Ultimately, as I suggested earlier, the contradictions of control in capitalism drive the political and economic systems towards crisis, and reform is but a stop-gap effort to stay one step ahead of crisis. In organizing work activities — whether in the factory, office, or classroom — systems models suffer from one overriding dilemma: greater control over the point of production is achieved only at the expense of a further alienation of workers from system goals. Highly predetermined and rationalized work is severely lacking in motivation that is internal or intrinsic to the task. Instead, work becomes perceived as a routine, drudgery, something that one does only when compelled and/or extrinsically rewarded.[27] In industry, the ascendancy of scientific management and systems management forms of work structuring have led to worker discontent, increased conflict in the workplace, resistances by workers, a decline in worker concern over product quality, high absenteeism and turn-over rates, and the so-called blue collar blues, a form of worker apathy that management suddenly discovered in the late 1970s.

School work, organized through curriculum planning along similar lines, encourages similar kinds of alienation reactions among both teachers and students. As learning becomes apprehended as merely a work routine, it loses much of its power to motivate and much of its meaning to the learner. Core problems in schooling at this point in time consequently have much to do with a general decline in student motivation and teacher morale. Instead of dealing head-on with this issue of motivation, systems planning models look for new ways of getting around the problem, of increasing classroom productivity in other ways, and at some point these cease to be very effective in dealing with a problem that has its roots in motivation. For example, one of the problems of approaches to increasing classroom productivity through more time on task is that they tend to overlook the phenomenon of diminishing returns in routine work. That is, at some point equal additions of time spent with the curriculum, all other factors held constant, will yield smaller and smaller incremental gains in achievement as fatigue and boredom begin to interfere unduly with progress in skill mastery. In this context, there is no reason to believe that more accountability systems and more predetermination of the curriculum will solve the basic problems that haunt public education. By locking teachers, students, parents, and the community out of the planning process, by emphasizing a reductionistic and inherently alienating conception of learning, and by treating teachers as interchangeable or substitutable units of instructional labor, the system generates problems that threaten system stability and that resist resolution within the systems management framework.

Towards an Alternative Model of Curriculum Planning

The first element of a critical appraisal of curriculum planning, as sketched in the preceding sections, involves an examination of existing models and forms, a description of their social and economic roots, their impact on the reproductive role of the schools, and an assessment of the contradictions and dilemmas that drive the system towards fundamental change. A second essential element in critical analysis is the formulation of a politically progressive response that works toward fundamental system change, including redirecting the goals of schooling to include personal empowerment within the context of a democratic society. This second element can, in turn, be broken down into two tasks. First, critical analysts of schooling must propose a coherent model of what curriculum planning might look like in a postcapitalist social context. To some extent, this will represent an idealized model, in that it is not immediately realizable given the constraints placed upon the schools in advanced capitalism. Its formulation, however, is essential if we are to have some idea of what to work for — and against. Second, we need to establish criteria for analyzing and reacting to current calls for reform within the schools, for working within the current social context to support limited but nevertheless worthwhile change. For example, we might conclude that reforms should be supported that seem likely to increase the benefits disadvantaged groups can derive from state institutions such as schools. What makes such support radical in some sense is that it is motivated by a concurrent concern to push the state to the limits of reform — to reveal, in fact, that severe limits *do* exist on school reform within the current system — and thereby to further demystify the workings of the schools and the state in the interests of socioeconomic elites. A democratic political agenda must pursue objectives that have a chance of being realized within existing political parameters; but it must also emphasize the fact that current reform efforts are not enough, that certain structures and beliefs stand in the way of a more fundamental transformation of the educational process, and that without such a reorganization and redirection of public education (which implies a broader reorganization and redirection of institutional control within the state) the system will continue to languish in a state of crisis.

Let me address more specifically several broad directions of school change that seem worthy of support from a critical perspective. First, a progressive model of curriculum planning might well continue to define the learning process as a work process; however, in this case, the emphasis would be on structuring the conditions for nonalienating school work by teachers and students. Work can be understood as experience that contributes to self-development and identity formation and that contributes to the "making" of a culture. Nonalienating school work might not always be "fun," as some "free school" educators believed it could be. It may entail a good deal of hard work on the part of both teachers and students. It may even involve some rather routine library reference work and sorting of data. What makes school work nonalienating, for students, is their sense that the system basically serves their interests, that it is preparing them for a responsible and productive adulthood in a society that they are helping to shape and that they are also helping to shape and direct their own learning. We may refer to this type of nonalienating curriculum as *personalized*, rather than individualized. While *individualization* implies the technical predetermination, rationalization, and routinization of the learning process compatible with top-down control, *personalization* implies a curriculum that is not totally determined in advance, that is open to modification in classroom practice, and that is more concerned with the development of higher-order critical thinking skills than with the acquisition of sets of reductionistically defined basic skills.[28] The objective must be to create a literate, democratic citizenry capable of self-governance, which absolutely requires that students be provided with opportunities to make choices and decisions. This is similar to what Wood means in his call for a "pedagogy of democratic participation." He writes:

> To enable students to attain the literacy skills needed for democratic action, critical-literacy work could help students uncover the reality of the current social relations. . . . Beyond the school, students can use the conditions of their daily existence in the search for critical literacy. . . . Thus students become critically-literate — not only able 'to read' and 'do math', but able to penetrate the very structures which oppress them. This is the first step towards a pedagogy for democratic participation.[29]

111

Aside from these changes in the curriculum's form and content, a more progressive model of curriculum planning would imply a far greater decentralization of decisionmaking generally in making curricular choices within the broad guidelines established for the schools by the community and the society. For teachers in particular this means more discretionary power over the actual organization, content, and evaluation of classroom lessons. It also means much more time for teachers outside of the self-contained classroom, working on various committees in the school and the community to help plan and revise the instructional program. Joseph Schwab writes of such a role for the teacher:

> Teachers must be involved in *debate, deliberation* and *decision* about what and how to teach. . . . Without such [involvement] . . . teachers not only feel decisions as impositions, they find that intelligence cannot traverse the gap between the generalities of merely expounded instructions and the particularities of teaching moments. Participation in debate-deliberation-choice is required for learning what is needed as well as for willingness to do it.[30] (Emphasis mine)

Teacher accountability might continue to be an important concern if the role of the teacher was changed in these directions, but it would certainly take on a very different form and function. Teachers' rights as craft practitioners must be matched with the rights of school client groups (students, parents, the community), as well as the needs of the broader society. All of these groups have a right to explanations and input into curricular decisions. Nevertheless, democratic conceptions of accountability suggest that room should be left for the broad exploration of a wide and differing range of options for teachers. As Maurice Kogan observes, "an accountability system can put as much emphasis on individual discretion as on authority conveyed by prescription."[31] Accountability systems themselves are not inherently evil or elitist. What is wrong with accountability systems as currently conceived by corporate and state planners is that they are undemocratic, they serve to depoliticize and thereby legitimate a whole range of inherently political planning issues, and they insist upon the quantification of learning outcomes following a production metaphor. Democratic accountability systems must be based on differing principles.

Finally, although I advocate here a participatory democratic model of curriculum planning with a good deal of decentralization of power and authority, I do not want to suggest that the state would simply "wither away" in some ideal Marxian sense in postcapitalist society. Rather, the state would continue to exercise some general control over the schools consistent with the concerns of the society as a whole, although this control would be less extensive and of a different form from that exercised by the state in advanced capitalism. Local districts might be prohibited, for example, from adopting textbooks that include racial or gender-based stereotypes and pejorative images, and they might be required to adhere to a planning process that effectively involves broad segments of the community or that includes qualitative as well as quantitative data for evaluation purposes. But because schooling would no longer be a process requiring a good deal of imposition, control, and subordination, the inherent conflicts and contradictions of planning in the current system would largely be overcome. State guidelines, therefore, would be the result of a decisionmaking process that ultimately begins at the local level and moves upward, rather than the result of top-down impositional decisionmaking.

Notes

1. I do not mean to pose "capitalist" and "democratic" as totally dichotomous terms, or to suggest that elements of democracy do not exist within the context of advanced capitalist society. I do mean to suggest, however, that the more complete realization of democratic ideals is fundamentally at odds with the continued domination of capitalist models of organization and control. To this extent, struggles to further democratize society must at some point challenge capitalist hegemony.

2. For a good overview of this critical perspective see Michael W. Apple, ed., *Cultural and Economic Reproduction in Education; Essays on Class, Ideology and the State* (Boston: Routledge and Kegan Paul, 1982).

3. See Gordon Clark and Michael Dear, *State Apparatuses; Structures and Language of Legitimacy* (Boston: George Allen and Unwin, 1984); Chapter 7, "The Local State," pp. 104–30.

4. *Ibid.*, Chapter 2, "The Problematic of the Capitalist State," pp. 14–35.

5. Nicos Poulantzas, *Classes in Contemporary Capitalism* (London: New Left Books, 1975); and Louis Althusser, "Ideology and Ideological State Apparatuses," in *Lenin and Philosophy and Other Essays* (London: New Left Books, 1971).

6. For criticism of the structuralist model see Anthony Giddens, *Central Problems in Social Theory* (Berkeley, Calif.: University of California Press, 1979); and Erik Olin Wright, "Giddens' Critique of Marxism," *New Left Review* (March–April 1983): pp. 11–35.

7. Jurgen Habermas, *Legitimation Crisis* (Boston: Beacon Press, 1975).

8. See James O'Connor, *The Fiscal Crisis of the State* (New York: St. Martin's Press, 1973); and Joan Weitzman, *City Workers and Fiscal Crisis; Cutbacks, Givebacks and Survival* (New Brunswick, N. J.: Rutgers University Press, 1979).

9. George H. Wood, "Schooling in a Democracy: Transformation or Reproduction," *Educational Theory*, 34(Summer 1984): pp. 219–39.

DENNIS L. CARLSON

10. For a discussion of the clean government movement in education see David Tyack, *The One Best System: A History of American Urban Education* (Cambridge, Mass. Harvard University Press, 1974).

11. See Harry Braverman, *Labor and Monopoly Capital* (London: Monthly Review Press, 1974). See also Craig Littler, *The Development of the Labor Process in Capitalist Societies* (London: Heinemann, 1982) for a detailed account of the spread of scientific management in Great Britain, Japan, and the United States.

12. Frederick Taylor, *The Principles of Scientific Management* (New York: 1967 reprint), p. 24.

13. This notion is developed by Maurice Kogan, *Education Accountability; an Analytic Overview* (London: Hutchinson, 1986), Chapter 2, "Normative Models of Accountability," pp. 25–54.

14. See Talcott Parsons, "The School Class as a Social System: Some of Its Functions in American Society," *Harvard Educational Review*, 29 (Fall 1959): pp. 297–318.

15. See Daniel Bell, *The End of Ideology* (New York: Collier Books, 1961). For a neo-Marxist critique of the "end of ideology" theorists see Michael Mann, *Consciousness and Action Among the Western Working Class* (London: Macmillan, 1973).

16. I lay out this historical development of systems management in the state in more detail in " 'Updating' Individualism and the Work Ethic: Corporate Logic in the Classroom," *Curriculum Inquiry*, 12, (1982): pp. 125-60.

17. Elaine Exton, "USOE Uses Computer-Based Models to Evaluate Education," *American School Board Journal*, 154(January 1967):pp. 15–6.

18. Leon Lessinger, "Accountability for Results: A Basic Challenge for America's Schools," *American Education*, 5(June–July 1969):p. 3.

19. Michael W. Apple, "State Bureaucracy and Curriculum Control; A Review Essay on *Legislated Learning: The Bureaucratization of the American Classroom*, by Arthur Wise," *Curriculum Inquiry*, 11, 4(1981):pp. 382–83.

20. Michael W. Apple, "Curricular Form and the Logic of Technical Control: Building the Possessive Individual," in Apple, ed, *Cultural and Economic Reproduction in Education*, pp. 247–74.

21. For an exposition of this "correspondence" between school and work norms, see Samuel Bowles and Herbert Gintis, *Schooling in Capitalist America* (New York: Basic Books, 1976). Although their treatment is overly deterministic, it nevertheless makes sense as a general description of the effects of schooling.

22. See Carlson, " 'Updating' Individualism and the Work Ethic: Corporate Logic in the Classroom," *op. cit.*, pp. 138–42.

23. Basil Bernstein, *Class, Codes, and Control*, Vol. 3 (London: Routledge & Kegan Paul, 1977).

24. Apple, "Curricular Form and the Logic of Technical Control: Building the Possessive Individual," *op cit.*, p. 255.

25. See Stephen Rubin and William Spady, "Achieving Excellence through Outcome-Based Instructional Delivery," *Educational Leadership*, 41(May

1984):p.38; and Charles Fisher and David Berliner, eds., *Perspectives on Instructional Time* (New York: Longman, 1985).

26. See *Making Do in the Classroom: A Report on the Misassignment of Teachers*, Council for Basic Education (Washington, D. C.: 1985); and Fred Hechinger, " 'Dirty Little Secret' of Unlicensed Teachers," *New York Times* (October 8, 1985):p. C8.

27. See Robert Dubin, "Industrial Workers' Worlds: A Study of the Central Life Interests of Industrial Workers," *Social Problems*, 3(1956).

28. Theodore Sizer develops this notion of personalization in *Horace's Compromise: The Dilemma of the American High School* (Boston: Houghton Mifflin Co., 1984).

29. Wood, *op. cit.*, pp. 234–35.

30. Joseph Schwab, "The Practical Four: Something for Curriculum Professors to Do," *Curriculum Inquiry*, 13(Fall 1983):p. 245.

31. Kogan, *op. cit.*, p. 36.

III

Curriculum and Knowledge Selection

SEVEN

Curriculum and Knowledge Selection

Philip H. Steedman

Developments in the field of curriculum studies in the last generation have been both various and spectacular, many of which are discussed in other chapters herein. This chapter focuses on the relations that exist between curriculum questions, issues, problems and theories, on the one hand, and different accounts of the nature of knowledge, on the other. But even this preliminary delimitation may be misleading. One should note that, in this field, isolating one constellation of issues and problems from others relating to it is not really possible. A fully developed and rigorous treatment of these topics would raise all the important issues educational theory comprehends, and understanding why this should be is easy. *Knowledge* is conceptually related to *education* and also to *curriculum*. Discussions of one at least imply the others. Selection is thus inevitable in this chapter. The first section outlines an account of what is characterized as the traditional conceptualization of the relations between curriculum and knowledge. A critique of this understanding is included as well. The second section examines several of the most influential candidates competing to replace the traditional account. Both sections aim to delineate the debates surrounding these positions and draw a map of this terrain.

The Traditional Account

Education and *curriculum* are both Greek in their origins. Our culture receives both as interpretations of our ancestors' understandings of aspects of Greek conceptions of social life. Specifically, our culture's comprehension of these matters is much filtered by English interpretations and idealizations of Greek social practice and theory. What the Greeks thought about these matters is, plainly, varied and often contradictory; indeed, the idea of "the Greeks" and their "thinking" about anything in particular of this sort cannot sustain careful scrutiny. More important, however, is the emphasis of interpretations of Greek thought that became widespread in the nineteenth century. As Matthew Arnold had a decisive influence on such conceptions in the nineteenth century, Paul Hirst has had a similar influence in our own, and this discussion focuses on his work.

Hirst's work, however, has not been confined to such questions. His writing in several areas has been influential. However, Hirst's work in curriculum justification has been the most influential[1] and has caused him to be regarded as one of the most celebrated and controversial philosophers of education of this day. In order to examine this work, the scene must be set by reviewing Hirst's intellectual "location."

First, Hirst is one of the principal members of the London School. The School is led by R. S. Peters and P. H. Hirst and lists among its members persons such as R. F. Dearden, J. P. White, P. A. White, and R. Pring.[2] The School is committed to the philosophical consideration of fundamental questions underpining educational practices, insisting that these questions be treated with the standards of academic rigor normally accorded other philosophical inquiries. Its technique has been, for the most part, *conceptual analytic*, inheriting the methodology of philosophers such as Gilbert Ryle and J. L. Austin and applying it with startlingly illuminating results in a traditionally opaque, even wasted, area. In this endeavor, Hirst and Peters have been closely linked. Their *The Logic of Education*[3] represented a rough summary of the London School's work up to the time of publication. In this partnership, Peters provides the ethical component[4] of the emerging educational theory, while Hirst contributes the epistemological component.

A second characteristic of Hirst's work, linked strongly to the first, is its conservatism. The London School, and Hirst with it, inherited the intellectual orientation of English academic conservatism. Oakeshott's work[5] has been influential as a foundation of the London School's work. Its most important characteristic is an absolute insistence on seeing persons as products and inheritors of their cultures, stressing traditional values such as those of respect for excellence. Indeed, they are central to this position. These values find the most explicit support in Oakshott's work, but they are also deeply embedded in that of Peters and Hirst, although less obviously.

The third characteristic of Hirst's intellectual position is his fundamental epistemological positivism, which is not discussed explicitly in his published work, but permeates the work nevertheless. The position Hirst adopts is to some extent that taken by Hamlyn[6] to whom Hirst acknowledges a debt. This positivism, despite being discredited as an epistemological theory, haunts much philosophical thinking to this day. The particular form this influence has taken in Hirst's work emerges in the following discussion.

Hirst's Curriculum Justification

Hirst's work in curriculum justification has been immensely significant. One might not agree with Peters's observation, "Whitehead once said that philosophy never really recovered from the shock of Plato. My guess is that curriculum theory will never recover from the shock of Hirst."[7] Or, one might regard this shock less favorably than does Peters. Nevertheless, Hirst's work has been the center of a sustained critical debate about the curriculum and its justification. This is the consequence of two factors. First, Hirst's scope has been vast. He has addressed, or has often been seen as addressing, the most fundamental questions of this sort. He has, one might say, faced the problem(s) and its (their) implications, head on. Regardless of what may be said in criticism of Hirst, it should be recognized and appreciated that his work was not simply a nit-picking tinkering with philosophical trivia but a genuine attempt to answer philosophical and educational problems of great depth and complexity. That he may have failed in some measure should not obscure the grandeur of the undertaking. Second, Hirst's writing style has caused great confusion. On the one hand, the problems he has discussed are vast and important and, in virtue of these facts, other philosophers have addressed themselves to his work. On the other hand, Hirst's writing style, together with his apparent unwillingness to provide a complete account (in print) of his position, has caused confusions and not a little frustration. A good deal of the critical debate has originated in this confusion.

Peters's ethical views are argued widely, but he *has* given a single, elaborated, well-argued account of them in one volume.[8] The same cannot be said of Hirst. He has not produced the companion volume to Peters's *Ethics and Education* that he might, and perhaps, should have. *Epistemology and Education* does not exist. Rather, Hirst's "Liberal Education and the Nature of Knowledge," which carried the burden of his argument, has been reprinted often.[9] Other papers have tended to fight a rearguard action to ward off critics. A more recent essay, "The Forms of Knowledge Revisited,"[10] adds little of substance to the argument. Thus, this discussion addresses the argument contained in "Liberal Education and the Nature of Knowledge."

In order to judge Hirst's work, one must have a clear idea of what he was setting out to do; that is, to provide an account of what logically must be included in a curriculum based on the nature of knowledge itself. Thus, his justification is an epistemological one. The criteria on which it is to be judged are also, therefore, epistemological. His defense is of a "liberal education," an education based on the nature of knowledge itself. Such a curriculum is anything but new. Its history reaches back to the time of Ancient Greece and a series of related doctrines that have their foundations in metaphysics. The mind, they argued, was an organ. Organs had functions — the eyes to see, the ears to hear, the nose to smell, and so on. The function of the mind was to know. This set of ideas fitted neatly with an account of human life, and also of education, in which perfectibility played a large part. It was fitting to perfect a person as far as this was possible. The final part of the educational theory was contributed by an account of knowledge that was deductive and that accorded knowledge a far more absolute and certain status than is common today. Educational questions could be answered by reference to these doctrines. Education perfected the mind by giving it knowledge. Overestimating the influence of this theory is difficult. Elements of it have continued to influence educational practices until the present, despite the fact that the metaphysics on which its constituent doctrines are based has long since been discarded by philosophers. Elements of the liberal education to which it gave rise have also survived until today. Hirst attempted to give this curriculum a new justification. Rather than metaphysics, he chose, or seemed to choose, the methods of the conceptual analyst.

In "Liberal Education and the Nature of Knowledge," Hirst rejects the justification of a liberal education and sets out a replacement of his own. Hirst's style is opaque, however; determining what he is saying or exactly what he means is often difficult. Hirst's justification rests on two interlocked theories, one of knowledge, the other of mind, and the following discussion explains his views.

The Theories of Knowledge and of Mind

Knowledge, Hirst claims, is organized into forms. *Forms of knowledge* are distinguished by their distinctive concepts. Science, for example, has concepts such as *mass, velocity, particle,* and *energy*. Mathematics has *point, line, set,* and *nested relations*. Religion has *God, sin, eternal life,* and *hell*. Morality has *good, right, obligation,* and *wrong*. Hirst is careful to point out that the forms are not *a priori* but rather that they are those which have happened to develop. Other forms might have developed. This view is challenged by E. Hindess,[11] but this criticism is examined later. Why, one must ask, have these forms developed? This question strikes at the heart of Hirst's argument, for his real commitment is to an account of the development of a rational mind. He sees rationality as a matter of justificatory activities. The developed forms enshrine the publicly recognized and accepted criteria of justification. Thus, *knowledge* and *rationality* are closely linked.

The forms have proven to be problematic. Perhaps the word itself was an unfortunate one. Philosophers have been fighting forms too long to be willing to allow a new generation of them to be born easily. Cooking could be a form because of its distinctive concepts (*sauce, recipe, menu,* etc.). So could sport, war, philately, and a very long list of other activities. In the face of such criticism, Hirst later reformulated the account of forms. They are distinguished by "fundamental, ultimate or categoreal concepts of the most general kind which other concepts of the most general kind in the category presuppose." Given this, he argues that,

> It is these categoreal concepts that provide the form of experience in the different modes. Our understanding of the physical world, for instance, involves such categoreal concepts as those of *space, time,* and *cause.* Concepts such as those of *acid, electron,* and *velocity,* all presuppose these categoreal notions. In the religious domain, the concept of *God* or *the transcendent* is presumably categoreal whereas the concept of *prayer* operates at a lower level. In the moral area, the term *ought* labels the concept of categoreal status, as the term *intention* would seem to do in our understanding of persons. The distinctive type of objective test that is necessary to each domain is clearly linked with the meaning of these categoreal terms, though specific forms the tests take may depend on the lower level concepts employed.[12]

The forms, then, are the results of the articulation of our modes of experience, and their logical structure reflects our experience of the world. This experience is not an individual one that a particular person may have, for true rationality is a matter of observing public criteria of testability.

Obviously much depends on what Hirst means when he refers to the "logic" of a form, and to state precisely what he does mean is not easy. In his "The Logical and Psychological Aspects of Teaching a Subject,"[13] Hirst gives some clues. A form is composed of concepts set in a distinctive set of relationships. These relationships are its logic. Within a particular form, two distinct but related levels of logical relationships are found. The first is the form's logical grammar itself, which is composed of the rules that, when obeyed, give meaning to the terms distinctive to the form. The second is the level of ". . . relations between propositions in terms of which valid historical or scientific explanation are formed."[14] Given that this is the most precise ac-

123

count we have of his views about the logic of the forms, what does Hirst draw from them? For the answer, one must return to "Liberal Education and the Nature of Knowledge." Here he is quite bold. Knowledge, he suggests, can be divided into two groups: (1) distinct disciplines or forms of knowledge (subdivisible): mathematics, physical sciences, human sciences, history, religion, literature and the fine arts, and philosophy; and (2) fields of knowledge: theoretical and practical, which may or may not include elements of moral knowledge.[15]

Mind for Hirst, as suggested earlier, is closely related to knowledge. He asserts quite positively, if less than clearly, that "[t]he achievement of knowledge is necessarily the development of mind in its most basic sense,"[16] and "[t]he achievement of knowledge is necessarily the development of mind — that is, the self-conscious rational mind of man — in its most fundamental aspect,"[17] and further, "[t]o have a mind basically involves coming to have experience articulated by means of various conceptual schema."[18] To answer the question raised by mentioning *conceptual schema* (what are they?) one must come to grips with the meaning of a sentence that seems to be fundamental to Hirst's account of mind, "to acquire knowledge is to become aware of experience structured, organized and made meaningful in some quite specific way, and the varieties of human knowledge constitute the highly developed forms in which man has found this possible."[19] Thus, mind is linked to the forms. The connection is a conceptual one; however, the forms themselves might have been different. The argument seems to be: (1) To have a mind (or, to use Hirst's strange language, to "have mind") is to have knowledge organized and structured in a way or ways, that people have developed. The forms are these ways. (2) To have knowledge is to be able to justify beliefs. (3) To justify beliefs, one must use the criteria (tests) established within the disciplines which constitute the forms. (4) Rationality is a matter of employing the tests established within the forms. (5) Mind (in its most basic sense) is a matter of being rational. Several features of this argument should be noted.

First, the accounts of knowledge and of mind dovetail neatly, perhaps *too* neatly, for it might be said that the argument tends to be circular. The reason for this is obvious: No full account has been given of either concept. A more substantial account would be needed before much could be made of what Hirst has said. Second, Hirst's argument dovetails well with Peters's account of *education*,[20] in which Peters tries to show that *education* refers to an individual's initiation into his cultural heritage represented by those worthwhile activities and knowledge enshrined in the disciplines. Peters has tried to weld the finest elements of both traditionalism and progressivism into an educational theory not flawed by the limitations of either. In this enterprise, Hirst's curriculum justification has provided the foundation of the curriculum and its content, the disciplines.

Third, Hirst's use of *mind* is worthy of attention. Even the sympathetic reader must wonder why Hirst has employed the concept in the way he has. Its meaning is too elusive to be very useful. What can be said of it is: (1) Whatever else it is, it is not a conceptual analysis of *mind*. Yet, it *seems* as if Hirst would like us to believe it is an analytic account that he is giving. (2) Hirst may, in fact, be asserting that that is what a desirable mind would be. If this is so he may be right but, once again, given what he has actually written, one can tell neither his intention nor his possible justification. (3) If Hirst's account of *mind* is viewed as a neutral analysis, then it plainly is not one. What is more, it is not even close to one. It is blatantly prescriptive. (This is the source of the readers' doubts. Hirst, one thinks, really could not expect his readers to accept, or perhaps swallow, *that*. Yet he does seem to expect just that.) (4) If, on the other hand, it is supposed to be an account of a *rational mind*, it is equally, if a little less obviously, wrong. One does not use *rational* in the way Hirst suggests, any more than one uses *mind* as he suggests. The language is altogether richer than that. It is not that rationality has nothing to do with the forms or the disciplines. One can be rational by virtue of one's initiation into and mastery of them. The point is, however, that one *need* not. These criticisms are devastating. Flying under the colors of the conceptual analyst, Hirst has misanalyzed concepts crucial to his argument and, what is more, failed to argue very much at all. Hirst often argues by simple assertion and little justification is provided for assertions of major importance; the reader is thus left perplexed.

How can one understand Hirst? What is he really doing if he is not analyzing concepts? One suggestion[21] is that Hirst's forms should be viewed under the aspect of Wittgenstein's later work in the theory of meaning. If this was the case, the terms employed in each form would gain their meanings by a refernce to each other. On the face of it, this view might be attractive to Hirstians, seeming to solve the problems raised by questions about what Hirst means by "publicly recognized and accepted criteria of justification" and "public criteria of testability." Additionally, border disputes between the forms seem much less important when a positivistic basis for them is denied.

A major objection to this interpretation is found, however. This argument runs counter to Hirst's apparent intentions. Indeed it could hardly be more opposed to what he seems to be trying to do. Positivism, so strongly denied by the later Wittgenstein, is the very foundation on which Hirst's argument rests.

It is worth pointing out, in addition, that the social context in which knowledge is produced, and indeed, as some would have it, by which knowledge is produced, is also ignored by Hirst. When he writes that "an adequate account of my views can be gained from reading the papers collected in *Knowledge and Curriculum*,"[22] the reader must conclude that, given what those views are supposed to account for, they are inadequate.

Hirst's Critics

I have already suggested that Hirst's work has received much critical scrutiny, most of which has been engendered by obscurities or apparent confusions in Hirst's thesis about the nature and number of forms. This section briefly reviews this literature, thereby highlighting these problems. No attempt is made to provide solutions to them, and the literature discussed here does not cover the full range of criticisms that *could* be made of Hirst's work.

"The Forms of Knowledge Revisited"[23] is Hirst's most recently published treatment of the forms. In it, he replies to his critics, writing from within philosophy of education. J. Wilson,[24] in a short paper, makes a number of interesting points. He notes that the concept of *justification* is rather tangled in Hirst's work. *Justifying, per se*, seems odd indeed, because any particular justificatory activity must be heavily context-related. This is an important point because Hirst's argument about the value of justification is a *conceptual* one. However, Wilson correctly points out that,

> In order to justify particular curricula for particular people, then, we have to have some external criteria. . . . Different types of truths or of rationality are important for different reasons, . . . which types are considered important will depend (*inter alia*) on what picture we have (a) of local conditions in particular instances, and (b) of the human condition in general. Thus (a) it is plainly absurd to teach Greek, rather than agriculture, to starving refugees. . . . Similarly (b) an Augustinian or Freudian picture of human life would stress very different types of rationality from those implied by, say, the picture painted by Aristotle or J. S. Mill. Because of this dependence on empirical fact, there is no quick 'philosophical' answer to the (mythical) question of how to 'justify curricular subject'.[25]

This criticism seems to undermine Hirst's argument at its most important point, for it denies that a conceptual argument would (logically) be used as Hirst wants to use it.

Wilson goes on to wonder what the nature of the "tests" Hirst describes is. He says quite simply, "I'm not clear how 'testable against experience' applies to, e.g., mathematics, formal-logic, or religion."[26] Nor, one might reasonably observe, is anyone else. Wilson suggests an appeal to the work of the later Wittgenstein might be helpful. For the reasons outlined earlier, this move seems of doubtful value.

Wilson's most telling criticism, however, is that of Hirst's account of *rationality*. He is concerned that ". . . *rational* is unduly tied down to cognitive activities,"[27] and gives an excellent summation of how it should be used:

> It must not be forgotten that rationality cannot be fully explicated in terms of ratiocination, conscious knowledge or awareness, or anything normally understood by such a phrase as 'initiation into forms of discourse.' The unreasonable man is not he who does not know enough scientific facts, or who cannot reason scientifically: it is he who refuses to face them, or who makes up pseudo-reasons to comfort himself. If we are concerned with educating *people*, it may be profitable to consider more closely the ways in which *people* can be rational and irrational, as well as considering more closely the abstract 'forms of discourse' and 'worthwhile activities' into which people can be justifiably initiated. This is not to deny the importance of the latter approach: it is rather to say that both are approaches to the same question.[28]

In sum, these criticisms are congruent with those advanced earlier. Each, individually, is important and requires a convincing reply. Taken together, they provide a good reason for a reconsideration of Hirst's whole enterprise of curriculum justification.

Hindess[29] has set out to "call into question the epistemological status of those forms of knowledge as described in Hirst's various contributions to the philosophy of the curriculum."[30] She is a careful critic who is not unsympathetic to what Hirst is trying to do. She distinguishes three different types of intellectual inquiry in which he might be engaged: Type A, a historical investigation of a contingent matter; for example, an enquiry into the reasons and events leading up to the "Charge of the Light Brigade"; Type B, a philosophical investigation of a contingent matter; for example, an investigation into the moral principles which informed the debate on sovereignty *vis-à-vis* Great Britain's entry into the Common Market; and Type C, a philosophical investigation of what is necessarily the case; for example, an enquiry into why $2 + 2 = 4$. Hirst is at pains to claim that the seven forms are not the only forms which *might* have developed. They are the forms which did *in fact* develop. Thus his investigation seems to fall into Type A. Hindess questions whether it, in fact, does. When discussing the forms, Hirst uses language such as "fundamental categoreal division" and "irreducible categories,"[31] which, as Hindess points out, "do not strike one as appropriate terms for describing a contingency."[32] The reader begins to suspect that what Hirst is really doing is an activity of the Type C variety. Hindess summarizes her criticism as follows:

> In discussing the limits of human experience, Hirst is no longer dealing with the question of the nature of knowledge in the way that that question was first

introduced in 'Liberal Education and the Nature of Knowledge.' . . . First, whereas Hirst claims to be answering the question 'How do we at present categorize or classify knowledge?', he offers answers to the question 'By virtue of what categories is knowledge, and all experience, possible?' Secondly, Hirst should, by his own theory, be interpreted as answering the question, 'What is it to have an educated mind?' but his language in places suggests that he is trying to answer the question, 'What is it to have a mind (at all)?' Thirdly, instead of sticking to the idea of forms of knowledge as skills which can be learned, Hirst treats them as categories without which no learning would be possible.[33]

This is an excellent summary of some of the major epistemological confusions and objections to which Hirst's position gives rise. It is interesting to see how he replies to them.

Hirst's reply[34] consists, in the main, of restating his case without illumination while trying to point out what he is not asserting. Even if this was done well, it would not be an especially useful thing to do. But it is not even done well. Indeed, Hirst says at one point, "It is I think a strange gloss on my procedure to see the thesis of which I have argued as an attempt to develop an answer to the question 'What is it to have a mind (at all)?' Such an undertaking would be vast and at a philosophical level on which I have never sought to operate."[35] While it is certainly true that such an undertaking would indeed be vast, it is precisely what Hirst has seemed to be doing. In respect of the debate about whether he has been engaged in a Type B or Type C enterprise, Hirst replies,

> If of course the question I am supposed to have answered is about the categories which all experience must necessarily take, or logically could take, I must insist I have neither asked that question nor ventured an answer to it . . . . I have never considered the categories I have outlined, as those to which all learning for all time, logically must conform. At present all learning is within these categories, that is all I think one can say.[36]

It seems clear that Hirst has then either changed his ground (for what he disclaims is what he certainly *seemed* to be doing, or trying to do) or has been misunderstood. The former seems more likely. Indeed, Hirst probably did not grasp the full implications of his thesis in "Liberal Education and the Nature of Knowledge." But that is not to say that the thesis was not there.

Simons[37] offers another fundamental criticism of Hirst's justification of a liberal education, examining Hirst's contention that the forms are rational, resting on a species of Kantian transcendental justification. It seems as if the forms should be taught because they are rational (and develop *mind*). But they are only rational in a formal "philosophical, descriptive and non-commendatory technical sense."[38] So why, Simons asks, should they be taught? This is an acute criticism, for it highlights Hirst's tendency to extract quite precise teaching recommendations from philosophical arguments at a high level of abstraction. One often has the feeling, reading Hirst, that he has performed a philosophical sleight-of-hand. Simons has identified one of the reasons for this. His attempt at a solution is reminiscent of Wilson's[39] in that he observes that a simple appeal to rationality itself will not suffice to provide a justification of a curriculum. The choice of what will be taught will depend on one's *purposes*. One cannot decide in advance and without reference to particular cases. Once that fact is admitted, one must agree with Simons that "[t]he whole question is thrown open again."[40] Just because rationality is such a formal principle, no appeal to a transcendental justification can logically tell one what should be taught.

A rather different, if related, sort of criticism is offered by writers such as Gribble[41] and Phillips,[42] whose works represent an attempt to elucidate Hirst's claim that logically distinct forms of knowledge exist. Gribble has argued that literary criticism rather than literature itself might constitute a form. Gribble's attack is mounted on the notion of truth criteria which, one will remember, Hirst maintains each form has. Gribble denies that literature and fine arts have such truth criteria but points out that literary criticism has. It is an interesting argument because it highlights the very great complexity of the epistemological questions which lie just under the surface of Hirst's central thesis. In his reply, Hirst[43] avoids answering the questions his original thesis posed. He is content to restate his case, then simply observe that "[w]hether or not there are indeed objective tests is a matter which I must leave to those far more expert than myself in literture, literary criticism and the philosophy of those domains."[44] This is an astonishing position to take, because the weight of his argument in "Liberal Education and the Nature of Knowledge" rests on there being such tests. Because he has asserted that such tests exist, it seems odd that he should, faced with Gribble's criticism, simply assert that such tests may or may not exist. What if they do not exist? Would literature and the fine arts be dropped from his list of forms? We are not told.

Phillips's criticism is in some respects of a similar kind to Gribble's, however, it is more general. Phillips attacks all four grounds on which the forms can, in Hirst's view, be distinguished. The four grounds are: (1) Each form of knowledge involves central concepts that are peculiar in character to the form. (2) In a given form of knowledge these and other concepts form a network of possible relationships. As a result the form has a distinctive logical structure. (3) Each form, then, has distinctive expressions that are testable against experience in accordance with particular criteria that are peculiar to the form. (4) The forms have developed particular techniques and skills for exploring experience and testing their distinctive expressions. To this four-part argument Phillips brings a barrage of objections. In the case of the first, he simply points out that in a field as narrow as physics, it is "difficult to see what they [concepts such as atoms, molecules, pressure, volume, mean kinetic energy, mass, temperature, gravitational constant, line of electrical force] have in common."[45] He is right, and even more obviously so when he points out that if science *in toto* is considered, its concepts do not have "peculiar character" in common. Indeed, concepts in one form may have more in common with some concepts in another form than they do with some others in their own form. His example is a good one. The concepts of *historical period* and *geological age* seem to have more in common with each other than they do with some others in history or geology.

In the second case, he notes that "at least some forms" do not possess "*a* distinctive logical structure." Algebra and geometry do not, for example, despite the fact that they are both included in the form mathematics. He also points out the confusion that exists about the meaning of *logic*. The "logic of a subject" is not its "logical structure." The "logic of a form of knowledge" is distinct from "formal logic." As so often with Hirst's work, understanding exactly what is meant by a subject or form or discipline's "logic" is difficult.

The third criterion is one mentioned by Gribble. Understanding the way "tests against experience" could be devised in the case of some of the forms is not easy. The two most difficult examples are religion and mathematics, which seem to defy such a specification. A more fundamental objection exists, however. Even Hirst's critics freely allow that in the case of science, tests against experience do occur. However, this issue seems much more complex upon careful examination. Amsterdamski,[46] for example, sees the relationship between scientific knowledge and empirical observation as a much more complex one than Hirst and his critics seem to assume it to be.

Hirst's fourth criterion meets a predictable objection. Phillips notes that investigators in any of the disciplines within the forms will use *any* methods of enquiry that seem appropriate. One should note that this problem has two faces, one historical, the other philosophical. Science historians,[47] for example, tell us that scientific progress is a far more random and less methodologically conventional matter than Hirst seems to allow. For their part, philosophers of science, or at least some of them, agree that this must (logically) be the case. The positivistic account of science Hirst seems to support with its "particular techniques and skills for exploring experience and testing their distinctive expressions"[48] seems far too restrictive on both historical and philosophical grounds.

Altogether, Phillips's criticisms succinctly summarize the weaknesses and, perhaps more important, confusions and ambiguities, inherent in Hirst's thesis as it appeared in "Liberal Education and the Nature of Knowledge." One might have expected Hirst to have answered these criticisms squarely in "The Forms of Knowledge Revisited."[49] He does not. Rather, he seems to restate his case and engage in something akin to philosophical shadow boxing. The reason for this is plain. A much more specific, less general, treatment of a particular form, or forms, would be needed to do justice to the now considerable body of criticism which he faces. Hirst seems unwilling to accept this challenge.

This brief review has not attempted either to make an exhaustive examination of the literature or even to recount all the arguments advanced by those writers mentioned. Rather, it has attempted to locate some of the central problems to which Hirst's general thesis has given rise. What should we conclude from this review? First, despite the passing years and a considerable cumulative literature, only a little progress has been made in clarifying what Hirst's thesis is and what its implications are. Second, that these things will be done in any single, unified way seems doubtful. This situation is most unsatisfactory, for the problem cannot simply be dropped. Curriculum justification is too important an issue for that. What is more, the epistemological concerns on which such a justification must rest are clearly central to many major concerns in the philosophy of education. While no one within this tradition seems satisfied with Hirst's attempt to solve these problems, they are, or at least have until recently, been unable to provide a satisfactory alternative solution, or solutions, of their own.

The New Sociology of Education

Ironically, during the very years in which Hirst's work was being formulated, published, and was most immediately influential, other literatures were also developed which would supercede it. In philosophy, Kuhn's work[50] was followed by that of Feyerabend[51] and Lakatos[52] and the whole positivistic research program on which the *forms* rested went into a rapid decline. Its tombstone must be the work of Rorty.[53] Simultaneously, Needham's great work was appearing, and indeed in 1962 his volume on physics was published,[54] further undermining Hirst's treatment of forms, knowledge, and curriculum.

Within the educational literature a number of developments were taking place that would not so much defeat traditionalism as supercede it. First were the historical and sociological studies that suggested the traditionalist account of what schools were doing, or even intended to do, were fantasy. An ever increasing number of writers attacked both the liberal ideology which supports schooling and its real social consequences. Works such as those of Karier[55] and Violas[56] exposed the ideological underpinnings of much schooling practice and the origins of curriculum. The decisive work, however, was Bowles and Gintis's paradigm marking study[57] which sought to demolish the myth of equality of educational opportunity as real social practice.

A second literature also attacked traditional conceptions of schooling but from other points of view. Illich,[58] Reimer,[59] and Freire,[60] among others, had powerful influences in undermining traditional curriculum theory by showing the political nature of supposedly apolitical curriculum. Various Marxist and neo-Marxist studies of schooling developed some of these notions and indeed provided systematic treatments of traditionalist curriculum theory in terms of an instrument of social class conflict and mystification. This has proven to be an especially potent literature with works by Apple,[61] Harris,[62] and Matthews[63] commanding extensive audiences, indeed, making a serious claim on providing a unified paradigm in place of the traditional one.

Many of these developments coalesce in a fourth, which is known as the New Sociology of Education. It is not that every element of these literatures is incorporated there; that could hardly be the case because many of these elements are contradictory. Rather, many of the assumptions of the traditionalist curriculum position are given one of the most serious critiques in the New Sociology for reasons sympathetic to much of the other criticism.

The New Sociology of Education grew, I believe, from long-term and increasing dissatisfaction with the apparent sterility of much serious academic writing, and especially philosophical writing, about education. The movement's work came together in a single volume edited by Michael F. D. Young, well-titled *Knowledge and Control: New Directions for the Sociology of Education*.[64]

Young begins his "Introduction" to *Knowledge and Control* by restating the distinction between *taking* and *making* problems. The fault of traditionalism was that it took problems, and their definitions, uncritically from educators, whereas the New Direction did not do so. What united the authors represented in this book is that "they hold in common . . . that they do not take for granted existing definitions of educational reality, and therefore do 'make' rather than 'take' problems for the sociology of education."[65] This *making* has many implications, and Young proceeds to mention what is perhaps the most significant one, one that has certainly been the most controversial:

> They [sociologists] are inevitably led to consider, often from widely different perspectives, 'what counts as educational knowledge' as problematic. The implication of this is that one major focus of the sociology of education becomes an enquiry into the social organization of knowledge in educational institutions. Thus, and this has important implications for the organization of sociological knowledge, sociology of education is no longer conceived as the area of enquiry distinct from the sociology of knowledge.[66]

What Young intends, then, is much more than a dispute within the existing Sociology of Education. His program is "revolutionary" in the Kuhnian sense:

132

Knowledge and Control is intended to destroy the existing paradigm by calling into question the very questions it generated, the meanings of the terms it employed (such as *knowledge, sociology, philosophy,* and *curriculum*), and what counted as answers to them within it.[67] Young seeks to "get behind" or "make problematic" the whole structure of meanings and values accepted in contemporary education. Apple, commenting on Young's program, and his own, summarizes the New Directions in this way:

> The study of educational knowledge is a study in ideology, the investigation of what is considered *legitimate* knowledge . . . by specific groups and classes, in specific institutions, at specific historical moments. . . . In clearer terms, the overt and covert knowledge found within school settings, and the principles of selection, organization, and evaluation of this knowledge, are value-governed selections from a much larger universe of possible knowledge and selection principles. Hence they must not be accepted as given, but must be made problematic — bracketed, if you will — so that the social and economic ideologies and the institutionally patterned meanings which stand behind them, can be scrutinized.[68] (Emphasis in original.)

Young focuses, most specifically, on the role of Sociology of Education itself and seeks to find "possible explanations of the failure of (traditional) sociologists to raise questions and develop research into the social organization of educational knowledge."[69] He sees as a "central issue" the "dialectical relationship between access to power and the opportunity to legitimize certain dominant categories, and the processes by which the availability of such categories to some groups enables them to assert power and control over others."[70]

This, then, is the program of the New Directions. But questions are at once apparent about the social constitution of knowledge and also about the nature of Sociology of Knowledge itself. The latter may be appropriately (given Young's context) characterized in Mannheim's terms, "The sociology of knowledge is concerned . . . with the varying ways in which objects present themselves to the subject according to the differences in social settings. Thus, mental structures are *inevitably* differently formed in different social and historical settings."[71] (Emphasis added.) Knowledge in this view is "inevitably" context dependent and is "seen not as having a permanent 'out there' nature but rather to be an essentially relativist artefact as are the qualities of 'truth' and 'objectivity' associated with it."[72]

Young, however, does not trace the descent of his position from Mannheim, but rather from Mills, who demonstrated that the "absolutist model of validity" can be traced to "the traditions of a centralized intellectual elite with close links to those holding economic and political power."[73] This, for Young, implies that "[f]or sociological research, the obvious empirical possibility of different sets of criteria of validity, which themselves only emerge and can be said to exist in the practice of actual enquiries and interaction,[74] is of considerable importance"[75] because "without any preconceptions about 'good explanations' or a 'higher order rationality,' we should then explore the possible origins of the particular explanation provided."[76] Within the New Sociology of Education this would mean, for example, that "questions might be posed about how young secondary school children with widely different backgrounds 'make sense of' a ten-subject, forty-period school week."[77] More generally, it challenges all the major tenets of the traditional position. The objectivity of the curriculum is no longer "given," and thus, by implication, the authority of the teacher is in peril. Indeed, Young sees quite a different role for the teacher under the New Directions. The banking model of teaching can no longer be justified, for *knowledge* and *reality* are "constructed" *by the knower* in particular historical settings. The teacher can, on this account, become an agent of change, "the author of her own speech,"[78] rather than the transmitters of "class-biased knowledge" forced on pupils in acts of "class domination." Most important, the New Challenge, as articulated in *Knowledge and Control*, sets out not simply to undermine the foundations of traditionalism but those of *all* knowledge. It is a position of "total relativism,"[79] and one of idealism, for *reality* is constructed by the knower.

Clearly, Young is making several claims, within the new critique, which should be distinguished. Lawton's[80] attempt to do so is a good one. He sees Young's claims, in *Knowledge and Control*, as falling into five "levels":

Level 1: That the present structure and organization in our society serves to preserve the status quo in an unjust society — this level is particularly concerned with questions such as the *social distribution of knowledge.*

Level 2: That in particular the *content* of education — the selection of knowledge for transmission by schools — should be *made* into a problem for critical examination rather than be taken for granted; this level is concerned with *what counts for knowledge in our society, and the stratification of knowledge.*

Level 3: That *subject barriers are arbitrary and artificial,* existing largely for the convenience of those in control of education.

Level 4: That *all knowledge is socially constructed.*

Level 5: That not only knowledge but *rationality itself is merely a convention.* (Emphasis in original.)

It is doubtful that Young would want his argument "filleted" in this way, especially because the force of "level" is unclear and because Young uses the arguments "on" the different levels together. Significantly, this classification also omits mention of the knower as *constructing, educational reality* or *reality*.

Conclusion

No neat, definitive way of drawing a set of conclusions from this literature is possible. Such matters defy easy summation. What cannot be doubted, however, is that between Hirst's traditionalism and Young's New Directions, a revolution has taken place. That *Knowledge and Control* could bear the imprint of the Open University is a mark of its success.

This revolution amounts to the sort of development within a discipline pointed to by Kuhn and, in a more sophisticated way, Lakatos. On the surface it seems that the developments in curriculum theory outlined by Young and those sympathetic to him can be evaluated by seeking to answer the questions raised about them. This, however, is misleading. At least from the point of view of knowledge selection, it hardly matters if Young and his sympathizers are eventually found wanting in every particular matter. What does matter is that the "location" of such questions has been altered — and decisively. By wedding curriculum itself to the sociology of knowledge, its isolated, contextless condition has been altered forever. The irony, of course, is that curriculum *always was* an integral part of questions about the social creation of reality and the social constitution of knowledge. But this understanding has been obscured by various sorts of systematic misunderstanding. It is now post-Young *et al.*, easier to see both how curriculum questions must be related to other educational questions *and* how a theory of education must relate to a broader social theory. Aristotle knew that, "What should be taught?" is a question that epistemology cannot answer but rather must find its answer in politics. Contemporary curriculum theory has returned to this truth. It is one which should not be feared. The schools are sites of personal creation and development, on the one hand, and social reproduction on the other. It is fitting that democratic people understand that both what their children learn and how they learn it must involve the most subtle and powerful questions of legitimation. To debate such issues is not to betray a heritage, but rather to act democratically.

Notes

1. See, for example, Paul H. Hirst, "What Is Teaching?" *Journal of Curriculum Studies*, 3(1971); and Paul Hirst, *Moral Education in a Secular Society* (London: University of London Press, 1974).

2. A representative volume of their own work is R. F. Dearden, Paul H. Hirst, and Richard S. Peters, eds., *Education and the Development of Reason* (London: Routledge & Kegan Paul, 1972).

3. Paul H. Hirst and Richard S. Peters, *The Logic of Education* (London: Routledge & Kegan Paul, 1970).

4. Peters's writing in this field has been very considerable, but his *Ethics and Education* (London: Allen and Unwin, 1966) is the centerpiece of his work.

5. See, for example, Michael Oakeshott, "Education: The Engagement and its Frustration," *Proceedings of the Philosophy of Education Society of Great Britain* 5(January 1971).

6. D. W. Hamlyn, *The Theory of Knowledge* (London: Macmillan, 1970).

7. Richard S. Peters, "Introduction," in Paul H. Hirst, *Knowledge and the Curriculum* (London: Routledge & Kegan Paul, 1974).

8. Peters, *Ethics and Education, op. cit.*

9. It appeared first in Reginald D. Archambault, ed., *Philosophical Analysis and Education* (London: Routledge & Kegan Paul, 1965).

10. Paul H. Hirst, "The Forms of Knowledge Revisited," in his *Knowledge and the Curriculum, op. cit.*

11. Elizabeth Hindess, "Forms of Knowledge," in *Proceedings of the Philosophy of Education Society of Great Britain*, VI (1972).

12. Hirst and Peters, *The Logic of Education, op. cit.*

13. Paul H. Hirst, "The Logical and Psychological Aspects of Teaching a Subject," in Richard S. Peters, ed., *The Concept of Education* (London: Routledge & Kegan Paul, 1967).

14. *Ibid.*, p. 51.

15. Paul H. Hirst, "Liberal Education and the Nature of Knowledge," in Archambault, *op. cit.*, p. 131.

16. *Ibid.*, p. 126.

17. *Ibid.*, p. 123.

18. *Ibid.*, p. 125.

19. *Ibid.*, pp. 124–25.

20. Richard S. Peters, "Eduction as Initiation," in Archambault, *op. cit.*

21. Made by John Wilson, "The Curriculum: Justification and Taxonomy," *British Journal of Educational Studies*, Vol. XVII (1969).

22. Hirst, *Knowledge and the Curriculum, op. cit.*, p. 100.

23. Hirst, "The Forms of Knowledge Revisited," *op. cit.*, pp.84–100.

24. Wilson, *op. cit.*, p. 36.

25. *Ibid.*, pp. 37–8.

26. *Ibid.*, p. 39.

27. *Ibid.*, p. 39.

28. Ibid., pp. 39–40.
29. Hindess, *op. cit.*, p. 164.
30. *Ibid.*, p.164.
31. Hirst and Peters, *The Logic of Education, op. cit.*, pp. 64–5.
32. Hindess, *op. cit.*, p. 170.
33. *Ibid.*, p. 171.
34. Paul H. Hirst, "Forms of Knowledge – A Reply to Elizabeth Hindess," *Philosophy of Education Society of Great Britain* 11(July 1973).
35. *Ibid.*, p. 267.
36. *Ibid.*, p. 267.
37. M. Simons, "The Forms of Knowledge Again," *Educational Philosophy and Theory* 7(1975).
38. *Ibid.*, p. 44.
39. Wilson, *op. cit.*, pp. 36–40.
40. Simons, *op. cit.*, p. 46.
41. James H. Gribble, "The Forms of Knowledge," *Educational Philosophy and Theory* 2(May 1970).
42. D. C. Phillips, "The Distinguishing Features of Forms of Knowledge," *Educational Philosophy and Theory* 3(October 1971).
43. Paul H. Hirst, "Literature, Criticism and the Forms of Knowledge," *Educational Philosophy and Theory* 3(April 1971).
44. *Ibid.*, p. 17.
45. Phillips, *op. cit.*, p. 31.
46. Stefan Amsterdamski, "Between Experience and Metaphysics," *Boston Studies in Philosophy of Science*, Vol. 35 (Boston: Reidel, 1975).
47. See, for example, Gerald Holton, "Einstein, Michelson, and the 'Crucial' Experiment," *Isis* 60(1969).
48. Phillips, *op. cit.*, p. 34.
49. Hirst, "The Forms of Knowledge Revisited," *op. cit.*, pp. 84-100.
50. Thomas S. Kuhn, *The Structure of Scientific Revolutions* (Chicago: University of Chicago Press, 1962); second edition, 1970.
51. Paul K. Feyerabend, "Against Method," in M. Radner and S. Winnokur, eds., *Minnesota Studies in Philosophy of Science*, Vol. IV (Minneapolis: University of Minnesota Press, 1970).
52. Imre Lakatos, *The Methodology of Scientific Research Programmes: Philosophical Papers*, Vol. I, John Worrall and Gregory Currie, eds. (Cambridge: Cambridge University Press, 1978).
53. Richard Rorty, *Philosophy and the Mirror of Nature* (Princeton, N.J.: Princeton University Press, 1979).

54. Joseph Needham and Wang Ling, *Science and Civilization in China*, Vol. IV, Part I, Physics (Cambridge: Cambridge University Press, 1962).

55. Clarence J. Karier, *Man, Society, and Education* (Glenview, Ill.: Scott, Foresman, 1967).

56. Paul C. Violas, *The Training of the Urban Working Class* (Chicago: Rand McNally, 1978).

57. Samuel Bowles and Herbert Gintis, *Schooling in Capitalist America* (New York: Basic Books, 1976).

58. Ivan Illich, *Deschooling Society* (London: Penguin, 1973).

59. Everett W. Reimer, *School Is Dead* (London: Penguin, 1971).

60. Paulo Freire, *Pedagogy of the Oppressed* (London: Penguin, 1972).

61. Michael W. Apple, *Ideology and Curriculum* (Boston: Routledge & Kegan Paul, 1979).

62. Kevin Harris, *Education and Knowledge* (London: Routledge & Kegan Paul, 1979); and *Teachers and Classes* (London: Routledge & Kegan Paul, 1982).

63. Michael R. Matthews, *The Marxist Theory of Schooling* (Atlantic Heights, N.J.: Humanities Press, 1980).

64. Michael F. D. Young, ed., *Knowledge and Control* (London: Collier-Macmillan, 1971).

65. *Ibid.*, pp. 2–3.

66. *Ibid.*, p. 3.

67. Peters, for example, an especially powerful force in shaping educational research, denies that there can *be* such a thing as a Sociology of Knowledge. All one can have is epistemology and a Sociology of Belief in his view. Richard Peters, private communication, 1972.

68. Apple, *op. cit.*, p. 45.

69. Young, *op. cit.*, p. 8.

70. *Ibid.*, p. 8.

71. Karl Mannheim, *Ideology and Utopia* (London: Routledge & Kegan Paul, 1926), p. 238; cited in John Eggleston, *The Sociology of the School Curriculum* (London: Routledge & Kegan Paul, 1977), p. 64.

72. Eggleston, *op. cit.*, p. 65.

73. Young, *op. cit.*, p. 6.

74. This (crucial) point is well illustrated by Lakatos's work on Newton and Feyerabend's on Galileo. See Imre Lakatos, "Newton's Effect on Scientific Standards," in John Worrall and Gregory Currie, eds., *Philosophical Papers of Imre Lakatos*, Vol. 1 (Cambridge: Cambridge University Press, 1978); and Paul K. Feyerabend, *Against Method* (London: New Left Books, 1975), especially Chapter 7.

75. Young, *op. cit.*, p. 6.

76. *Ibid.*, p. 6.

77. *Ibid.*, p. 6.

78. J. White and M. Young, "The Sociology of Knowledge: Part I" *Education for Teaching* 98(Autumn 1975), p. 7.

79. J. Clark and H. Freeman, "Michael Young's Sociology of Knowledge: Epistemological Sense, or Non-Sense?" *Journal of Further and Higher Education* 3(1), (Spring 1979), p. 7.

80. Dennis Lawton, *Class, Culture and the Curriculum* (London: Routledge & Kegan Paul, 1975), p. 58.

EIGHT

Curriculum Platforms and Literature

Thomas E. Barone

urricularists have historically conceived of the curriculum planning process in rather narrow terms. The focus has been on the task of development — whether as a linear, theory-driven, rational process, or, *apres* Schwab,
as the practical activity of deliberation. Without denying the need for continued attention to the nature of planning and policymaking episodes, especially
to the analysis of deliberate engagements, I want to consider how curriculum
workers can prepare for such engagements. In this essay, I wonder less about
what curriculum developers *do* in the development process than with what
they *bring* to it.

I have in mind a notion similar to what Decker Walker, in delineating his
"naturalistic model" for curriculum development more than one decade ago,
called the *platform* of the individual designer. For Walker,

> the word *platform* is meant to suggest both a political platform and something to
> stand on. The platform includes an idea of what is and a vision of what ought to
> be, and these guide the curriculum developer in determining what he should do to
> realize his vision.[1]

Walker's metaphor is insufficient insofar as it conveys an image of a fixed,
enduring structure rather than the fragile nexus of vague attitudes, tentative

140

beliefs, complex dispositions, and ideologies perhaps only partially congealed, within which most curriculum workers operate. Nevertheless, the concept is enormously helpful insofar as it reminds us that the entire process of curriculum planning or policymaking must be contingent upon these individually held conceptions of what is (in Walker's words) educationally "good, true, and beautiful." Indeed, I explore herein the process of platform growth, the manner in which individual planks are crafted and placed in (at least a temporary) position.

Of course, the formation of images of educational virtue is an enormously complex process occurring within the entire fund of experiences that constitute a biography. Still, the guidance of curriculum planners, policymakers and practitioners toward the formulation of personal educational theory — the erection of a platform, if you will — surely lies at the heart of what those of us who are teacher educators continually attempt to accomplish. And so I want to imagine some tools that might be helpful in this endeavor.

These tools are *educational research documents*. Now, this may seem exceedingly odd, insofar as many curriculum workers, like other practitioners, have long greeted the claims of educational research with disinterest, skepticism, and even cynicism. Anyone with more than a passing acquaintance with the field is aware of a new generation of educationists — theorists, philosophers, even researchers themselves — who have also grown increasingly critical of the nature and purposes of mainstream educational research. But, of course, I do not have those modes of research in mind.

I also want to move beyond most of the alternative forms of inquiry — methodologies often labelled *qualitative, holistic* or *idiographic* — that have been advanced over the last decade. These represented steps taken in the right direction, but now appear incomplete and timid. Credibility and enthusiasm for the fruits of research among nonresearchers will demand more fundamental replacements for certain assumptions about the research enterprise and the creation (or at least discovery) of radically different studies of school life. Only then will educational research speak authoritatively to curriculum planners and policymakers whose ultimate aim is nothing less than the reformation of schooling in our society.

My thesis, therefore, will most likely cause many research traditionalists to blink in disbelief, while some literary critics may grimace at (what is to them) the painfully obvious. The thesis is straightforward and its components are these:

1. that works within literary genres such as the novel and short story have traditionally resulted from careful observation and even field research;
2. that, indeed, all research is, in a certain sense, fictive;
3. that, when an educational theme is effectively treated in literary-style

141

fiction, the work may possess certain aesthetic qualities that make it potentially enticing to and broadly useful for curriculum planners, including teachers;

4. that the purposes for crafting such fiction are in accord with the fundamental emancipatory aims of education; and
5. that, therefore, the legitimation and use of these documents as educational research texts will be crucial steps toward educational reform.

Leaving School or Staying In?: Three Research Texts

I offer first three articles of evidence, each a product of a different research genre and each touching upon the same profound educational theme: the adolescent's commitment to being schooled. One is a recent paper that reviewed the social-science-based research literature on factors influencing school drop-out rates and their implications for drop-out prevention.[2] Three broad interacting factors were cited as contributing causes: economic conditions, family factors, and student experiences in school. Included in the last was "by far, the most common reason for student drop out . . . poor academic performance." The author elaborates on this point:

In surveys of dropouts, this poor performance is expressed in terms of "I disliked school" or "School was not for me." . . . Expulsion, suspension, truancy, and absenteeism, in-school delinquency, and inappropriate classroom behavior can be identified as other school factors related to student drop out, but these factors are heavily associated with poor academic performance. Poor academic performance in school means no rewards in school, no sense of accomplishment, low self-esteem, constant feelings of failure.[3]

And what is the author's interest in this area of research? Hollifield's response recalls the familiar purposes of most educational research:

We shouldn't downplay the importance of other factors, but [student experiences are] the crux of the problem. And we should be thankful . . . because student experiences in school are, at least theoretically, very much subject to our control. We can't change economic factors very easily, and family socioeconomic background is something students bring with them to school, but the school factors themselves we can get a grip on and change.[4]

Hollifield, in the mainstream of social-science research, aspires to link cause and effect for purposes of reliable prediction and control. He assumes, for example, that "intervention programs" can be designed to stimulate academic achievement, which tends, at least theoretically, to increase retention rates, thereby promoting educational progress.

The other two documents were composed by authors (whom I expansively call *researchers*) with different intentions. The authors of these texts did not aspire to control their subjects. Instead, the aim of each was to tell a story about the schooling experiences of his protagonist. Consider the second example, the richly textured portrait of a British adolescent who did indeed drop out — albeit in an extraordinary fashion: Guy Bennett is the central character in Julian Mitchell's historical drama *Another Country*.[5]

Bennett later became an infamous spy who actually defected to Russia in 1955, but the play and film recount certain key incidents in his life as a 1930s youth in an upper-class, all-male public school. Despite his awareness of homosexual tendencies, Bennett is initially devoted to the acquisition of status and power within the rigid hierarchial system of the school; he craves membership in the ruling elite of students called the *gods*; Bennett's ultimate aspirations are even grander, for "[l]ife is ladders . . . that's all! Prep school to here, first form to sixth, second assistant, junior under-secretary, to ambassador in Paris: Sir Guy Bennett, K.C.V.O., K.C.M.G." But that is not to be, for his reputation is ruined upon the revelation of an indiscreet liaison with a schoolmate for whom he cares deeply. Disillusioned and embittered, he finally accepts his "true nature," and abandons what now appears as a hypocritical way of life. He will be no "god"; he will abandon school along with the repressive system that feeds and is fed by it. An alternative to the ambassadorship is provided by a fellow "outcast." Bennett embraces the Marxist ideology of a heterosexual friend, Tom Judd, and sets about living a life of revenge through "total indiscretion."

The third example is, like *Another Country*, a masterfully rendered story, but describes virtual rather than actual events and characters.[6] It is a novelistic short story by John Updike entitled "A Sense of Shelter."[7] Through its vivid portrait of a counterexample to the scholastically alienated, this tale considers the attractiveness of schooling for one type of teenager. It poignantly depicts the sudden realization of a shy, socially awkward adolescent named William Young, that, having mastered the academic environment and feeling really safe only therein, he would *never* leave school. Instead of facing life in an unfamiliar and uncertain realm outside, he reminds us of the early Guy Bennett as he vows to remain sealed in and secure forever,

> high school merging into college, college into graduate school, graduate school into teaching at a college — section man, assistant, associate, *full* professor, professor of a dozen languages and a thousand books, a man brilliant in his forties, wise in his fifties, renowned in his sixties, revered in his seventies, and then retired, sitting in the study lined with acoustical books until the time came for the last

143

transition from silence to silence, and would die, like Tennyson, with a copy of *Cymbeline* beside him on a moon-drenched bed.[8]

Each of these three texts, in its own way, involves the crucial theme of adolescent attitudes toward their schooling—a theme that surely pierces the core of the educational enterprise. My ultimate concern is the potential usefulness of these texts for shaping the platforms of curriculum workers. These texts individually and, more important, as representatives of distinct genres, are designed to further different research aims. But first, how dare I characterize literary works—including plays and short stories such as those mentioned above—as legitimate products of educational research? Certainly this is tampering with the widely accepted definition of research, the one legitimated and sanctified by the history of the field? Probably so. But to ascertain whether this is molestation or warranted adjustment, consider the prerequisite activities to writing novelistic fiction.

Aesthetic Criteria Versus the Necessity of Method

Only the naive can believe that novelists spin their imaginary webs from within a world of pure illusion and fantasy. On the contrary, at least since Henry Fielding, novelists have relied upon observation of the minutiae of human activity, attending to specific characters in particular physical, cultural, and sociohistorical contexts. From its inception, the novel has been drenched in social realism. Or as Cooke states, "The basic talent of the novelist is to observe social behavior—the way a person furnishes his house or makes love or reacts to death or folds an envelope or constructs his sentences or plans his career."[9]

Often these observations arise from within the process of daily lived experiences, lending an autobiographical flavor to the storytelling. Consider the following excerpt from Updike:

The sky behind the shreds of snow was stone-colored. The murk inside the high classroom gave the air a solidity that limited the overhead radiance to its own vessels; six globes of dull incandescence floated on the top of a thin sea. The feeling the gloom gave him was not gloomy but joyous: he felt they were all sealed in, safe; the colors of cloth were dyed deeper, the sound of whispers was made more distinct, the smells of tablet paper and wet shoes and varnish and face powder pierced him with a vivid sense of possession. These were his classmates sealed in, his, the stupid as well as the clever, the plain as well as the lovely, his enemies as well as his friends, his. He felt like a king and seemed to move to his seat between the bowed heads of subjects that loved him less than he loved them. His seat was sanctioned by tradition; for twelve years he had sat at the rear of classrooms, William Young, flanked by Marsha Wyckoff and Andy Zimmerman. Once there had been two Zimmermans, but one went to work in his father's greenhouse, and in some classes — Latin and Trig — there were none, and William sat at the edge of the class as if on the lip of a cliff, and Marsha Wyckoff became Marvin Wolf or Sandra Wade, but it was always the same desk, whose surface altered from hour to hour but from whose blue-stained ink-hole his mind could extract, like a chain of magicians' handkerchiefs, a continuity of years.[10]

This passage is clearly not a product of innate knowledge or divine revelation, but accomplished out of experience and reflection. Updike's precise location of sensory details — sights, sounds, and smells — within a meaningful landscape convinces the reader of (at least) the possibility of this classroom's and this character's existence. The details seem lovingly drawn from Updike's own school life, or from other school settings (a son's? a friend's?) to which circumstances had later drawn him. But while the basis for this fictional description may be the author's casual reflection upon his past encounters with the world-as-lived, such is not always the case. Indeed, accounts exist of prominent literary figures engaging in rather elaborate forms of what social scientists might call *field research*. These range from Charles Dickens's attempts at gathering material for *The Life and Adventures of Nicholas Nickelby* — in order to gain admittance to the notorious Yorkshire boarding schools, he assumed the false identity of someone seeking a school for the son of a widowed friend — to James Michener's gathering the sociohistorical particulars that saturate his massive works on geopolitical entities such as *Poland*, *Texas*, and *Chesapeake*.

Still, even these journalistic-style forays and other quasianthropological ventures (like George Orwell's participant-observation approach to his research for *Down and Out in Paris and London*) are too casual and brief for the taste of the more tradition-bound segments of the educational research community — despite their rough equivalence to the efforts of some of today's respected qualitative educational researchers. Consider, for example, Sara Lawrence Lightfoot's visits to some of the schools she insightfully portrayed in *The Good High School*. Her fieldwork, though relatively informal and limited in duration, did not decrease the power or significance of her work — at least not in the judgment of the American Educational Research Association (AERA), which presented her its Outstanding Book Award for 1984. Nor, suggests a consensus of the literary world, did Orwell's work suffer from inadequate research methods. Nor Dickens's. Indeed, it is the difficulty in reconciling the traditional insistence on highly systematic forms of data-gathering with the clarity and forcefulness of the informally acquired observations of great writers that draws us to this radical rethinking of certain assumptions of social research methodology. How much, after all, does the

THOMAS E. BARONE

manner in which Herman Melville learned about the intricacies of the whaling industry really matter? Could Updike have possibly revealed more about the hidden curriculum at William's high school by providing an afterword on "methods employed?" We judge the tales of Melville and Updike on their own purposes — on their potential for enlightenment — and not on the manner of their preparation. While an attentiveness by the writer to the details of his or her encounters with the world is important, these nonmethodical observations and recollections do not serve traditional research ambitions of verbally mirroring an objective reality. Dickens and Orwell did not embark upon experience-enhancing field trips merely to comfort potential publishers concerned with literal truth. Rather, their aim was to position themselves more effectively for bestowing meaning upon facets of an unfamiliar social landscape. They knew that a broader and deeper experiential background can increase the available array of perceptions from which the author may draw for effective arrangement into a form that enhances their meaning. Personal familiarity with the milieu of an intended story tends to ensure its embroidering in rich and significant detail, yielding a more plausible and powerful work.

The degree of power will also depend, to some extent, upon the structure into which these details are placed. Geertz[12] has reminded us that the original meaning of *fiction* (*fictio*) is "something fashioned," and the process of imaginative arrangement of revelations into a structure that intensifies and dramatizes meaning is indeed central to all good fiction. Such a dynamic aesthetic form can be quite alluring, promoting in a reader that which philosophers and aestheticians such as Dewey,[13] Beardsley,[14] and Dilthey have called an *aesthetic experience.* This coherently patterned "reaction of a whole self to a situation confronting it"[15] proceeds through the phases of a drama, from an enticing opening in which characters and settings are introduced and a dilemma is posed, to a heightening of suspense as the complications of plot unfold, to the ultimate climax and resolution. Dewey and Dilthey have suggested that such a kinetic form is structurally isomorphic with the dynamics of more ordinary human experiences. Dewey's example was the experience of a storm approaching and passing; Dilthey discussed the unified structure in the process of having a child and the ensuing changes in the parents' lives. And Langer noted that such a dynamic form even mimics the rhythms of human physiology, the ebb and flow of life itself.[16] Because of the elemental nature of this kinetic structure, its unfolding in a work of literature can seduce a reader into interaction with the text. But the perception of a well-crafted form is only one of two coequal criteria necessary for an experience to be aesthetic. Indeed, an artfully fashioned story about the experience of schooling risks dismissal as mere entertainment unless it thematically addresses important educational concerns. Such a work must not merely dazzle; it must also enlighten through the careful development of the significant message that is the *aesthetic content.*

146

This "content" component of the aesthetic response has been historically undervalued.[17] For example, prominent aesthetic theorists such as Kant, Schopenhauer, Croce, and Bergson have advanced the notion of *aesthetic disinterest*. In this view, the aesthetic object is self-contained and autonomous. Within an *aesthetic attitude* one apprehends the relationships of the work's formal properties to each other. Aesthetic response is seen as sealed off, occurring for its own sake within the psyche of the experiencer and detached from any cultural context. Impulses to action and all thoughts of the practical are viewed as anaesthetic, deforming the holistic nature of the act of contemplation.

But this notion of art as sublime and remote is enormously debilitating, for it is in its connectedness with the mundane and the nearby that art acquires its true power. Its vitality is linked to its capacity to convey a message relevant to the concerns of the experiencer of the work and thereby to edify. Thus the profundity of a narrative about life in classrooms depends as much on the contents of the story — the meanings attached to features of the classroom landscape — as on the manner of its telling. Indeed, it is *aesthetic* only insofar as it is able to challenge and persuade the reader to consider an alternative formulation of these meanings, to seek out these features in landscapes nearby, and to look upon them in a fresh and novel way. This proposed formulation of meaning is the *thesis* of the work.

The thesis of a literary work can be advanced either directly, as in an essay or work of critical theory, or implicitly, as in most novelistic fiction. One might, for example, formulate the implicit thesis of *Another Country* as follows: "Schooling institutions that demand loyalty from students while serving to perpetuate certain repressive features of the society-at-large can foster extreme forms of alienation from both school and society in students who choose to honor a greater loyalty to their own authenticity as human beings." This thesis, like every literary "message," is developed within the dynamic structure of a literary work, while itself serving as a criterion for a rigorous selection of insights for inclusion in the narrative. An example of this synthesis of aesthetic substance and form can be found in "A Sense of Shelter."

First, there is the early recognition of a dilemma by the reader, the discovery of a problem in whose solution one quickly develops an interest. The reader is swiftly initiated into the world of William Young, "not popular . . . never had a girl," but so adept on the academic playing fields of the classrooms that in this domain "he was a kind of king." And now today he would tell fellow senior Mary Landes — an attractive social sophisticate who at once symbolizes and embodies for William the alien nature of life outside the institutional walls — "that he loved her."

Next comes a building phase. In it the reader experiences a sense of growing meaning, conserved and accumulating toward the full ripening of the thesis. Here Updike feeds us clues about the deep importance of William's classroom status to his self-concept, and reveals his "love" for Mary as a childish infatuation stemming from his mother's approval of her. The reader interprets this new information, of course, in light of what he or she has already learned about William's life situation and in light of what is believed about human motivation in and out of school settings.

Finally, a climax is reached and a *denouement* ensues. As William's advances are rebuffed, the inevitable incompatability with Mary becomes obvious. His self-concept as a successful student intact, he then proceeds to joyously consider that which *will* be his: "he felt so clean and free he smiled. Between now and the happy future predicted for him he had nothing, almost literally nothing, to do."

"A Sense of Shelter" compellingly conveys an important message about one kind of life lived in schools. The aesthetic experience it offers is relevant beyond its own context and so is potentially intriguing, persuasive, and useful for educators. Before exploring the importance of such an accomplished fictionalization of aesthetic content for platform development, however, consider a less successful form of compulsion implicit in traditional research studies.

Abandoning Traditional Attempts at Compulsion

Anyone acquainted with traditional educational research reports is aware that the twin criteria of aesthetic substance and form are *not* honored therein. Works within the scientific genre have, nevertheless, attempted — rather unsuccessfully, I argue — to compel the attention (and allegiance) of members of various educational constituencies. But I have already noted how many educators often perceive these works as being less than interesting and helpful.[18] The lack of success seems related to the misguided practice of methodically manipulating data while tacitly suggesting that no such fashioning has occurred. Let me elaborate.

Whatever the profundities of great works of literature, researchers in the human studies, including educational inquirers, have been professionally socialized to regard fruits so casually harvested with disdain. Storytellers, prone to unruly flights of the imagination, are viewed as operating within the ephemeral "context of discovery"; only scientists possess the tools appropriate for toiling within the quite distinct, and hallowed, "context of justification." Prediction and control require trustworthy knowledge free from personal fantasy and prejudice. When verbally stated, findings must correspond directly to objects in the real world and ensure the validity necessary for making policy and guiding practice. Only through methodical observations of phenomena, preferably in a controlled environment, can such absolute impersonal knowledge be secured.

Certain social-science philosophers have, for some time, been attempting to expose this correspondence theory of knowledge for what it is: the subtle rhetoric of a discredited positivistic epistemology.[19] It has been a rhetoric whose persuasive power, according to Rorty, is based upon *fear*, upon an anxiety that "the manifold possibilities offered by discursive thought will play us false, will make us 'lose contact' with the real." The fear is clearly reflected not only in the systematic method but also in the discursive language of scientific-style research: the objective, detached, passionless voice favored by the positivists, striving toward (in Rorty's phrase) the impossible language "which the universe uses to explain itself." To locate the historical origins of this dread (first sensed by Heidegger as pervading the Western philosophical tradition) Rorty refers us all the way back to Parmenides:

> Parmenides' fear of the poetic, playful, arbitrary aspects of language was so great as to make him distrust predicative discourse itself. This distrust came from the conviction that only being seized, compelled, gripped by the real could produce Knowledge rather than Opinion.[20]

This fear has so pervaded our research communities that even the preponderance of so-called qualitative researchers have shown reticence in abandoning the positivistic underpinnings of their research efforts. This is especially so among those claiming to work within the hermeneutical or interpretive tradition of social inquiry. Originated by Wilhelm Dilthey, the eminent eighteenth-century German scholar of the human studies, this branch of inquiry centers not around questions of fact, but around the meaning of phenomena. Its primary purpose has thus often been stated as the empathic understanding of human actions (*Verstehen*) rather than the detached explanation of behavior (*Erklaren*).[21] But most educational hermeneuticists — ethnographers, ethnomethodologists — have demonstrated a susceptibility to the same positivistic anxieties about knowledge tainted by human judgment. These fears now seemed reinforced by a concern about the respectability of any discipline that could not measure up to the confident knowledge claims of the physical sciences. Hence, they chose to follow the lead, not of Dilthey, but of Max Weber, who strove toward an "objective science" of interpretation — "one undistorted by our value judgments."[22] They felt compelled to justify the worthiness of their findings by relying on this Weberian separation of *facts* and *values*.[23] Many still cling to the correspondence theory of truth and yearn for objective criteria that clearly discriminate between the literally true and the false. Honor is explicitly accorded to the realist epistemology in their methodological meta-talk,[24] and implicitly, in the methods employed and the manner of presenting findings.[25]

But if progress in recognizing the inevitably fundamental role of human agency in educational research has been slow, movement over the last decade has nevertheless been incessant. Foremost among the fearless were relatively small groups of scholars that included the so-called reconceptualists in the curriculum field, the critical theorists, and the "new" sociologists of education. For a while, their voices remained outside of the educational research mainstream, preaching primarily to the converted in sympathetic journals and at "splinter" conferences. While even today the educational research establishment remains largely impervious to their criticisms, the messages of Michael W. Apple, Henry Giroux, William F. Pinar, and many others, are reaching wider audiences. They have been joined by others in a more liberal tradition (e.g., Elliot Eisner, Gail McCutcheon, Robert Donmoyer) who share their skepticism about the epistemological and methodological assumptions of mainline educational research. Recently even journals as fundamentally staid in methodological preferences as *Educational Evaluation and Policy Analysis*, *Educational Researcher*, and *Review of Educational Research* have published critiques of those assumptions.[26]

To my mind, these scholars (and others) have performed an invaluable service in advancing the notion (without using this precise terminology) that *all* educational research is essentially *fictive*, fashioned by the researcher. Still, having so effectively exposed the pretensions of the dominant style of educational research, they have largely failed to promote the legitimacy — let alone the primacy — of the novelistic mode of storytelling as a means for studying classroom life. Such a promotion lies at the heart of my agenda here.

Modes of Fiction and the Purposes of Research

We are now free to imagine, in lieu of customary conceptual categories of fiction and nonfiction, a continuum of research genres, the products of which are viewed as equally fictional. According to this schema, Fyodor Dostoevsky's *Crime and Punishment* is no more fictional than, say, the work of Sigmund Freud; Rumberger's[27] report on his standardized survey of high school dropouts is no less fictional than "A Sense of Shelter." What varies is not the degree of human agency involved in the research processes, but rather the *modes of fiction* employed by the researcher. At one end of the continuum we find fiction within the social science genres employing modes that guide the creation of research texts in accordance with the "foundationalist" tenets of positivism, including methods designed to camouflage subjectivity, and a supposedly value-free, dispassionate style of communicating findings. But fiction it is, for as McCutcheon has noted, value judgments are unavoidably required in several phases of scientific educational research: in the formation of the research question, in the choice of research tools employed, in the interpretation of information collected, and in the language and format used in disclosing the interpreted results.[28] Toward the opposite end of the spectrum, fiction within more "artistic" or "literary" genres offers phenomena selected for the advancement of a personal thesis and conveyed in accordance with the kind of aesthetic criteria discussed earlier.

On what grounds will the researcher base his or her choice of fictional modality? The modes of fiction employed within each genre are selected in order to further the fundamental purpose for which the research effort is undertaken — even if no guarantee is given that the selection process will be guided by wisdom. Indeed, Donmoyer has proposed that one order of mistakes made by researchers relates to the inadequacy of the research purpose.[29] I want to suggest and illustrate *two forms* of such inadequacy. In the first case, the researcher's purposes are problematical because they are unachievable *on their own terms* — because they have severely misjudged the nature of the phenomena they are studying and have selected modes of fiction inappropriate to their research focus.

Consider an example from the scientific end of the continuum, a set of research studies that attempt to uncover one portion of the presumably stable, transcribable reality of schooling. Its ultimate purpose is that cited by Hollifield[30] — to provide curriculum planners and other practitioners with the theoretical knowledge necessary for the control of student learning outcomes. The studies would aim to locate those instructional treatments that most reliably produce the desired academic achievement in individual students, thereby serving to increase student retention rates.

But some readers may recognize the redundancy of such an attempt, recalling one of the most gargantuan efforts in the history of educational research: the Aptitude/Treatment Interaction (ATI) studies of the 1960s and 1970s. The cumulative outcome of these studies has been frequently cited by critics of the traditional research paradigm, and the startling conclusions of Cronbach, the prominent educational psychologist and coauthor of the ATI approach, were set forth in a landmark paper more than one decade ago.[31] Nevertheless, in light of Hollifield's efforts — and those of others engaged in related research aimed at producing more "effective schools" or "efficient instruction" — Cronbach's comments apparently bear repeating. We can, he said, *never* acquire the scientific knowledge necessary for the control of learning outcomes. Why not? When an aptitude for learning interacts with a specified instructional tactic (treatment), the

> result can be taken as a general conclusion only if it is not in turn moderated by further variables. If Aptitude × Treatment × Sex interact, for example, then the

151

Aptiude × Treatment effect does not tell the story. Once we attend to interactions, we enter a hall of mirrors that extends to infinity. However far we carry out analysis — to third order or fifth order or any order — untested interactions of still higher order can be envisioned.[32]

Now, Hollifield himself has admitted that "most dropout problems are a long-term, complex mixture of school, home, and economic pressure interacting with the psychological make-up of each individual student,"[33] and indeed, as we revisit the psychological landscapes of Guy Bennett and William Young, we begin to understand Cronbach's reluctant conclusions about traditional research hopes for control of learning outcomes — even "in-school" outcomes. We comprehend the utter impossibility of successfully manipulating specific variables for managing the learned behavior of individual students.

Moreover, it is not merely the enormous complexity of educational phenomena that render them uncontrollable within the social science modes of fiction. Other thinkers, most notably Schutz[34] and Habermas,[35] have emphasized a fundamental difference in the "object domains" of the physical scientist and social inquirer. Unlike the natural world, "which does not mean anything to molecules, atoms, and electrons," social reality, argues Schutz, "has a specific meaning and relevance structure for the human beings living, acting, and thinking within it."[36] Modes of fiction that demand objective explanations using constructs predefined by the researcher, rather than explaining the constructs made by the actors on the social scene, seem particularly unsuited to their task. True, formalized student surveys and questionnaires are common in drop-out research,[37] but, as in other branches of traditional survey research, subjects confront highly prestructured questions, their responses elicited for purposes of statistical compilation and manipulation. The data is abstracted, torn apart from the contexts of specific lives. Such modes of fictionalization obviously do not promote in readers (including curriculum planners) a vicarious participation in those real (or virtual) lives, nor therefore, a sense of the relevance structures that make them coherent.

Perhaps Eisner most clearly summarized these concerns about the ineffectuality of social-science-based educational research in fulfilling its own stated purposes:

There is little in research that can be used to guide practice; for example, the descriptions of the methods used in experimental research are minimal, dependent measures that almost always underestimate the range of outcomes with which teachers are concerned, and one is almost always forced to violate the limit of scientific generalization in applying research findings to one's own teaching circumstances. . . . [So] what function do [research conclusions] have in guiding practice at the elementary and secondary levels? Educational research provides not so much conclusions or recipes for practice as it does analytical models for thinking about practice. I believe the models that are most readily used are those that are consistent with the educational views one already holds. Rogerians are seldom converted to a Skinnerian world on the basis of data.[38]

The same certainly holds true for the practices of curriculum planning and policymaking. The products of traditional research do not seem made of the stuff that significantly contributes to the building or the renovation of platforms.

The second form of inadequacy of purpose in scientific educational research is less pragmatic in nature. It stems from the dubious value structure undergirding the research purpose. Certain phenomenologists and critical theorists have questioned the manipulative, control-oriented values upon which traditional educational research is premised. Apple in particular has effectively articulated the manner in which these premises serve to orient us toward scientific rationalization and technical control, outcomes most likely to further the interests of our dominant political and economic groups rather than those of the individual child.[39] For, education is surely an enterprise whose fundamental purposes must be to grant to each student empowerment over his or her life. This is accomplished not by total control of the student and his or her environment but by creating situations that encourage what Dewey called *educational experiences*.[40] An educational experience is a growth-inducing experience that fosters self-control over one's relations with the world and therefore a capacity for having even richer experiences in the future. In the next section, I propose a research purpose consonant with this emancipatory view of education and to imagine the modes of fiction most likely to further it.

The Crafting of Likely Stories: Beyond Objectivism and Relativism in Studies of Classroom Life

We have seen that in traditional research the modes of fiction dictated by the purpose of scientific genres favor standardized criteria for neatly distinguising between reliable knowledge and mere belief. We have noted the resulting illusion of epistemological certainty so compelling in its offer of psychological safety against the potential anarchy of relativism. This was a comfort preservable only by refusing to overturn the research stone and uncover the dubious epistemological premises and troubling values that lay underneath. With that stone now overturned and with the narrow criterion of literal truth no longer available, how can a curriculum worker distinguish the worthwhile research text from the worthless? Is the antithesis of foundational knowledge not intellectual chaos? I cite a variety of sources to offer reassurance that it is not — from pragmatist philosophers such as John Dewey and William James, to neopragmatist Richard Rorty, social philosophers such as Hans-Georg Gadamer and Hannah Arendt, and a school of modern literary theorists.

We begin with a bow to pragmatist epistemology. Reality for thinkers like Dewey and James is located neither in a realm totally distinct from the mind of the knower, nor solipsistically within that mind. No, experiencing is always a process that is anticipatory, open to the world; reality resides within the communion of subject and object which comprises that experiencing. This epistemological premise is also fundamental to the work of a group of literary theorists known as *intertextualists*.[41] For these critics, a text is not a static, self-enclosed object that exists when not being read; rather, it exists only as the act of reading occurs. This process is a dynamic one in which the individual reader "assents to confer meaning on the text in terms of his own complex of expectations, understandings and desires."[42]

Educational research literature may indeed be viewed as texts, and its readers — curriculum practitioners, policymakers, and others — as engaged in sensemaking transactions with that literature. The potential of any particular text is realized, therefore, only within these intertextual acts of human understanding. Only then is the text's message in existence, and its thesis potentially useful.

The most helpful research texts are therefore those composed in a manner that invites "completion" by the reader, luring him or her into this construal of meaning. Unfortunately, mainline research provides documents that do not facilitate this sensemaking process, texts that are jargon-laden, graceless, often lacking in educational significance, and therefore aesthetically unappealing to educators not initiated into the research class. Ironically, the opposite qualities have been sacrificed in the name of an impossible "truth." These texts are still fictional, but as fiction they are usually unsatisfactory. More useful for the purposes of an emancipatory view of education are research texts that I call *likely stories*.

A *likely story* is a carefully (if nonmethodically) researched story that throbs with vivid, contextually detailed, dramatically fashioned aesthetic content. This content is comprised of observations that lay bare the meaning and significance of selected educational events from the characters — and, of course, the author's — points of view. Building upon each other, these dabs of literary paint can yield a coherent picture with an internal logic that persuades us of the possibility of its essential message, its thesis. In this manner, likely stories dramatically introduce the curriculum worker to new forms of life in schools, forms that once were largely alien, beyond what Gadamar would call the reader's "horizon," or the "range of vision that includes everything that can be seen from a particular vantage point."[43] Indeed, likely stories are premised on the *openness* of horizons, on Gadamer's fundamental notion that while we cannot entirely escape our own ontological situation, we do indeed seek to understand landscapes other than our own. A story that lends itself to this process of understanding is more likely to render the horizons of others more accessible to the reader.

In reading a likely story, the curriculum worker can thus perceive anew. Upon encountering a powerful union of aesthetic content and dynamic structure, he or she is pulled into the perception of relationships between a fund of ideas in his or her own horizon — a portion of which will contribute to his or her educational plaform — and new ones from the text which seek a place in his or her belief and value nexus. Dewey called this act of perception "an act of reconstructive doing wherein consciousness becomes fresh and alive."[44] Or in Gadamer's terms, a fusion of horizons is achieved wherein the reader's perspective is enlarged and enriched. In this enlargement, the curriculum planner is pushed forward, projected outward into the realm of the virtual. In *Another Country*, we meet a particular stranger in a distant land and era but whose story vivifies a universal form of adolescent alienation. And "A Sense of Shelter" introduces us to a human "hothouse plant" who can blossom only in the rarefied atmosphere of a classroom: William Young closets himself away from the disappointments that he fears await him in an inhospitable outside world. He is not a school dropout; he is a school shut-in. His virtual being is also a challenge to our sensitivities, for it raises the possibility of others in our own landscapes who are actually like him.

Each of these likely stories possesses the enticements of aesthetic form shaped within the personal vision of the researcher. This dynamic structure effectively merges with aesthetic substance (as a developed thesis) to yield intriguing configurations of human phenomena. Each illustrates how likely stories can serve two important functions in the growth of educational platforms. First, they can broaden the vision of curriculum planners, including teachers, concerning "what is," i.e., the range of personal relationships, social patterns, and multiple meanings that adhere to classroom phenomena. Secondly, in their creation of virtual worlds they can promote platform reconstruction by challenging comfortable, existing notions of "what ought to be." Thus, likely stories can be broadly useful, as they advance the emancipatory purposes of education mentioned earlier; that is, they serve to extend the scope of our personal knowledge of the wide variety of schooling experiences, thereby enhancing our sense of the possibilities for the educational community.

THOMAS E. BARONE

Communal Nature of Judgment and Taste

This criterion of broad usefulness suggests a means of escape from a false dichotomy of objectivism and relativism in studies of school life. While offering no false hope of a neutral descriptive language or a permanent standard of rationality for finally discriminating between Absolute Truth and mere belief, it does not ignore the need for guarding against the kind of cynicism fostered by a reliance on shifting tastes and opinions. Bernstein has noted that Gadamer's main concern in *Truth and Method* is indeed a critique of the "radical subjectivisation" of judgment in all domains of life, the notion that taste is *only* private and idiosyncratic.[45] Building on the transactional epistemology of the pragmatists, Gadamer argues cogently that relativism can only make sense as an antithesis to objectivism, and if positivistic objectivity is implausible then we must simultaneously question the intelligibility of the concept of relativism.[46] It is impossible, therefore, for the content of each person's experiencings — for example, my own intellectual and emotional interplay with Updike's text — to be unique and utterly idiosyncratic. I belonged to a shared tradition and culture — including common schooling experiences — before they belonged to me. My belief and value system cannot fully escape the prejudgments that are inherent in that tradition; they also, to some extent, constitute who I am. Horizons (and platforms) inevitably overlap, and in this commonality we bring to a text proclivities for interpretations that cannot be totally arbitrary exercises of purely independent will. But as Gadamer noted, no understanding — scientific or otherwise — is "free of all prejudices, however much the will of our knowledge is directed toward escaping their thrall." No, scientific method cannot provide that escape, but a spirit of skepticism, a "discipline of questioning and research," can. This "escape," of course, is not into a realm of impersonal Truth, but toward a precious intersubjectivity.

And as Gadamer emphasizes this communal sense (*sensus communis*) of taste, so Hannah Arendt makes an analogous point about the intersubjective nature of opinions.[47] Opinions must not be private feelings but rather formed through *judgment*, "one, if not the most, important activity in which a sharing-the-world-with-others comes to pass."[48] Judgment is also *communal*, requiring an "enlarged mentality" achieved through "representative thinking" — or Gadamer's "fusion of horizons." In Arendt's words:

The power of judgment rests on a potential agreement with others, and the thinking process which is active in judging something is not, like the thought process of pure reasoning, a dialogue between me and myself, but finds itself always and primarily, even if I am quite alone in making up my mind, in an anticipated communication with others with whom I know I must finally come to some agreement. From this potential agreement judgment derives its specific validity. This means, on the one hand, that such judgment must liberate itself from the 'subjective private conditions', that is, from the idiosyncrasies which naturally determine the outlook of each individual in his privacy and are legitimate as long as they are only privately held opinions, but which are not fit to enter the market place, and lack all validity in the public realm. And this enlarged way of thinking, which as judgment knows how to transcend its own individual limitations, on the other hand, cannot function in strict isolation or solitude; it needs the presence of others 'in whose place' it must think, whose perspectives it must take into consideration, and without whom it never has the opportunity to operate at all.[49]

Texts greatly deficient in necessary judgment — such as those composed or interpreted by a schizophrenic — do not communicate and so suffer in usefulness (and truthfulness). It is, therefore, our responsibility as curriculum workers and educators to approach likely stories carefully with a spirit of intellectual openness that encourages a risking of our own belief-and-value systems as we test them against those within other horizons. The resulting "enlarged mentality" means — as we have seen — the extension and refinement, the elaboration and reconstruction of that which a teacher or other curriculum planner brings to the development process: his or her platform. The ultimate result should then be an enhanced quality in the deliberative activities wherein curriculum judgments derived from these platforms are communally tested.

Today's Educational Storytellers: Potential Partially Realized

The genres of fiction with the greatest potential for fostering such an enhancement are indeed those found toward the literary-based end of the research contiuum. But can the products of nonnovelistic (or what are commonsensically called *nonfictional*) forms of storytelling also serve as likely stories? To answer that question, consider the works of two groups of storytellers already in our midst.

Autobiography and Biography

Members of the first group boldly embrace the philosophical premises of existentialism and phenomenology and are broadly labelled *reconceptualists*. Foremost among many are scholars such as William F. Pinar, Madeleine Grumet, and Max van Manen. Examples of their works can be found (among other places) in *Phenomenology & Pedagogy* and the *Journal of Curriculum Theorizing*. These researchers often employ autobiographical or biographical approaches to studying educational experiences.[50] Through careful introspection and retrospection the individual inquirer attempts to imbue present and past real-life events with meaning. As research documents, these life stories are offered to those of us who are also seeking to more fully understand ourselves and our world, especially that portion related to education and formal schooling.

Aware of the inherently subjective nature of the inquiry process, these writers eschew the technical, conventional, or (as William James states) "privileged" language of the positivists, in favor of a conversational or vernacular style more attuned to their storytelling purpose. This purpose is indeed concerned with the emancipation of the student: enticing others to reconceptualize the meaning of the educational process through intimate disclosures from the lives of individual educators and students. In my judgment, overcelebrating the development of this educational inquiry genre as a potentially powerful alternative to traditional modes of research is difficult. In actuality, however, the potential remains at least partially unrealized. For while a few of these writers have composed with a remarkable deftness and sensitivity, most have failed to achieve the compelling power witnessed in the stories of Mitchell and Updike.

Part of the reason, I believe, is that they honor only one of the twin necessities for truly enticing fiction. Present has been a healthy fascination with aesthetic substance, profound personal insights into educational growth, and commitment to a life of learning. But a powerful shaping of those insights into a satisfying aesthetic form has often been missing. Discursively recounting actual life incidents and events, they fail to lift this raw biographical data into the realm of the virtual. The failure becomes more obvious when one confronts the unity of form and substance provided by masters like James Boswell, Henry David Thoreau, and James Joyce, or even in works like Alex Haley's biographical *The Autobiography of Malcolm X*, or Elizabeth Hardwick's autobiographical *Sleepless Nights*.[51] Of course, not everyone can compose with such eloquence and finesse, but many of the educational autobiographers seem unconcerned with the dramatic shaping that is at the heart of the novelization process. A point made by Scholes and Kellogg seems pertinent here:

> If any distinction can be said to exist between the autobiography and the autobiographical novel it resides not in their respective fidelity to facts but rather in their respective originality in perceiving and fashioning the facts. It is in the knowing and in the telling, and not in the facts, that the art is to be found.[52]

Indeed, one finds such art in Mitchell's *Another Country*. Although a biographical drama, it nevertheless illustrates the potential to be unleashed when an educational theme is effectively treated within this novelistic genre. With details clearly at the service of a personal vision (as expressed within a thesis), Mitchell has fashioned a story that is truly compelling fiction. If the potentials of the biographical and autobiographical approaches to telling education-oriented stories are to be fully realized, their authors must likewise learn not to fear novelization of their insights. Otherwise, in comparison with the best novelistic fiction, works within these genres will surely pale.

Educational Criticism

Perhaps those who have travelled farthest from the positivistic style of cool, dispassionate, literal research language are the proponents and authors of what is known as *educational criticism*. The brainchild of Elliot Eisner, this *avant-garde* approach to educational research looks to the fields of art and literary criticism for the tools to investigate educational phenomena. And as in art criticism, the actual products of this educational research genre have indeed employed a rich, evocative, vernacular language, but now for depicting qualities in classroom experiences.[53]

As in many of the autobiographical works, a personal voice does forth-rightly convey the sense of human perspective. Critiques carry a tacit admission to being fictive in the broad sense, i.e., fashioned by a human mind with certain purposes and inherent emotional qualities. Moreover, some examples of educational criticism have indeed plotted their observations around a controlling thesis that provides the text with a kinetic literary form.[54] The stories they tell can be simultaneously informative and entertaining, even intriguing. They are, therefore, potentially very useful as research texts for educational practitioners. Still, as for the autobiographical genre, the modes of fiction employed are somewhat hazardous to the full realization of its ultimate educational research purpose. As an advocate and practitioner of educational criticism, I have in the past attempted to identify certain canons of fiction appropriate to this genre. I have cautioned against overstepping the (old, commonsense) boundaries between fiction and nonfiction, urging that care be taken "not to produce composite characters . . . or to distort incidents to further a theme, or to invent dialogue, or even to suggest that certain activity of a particular child is typical if it is in fact unusual."[55] I now believe that obedience to these canons can place unnecessary constraints on the researcher-writer. The rules demanded that the critic remain on the "factual" side of a continuum that, we now see, actually ranges from one form of fiction (scientific) to another (novelistic). They urged that one's thesis be served only by actual particulars experienced in the present context and not through the creation of a virtual experience. As a sometime-author of this kind of story, I

THOMAS E. BARONE

have felt the tension created by the need for my research narrative, tacitly advertised as a "true story," to be shaped nevertheless into a dynamic form. I have felt the self-imposed restrictions that prevent the fashioning of the mundane experiences-at-hand into a story of much greater power and usefulness. But I also admit to occasional feelings of security and comfort in knowing that, lacking the ability to novelize my work of fiction, I can easily put forth a more literal exposition of my experiences.

By no means is such a rendering necessarily worthless. The best educational criticisms have approached the power of works in other literary forms that blur the boundaries between the actual and the virtual — to name a few: the "nonfiction novels" of Norman Mailer,[56] Tom Wolfe,[57] and Truman Capote,[58] the historical novels of Gore Vidal,[59] the biographical and autobiographical novels mentioned earlier, and the historical drama *Another Country*. In principle, of course, one who writes *novelistic* fiction exchanges a dependence on literal canons of fiction for a release of even higher orders of the imagination. One is freed from recounting empirical particulars experienced in a specific setting but is thereby challenged to create and dramatically convey more profound and enticing insights. It is he or she who, at least theoretically, honors more fully Jean Paul Sartre's dictum that we must lie in order to tell the truth. Nevertheless, while as a genre novelistic fiction may hold a greater potential for the crafting of likely stories that will be enticing to educators, each story, regardless of genre, must still ultimately be judged on its individual potential for usefulness. So particular works within a nonnovelistic genre — such as Lightfoot's "social science portraits," or Marianne Amarel's educational criticism, or Grumet's biographical/autobiographical efforts — can be more illuminating fiction than a novelistic short story that is poorly researched and unimaginatively plotted.[60] Yes, stories that claim a literal truth can also be *likely stories*, but only to the degree that the pursuance of this narrow illusion does not distort the aesthetic fashioning of the story.

The Task Ahead

Whatever its genre, a fictional account with an educational theme that offers the kind of reconstruction suggested by Gadamer and Arendt fulfills the emancipatory purpose of educational research suggested earlier. It does not aspire to the standard goals of traditional research: it is not absorbed in the technical and will not directly communicate operational strategies to curriculum workers or other practitioners. It heeds, instead, the recommendations of Scheffler that the education of policymakers move beyond the techniques offered by traditional research texts that are entranced with the "pervasive drive to simplify, to objectify, to reduce." Policymakers, argues Scheffler,

160

must acquire a kind of critical reflexivity that promotes a deeper self-aware-ness relevant to the policymaker's role:

> Students of human culture and history are learning about themselves as well as about others. . . . As creatures of intention and action they pursue their special goal of understanding intention and action by studying the self-conceptions of creatures like themselves.[61]

I believe that the development of such vital self-awareness must be at the very center of any efforts to reform our schools. But until educational re-search — as exemplified by the so-called drop-out literature — abandons its reliance upon modes of fiction that are undergirded by an outdated episte-mology and mistaken purposes, our hopes for such vital self-awareness appear rather dim.

I have attempted here to scout out a new direction for the studying of classroom life, encouraging the crafting and use of research texts that are highly accomplished in aesthetic form and substance and that therefore pro-mote the refinement and reconstruction of educational platforms. We must not minimize the difficulty of gaining legitimacy for such texts in a culture like ours that is so pervaded by a technocratic ethos. True acceptance will require drastic changes in myriad areas — from the kinds of research talents that we recognize as important (and therefore attempt to promote), to the creation of professional journals dedicated to the publication of collections of good educational fiction (at least one of which could deal thematically with student affection/disaffection for schooling — we sorely need many more such stories) to the use of these anthologies as texts in the formal education of practitioners. Teachers and other curriculum planners who have heretofore felt alienated from educational research may then be enticed to view its products (as I did upon reading "A Sense of Shelter" and viewing *Another Country*) as a useful means for understanding more adequately the daily classroom events in which they partake.

The task is indeed formidable. But if the intellectual and emotional sustenance gained by curriculum workers from excellent studies of life in schools is, as I believe, crucial to the efforts of educational reform, then what is the alternative? Let us therefore imagine the possibilities of educational fiction that honors criteria not unlike those used, coincidentally, by novelist Gail Godwin as she edited *The Best American Short Stories 1985*. The motto of her collection, she said, is this: Give me well-crafted stories that "tell me something I need to know — about art, about the world, about human behav-ior, about myself."[62] Give me, Godwin seems to be asking, pieces of compel-ling and useful fiction. Tell me likely stories.

161

Notes

1. Decker Walker, "A Naturalistic Model for Curriculum Development," *School Review*, Vol. 80, 1(1971).

2. J. H. Hollifield, "Creating Effective Schools for All Students: Implications of Educational Research for Dropout Prevention," paper presented to the Regional Leadership Conference, Secretary's Secondary School Recognition Program, Atlanta, Ga., April 1985.

3. *Ibid.*, p. 7.

4. *Ibid.*, p. 7.

5. Julian Mitchell, *Another Country* (Ambergate, England: Amber Lane Press, 1982).

6. This notion of virtual events is adapted from Suzanne Langer's *Problems of Art* (New York: Charles Scribner's Sons, 1957). Her conception of a virtual entity is one in which actual physical particulars are given over to an artistically created apparition, a perceptible form that expresses the "complexity and richness of what is sometimes called man's 'inner life', the stream of direct experience, life as it feels to the living."

7. John Updike, "A Sense of Shelter," in *Pigeon Feathers and Other Stories* (New York: Fawcett Books, 1959).

8. Ibid., pp. 73–4.

9. A. Cooke, *The Meaning of Fiction* (Detroit, Mich.: Wayne State University Press, 1960), p. 84.

10. Updike, *op. cit.*, p. 63–4.

11. Sara Lawrence Lightfoot, *The Good High School: Portraits in Character and Culture* (New York: Basic Books, 1983).

12. Clifford Geertz, *The Interpretation of Culture* (New York: Basic Books, 1973).

13. John Dewey, *Art As Experience* (New York: Capricorn Books, 1958).

14. Monroe Beardsley, *Aesthetics: Problems in the Philosophy of Criticism* (New York: Harcourt, Brace & World, 1969).

15. Cited in H. A. Hodges, *Wilhelm Dilthey: An Introduction* (New York: Oxford University Press, 1944).

16. Langer, *op. cit.*

17. Landon E. Beyer, "Aesthetic Experience for Teacher Education and Social Change," *Educational Theory*, Vol. 35, 4(Fall 1985).

18. For the views of teachers, see Robert Dreeben, *The Nature of Teaching* (Glenview, Ill.: Scott, Foresman, 1970), and Dan Lortie, *School Teacher: A Sociological Study* (Chicago: Unviersity of Chicago Press, 1975).

19. See J. Bergner, *The Origins of Formalism in Social Science* (Chicago: University of Chicago Press, 1981).

20. Richard Rorty, *Consequences of Pragmatism* (Minneapolis: University of Minnesota Press, 1982), p. 130.

21. G. H. von Wright, *Explanation and Understanding* (London: Routledge & Kegan Paul, 1971).

22. R. Aron, *Main Currents in Sociological Thought 2*, R. Howard and H. Weaver, trans. (New York: Penguin Books, 1967).

23. J. Smith and L. Heshusius, "Closing Down the Conversation: the End of the Quantitative-Qualitative Debate," *Educational Researcher*, Vol. 15, 1(1986).

24. See, for example, M. Miles and M. Huberman, *Qualitative Data Analysis: A Sourcebook of New Methods* (Beverly Hills, Calif.: Sage Publications, 1984).

25. See, for example, E. Guba, *Toward a Methodology of Naturalistic Inquiry in Educational Evaluation* (Los Angeles: Center for the Study of Evaluation, University of California, Los Angeles, 1978); and M. LeCompte and J. Goetz, "Problems of Reliability and Validity in Ethnographic Research," *Review of Educational Research*, Vol. 52 (1982). For a discussion of these ideas, see J. Smith, "Quantitative versus Qualitative Research: An Attempt to Clarify the Issue," *Educational Researcher*, Vol. 12 (1983).

26. See Robert Donmoyer, "The Rescue from Relativism: Two Failed Attempts and an Alternative Strategy," *Educational Researcher*, Vol. 14, 10(1985); Smith and Heshusius, *op. cit.*; Elliot W. Eisner, *The Educational Imagination: On the Design and Evaluation of School Programs*, second edition (New York: Macmillan, 1985); Smith, *op. cit.*; and J. S. Allender, "Educational Research: A Personal and Social Process," *Review of Educational Research*, Vol. 56 (Summer 1986).

27. R. Rumberger, "Dropping Out of High School: The Influence of Race, Sex, and Family Background," *American Educational Research Journal*, Vol. 20 (1983).

28. Gail McCutcheon, "The Disclosure of Classroom Life," unpublished doctoral dissertation (Stanford, Calif.: Stanford University, 1976).

29. Donmoyer, *op. cit.*

30. Hollifield, *op. cit.*

31. Lee Cronbach, "Beyond the two Disciplines of Scientific Psychology," *American Psychologist*, Vol. 30, 2(February 1975).

32. *Ibid.*, p. 119.

33. Hollifield, *op. cit.*, p. 4.

34. Alfred Schutz, *The Collected Papers, Volume 1*, B. Natanson, ed. (The Hague: M. Nijhoff, 1962).

35. Jurgen Habermas, *Knowledge and Human Interests*, Jeremy Shapiro, trans. (Boston: Beacon Press, 1971).

36. Schutz, *op. cit.*, p. 11.

37. See, for example, S. Peng, R. Takai, and W. Fetters, "High School Dropouts: Preliminary Results from the 'High School and Beyond' Survey," paper presented at the annual meeting of the American Educational Research Association, Montreal, 1983; Rumerger, *op. cit.*; and A. M. Pallas, "The

Determinants of High School Dropout," unpublished doctoral dissertation, (Baltimore, Md.: Johns Hopkins University, 1984).

38. Eisner, *op. cit.*, pp. 358–59.

39. Michael W. Apple, "Scientific Interests and the Nature of Educational Institutions," in William Pinar, ed., *Curriculum Theorizing: The Reconceptualists* (Berkeley, Calif.: McCutchan Publishing Corporation, 1975).

40. John Dewey, *Experience and Education* (New York: Collier Books, 1963).

41. Intertextualism is closely associated with the New French Critics such as Roland Barthes and J. Kristeva, and the American Stanley Fish.

42. R. Adams, "The Sense of Verification: Pragmatic Commonplaces about Literary Criticism," *Daedalus*, Vol. 101, 1(Winter 1972).

43. Hans-Georg Gadamer, *Truth and Method*, G. Barden and J. Cumming, trans. and ed. (New York: Seabury Press, 1975).

44. Dewey, *Art as Experience, op. cit.*

45. Richard J. Bernstein, *Beyond Objectivism and Relativism: Science, Hermeneutics, and Praxis* (Philadelphia: University of Pennsylvania Press, 1983).

46. *Ibid.*, p. 167.

47. *Ibid.*, p. 217.

48. Cited in *Ibid.*, p. 217.

49. *Ibid.*, p. 218.

50. The growing body of literature that discusses and provides examples of biographical and autobiographical narrative includes the following: William Pinar, "Life History and Educational experience," *Journal of Curriculum Theorizing*, Vol. 2, 2(1980) and "Life History and Educational Experience: Part Two," *Journal of Curriculum Theorizing*, Vol. 3, 1(1981); Leonard Berk, "Education in Lives: Biographic Narrative in the Study of Educational Outcomes," *Journal of Curriculum Theorizing*, Vol. 2, 2(1980); Madeleine Grumet, "Songs and Situations: The Figure/Ground Relation in a Case Study of *Currere*," in George Willis, ed., *Qualitative Evaluation* (Berkeley, Calif.: McCutchan Publishing Corporation, 1978); R. L. Butt, "Arguments for Using Biography in Understanding Teacher Thinking," in R. Halkes and J. K. Olson, eds., *Teacher Thinking* (Lisse, Holland: Sevets and Zeitlinger, 1984); R. Butt, D. Raymond, G. McCue, and L. Yamagishi, "Interpretations of Teacher Biographies," paper presented at the annual meeting of the American Educational Research Association, San Francisco, 1986; F. M. Connelly and D. J. Clandinin, "On Narrative Method, Personal Philosophy, and Narrative Unities in the Study of Teaching," *Journal of Research on Science Teaching*, Vol. 23, 3(1986); Thomas E. Barone, "Educational Platforms, Teacher Selection, and School Reform: Issues Emanating from a Biographical Case Study," *Journal of Teacher Education*, Vol. 38, 2(1987).

51. Elizabeth Hardwick, *Sleepless Nights* (New York: Random House, 1979).

52. R. Scholes and R. Kellogg, *The Nature of Narrative* (New York: Oxford University Press, 1966).

53. Educational criticism has been discussed more than it has been practiced. Examples are found, however, in Eisner, *op. cit.*; Willis, *op. cit.*; and the Fall 1981 and Summer 1983 issues of *Daedalus*.

54. See, for example, Thomas Barone, "Of Scott and Lisa and Other Friends," in Eisner, *op. cit.*

55. Thomas Barone, "Effectively Critiquing the Experienced Curriculum: Clues from the 'New Journalism,'" *Curriculum Inquiry*, Volume 10, Number 1, 1980.

56. Norman Mailer, *The Executioner's Song* (New York: Warner Books, 1979).

57. Tom Wolfe, *The Right Stuff* (New York: Warner Books, 1979).

58. Truman Capote, *In Cold Blood* (New York: Signet Books, 1965).

59. Gore Vidal, *Burr* (New York: Bantam Books, 1973); and Gore Vidal, *Lincoln* (New York: Ballantine Books, 1984).

60. Lightfoot, *op. cit.*; Grumet, *op. cit.*

61. Israel Scheffler, "On the Education of Policymakers," *Harvard Educational Review*, Vol. 54, 2(1984)155.

62. C. Romano, "Short Stories' Collection of Characters." *Cincinnati Enquirer*, December 29, 1985.

NINE

Democracy and the Curriculum

George H. Wood

A s other selections in this collection have made clear, the curriculum arises as a product of choice: curricular decisions are political decisions. At times, as shown in the two previous selections, the political nature of curricular choices is hidden by appeals to the neutrality of science or social need. However, choosing from among many curricular possibilities is always first and foremost a political act.

Political debates are usually generated by competing views of the way the world "should" be. Thus, we argue for competing conceptions of the curriculum (or school organization, pedagogy, control, etc.) on the basis of our view of a just society and good life. What this means is that behind arguments for particular curricula is more than the intention that students gain particular academic skills. In addition, each proposed curricular formation carries with it a distinct social outcome—a notion of what body of knowledge, skills, attitudes, and values students should gain in order to live in a particular social order. This essence of the curriculum leads to the vociferous debates over what schools should do.

These questions become especially difficult in a democracy, given democracy's essentially fluid character. Primary to any sense of democratic life is the notion that individuals are free to remake the social order in ways that best suit collective needs. On the other hand, concern is always present regarding the stability of the social order which requires that citizens accept the status quo in terms of social organization. These are questions not faced in terms of education in more centralized political orders. Autocracies, monarchies, and dictatorships all are preoccupied with stability and have little concern with the ability of the general populace to be self-governing. A democracy, however, faces directly the need for the democratic empowerment of its citizens.

In the early days of the Republic, Thomas Jefferson laid out the rationale for public schooling in a democratic society.

> In every government on earth is some trace of human weakness, some germ of corruption and degeneracy, which cunning will discover, and wickedness insensibly open, cultivate and improve. Every government degenerates when trusted to the rulers of the people alone. The people themselves therefore are its only safe depositories. And to render even them safe, their minds must be improved to a certain degree.[1]

Jefferson's ideas have been criticized for their elitism and limited view of the public. Yet within his proposals for free, public education are the seeds of the most important task before the school — to be the site where democratic citizens are empowered.

Indeed, the ongoing debate over schooling in America has historically focused on the school's social mission. The question is how can we best meet a democracy's need for informed, active, and productive citizens? Of course, this invokes a series of prior issues as well, most importantly the issue of how we are to define democracy and citizenship within it.

The resolution of this debate is central to thinking about and formulating educational decisions — including those regarding the school curriculum. Simply put, we need to know *what* we intend to do before we try and do it. Only after we are sure we undestand the school's role in a democracy can we begin to approach the question of curriculum. Only after we understand what it means to be a citizen, to participate democratically, can we begin to sort out the shape and scope of the curriculum.

Unfortunately, the contest over a curriculum for empowerment or control in a democratic society is often lost in curricular debates. We assume that the way the world as it currently exists is the way it should be; the curriculum is, thus, merely a tool to prepare students to fit into the existing social order. However, this begs the question of what it means to live and act democratically. This chapter addresses the meaning of democracy and its centrality as an organizing principle for curricular action.

In particular, three issues are explored. First, what do we mean by democracy and why should it be invoked as an organizing principle for schooling?

Second, what can we say about the nature of many current curricular reforms in light of this discussion of democracy? And finally, what would a curriculum for democratic empowerment, as opposed to social control, look like?

The Meaning of Democracy

What do we mean when we say the purpose of schooling is to prepare democratic citizens? Certainly much of what we mean is found in how we define democracy. Often, the definition invoked is merely a reflection of current social and political practices. However, other choices are possible when deciding whether to judge a system or action democratic. In fact, there are ways to conceive of democracy which run directly counter to our present practices. A discussion of educating for democracy thus must begin with a clear understanding of democracy itself.

In the last 30 years a concerted effort has been made to bring definitions of democracy into line with its contemporary practice. Intended here was a move away from direct public participation in governance to making representation democracy's central characteristic.[2] These theories of democracy, referred to as either "weak" or "protectionist" theories, argue that we all engage in politics, or governance, only when we have personal interests to protect. Thus, we elect representatives to protect those interests from being violated.

To justify this vision of democracy, contemporary theorists of democracy draw on a variety of sources. First, the argument is made that the populace is composed of people who generally do not possess either the democratic attitudes or the intellectual capacity needed for self-governance. We are not willing, the argument goes, to invest the time necessary for democratic self-governance. Beyond that, the intellectual skills needed to resolve the problems of governance are not widely found in the general population. Therefore, democratic politics should be primarily a process of our choosing those who will make decisions rather than making decisions ourselves. Democracy is to be a competition between social and/or intellectual elites for the right to govern.[3]

Given this model, the central criterion for judging a system democratic is a system of open and free elections. If some public system exists through which social or political elites can compete for the right to represent individuals and their interests, that system must be judged democratic. As for those who do not vote, they also play a vital political role.

The positive contribution of political apathy is twofold. First, it demonstrates the general level of satisfaction with the system — it is simply assumed that those who do not vote are satisfied with the way things are. The second

(2)

function of apathy is to keep to a minimum the demands upon the system. Some individuals will refrain from voting not because they are satisfied, but because no elite is articulating their interests. This implies that the interests held by the individual are not widely shared, and thus do not deserve a place on the ballot.

→This second function of political apathy is the key to understanding the main concern of proponents of protectionist democracy's stability. Any political system that claims to be "by, of, and for" the people does have inherent in it some instability. The greatest fear of those who advocate protectionist democracy is that this instability will be carried as far as it was in the Weimar Republic in Germany. As George Will states:

> In two presidential ballotings in Germany in 1932, 86.2 and 83.5 percent of the electorate voted. In 1933, 88.8 percent voted in the Assembly election swept by the Nazis. Were the 1932 turnouts a sign of the health of the Weimar Republic? The turnout reflected the unhealthy stakes of politics then; elections determined which mobs ruled the streets and who went to concentration camps.
>
> The fundamental human right is to good government. The fundamental problem of democracy is to get people to consent to that, not just to swell the flood of ballots. In democracy, legitimacy derives from consent, but nonvoting is often a form of passive consent. It often is an expression not of alienation but contentment . . . the stakes of our elections, as they affect the day-to-day life of the average American, are agreeably low.[4]

(*)   An alternative, "strong" or "participatory" conception of democracy, focuses upon public participation as opposed to representation. This classical notion has posited that democracy, in the words of John Dewey, "is more than a form of government; it is primarily a mode of associated living, of conjoint communicated experiences."[5] That is, democracy is a way of living in which we collectively deliberate over our shared problems and prospects. It is conceived as a system in which decisions are made by those who will be directly effected by the decision.

The rationale for this notion of democracy comes from Rousseau's *The Social Contract*: (1) Participatory systems are self-sustaining because the very qualities required of citizens if such a system is to work are those that participation itself fosters; (2) participation increases one's "ownership" over decisions, thus making public decisions more acceptable to individuals; and (3) participation has an integrative function—helping integrate individuals into the social order.[6] These premises were further developed by John Stuart Mill and G. D. H. Cole.[7] Mill argued that the primary consideration in judging a society or government to be good was the effect that system had upon individuals. Rather than concern himself with efficiency, Mill argued that participatory democracy fostered within individuals the psychological attributes needed in self-governance. In addition, Mill and Cole argued that these characteristics are best developed at the local level. Through such local participation, citizens come to formulate and take seriously decisions made on an immediate level, and develop those skills and attitudes necessary for self-governance at the national level.

What in particular is meant in referring to attributes needed for self-governance? J. S. Mill argued that an active character would emerge from participation and Cole suggested that a nonservile character would be generated. What this means is that individuals should have the confidence that they are fit to govern themselves. The term often used to describe such a state is known as a *sense of political efficacy*. That is, the belief that individual political action does have an impact on decisionmaking; therefore, performing one's civic duties is worthwhile.

Empirical evidence suggests that participation does enhance feelings of political efficacy. Studies by Almond and Verba, Carnoy and Shearer, and those cited by Wirth, point out that participatory models in local governments, workplaces, and associations do lead to higher levels of participation in national politics. In all of these studies, local participation in self-governance increased a sense of control over the immediate political environment and a concurrent desire emerged to participate in controlling the national political agenda.[8]

Let me clarify what these theories and studies mean when the term *participation* is used. Three conditions must be obtained: First, the participants must be in the position of decisionmaker rather than decision influencer; second, all participants must be in possession of, or have access to, the requisite information on which decisions can be reached; and third, full participation requires equal power on the part of participants to determine the outcome of decisions. When individuals experience participation in this sense at a local level, the research suggests that they will gain a greater sense of political efficacy in the national arena.[9]

This implies, contrary to claims made by protectionist theorists, that democracy best functions as a lived process of participation, a process in which citizens do not merely choose between elites but actually transform themselves through debate and contestation over public issues. This was the original vision of democracy upon which the foundations of our political practice were laid. Additionally, as has been pointed out in Wirth's review of workplace democracy, it is a vision of democracy that continus to be relevant as it humanizes shared social spheres, empowers democratic citizens, and leads to more effective and efficient decisionmaking. Ongoing debate into the way such participation is facilitated in our evolving society is necessary. The point here is that *participatory theory* holds us closer to a democratic society than does *protectionist theory*.[10]

Educators should realize that the social role they play depends upon the conception of democracy, participatory or protective, they choose. On the one hand rests a conception of democracy within which the participation of the minority elite is crucial and the nonparticipation of the apathetic ordinary individual is necessary to maintain the system's stability. On the other hand, democracy is conceived as encompassing the broadest participation of the people working to develop political efficacy and a sense of belonging in order to further extend and enhance more particpation.

Schooling and Protectionist Democracy

Given the above outline, it seems clear that the most broadly publicized and debated of the current reports on curricular reform are based upon protectionist democracy. Both in substance and implementation, recommendations for change seem destined to limit democratic participation rather than expand it. It is important to see how this happens before turning to curricular action based upon participatory democracy.

Perhaps the most glaring democratic indictment of the reform effort of the 1980s is its top-down nature. A simple survey of the make-up of commissions that have issued curricular proclamations demonstrates the elite make-up of the recommending committees: In the six most publicized and promoted reports, 132 individuals played a part, among whom were three teachers.[11] This top-down reform is carried out in the best traditions of protectionist democracy, with self-selected elites choosing the curriculum to be followed by teachers and students. Perhaps Susan O'Hannian's biting sarcasm most clearly summarizes the nature of such curricular mandates:

> The good gray managers of the U.S., the fellows who gave us Wonder Bread, the Pinto, hormone-laden beef wrapped in Styrofoam, and *People* magazine — not to mention acid rain, the Kansas City Hyatt, $495 hammers, and political campaigns — are now loudly screaming that we teachers should mend our slothful ways and get back to excellence.[12]

Such curricular action is a continuation of the trend to "teacher-proof" the curriculum; that is, a desire to standardize and routinize the curriculum in ways that dictate teacher behaviors, leaving little or no room for creativity, individuality, or spontaneity. Only in that way will the top-down reformers be assured that they, not teachers, are in control.[13]

Additionally, these reforms are to be implemented by state or national mandate. Most of the national commissions do not see a need for local control of, or diversity in, the curriculum. Rather, standardization is to be imposed on teachers from the highest levels of the educational bureaucracy. Again, the theme is centralization of both power and control as opposed to any notion of public participation and community control. If this is how reform is to be implemented, what end does it serve?

The answer to this seems to be the narrowing of what counts as worthwhile knowledge, linking schooling to work, and avoiding issues of equity in pursuing what is loosely called *excellence*. Some examples of each of these trends are in order here.

In each report, the sentiment is that it is time to get back to the basics. All focus on what is believed to be a set of basic skills to be mastered and then tested on standardized measures. The Twentieth Century Fund calls for a core of reading, writing and calculating; technical capability in computers; training in science and foreign languages; and knowledge of civics. The National Science Board (NSB) couples the "three R's" with communication and higher problem-solving skills, and scientific and technological literacy. The President's Commission on excellence in Education's much discussed report, *A Nation At Risk*, calls for concentrating in the "Five New Basics," English, mathematics, science, social studies, and computer literacy.

Objecting to the notion that these should all be valued components of any curricular reform is difficult. However, upon careful examination, two problems of intent arise. First, these proposals all seem to define narrowly what is considered *an education*. Under the guise of returning to "basics," a great deal is eliminated—such as the arts, music, and humanities in their broadest sense. Of course, given that these proposals all carry with them an intent to test student achievement, we can expect a narrowing even within the basics. In English, for example, the ability to find a verb in a list of words becomes more important than crafting a clear sentence or paragraph. Given the very nature of standardized testing, the process of teaching to the test forces a narrowing of the curriculum.

But the curriculum always has some intent—and the intent in these reports is clearly to produce a steady source of workers. The concern that motivates each report is with the failure of American industrial strength: "Our once unchallenged preeminence in commerce, industry, science, and technological innovation is being overtaken by competitors throughout the world."[19] "Japan, West Germany, and other relatively new industrial powers have challenged America's position on the leading edge of change and technical innovation."[15] "Already the quality of our manufactured products, the viability of our trade, our leadership in research and development, and our standards of living are strongly challenged. We must not let this happen;

172

America must not become an industrial dinosaur."[16]

Given these problems, the need for "more skilled young people [is greater] than ever before...."[17] And the origination of these demands for well-trained workers comes directly from business: "Business will require, to an increasing degree, people who are knowledgeable about science and technology."[18] The purpose of these reforms, the motivation behind the narrowing of the curriculum, is simply to prepare children for work (and, in *A Nation At Risk*, for the military).

In analyzing this trend, David Cohen has called it part of the "Toyota Problem."

> We have not always had Toyotas, but schools have long had the problem of improving productivity, or efficiency, or both — at least schools have long thought they had that problem. Since the 1890s we have thought of schools as a chief means for making America more productive, more efficient, more competitive. This is an idea that becomes increasingly problematic the deeper one digs into the relationship between education and productivity, yet few seem inclined to question the notion that schools are responsible for the many failures of General Motors, or Ford, or Chrysler. It is odd since schools never were praised for causing earlier success in that industry.[19]

It is important at this point to note that this is not a new trend. Rather, it derives directly from the scientific management ethos forced on schooling in the early 1900s. The attempt in these early decades was to mold the schools in the model of scientifically managed industry. Here, work was fragmented into small parts with each worker a cog in a larger machine controlled by the foreman. Workers did not control either the speed or nature of their work because the goal was a tightly controlled process which generated the greatest amount of production in the shortest time possible.

Schooling, molded in this image, was a process of mass producing workers in the most cost-effective, or efficient, manner. Minimum standards were set both for job performance and student achievement. Teaching was to be controlled by an administrative hierarchy applying the latest techniques of scientific measurement and analysis. The results of this "cult of efficiency," as Raymond Callahan has called it, depended upon where one sat.[20] Ellwood P. Cubberly, an administrator and proponent of the application of scientific management to schooling, saw the movement this way in 1916:

> The [efficiency] movement indicates the growth not only of a professional consciousness as to the need of some quantitative units of measurement, but also, to a limited extent, of a public demand for a more intelligent accounting by school officers for the money expanded for public education.[21]

173

As opposed to this in 1911, Margaret Haley, an elementary teacher and organizer of the Chicago Teacher's Association, saw the "Factory System" of education as needing "only the closing time whistle to make complete its identification with the great industrial plants."[22]

Indeed, as Arthur Wirth and others have recounted, the attempts to scientifically control education, to mandate from the top down, worked to limit the educative function of schooling. Rote learning was valued over critical thinking, group recitation took the place of individual inquiry, and bland, standardized textbooks replaced reading the classics or the legitimate literature of the day. This is not to suggest that there was some "Golden Age" of schooling that the scientific management craze displaced. Rather, while alternatives did exist (often in school districts under more localized and populist, as opposed to bureaucratic and professional, administrative forms) they were eliminated in the name of science.

To return to the theme of this essay, it could also be claimed that such school reform was profoundly antidemocratic. School control was removed from the public and put in the hands of administrators (never teachers). The curriculum was structured to meet national or local manpower needs, not the preparation of active citizens. Lessons learned focused on rote repetition, obedience, and compliance as opposed to inquiry, self-government or control, and active involvement. All in all, it was schooling for passive control, not for democratic involvement.

The mainstream reform documents of today seem to echo the words of these scientific management educators and efficiency experts. (Exceptions to this are highlighted in the following section.) As opposed to restructuring the antidemocratic nature of many curricular practices, including rote memorization, passive learning and tightly controlled school environments, we hear calls for more of the same. More is frequently the actual prescription: more days, more hours, more homework, more tests, more, more, more.[23] Additionally, control of the curriculum is to continue to be centralized — mandated by state or professional bodies and carried out by the lowly teacher (worker). In this new manifestation of schooling for work, the scientific management of the curriculum enters not a new, but a merely expanded, phase.

The consequence of schooling that seeks merely to respond to the demands of the workplace seems all too clear: Individuals patterned to take their place unthinkingly in a world that operates beyond their control with no respect for their needs. We become cultural and political isolates — with little sense of community or cooperative effort. And most essentially, we adopt a position of passivity, waiting to be "done to" rather than acting ourselves.

The broadest, most public agenda for schooling is thus abandoned. The issue of preparing a public to live democratically, to share in collective decisionmaking, to participate broadly in public affairs, is lost to the simple

174

memory tasks of mandated minimum competencies. It is not simply an ignorance of the school's democratic mission that brings about these trends.
Rather, it is a decidedly antidemocratic spirit that motivates reforms designed
to keep the public ignorant and passive as opposed to enlightened and active.
"The public schools of America have not been corrupted for trivial reasons,"
writes Walter Karp.

> Much would be different in a republic composed of citizens who could judge for
> themselves what secured or endangered their freedom. Every wielder of illicit or
> undemocratic power, every possessor of undue influence, every beneficiary of
> corrupt special privilege woud find his position and tenure at hazard. Republican
> education is a menace to powerful, privileged, and influential people, and they in
> turn are a menace to a republican education. . . . Merit pay, a longer school year,
> more home work, special schools for 'the gifted,' and more standardized tests will
> not even begin to turn our public schools into nurseries of 'informed, active, and
> questioning citizens.' They were not meant to. When the authors of A Nation At
> Risk called upon schools to create an 'educated work force,' they are merely
> sanctioning the prevailing corruption, which consists precisely in the reduction of
> citizens to credulous workers.[24]

A Curriculum for Democratic Empowerment

Is it possible for public schooling to achieve its democratic promise?
Rejecting recent reform proposals is not enough if schooling is to take a
democratic direction. Additionally, parameters (as opposed to prescriptions)
of what would count as democratic curriculum, school organization, and
pedagogy need to be set forth. In what follows we consider solely the issue of
the curriculum. Yet this does not mean curricular reform can stand alone. If
the curriculum is to become a source of democratic empowerment, it will
need the support of changing administrative and pedagogic structures. But
these are beyond the scope of this chapter. Here, my concern is with the
notions of democratic empowerment, democratic values, and a democratic
curriculum.

Historically, the assumption was that a liberal arts curriculum was all that
was required to educate for democratic citizenship. The political tools were
there to be utilized by those literate enough to engage in political matters.
This is no longer a viable approach to public education for democratic life for
two reasons. First, the complexity of the issues that face the public often seem
to paralyze popular democratic action. We turn too often to technical experts
to solve what are more genuinely political problems. Second, strong, antidemocratic forces are at work today that must be contained if democratic life is
to have a future. Institutionally, we are witnessing broad areas of public

175

concern (foreign policy, local economic development, the environment) coming under increasingly private or, if public, bureaucratic control. Attitudinally, vast numbers of citizens refuse to participate politically due to despair, apathy, or a refusal to take responsibility. The complexity and antidemocratic nature of our social lives will not be overcome by traditional liberal arts curricula, as valuable as they may be.

This is not to suggest that the alternative curricula proposed herein for democratic empowerment will resolve all of the foregoing problems. Certainly, the revitalization of democratic life requires action in a variety of spheres, economic, cultural, social, political, as well as educational. Yet the value of engendering a democratic disposition among youth in schools cannot be underestimated. If Dewey and the pragmatic philosophers are correct, if indeed we learn what we experience, then the only way to guarantee a reservoir of democratic sentiment in the culture is to make public schooling a center of democratic experience.

What is meant when we speak of a curriculum for democratic empowerment? To begin with, let us define what is meant by democratic empowerment. Gaining a sense of democratic empowerment involves the following cognitive, personal, and communal skills and understandings:

1. believing in the individual's right and responsibility to participate publicly;
2. having a sense of political efficacy, that is, the knowledge that one's contribution is important;
3. coming to value the principles of democratic life — equality, community, and liberty;
4. knowing that alternative social arrangements to the status quo exist and are worthwhile; and
5. gaining the requisite intellectual skills to participate in public debate.

A wide body of literature, as well as actual curricular practices, have recently focused on school reform geared to democratically empower students. There have been proposals, such as those from the American Educational Studies Association (AESA) and the Public Education Information Network, that argue for more democratic school structures.[25] In both cases, the argument is that autocratic forms of school organization foster passive, nonparticipatory models of citizenship. Students, with no role to play in decisionmaking within the institution, learn through experience that the role of the good citizen is to passively obey, not to question.

Opposed to this are offered models of school organization that actively engage students in making decisions about their lives. From the AESA document:

Moreover, a democratic commitment demands a pedagogy which does more than effectively transmit the cultural heritage, extend bodies of knowledge, or vocational skills. It must teach students how to think, how to order their own affairs rationally, how to function as competent citizens, and how to accept, value, and respect others. It must develop the exercise of those capacities central to understanding one's own interests, those of others, and how to effect decisions. . . .

It is unreasonable to expect school graduates to behave responsibly unless they have learned to exercise the judgment that yields such behavior and to practice the examining and choosing of alternative courses of action. . . . If we want adults who can outgrow the bonds of their personal dependency, and who are capable of the freedom a democratic society expects them to exercise, the school must explicitly concern itself with the development of individual autonomy.[26]

Other proposals focus on reforming the curriculum in ways that would better equip students to participate democratically. They argue against ability-segregated school organization that creates a political underclass through differentiated knowledge acquisition. Furthermore, they suggest that the entire curriculum should target political and social as opposed to vocational life. Such is the argument of curricular proposals put forth by a wide range of individuals, from Mortimer Adler to John Goodlad and Ernest Boyer.

The one-track system of schooling *The Paideia Proposal* advocates has the same objectives for all without exception. These objectives are not now aimed at in any degree by the lower tracks onto which a larger number of our underprivileged children are shunted—an educational dead end. It is a dead end because these tracks do not lead to the result that the public schools of a democratic society should seek, first and foremost, all its children—preparation to go on learning, either at advanced levels of schooling, or in adult life, or both.[27]

Civic literacy is decreasing, and unless we find better ways to educate ourselves as citizens, we run the risk of drifting unwittingly into a new kind of Dark Age—a time when, increasingly, specialists will control knowledge and the decisionmaking process. In this confusion, citizens would make critical decisions, not on the basis of what they know, but on the basis of blind belief in one or another set of professed experts.[28]

At the center of all five proposals is some sense, more explicit in the first two, of educating for democratic empowerment. They set forth the broad outlines of the necessary schooling arrangements to generate the social, intellectual, personal, and cultural skills to embrace democratic citizenship. The issue now is to move more directly to what a curriculum for democratic

(What would the cur. for democr. empowerment look like?)

empowerment would look like. Such a curriculum includes critical literacy skills, developing student's stock of cultural capital, actively engaging students in decisionmaking, providing for social alternatives, and embacing democratic values. Each of these is set forth in what follows.[29]

Critical Literacy

Any curriculum focusing on democratic empowerment must find at its base a foundation in critical literacy skills. This does not mean, however, the limited "back to basics" approach that dominates so much of the literacy literature. The workbook, basal approach to reading, writing, and speaking presents only a fragmented and technical approach to these skills. Not only do these approaches not work, they restrict the ways children come to see literacy as a tool for their own empowerment. Language is seen as a decoding device, useful for understanding what we are told, but not for making our own voices heard.

(crit. lit.
know to
able to
eval.
what's
read or
heard into
req. to
being
served
positions
taken)

In opposition to that prescription, a curriculum for democratic empowerment needs to enhance critical literacy skills that give children personal and political facility with the language. Critical literacy invovles the ability to evaluate what is read or heard with respect to the interests being served or the positions taken. Furthermore, critical literacy enhances the ability to mold one's own world through naming and constructing models of preferred social and personal life.

What this means in practice is helping students come to see the written word as something other than truth incarnate. Working toward an understanding that all writing and speaking is nothing more, and nothing less, than an attempt to communicate and persuade — a process open to all. Several examples help illuminate this process.

For younger children, critical literacy involves building reading skills around students' own reading agendas. Having them read about things in which they have an interest and helping them write their own reading material are key components in this process. Several teachers with whom I work approach this in a variety of ways. One has children extend the books they read, either writing new endings or going beyond the ending to continue the story. Another builds entire curricular units around topics of student interest. Called *webbing*, the teacher and students gather real books, not basals, on the topic at hand and read, share, write about, construct models, present plays, and so forth on topics based on their readings. Moving beyond webbing, one teacher has students write their own textbooks in the academic areas, drawing together student learning in their own words.

At the elementary level, some of this is just sound teaching practice. Reading and writing, when taught as interconnected processes and not just technical skills, become things students enjoy and continue to engage in over time. Beyond that, these children are learning that they can control words so as to build their own reality. They do not have to rely upon the words and images of others.[30]

With older children, critical literacy means interrogating the text and writing about the real. In one social studies class, the teacher has students read competing accounts of the same event. The questions then addressed are why these accounts differ, what counts as a trustworthy source, and whose interests these competing accounts serve. Several English teachers are engaged in a project involving students writing about community affairs. Students research issues in their communities that concern them and then write about them for publication from an advocacy position.

Such activities develop critical literacy skills in two ways. First, students come to see that what is written down is never "plain truth" but rather attempts to persuade. Second, they find their own voices to speak and persuade others. In so doing, they move well beyond basic skills and become what Moffit has termed "dangerously and democratically literate."[31]

Cultural Capital — cult. awareness that an indiv. poss. @ his/her own history — — can act w/ autonomy

The term *cultural capital* means that stock of cultural awareness that an individual possesses about his or her own history, and this knowledge makes acting as autonomous human beings possible.[32] As Black history advocates have so clearly argued, without a sense of one's roots it is hard to act in ways that are in one's self—or group—interest. Feminists as well have worked to rediscover the historic, social, political, and economic contributions of women, in order to foster a deeper sense of possibility and unity among women.

What this means for a democratic curriculum is the use of students' own histories as the focus of historical inquiry. Rather than the endless parade of great white men and large-scale wars, history should contain a focus on the daily lives and contributions of the average citizen. Already available are commercially prepared history texts for older students focusing on the contributions of citizens' groups and popular protest.[33] More important is the example of the *Foxfire* program in Rabun Gap, Georgia.[34] In what began as an English curriculum, students explore local folk ways through oral interviews and publish those in the now highly successful *Foxfire Magazine* and books. This English curriculum has branched out to include music and radio/television work. Many additional examples of such a localized approach to history or English can be found.[35]

What history should do fu kids

With younger students, the focus is often on their own lives and surroundings. In the *"Perspectives"* series, produced by Educators for Social Responsibility, a text entitled *Making History* provides ways of students understanding and investigating their own histories.[36] From personal to family to community frameworks, the focus is on expanding the historical investigation

179

while maintaining a personal sense of location within that history.

Teachers who have worked on such projects find their students have a new sense of empowerment and possibility. For example, one young student summarized the feelings of an entire class when she expressed shame at her racism in the face of her own town's history of involvement in the underground railway during the Civil War. Other students have felt and acted upon a sense of personal power when they connect their own concerns with those of ongoing movements for social justice or change in their own communities. Perhaps nothing is more personally inspiring than finding in one's own family history an example of democratic participation in order to make the world a better place.

Such approaches to social studies, history, English, the arts, and other areas all have as their focus one agenda — personal empowerment. To participate democratically requires a sense of political efficacy — the belief that each individual's engagement is both required and has an effect. One side of efficacy is a historical sense of being part of a larger participatory tradition. The other is practical experience in decisionmaking.

Student Decisionmaking

The literature on efficacy clearly states that the desire to engage in democratic participation is generated by actual experiences with decisionmaking. Beginning at the local level, when individuals participate in decisions that directly effect them, they both develop the confidence that such action is possible as well as the desire to participate in even broader public debates. Harry Boyte and Sara Evans have recently called sites of such participation "free spaces" where "people are able to learn a new self-respect, a deeper and more assertive group identity, public skills, and values of cooperation and civic virtue."[37] I return to this larger notion of free spaces later, but here it is the focus on exercising control in such environments that concern us.

Students often have litttle, if any, control over their lives inside the institution called school. Curriculum, school rules, time schedules, texts, and on and on are all set long before students arrive inside the schoolhouse door. There are usually no free spaces within which students can practice and thus develop the skills needed for public participation in decisionmaking.

Any curriculum with democracy at its heart needs to include expanding spheres of free spaces for decisionmaking on the part of students. Perhaps the most straightforward way to approach this is to suggest that whenever the teacher has the latitude to make a decision, an opportunity is also present for students to enter into the decisionmaking process themselves. In conversations with and observations of classroom teachers, I have learned that the possibilities here are endless.

With younger children, seemingly simple issues like room decoration provide excellent free spaces to begin the development of decisionmaking skills and potential. Additionally, such activities as choosing reading materials, group activities, and the focus of reading webs, are all well within the abilities of children. As students get older, spheres of decisionmaking can expand to include room management, curricular focus (as seen earlier with local history and writing), and the organization of social life in the school.

A word needs to be said here about classroom management. The way a classroom or school is run has a great deal to do with the way students perceive their place in the life-world of the school. Recently, an entire school of classroom management has developed that argues for a reassertion of the teacher's power to dominate and control the classroom. The most widely embraced of these models is Assertive Discipline which operates from a behavior modification agenda in stipulating that behavior rules and punishments (sometimes awards) are to be set by the teacher and followed by the students. Aside from *not* teaching self-discipline, this system takes away the experience of decisionmaking and disempowers students who face almost total institutional control.

As an alternative to such antidemocratic schemes, a variety of collaborative possibilities have been offered as ways of enhancing both self-discipline and decisionmaking. While I do not have space to catalogue all of these suggestions here, their broadest outlines can be traced. First, they all argue that developing genuine self-discipline comes from the experience of making and holding oneself to rules that are collectively established. Second, the parameters of behavior can only be set in an atmosphere of cooperation between all parties, including the adult teacher who plays the role of facilitator and guide. Finally, rules must be flexible enough to allow for change as participants learn more about the consequences of their action. In such settings, classroom management becomes a collaborative, democratic experience as opposed to an autocratic, antidemocratic one.[38]

Coupled with a sense of personal and community history, such decision-making structures offer the possibility of developing genuine personal efficacy. The curriculum develops both personal power and participatory skills within a collaborative environment. Within such free spaces students learn to act for the common good.

Social Alternatives

However, if students are to act for the common good, they need some notion that such action is likely to yield results — that alternatives to the way we currently organize social life exist. The curriculum is often presented to students as a given, a set of established facts. There seem to be only one

181

answer to each question and only one approach to each problem — the right one. If students are to make decisions, which of course involve choices, they need to be aware of the range of choices they face.

Teachers concerned with such choices operate in two ways. First, the curriculum can offer choices to students. For example, the teaching of science can offer multiple approaches to uncovering the same principles. The teaching of writing can consist of a variety of ways to learn the rules of grammar through students' own modes of expression. Throughout the curriculum, using multiple sources as opposed to a textbook format exposes students to the notion that multiple approaches to a variety of ends are possible.

In addition, students deserve to see that the ways in which we order our social lives are not written in stone. Rather, they are human choices which, in a democracy, are always open to change. The point then is to present to students through the curriculum alternatives to the existing order. Herbert Kohl states:

> The most important thing we can do is have our students understand that social-ism, communism, anarchism, and other noncapitalist forms of organizing human life are serious, and must be thought about; and that people have a right to choose the social systems they believe will meet their needs and the needs of their communities. Young people also ought to be given an opportunity to know that people fight for such abstractions as justice and for such concretions as the elimination of poverty and oppression.[39]

Peter Dreier additionally suggests that students be exposed to attempts in the Third World to transform a harsh reality into a humane society as examples of what people, through cooperative action, can accomplish.[40] Making the connection between the Third World and our technological society can be enhanced by exploring examples of similar social alternatives in our society. Such examples range from the publicly owned and operated plants and utilities in the United States to such large scale projects as Canadian socialized health systems, England's nonprofit housing system, and Sweden's mass-transit system. Coupling these two sets of examples provides alterna-tives to the existing order and demonstrates the means by which such alterna-tives arise and take their place in a transformed social order. It further confronts students with a variety of concepts of the "social good," offering choices around which decisions can be made.

Democratic Values

Finally, the curriculum should be structured so as to embrace the values of democratic life. These include the essential values of equality, liberty, and community. All of these are best taught through lived experiences as opposed to the disembodied accounts in textbooks of the founding fathers' pronouncements regarding freedom, liberty, justice, and similar concepts. We have already discussed liberty in the context of student decisionmaking. Here I turn more explicitly to issues of equality and community.

As for equality, curricular practices that are based on notions of inequality should be abolished. First and foremost, this means eliminating from the curriculum all ability grouping and tracking. Not only is this practice clearly antidemocratic, it simply does not work. As Jeannie Oakes states:

> [T]racking is *not* in the best interests of most students. It does not appear to be related to either increasing academic achievement or promoting positive attitudes and behaviors. Poor and minority students seem to have suffered most from tracking — and these are the very students on whom so many educational hopes are pinned. If schooling is intended to provide access to economic, political, and social opportunity for those who are so often denied such access, school tracking appears to interfere seriously with this goal. Yet, despite what we know about the effects of tracking, the practice persists.[41]

Of course, beyond this is the clearly inegalitarian and thus antidemocratic bias in ability grouping. The practice of ability grouping segregates students and prepares them for decidedly different futures. In so doing, the clear message is that some students should have access to higher-status knowledge because they will be expected to occupy higher-status social positions. The notion of political equality, fundamental to a democracy, gets lost in the rush to label and segregate young learners. Alternatives to such inegalitarian, antidemocratic practices are those that focus on the classroom as a cooperative community. A wide variety of approaches to the curriculum are available that embrace community and cooperation over competition and tracking, including grouping students by interest as opposed to ability in all subjects. In elementary grades, this can be as simple as reading groups based on topics in which a wide range of ability-level texts are available. In upper grades, collaborative projects such as those involved in the Foxfire Program can be undertaken. The point in all of these is to structure the classroom so that cooperation is valued over individualistic competition. As Johnson and Johnson have argued, it is only in classrooms directed toward cooperative learning that those interpersonal skills necessary for democratic life will be developed. Furthermore, it is only in cooperative settings that higher-order cognitive skills are obtained. According to Johnson and Johnson:

> When the instructional task is some sort of problem-solving activity, a cooperative goal structure clearly results in higher achievement than does a competitive or an individual goal structure. There is evidence that factual material will be re-

183

What Cooperative goal Structures?

membered better if it is discussed in a cooperatively structured group. Cooperative goal structures also facilitate mastery of concepts and principles and of creative processes (such as divergent thinking, risk-taking thinking, and entering into controversy). They are effective in developing verbal and problem-solving skills, cooperative skills, and the ability to see a situation from someone else's perspective (an ability that is essential to empathy, social adjustment, communication and autonomous moral judgment). In turn, the development of cooperative skills is essential to a person's self-actualization, i.e., the development of one's potentialities and the utilization of those potentialities.[42]

Certainly, students will only cooperate well when the teacher takes the time to structure the curriculum so that it requires cooperation and prepares students for the task. Given the cognitive and social benefits of such an effort it seems undemocratic and miseducative to do anything else.

Conclusion

How we school is a direct reflection of what we believe our social life should be. I have argued that fundamental to our best social intentions is a participatory form of democratic life. If we are to live democratically, the way we induct the young into the culture must be democratic as well. The emphasis on protectionist democracy currently a part of reform efforts in education must be resisted.

In terms of the curriculum, this suggests that both in content and form we embrace democracy. In content, we provide students with the tools to live a democratic life and the visions of what is possible in our shared social context. In terms of form, the curriculum should engage students in actual decisionmaking in a shared community of equality and justice.

What this suggests is that schools, and the classrooms within them, become islands of democracy. Locations where, in an often undemocratic society, children gain a strong sense of both their own autonomy as well as interconnectedness. That is, there should be the type of free space Boyte and Evans described — one where students gain a sense of self-respect, assertiveness, democratic values, and public skills that enable them to act democratically. It is only in so doing that they will come to value their own right and obligation to participate publicly, without which democracy has no future.

Notes

1. Andrew A. Lipscomb, ed., *The Writings of Thomas Jefferson*, Vol. 2 (Charlottesville, Va.: Thomas Jefferson Memorial Association, 1903), p. 207.

2. For a more detailed discussion of democratic theory see Carole Pateman, *Participation and Democratic Theory* (Cambridge: Cambridge University Press, 1970) and Benjamin Barber, *Strong Democracy* (Berkeley, Calif.: University of California Press, 1984).

3. See, for example, R. A. Dahl, *Preface to Democratic Theory* (Chicago: University of Chicago Press, 1956).

4. George Will, "In Defense of Non-Voting," *Newsweek*, October 10, 1983.

5. John Dewey, *Democracy and Education* (New York: MacMillan Company, 1916), p. 87.

6. Pateman, *op. cit.*

7. John Stuart Mill, *Essays on Politics and Culture* (Toronto: University of Toronto Press, 1965); and John Stuart Mill, *Collected Works* (Toronto: University of Toronto Press, 1963); and G. D. H. Cole, *Social Theory* (London: Methven, 1920).

8. G. A. Almond and S. Verba, *The Civic Culture* (Boston: Little, Brown, and Co., 1945); Martin Carnoy and Derek Shearer, *Workplace Democracy: The Challenge of the 1980s.* (White Plains, N. Y.: M. E. Sharp, Inc., 1980); Arthur Wirth, *Productive Work — in Industry and Schools* (New York: University Press of America, 1983).

9. See also Harry Boyte, *The Backyard Revolution* (Philadelphia: Temple University Press, 1980).

10. To claim one vision or theory of democracy to be "truer" to the original intent of our cultural heritage is most certainly tenuous business. For example, in practice our democratic origins excluded women and Blacks from the political process. If, however, it is fair to claim that our entire cultural heritage is based upon the expansion of political rights and freedoms then participatory theory does seem to have a more legitimate claim to our loyalties. Organizing social life along the lines of participatory democracy moves us along a continuum toward the more as opposed to the less democratic. Social institutions come under more direct as opposed to representative control and the process of governing is broadened to embrace the widest possible number of participants. Certainly this comes closer to a government of, by, and for the people than do notions of an elected autocracy.

11. The commissions, their reports, and membership were as follows: National Commission on Excellence in Education (*A Nation At Risk*) — 18 members, 1 teacher; Twentieth Century Fund (*Making the Grade*) — 11 members, no teachers; National Science Foundation (*Educating Americans for the 21st Century*) — 20 members, 1 teacher; Education Commission of the States (*Action for Excellence*) — 41 members, 1 teacher; The Paideia Group (*The Paideia Proposal*) — 22 members, no teachers.

12. Susan Ohanian, "Huffing and Puffing and Blowing the School Excellent," *Phi Delta Kappan*, January 1985, p. 316.

13. Michael W. Apple, "Curricular Form and the Logic of Technical Control," in Michael W. Apple, ed., *Cultural and Economic Reproduction in Education* (London: Routledge & Kegan Paul, 1982); Henry Giroux, *Theory and Resistance in Education* (South Hadley, Mass.: Bergin and Garvey Publishers, Inc., 1983).

14. National Commission on Excellence in Education, *A Nation at Risk* (Washington, D. C.: Government Printing Office, 1983), p. 5.

15. Education Commission of the States, *Action for Excellence* (Washington, D. C.: Education Commission of the States, 1983), p. 13.

16. National Science Foundation, *Educating Americans* (Washington, D. C.: National Science Foundation, 1983), p. v.

17. Twentieth Century Fund, *Making the Grade* (New York: The Twentieth Century Fund, 1983), p. 3.

18. National Science Foundation, *Educating Americans, op. cit.*, p. 44.

19. David Cohen, ". . . the condition of teachers' work . . ." *Harvard Educational Review* 54:1(February 1984), p. 11-12.

20. Due to space restraints, the historic origins of scientific management as applied to schooling cannot be discussed fully. For a detailed analysis see Arthur Wirth, *Productive Work in Industry and Schooling* (Lanthan, N.Y.: University Press of America, 1983); Raymond Callahan, *Education and the Cult of Efficiency* (Chicago: University of Chicago Press, 1962); and the chapters by Kliebard and Carlson herein.

21. Ellwood P. Cubberly, *Public School Administration* (Boston: Houghton Mifflin Co., 1916), p. 325.

22. Margaret Haley, "The Factory System," *The New Republic*, November 12, 1924, p. 19.

23. Christopher Lasch points out how these are actually calls for more mediocrity and operate against education for citizenship. See " 'Excellence' in Education: Old Refrain or New Departure?" *Issues in Education*, III: 1(Summer 1985), p. 1-12.

24. Walter Karp, "Why Johnny Can't Think," *Harpers*, June 1985, p. 73.

25. Public Education Information Network, *Education for A Democratic Future* (St. Louis: Public Education Information Network, 1985), p. 3. Mary Ann Raywid; Charles A. Tesconi, Jr.; Donald R. Warren, *Pride and Promise* (Westbury, N.Y.: American Educational Studies Association, 1984), p. 10.

26. Raywid, *et. al., op. cit.*, pp. 11, 12.

27. Mortimer J. Adler, *The Paideia Proposal* (New York: MacMillan, 1982), p. 15.

28. Ernest Boyer, *High School* (New York: Harper and Row, 1983), p. 105. See also John Goodlad, *A Place Called School* (New York: McGraw Hill, 1984).

29. I am indebted to the teachers involved in the Institute for Democracy in Education for their work with democratic alternatives that have provided me with the examples in the following sections of this paper.

30. See Marcia M. Burchby, *The Whole Language Alternative to Basal Instruction*. Occasional Paper #1, Institute for Democracy in Education Series (Athens, Ohio: Institute for Democracy in Education, 1986). For information about these or other materials mentioned herein, please contact the Institute for Democracy in Education, 372 McCracken Hall, Ohio University, Athens, Ohio 45701.

31. James Moffitt, "Hidden Impediments to the Teaching of English," *Phi Delta Kappan,* (September 1985), p. 50-56.

32. It is important to note that by *autonomous individuals* I am not arguing for an individualized or privatized notion of the citizen. Rather, what is suggested is the notion of autonomy within a community—the ability to be a free and equal contributor to collective and collaborative social life. For an extensive discussion of this concept, see Landon E. Beyer and George H. Wood, "Critical Inquiry and Moral Action in Education," *Educational Theory 36:* 1(Winter 1986), pp.1–14.

33. See, for example, D. Cluster, *They Should Have Served That Cup of Coffee: Seven Radicals Remember the 1960s* (Boston: South End Press, 1979); R. Cooney and H. Michalowski, *The Power of the People: Active Nonviolence in the United States* (Culver City, Penn.: Peace Press, 1977); and H. Zinn, *A People's History of the United States* (New York: Harper and Row, 1980).

34. Eliot Wigginton, *Sometimes A Shining Moment: The Foxfire Experience* (New York: Anchor Press, 1985).

35. The best compendium of such examples are published in *Hands On: Newsletter for Cultural Journalism.* Published by the Foxfire Fund, Rabun Gap, Ga., 30568.

36. See the "Perspectives" series, especially the volumes *Taking Part, Making History,* and *Investigations: Toxic Wastes* published by Educators For Social Responsibility, 23 Garden St., Cambridge, Mass., 02138.

37. Harry Boyte and Sara Evans, *Free Spaces* (New York: Harper and Row, 1986), p. 17.

38. See Albert Alschuler, *School Discipline: A Socially Literate Solution* (New York: McGraw Hill, 1980); Rudolf Dreikurs, Bernice Grunwald, and Floy C. Pepper, *Maintaining Sanity in the Classroom,* second edition (New York: Harper and Row, 1982) and "Teaching Self-Discipline," special issue of *Theory Into Practice,* XXIV: 4 (Autumn 1984).

39. H. Kohl, "Can the School Build A New Social Order?" *Journal of Education* 162:3 (Summer 1980), p. 63.

40. P. Dreier, "Socialism and Cynicism," *Socialist Review* 10:5 (September-October 1980).

41. J. Oakes, *Keeping Track: How American Schools Structure Inequality.* (New Haven, Conn.: Yale University Press, p. 2.)

42. D. Johnson and R. Johnson, *Learning Together and Alone* (Englewood Cliffs, N. J.: Prentice-Hall, 1975), p. 32–32. See also Johnson and Johnson, *Circles of Learning: Cooperation in the Classroom* (Alexandria, Va.: Association for Supervision and Curriculum Development, 1984).

IV

*Curriculum and the
Work of Teachers*

TEN

Curriculum and the Work of Teachers

Gail McCutcheon

This chapter contains a discussion of alternatives regarding the relationship between the curriculum and the work of teachers. One way of understanding what is meant by curriculum and teaching is to separate them, where curriculum is the intended fare of the schools, and teaching is its vehicle. However, they are more closely entwined; curriculum affects and is affected by teaching, and the opposite is also true. So, the medium and the message have a close relationship rather than being neatly separable.

Curriculum can also be thought of as what students have an opportunity to learn under the auspices of schools. In this case, the overt curriculum constitutes what school people intend that students learn and what teachers say they intend to teach — the publicly-advertised fare of the schools. The hidden curriculum is what students have an opportunity to learn through everyday goings-on under the auspices of schools, although teachers and other school people do not intend those learnings.

One facet of the overt curriculum is the graded course of study or written curriculum of the school. This is the *formal*, policy-level curriculum. The less formal, but perhaps more important, curriculum is the curriculum enacted in the classroom.

The hidden curriculum can be thought of as bearing two characteristics: (1) it is not intended, and (2) it is transmitted through the everyday, normal goings-on in schools. For example, through the hidden curriculum, students may receive stereotypical messages about minority and ethnic groups, and male and female roles, due to messages implicit in a teacher's actions, everyday occurrences in the schools, or from textbooks. The hidden curriculum may arise out of school policies. For instance, Mr. Bryant teaches mathematics in the eighth grade at Clearwater Middle School, where a policy states that students are to pass tests at a proficiency level of 80 percent or above before moving ahead to a new chapter. If they do not pass at this level they are to have a review and a retest. He and other teachers worry that through the hidden curriculum, students seem to be learning that even if they are not prepared today for the test, it does not really matter, for a retest is always given. For instance, students have asked *before* the test, "When's the retest, Mr. Bryant?" in what he describes as a cavalier or nonchalant manner. He and some colleagues fear that students might come to believe that they really do not have to study hard for the first test, for they can always depend upon the retest. Translated into everyday life, Mr. Bryant fears students might come to believe there is always a second chance, which is not always the case.

The hidden curriculum may also consist of the development of a work ethic, transmitted by teachers' admonitions such as those observed recently in another middle-school mathematics classroom:

Lois, keep your eyes on your own work.

Mark, let's get busy here. Get your work done on time.

Nancy, I know you can do better. Sit down and recopy this so it's neater. You need to turn in work you can be proud of, not this messy trash.

Alexander, you have to be more responsible. You can't leave your homework at home every night like this. Now, grow up. If you can remember your baseball glove, you can remember to bring your homework.

Some teachers in the elementary school where Mrs. Faye is a librarian reward their students. When the class is behaving well, these teachers put a marble in a jar and when the jar contains ten marbles, the teacher brings in a cake. Mrs. Faye does not do this in the library, and reflects, "Aren't my congratulations enough? What are the kids learning if you always reward them extrinsically with something material — in this case a cake? Life's not like that, and where do you ever learn self-control and patting *yourself* on the back in this kind of situation?"

As a final example of the hidden curriculum, Ron Comfort notes in a recent case study:

Broadly speaking, the environment of Fielding [School] 'teaches' that being a student involves hard work, high expectations for one's performance, deference to teacher authority, and a balance between cooperation and competition. Despite an ambiance of informality and openness among students and teacher participants in the setting, behavioral boundaries and seriousness of purpose are conveyed. These are communicated through the myriad of daily interactions rather than on the basis of codified rules. Indeed, they are a function of a sense of values which are held in common among teachers and to which students are socialized.[1]

An important role teachers have *vis-à-vis* the hidden curriculum is observing and reflecting on its nature and the possible effects of such an opportunity for learning. Through doing this, teachers can improve the hidden curriculum, thereby rendering more of it overt; because it has been reflected upon it moves into the intended realm.

The *null curriculum*[2] constitutes what students do not have an opportunity to learn under the auspices of schools. The null curriculum is virtually infinite; some aspects are consciously decided upon when school people deliberately elect *not* to include a particular matter in the curriculum due to its controversial nature, a lack of proper equipment or time, or other reasons. For example, following a recent conference about acquired immunization deficiency syndrome (AIDS), an authority suggested on network news that one implication of the increase in AIDS in both the homosexual and heterosexual community is to teach about safe sex in high school. As an aside, he noted that there really is not such a thing as "safe" sex, so he amended his proposition to "safer" sex by teaching about the use of the condom to prevent the mingling of vaginal and seminal fluids. This would be a fairly controversial topic to include in the high schools of many communities, so it will probably remain a part of the null curriculum. The null curriculum is also different for different students. Girls were not permitted to enroll in certain courses (such as metal, electric, carpentry, and industrial arts classes) and had little experience with certain sports until recent legislation aimed at providing more equity.

One example of null curriculum comes from a high school in a system where the superintendent is concerned about high unemployment rates in the community. He is convinced that all students should be qualified to attend college so they will be able to find employment. In the foreign langauge department, the French and Spanish teachers have been proposing that their courses have a large conversational component, but the proposal has fallen on deaf ears because the idea is not seen as one likely to enhance students' opportunities to enter college.

Another example comes from the arts, where an elementary school art teacher's requisition was severely slashed, leaving her students few opportunities for three-dimensional work, which she believes should be an aspect of the art curriculum at all grade levels. "Oh, sure," says Ms. Nash, "kids can make sculptures out of cardboard and other things they can bring from home, but unless I make dough for them to use, they can't have a three-dimensional experience with a plastic medium because I have no clay, no glazes, and very limited access to the kiln [at the high school]." She worries this may affect the experiences in which students are willing to invest themselves in upper grades because they are having such limited experience with three-dimensional media, which could ultimately affect their work as artists, museum attenders, and consumers. "This may always remain mysterious to them," she fears.

Other teachers have also cited the lack of particular materials as a factor contributing to the null curriculum: no sets of paperback novels for reading groups, no alcohol burners and test tube holders in an elementary school using a science text containing experiments where they are to use them, too few computers, a lack of storage space leading to disorganization or damage of art materials in elementary school classrooms, and being permitted to hire a piano tuner only at five-year intervals.

Another case concerns alterations in the curriculum in different areas of a city due to parents' expectations of their children. Here, an eighth-grade English teacher musing about one of his students remarked,

> Now, you take Leigh. She lives here in the Horlicks area of town—you know, a blue-collar area if I ever saw one. But Leigh could easily go to college. Now, don't get me wrong. She's no Einstein or Madame Curie, but she's got enough on the ball to go to State or somewhere. She'd be a great teacher, and she loves computer work. But her parents are sure she should get married or be a secretary or a hairdresser or nurse or a dental hygienist. Now, there's nothing wrong with those jobs, but it's too bad about Leigh. I've talked to the MacDonalds a lot, but in high school they're putting her in that business track—you know, typing, accounting, more typing, and office skills. The problem is, look at all the stuff she won't get to learn! It's amazing. You talk about how people's expectations affect education! Leigh's going to have to live down to her parents' expectations!

Just as the overt curriculum changes, so does the null curriculum. Part of this change is because of new discoveries, while others can be attributed to cultural change in general. So, for instance, until recently computer education was in the null curriculum, obviously because we were not using computers widely. A recent change in business colleges has been a call for international business matters to be addressed in undergraduate courses about business law, finance, marketing, and administration, because virtually every business is now in some ways international. Until recently, this was generally not treated to any extent in business college courses, so it was part of the null curriculum. Societal changes have brought that to the attention of these professors, just as problems of unwanted teenage pregnancy and AIDS concern many involved in secondary schools. Here again, an important role for teachers is to reflect on what constitutes the null curriculum and whether it is advisable.

The broad definition of *curriculum*, what students have an opportunity to learn under the auspices of schools, will be used in this chapter.

Teachers and the Overt Curriculum: A Traditional View

Returning to the overt curriculum, a traditional view is that teachers' work involves transforming that which is intended into a set of activities in order to make intended skills and knowledge accessible to students. That is, the formal curriculum and the enacted curriculum are to be the same.

While possibilities for activities are virtually endless, teachers tend to select textbooks and other two-dimensional, print-based materials for these purposes. Perhaps this is due to tradition; to visions of what school is supposed to be; to assumptions that they are to use the materials because the school system bought them; to parental pressure; and to systemwide mandates that virtually preclude the use of any other materials. One example of the latter might occur if a school system mandates that Ginn tests be used in reading — the teacher is virtually bound to use the accompanying textbooks.

This fairly traditional view that teachers are to teach the overt curriculum as mandated from above has its roots in the movement of the administrative progressives, such as Elwood P. Cubberly, who attempted to overlay a corporate model of scientific management onto the schools, a movement dating back to the turn of the century. An elite board and expert manager were to oversee the workings of the school and strive for efficiency. This result depended on obtaining accurate information and channelling it to the superintendent and his/her board; careful budgeting, relying on the review of programs to determine their efficiency and cost-effectiveness, and using that data to plan ahead; and specifying precisely how teachers were to turn out students whose skills and attitudes were consonant with those deemed important by society.[3] This last characteristic gave rise to the organized field of curriculum. Early curriculum scholars such as Franklin Bobbitt strove to formulate such curricula. Hence, the field of curriculum has its roots in management to better support administration; its original function was one of control.

More recently, this trend was perpetuated by the major curriculum reforms of the 1950s and 1960s. During this period teachers were asked to implement the nationally-produced programs and found, for a variety of reasons, that they did not work. These reasons included a lack of fit with local conditions, including values that were at odds with the local community's;

programs that were beyond the comprehension of their students; and the inclusion of experiences removed from their students' lives. Perhaps this difficulty was partly the result of teachers' minimal involvement with the national reforms and a preponderance of subject-matter experts' involvement.

During the structure of the disciplines movement when we were to teach "new" mathematics, parents were unable to help children with homework and did not understand why a new way of working the same problems was in order, for their way worked. Some teachers did not possess the mathematical knowledge needed to enable them to field students' questions. Hence, due to a lack of ease with ideas presented in the mathematics books, some teachers may have elected not to use them; others may have left unanswered the students' questions (and thereby rendered them part of the null curriculum).

Harking back to my own teaching experience during this time, a science kit had been adopted by our school system. In one lesson, eight sets of various balls — super balls, golf balls and tennis balls — eight meter sticks, and large pieces of paper were contained in the materials box. In this case, we were to divide our third-grade classes into eight groups of three or four students and have them drop each ball from shoulder height while another student metrically measured the first, second, and third bounce. For some teachers who virtually never taught with small groups or through activities, such a lesson was unthinkable. Others questioned the metric system. One colleague, for instance, taught this lesson through her own demonstration while a student measured the bounces under her direction. Another said that the primary matter dealt with in the lesson was discipline. Chaos did not reign, according to her, but it came close as children *bounced* (not dropped!) the balls and they flew everywhere for a while. The act of placing 24 balls in the hands of third-graders and then restraining their use in a classroom calls for one to believe the pupils had tremendous self-control; it also assumed teachers had organized their teaching around self-discipline and activity-centered learning, which was often not the case. It was no wonder that many teachers either did not use that activity or turned it into a demonstration. Perhaps many thought, "Too much!" as they were to reorganize science class in a drastically different manner, teach the use of metric sticks, and try to control the class as well. The idea may have been sound, but it probably did not fit many teachers' belief systems — their theories of action — so they altered the lessons to fit their belief systems and thereby subverted the program.

For many teachers, the new programs' content and their suggested use were substantially different from previously used programs, necessitating drastic shifts in classroom organization, beliefs about learning, and the accumulation of more knowledge to understand or implement the program. As a result of those features, many programs were difficult to implement unless extensive inservice programs were held or lengthy, highly detailed teachers' manuals were written. Because developers were outlining new content and innovative ways of teaching, they delineated quite specifically what was to occur in a given lesson. While some teachers were secure with such specificity, others resented it; for example, one teacher stated, in reflecting about her planning, "Going to college for five years to learn how to follow directions is pretty ridiculous." A lack of thorough understanding, such resentment, and an impracticality for the setting may be examples of why teachers used materials as they saw fit rather than as prescribed by teachers' guides, thereby substantially altering the nature of the course. This trend of specifying the curriculum to teachers in an attempt to control it — by administrators or by national reformers — continues to the present day. For example, teacher competency tests and demands for high student achievement test scores, and teacher accountability (as determined by students' achievement test scores, for example, in St. Louis) further support the efficient running of schools and focus our attention on ends as defined by the tests themselves.

This view is understandable in light of a current mood in the country for the public to be sure it is getting its money's worth from social institutions. Many teachers and administrators probably agree with the traditional view that the administration and board are to dictate the overt curriculum and that the teachers' role is merely to implement it. Indeed, teacher-proof curricula follow this same scheme. An extreme example can be found in DISTAR, an elementary-school reading program. In the 1962 edition, authors cautioned teachers:

> Follow the presentation as closely as possible. Don't improvise on the presentation materials. . . . Don't introduce variations of the instructions. Don't wander off onto other tasks. Don't present additional exercises that may come to mind. Don't use the material as a point of departure for free-association teaching. And above all, don't become involved in lengthy explanations. The directions for each of the tasks are designed to explain by showing. Resist the impulse to 'tell' the children. Chances are they won't have the faintest idea what you are talking about; you will unfortunately demonstrate that you cannot be relied on to clarify, that you only confuse.[4]

Since then, the authors have softened their tone somewhat, although the materials are still scripted. What teachers are to say appears in red type, what they are to do is in black type, and expected responses are in italics.

However, even in the case where we conceive teaching to be merely determining how to implement goals, the teacher's role is powerful in influencing what students have an opportunity to learn, in a variety of ways. Teachers can emphasize certain materials over others. Further, teachers may be more enthusiastic about a certain topic, skill, or understanding, which may permit them to provide more intriguing lessons and assignments than when a topic, skill, or understanding is of less interest to them. Mrs. Cabot, a fourth-grade teacher, reflects: "We have to teach from this reading series. But reading's more. Reading's joy as well as just word-calling. Maybe *more* joy. So I give the kids lots of independent reading time. They choose books from the library, and I schedule appointments with them so we can chat."

Teachers are the filters through which the mandated curriculum passes. Their understanding of it, and their enthusiasm, or boredom, with various aspects of it, color its nature. Hence, the curriculum enacted in classrooms differs from the one mandated by administrators or developed by experts.

Regarding the overt curriculum, then, teachers' influence is manifold. Teachers filter the objectives; it is up to them to understand what is to be taught and then conceive of ways to enact it and make it accessible to students. Teachers must also make sense of the context—the neighborhood, their students, parents' hopes and dreams, the social setting within the school, as well as the shape of the nation itself—and fit the objectives into these understandings. In this manner, such decisions are moral ones, going beyond an objective management activity. It is also the teachers who contend with policies and other phenomena within which the curriculum operates. So, when the schedule allots 53-minute class sessions or classrooms are lacking in particular equipment or materials needed for a lesson, teachers are the ones who reshape lessons accordingly. When the teachers themselves have only a superficial understanding of the content to be presented, their decisions about the importance of various lessons and what to stress are affected. In this case, the curriculum is also filtered by how articulately teachers are able to respond to questions, to embroider on points in lessons, and to conceive of relevant activities and assignments.

Teachers and the Hidden Curriculum: A Traditional View

Because teachers have their own personalities, values, interests, strengths, and weaknesses, they also affect the hidden curriculum. As teachers, we do not shrug off these aspects of ourselves as we remove our coats and hang them on pegs outside our classrooms. Hence, the hidden curriculum is primarily the purview of the teacher with the exception of latent messages in curriculum materials and school policies, as teachers communicate their values, expectations and other messages through the hidden curriculum while they teach the overt curriculum, manage their administrative tasks, maintain discipline, and attend to their other responsibilities.

So, in a traditional view where teachers implement an already-established curriculum, they still influence what students have an opportunity to learn because they must interpret curriculum mandates themselves in order to implement them and because they have an impact on the classroom's hidden curriculum.

A Deliberationist View

One alternative to this traditional, positivistic, top-down, control-oriented position is the deliberationist perspective,

> the method by which most everyday practical problems get solved . . . an intricate and skilled intellectual and social process whereby, individually or collectively, we identify questions to which we must respond, establish grounds for deciding on answers, and then choose among the available solutions.[5]

Following this perspective, then, teachers identify problems — perhaps tentatively — and progress to define them and their parameters more clearly, moving toward resolution of some critical issues. Deliberation is more an attitude than a series of steps — the quest for as ideal a curriculum as possible for *these* students in *this* location. Difficulties arise from concrete, specific situations and are reflected upon; data is gathered that sheds further light on the reflections; new action is taken if warranted, and further reflection ensues. Teachers negotiate the curriculum in an intricate, skilled intellectual manner. This cycle is never ending, and deliberation in this case is a private weighing of the nature of the situation and whether certain courses of action are warranted.

For example, an upper-grade elementary school teacher critiquing an earlier draft of this chapter reflected on his approach to teaching spelling.

> In going over the spelling books, I see lessons based on phonics with words using those sounds. Now, I brush over the phonics part lightly because first, I'm not positive I understand it all that well myself, and, second, I don't think that understanding phonics itself necessarily leads to a word sense. I think having a word sense may lead to an understanding of phonics. English is based on so many different languages that there are so many exceptions to rules, that phonics doesn't even work a lot of the time. I cover the material, but deemphasize phonics and concentrate more on the words themselves along with meanings and uses. If students can recognize a word and use it, they'll learn how to spell it. Once you learn how to speak, you use words and start to hear similarities — the *dis* in *discover* and *dissimilar* sound alike. If you don't understand the meaning and use of a word, it doesn't matter if you can spell it phonetically or not because you won't use it. But if you use it — even aloud — chances are you'll use it in written form and therefore learn its spelling.[6]

In this example, the problem is how to teach spelling. The teacher has begun to clarify for himself how he believes students learn words — through use, not phonics, in his view — and to develop strategies to facilitate students' using the words. He concedes that he's not sure that he's right and characterizes it as a sort of "hunting in the dark" in that it is probably more difficult to understand yourself than other people, and that while many people have written texts and articles about such a matter, he's not sure they are right; and while they are writing in an abstract, theoretical vein, he's there, on the spot, and the system does not seem to work. Learning it because you have learned how to use it is important, not learning it to pass a test. He continues:

> When I see children who get A's on the tests, but they can't write a paper and spell correctly — there's something wrong there. They've learned how to spell it on the test, but their language use does not increase in proficiency the way the tests indicate they should. I don't see sophistry (is that the word for it?) — I'm smart because I know how to spell these words — as the aim of schools. Maybe lots of the texts are set up for the convenience of textbook writers and teachers, not to educate children.

He suggests that he continues to watch whether students are spelling well with his system; if they do not, new actions will probably ensue.

A deliberationist perspective rests on the precondition that the teacher is a dedicated, responsible, morally-committed professional; whereas, in the traditional view, the precondition is that the curriculum is to be used because it is assumed to be the result of decisions by experts, and a trained person uses it by going through the motions dictated by the materials, much as an apprentice operates a machine in an assembly line. Hence, the traditional view strips teachers of professional judgment.

The deliberationist perspective is well complemented by action research, where teachers inquire into matters critically in order to improve their own practice.[7] Through this process of inquiry, information comes to light that informs the deliberation. In preactive mental planning of lessons, as teachers weigh alternatives and select what appears most propitious, given their experiences — what they know of these students, *this* particular content and context — they deliberate.

Deliberation also occurs interactively, during the lesson itself, as teachers notice such phenomena as the glazed eyes of disinterest, the excited look of curiosity, or puzzlement about a particular point. Each of these observations brings about questions for teachers about how to proceed, and they adjust the preactive plans.

As an experienced teacher reflects:

I can say that teachers make adjustments continuously, not only before and after the lesson, but also during the lesson . . . when a teacher changes the teaching strategy that has been planned initially, or even discontinuing a lesson that is not effective. Teachers must be able to make adjustments during the lesson for it to be most effective. This is not to say that deliberation during the planning of the lesson and after the deliverance of the lesson are not equally important.

Deliberation also occurs afterward, as teachers wonder how it went, what should be retaught to whom and how. In this postlesson reflection, teachers wonder if they actually took the best course, and this reflection may indeed alter plans for next year, and their theory of action[8] – and hence, further actions – when confronted with similar situations. Reading educational literature, talking with trusted colleagues, and attending graduate courses may widen the array of matters considered in deliberation.

Were this deliberationist perspective used in a school system to organize the curriculum, it would involve teachers collaboratively across the grade levels, within and across subject matters, to wonder together about scope, sequence, and integration. The process of deliberation and action research would lead to a sense of ownership of the curriculum, and this vested interest in it would bring about reformulations of it as problems were identified. Three teachers reacting to an earlier draft of this chapter discussed action research and deliberation. The following represents their dialogue:

Teacher I: Teaching amounts to ideas in action. It takes place in real time, encounters are immediate, and is encumbered by political and material constraints . . .

Teacher II: Some arising suddenly and unpredictably due to changes in the political and social life of the setting, and others more long-term and predictable.

Teacher III: When planning, plans for action are bound by practice because prior practice has taught us what works and does not work.

Teacher I: Teaching itself is fluid, dynamic, and requires instant decisions and practical problem-solving and judgment.

Teacher III: So it is deliberative in that it is purposive, pros and cons of action are weighed, and self-observation occurs to provide sound bases for critical self-reflection about processes, problems, issues, constraints and supports manifest in the practice.

Action research provides data that informs deliberation. This leads to *praxis* and improvement because it allows teachers to question their own practice and to formulate actions and a theory of action upon which they have deliberated carefully, as exemplified by this quote from one of the three teachers cited above.

Teacher II: Action research and deliberation permit us to articulate teaching experiences and bring them under self-conscious control, so we can organize our own self-enlightenment by engaging ourselves in private deliberation about practice. Teachers are professional this way because they try to be perfectionists.

Hence, the deliberationist perspective rests on intense teacher involvement, and teaching is a serious, professional enterprise.

Teachers adopting a deliberationist attitude are mature and secure enough with their roles as teachers to have abandoned a starry-eyed, romantic love of teaching and progressed to seeing teaching as challenging, difficult, enjoyable work where problems exist that are murky but can be resolved. Perhaps we can think of this as a loss of innocence, and perhaps this loss of innocence is needed for genuine improvement in what students have an opportunity to learn as we recognize the active, deliberative mental planning teachers do and its importance in shaping what students have an opportunity to learn. This position further implies the development of curriculum materials that engage teachers in deliberation rather than materials that assume teachers are a direct pipeline from the expert developer to students' minds. One example of materials that invite teachers' deliberation is *Project WILD*, a set of supplementary, interdisciplinary activities about the environment and conservation for educators of kindergarten through high school age young people. The *Elementary Activity Guide* invites instructors to

pick and choose from the activities. Each activity is designed to stand alone, without other *Project WILD* activities. There is no need to do the activities in order, nor to do all activities, even for a given grade level. However, the activities have been placed in a thematic and developmental order that can serve as an aid to their use.... Instructors may use one or many *Project WILD* activities. The activities may be integrated into existing courses of study, or the entire set of activities may serve quite effectively as the basis for a course of study.[9]

Such a perspective also assumes graduate courses and a supervision approach that engage teachers in public deliberation to facilitate the process itself and that raise issues to consciousness.

The picture painted in this chapter is one of teachers as thinkers who make many decisions that create the curriculum in classrooms. Rather than having the role of rather passive people who implement the curriculum, teachers have an important function in shaping what students have an opportunity to learn.

Notes

1. Ronald E. Comfort, "Analyzing the Operational Curriculum of a School: A Case Study." Paper presented at the Annual Conference of the American Educational Research Association, New Orleans, April 1984, p. 31.

2. Elliot Eisner coined this term. See Eisner, *The Educational Imagination* (New York: Macmillan Company, 1979), pp. 83–84.

3. See David Tyack and Elisabeth Hansott, *Managers of Virtue* (New York: Basic Books, 1982), for elaboration on the development and influence of the administrative progressive movement; also see the chapter by Carlson herein.

4. Seigfried Englemann and Elaine C. Bruner, *DISTAR Reading I, Teachers Guide.* (Chicago: SRA, 1969), p. 12.

5. William A. Reid, *Thinking about the Curriculum.* (London: Routledge & Kegan Paul, 1978), p. 43.

6. I am endebted to my husband, George L. Disch, for this example and reflections.

7. See Wilfred Carr and Stephen Kemmis, *Becoming Critical* (Victoria, Australia: Deakin University Press, 1983), for a discussion of action research.

8. See Donald P. Sanders and Gail McCutcheon, "On the Evolution of Teachers' Theories of Action through Action Research" *Journal of Curriculum and Supervision.* II:1(Autumn 1986):50–67, for a discussion of action research and the development of teachers' personal theories of action.

9. *Project WILD.* Western Regional Environmental Council, 1983.

ELEVEN

Teaching, Gender, and Curriculum

Sara E. Freedman

"Hurry up, hurry up, hurry up." I would stand in my classroom and hear myself repeating that phrase to the students, over and over again, several times a day. Hearing myself say those words set me trying to figure out why: What was compelling me to force myself and my students to think faster, to move faster, to tidy up faster, quietly to stand at the door faster? The "hurry up, hurry up, hurry up" in my own mind implied that somehow what we were doing within our own four tight walls had to catch up with the world outside the classroom. I was obviously anxious to make sure we made those connections in time, even as I sensed that the world outside would never know how we had reached the correct stage at the appropriate time, nor how we had changed in the process. No one came in and stood by my side to see what page we were on in the workbook, and no one timed my reading groups to calculate the speed of the children's reading, or how quickly they answered comprehension questions or completed their SRA worksheets. I simply knew that that phrase had become part of the day's lessons, and that I was now recognizing the presence of something whose shape and origin were invisible and utterly domineering, yet so impersonal that I did not know its shape, its voice, or its demands.

The major thing I did know was that it had to do with the school work —

either it was not being done fast enough or it was not being put away quickly enough or there was time wasted between one activity and another. There were moments of unproductivity in the classroom, times when children were not concentrating intensely on reading or writing or learning their multiplication tables.

Of course I felt bad. Not so much about those lapses of productivity, which did not seem to cause lower year-end test scores. My own education had made me appreciate the moments between "time on task." I cherished the students who would come up to me two hours after a classroom discussion and say, "Does that mean . . . ?," obviously having continued to mull over a whole new concept of life, relishing the chance to tell me what they had been trying to figure out for the last hour or so when they were supposedly sharpening pencils or filling in the blanks in their workbooks.

What made me feel bad was that I could not help pushing them away from that kind of thinking, away from that kind of personal musing, and away from sharing of the moment when teacher and student sense that a new leap has been taken. Those connections — between myself and the students, be- *Author's* tween past ways of thinking and an emergent understanding — sprang out of a *concern* particular classroom discussion, and the desire to share with one who had participated in it the sense of excitement that had sparked thought. Those connections, as well as the discussions that led to them, simply had less and less place in my classroom. Why? What was taking their place? What ideas about how learning should take place were constraining life in the classroom? Where were those ideas coming from?

This chapter is an attempt to answer these questions. I have come to believe that considering them seriously can challenge both the way curriculum is defined and who does the defining. For those of us who want to transform the schools, such a redefinition is essential.

Two major ways of defining curriculum exist within current educational literature, each with its own group of adherents. One group sees curriculum as a body of knowledge that is divided by subject matter and complexity according to the ability levels of students who, moving through the divisions in order, will master the whole body of knowledge by the time they finish school. This camp sees curriculum eroded by the other group: educational technocrats, who replace the emphasis on knowledge with one on methods and form.

Both of these emphases take knowledge to be a product, either a body of knowledge I was supposed to have mastered myself or a set of discrete steps and procedures that, if carefully studied and followed, would ensure that my students learned a body of knowledge. In both definitions, curriculum is something developed *outside* the classroom. It may be refined and tested within classrooms but the purpose of the testing is not to modify it so that it is specific to that classroom, but rather to ensure that it can be moved from classroom to classroom, or across state lines, and be recognized everywhere as the same set of ideas or facts.

What goes on in the classroom that is not part of that transportable set of concepts and facts, is simply irrelevant by either definition. Missing from both is a recognition that what one learns, and what one teaches, is transformed within the classroom, and to a great extent can only be understood by honoring that context. As a teacher, I was also losing track of that recognition. This chapter attempts to renew it, arguing that to define curriculum as an object, something that can be abstracted from a specific group of people, trivializes the role of the teacher and the pupil in shaping curriculum, and causes much of the resistance curriculum reformers face when they attempt to introduce yet another set of books, concepts, or schedules.

For the one thing they do *not* consider part of *curriculum* is the personalized adaptation of those ideas or stories by the teacher and her students, the establishment of a rhythm and a tone that matches that special time and place. Curriculum designers see those rhythms as corruptions, or at best as slight modifications by a gifted or assertive teacher. When such personalizing takes over, the results cannot be cross tabulated, they are hard to measure, they mess up time tables and schedules, and they raise the possibility that what goes on in the classroom is as important as, and potentially as exciting, as what happens in the university curriculum laboratory or textbook company.

When curriculum experts do allow that "classroom climate" can contribute to pupil progress (i.e., enhanced test scores) they generally credit the teacher with providing the emotional sustenance, the reassurance, and the personal incentive that makes learning possible. Conversely, when they see learning as arrested, they often cite the teacher's personal traits as obstacles to student progress. She has withheld approval, been overindulgent, neglectful, or too demanding. In short, she has *burned out* — a phrase that emphasizes the teacher's emotional makeup, implying that the teacher has become too numb to feel and that the core of who she used to be has somehow evaporated due to a reckless disregard for self-preservation. (The idea that a teacher's dissatisfaction might be tied to a lack of intellectual stimulation and/or recognition in schools is generally absent from the numerous discussions of burnout, underlining the common assumption that the ability of a teacher to use her mind is irrelevant to her self-esteem as a teacher.)

So curriculum people define teachers, successful as well as failed, as the emotional components, the heart if you will, of learning. The curriculum and those who develop it are the mind, contributing the intellect, the abstract concepts, and the clearly delineated sequences. To use the language of schools, teachers provide "affect," the personal, emotional, spontaneous, instinctual, private, and therefore secretive dimension. Those who work outside the classroom provide the curricula: the "cognitive," intellectual, abstract, public, rational dimension.

It is crucial to recognize that the division between affect — thought to be rooted in classroom life — and cognition — imported into the classroom — is structurally embodied in schools in a very clear-cut way. The principal adult actors *inside* the classroom are women, while the principal actors *outside* the classroom are men. This arrangement has held since the beginning of the common school movement. Nor is the belief that men and women properly have different and separate roles an anamoly of the educational system. Schools replicate and publicly sanction the division of labor and the power structure that distinguish men's and women's spheres of influence outside of schools. Bringing this knowledge to bear on a discussion of curriculum helps understand how curriculum has developed, what role it plays in schools, and how to change it.

A large and growing body of scholarship describes this division of labor, which is known in the literature as the *doctrine of the separate spheres*. The economic basis for this division of labor, with its accompanying difference of values and ideological supports, was the rise of modern industrial capitalism. New economic conditions removed the father from the home, required him to earn a wage in factory or office, assigned the responsibility for raising the family solely to the mother, thereby dividing life into the *public sphere* of the market and the *private sphere* of home. "As fathers moved off the farm into wage labor in factories and offices, women's maternal instincts were 'discovered', and mothers became increasingly associated with child care."[1] The divisions were both mutually reinforcing and antagonistic. "Life would now be experienced as divided into two distinct spheres: a *public* sphere of endeavor governing ultimately by the Market; and a *private* sphere of intimate relationships and individual biological existence."[2] In the home, people were valued "for themselves rather than for their marketable qualities"[3] and women were expected to provide to family members the sense of self-worth and unquestioned duty missing from the market place. In contrast, the definition of masculinity, at least for the rising bourgeoisie, was increasingly linked to managerial ideologies and practice. "The two spheres stand, in respect to their basic values, opposed to each other, and the line between them . . . charged with moral tension."[4]

The belief in women's maternal destiny affected not only mothers by confining them within their families, it also provided the ideological justification for encouraging women to export their supposed natural qualities of nurturance outside the home.

Women's maternal destiny now seemed to educators' satisfaction to prove their fitness as instructors and influencers of youth. Emma Willard argued not only that women were "naturally" suited to teach but that they could be hired at lower salaries in the common schools and that their employment would free more men to increase the wealth of the nation. In Joseph Emerson's estimation, the schoolroom ranked next to the home as a sphere of women's work. He 'suspected' that nature had designed the teaching profession to be women's, since the law, medicine, religion, and politics were exclusively (and appropriately) men's. Catherine Beecher drew tighter the link between motherhood and schoolteaching by asserting that "women's profession," inside and outside the family, was to form pure minds and healthy bodies. Along with an increasing host of educators, Beecher believed that the most direct path to the regulation of conscience and reason ran through the 'affections', or 'heart', the realm in which women's influence reigned. In these natural facts she discerned the efficacy of training women to be teachers.[5]

Beecher's arguments were eventually accepted by the architects of the common school movement, who desperately needed to expand the teaching workforce to accommodate the growing numbers of children now required to attend school.

Women filled a desperate need created by the challenge of the common schools, the ever-increasing size of the student body, and the westward growth of the nation. America was committed to educating its children in public schools, but it was insistent on doing so as cheaply as possible. Women were available in great numbers, and they were willing to work cheaply. The result was another ideological adaptation: in the very period when the gospel of the home as woman's only proper sphere was preached most loudly, it was discovered that women were the natural teachers of youth, could do the job even better than men, and were to be preferred for such employment. This was always provided, of course, that they would work at the proper wage differential — 30 to 50 percent of the wages paid male teachers was considered appropriate.[6]

Being identified with nurturance gave middle-class women entry to one of the few wage earning jobs open to them, and let many working class women move up. Once hired, however, they found it was not so much their "natural" abilities with children as their willingness to work for lower wages and their supposed acceptance of male authority that made them so attractive to school committees and school bureaucrats. The latter supervised their work strictly, making sure they taught prescribed curriculum, following mandated techniques.

While today there is more of a willingness to nostalgically grant old-time teachers a degree of intelligence assumed lacking from present recruits, to the teachers themselves, their now much vaunted intelligence was never mentioned. Instead their "natural ability" to work with children was emphasized, a trait that earned teaching the label "women's true profession." The emphasis on nurturing, as distinct from intelligence and analytical ability, if not their opposite, made irrelevant any discussion of the intellectual abilities of teachers.

Philip W. Jackson, in *Life in Classrooms*, provides a more updated insight into the role divisions between teachers and administrators/educational experts. In describing a group of teachers he has chosen to interview on the basis of their ability to work effectively with children, he states,

> If teachers sought a more thorough understanding of their world, insisted on a greater rationality in their actions, were completely open-minded in their consideration of pedagogical choices, and profound in their view of the human condition, they might well receive greater applause from intellectuals, but it is doubtful that they would perform with greater efficiency in the classroom. On the contrary, it is quite possible that such paragons of virtue, if they could be found to exist, would actually have a deuce of a time coping in any sustained way with a class of third graders in a playyard full of nursery tots.[7]

This quotation shocks us today in its patronizing attitude. Yet it baldly exemplifies a still-common belief in the necessary distinction between "pedagogical choices" — here equated with rationality and open mindedness — and the unique, personal, and idiosyncratic wisdom of teachers, considered essential for "coping with" children. Furthermore, the quote suggests that these two ways of viewing the world cannot be found in the same person. Indeed their combined presence in one person or group of individuals would make life in schools extremely problematic. Jackson suggests that here he has the teachers' own interests at heart. They would make their lives easier by just accepting the curriculum that is imported into the classroom and adjusting the students to it.

But if so, what does that tell us about what counts as learning in our schools? Can we actually separate what is taught from who does the teaching and who does the learning? Can a curriculum be devised outside the classroom that will work inside the classroom? And if so, who benefits from such a system and who suffers?

To address these questions, I now turn to the way teachers themselves view these divisions and the effect of the divisions on their work both in and out of classrooms. At first glance, some teachers appear to agree with those who say that teaching is fundamentally emotional labor, and intrinsically distinct from intellectual pursuits.

"It's funny. You don't use your mind when you're teaching kids. Now, I know that sounds really dumb, but you don't. It's not intellectual. It's a lot of

209

emotion. I'd put out a tremendous amount of emotional energy when I work with the kids, but it's not intellectual."[8]

Yet the same teacher, when talking about what children learn in her classroom, gives a rather different view of her own contribution to their learning, and in the process questions the way curriculum is normatively defined. This teacher explains that the skills she uses in her present position, and that she sees as essential, are individual to her classroom. For her, the official curriculum of the school system is abstract, it is not a "lived" curriculum. Even when a curriculum emphasizes such issues as social awareness or cultural diversity, there is pressure to implement it through a factual, teacher-manual type of approach:

> The affective kinds of things that I did with my kids aren't in the curriculum. The health curriculum talks about self-identity and finding yourself as a person, but I always felt it went much deeper than that and I spent a lot of time and a lot of energy getting kids to be good to each other and good to themselves by talking about their differences and similarities. That's not in the curriculum. Because the core curriculum deals with content—short *a* says *a*, Boston is the hub of the commonwealth, that type of thing. That's different from the kinds of things I thought were going on in my classroom that you just don't find in curriculums.[9]

Experts see the books, not the teacher, as defining the curriculum and determining the education—or miseducation—of the child. If the teacher adheres strictly to the text, the child should learn. But frequently there is a price to pay, both intellectually and emotionally, like my own "hurry-up" voice. Another teacher says,

> I think sometimes I get into a panic and panic the kids, cramming work down their throats in an effort to get them up to grade level. One of the problems I have is that I've got to complete all this work. I do feel that their books have gotten harder. The basal uses language arts a lot. A lot of adjectives, synonyms, naming words, action words. They are very much concerned with the technicalities, with sentences, periods, question marks. I have to introduce the vocabulary from that book, so whatever I do with them whether it's in the basal reader or outside the basal reader I still have to make sure that they can pick up the 'green book' in the next grade. If I don't, no matter how great their vocabularies are, then the second grade teacher will say, 'Hey, they didn't get this specific skill and they don't know these specific words'. I think they'd be able to tell.[10]

Still another teacher, on the theme of pace and panic:

> The principal started another program in kindergarten that he wanted to adopt, working with small groups, using electronic equipment like head sets and things,

very carefully planned individualizing instruction with the children. He was structuring, planning 15-minute segments. He wanted to try something new. We would have one-half hour of concentrated teaching in small groups. So you worked on listening to sounds or you worked on your workbooks in small groups and then after 15 minutes it was [clap hands] change groups. And no matter what, you had to stop at that point. There was one little girl in my room who had had kidney surgery who really wasn't learning and had a lot of problems and I felt couldn't sit and do the work like that. And I remember one day when I said, 'You know, she just had kidney surgery'. He said, 'I'm tired of hearing about her kidney surgery. I'm tired of hearing emotional things blamed for reading problems'. It's a very cut-and-dried thing.[11]

As speed-up and imposed structure increase, teachers, one would suppose, need less and less education to work well at the job, even though — ironically — they need more and more to get it in the first place. Needless to say, this disparity has exacerbated teacher alienation and increased resistance to curriculum reforms.

A teacher with a master's degree in reading talks about her efforts to use her experience both with curriculum and with a particular child to improve his learning.

The director [who has no experience in elementary education] has sent word down to the building that everybody is supposed to be reading in the Ginn series and if they're not, he wanted the names of teachers and children sent to the office. So he was keeping in touch. I got into hell for saying some kids couldn't read that book and I wanted to use the other one, that I knew really worked. He kept saying, 'No, put 'em in the Ginn.' He wanted them in that book and that was the end of it. He doesn't take his own teachers' expertise into consideration at all. Maybe he really believes his own teachers don't have any expertise or at least he doesn't value it.[12]

That belief seems implicit in the more and more common practice of mandating a basal reading series for an entire school or school system.

We were mandated to develop a program that within the building we had to use the same text. So we had to find a reading system that quote unquote met the needs of every kid in that building, kindergarten through eighth grade. Well, we chose a textbook that was excellent for teaching skills in the primary grades, but was not a good transitional text. I developed a transitional reading program for my classroom, and I wasn't unique in that. Our kids weren't ready to begin that fourth grade reader. And the answer was, 'Directive number such and such from the school department dictates that there must be one basal reading series in the building, so therefore you must order materials'.[13]

Teachers are told that these books are the most educationally sound on the market but the grapevine sometimes suggests other reasons:

> They hired a new reading coordinator. He was a writer for the American Book Company. He wanted to bring workbooks into the school for the kindergarten. I said I didn't want reading readiness workbooks. He said. 'Studies have shown that children who use books do better later', and he kept quoting those studies. So the second year, he introduced the American Book Company books, K through 6. All the other books were thrown out.[14]

Even when no crass interest of this sort is present, the impulse is toward uniformity:

> Some neat things might be happening next door with two teachers, but [administrators can't boast] this is what we're doing for the whole school or the whole town — so it doesn't have as much value. So, they're under pressure to show the community that this is how we are handling curriculum development. The easiest way is to use commercial materials such as a beautiful SCIS kit, lovely, big expensive kits, and easier to do it like that.[15]

Children learn, of course, that the knowledge they possess comes from and is only legitimately validated by the anonymous authority of the textbook. When they fill in the blanks, they are not responding to their own needs but to that of an authority whose interest in the child is not personal. Tacit acceptance by teacher and child that their skills are simply reactive is a strong means of control. Without an awareness of their own contributions, and without the public's awareness, they are easily blamed for any breakdown, and hiring a teacher becomes a question of choosing the person who will most strictly adhere to the one best system.

Even when teachers' work has created a major program their contribution appears publicly as negligible, secondary, or an exception to the rule. Their isolation from each other is perpetuated by the need to funnel any request or information up through the levels of the hierarchy and back down again rather than directly to each other. This prevents teachers from using their special knowledge of classroom life, which they alone possess, as a basis for determining systemwide, or even schoolwide, policies.

> After working for months on the fourth grade reading curriculum, we brought it up to the Assistant Superintendent. We had put a blanket statement at the beginning stating that we would assume that the teachers would be responsible by consulting the textbooks and other resource materials and their expertise and so on. . . . He made it quite clear that he didn't think they were capable of going over anything by themselves, finding the materials, using them appropriately. . . .

> We're smart enough to do all the busy work but not smart enough to carry it
> out. . . . All the teachers did all the work, but I haven't seen any acknowledgment
> of that publicly or any published words of praise for the teachers.[16]

In fact, teachers' ability to innovate frequently depends upon their skill in
concealing their originality, even their successes, so that they do not appear to
consider their own judgment on intellectual matters equal to that of principals or other administrators.

Many teachers, however, do develop imaginative, creative, and intellectually rigorous curricula. How do they fare within the educational system?
Some teachers, who can more openly acknowledge their curricular efforts,
depend upon a benevolent principal who is usually seen by both other administrators and by the teachers themselves as the exception to the rule. Teachers'
efforts are tolerated, for instance, in affluent school systems with access to
enrichment resources or in situations that include students from more privileged backgrounds, or in pilot programs, or in environments comprised of an
unusually cohesive group of pupils. Yet there is a danger that such teachers
will be seen as an example and a rebuke to other teachers.

> I was hired originally because open classrooms were popular at the time, and was
> interested in that kind of thing, even though I really didn't know what it was. I did
> try all kinds of things, and I was lucky because I also had an unusually bright
> classroom. The principal used to send all of the newspaper reporters to my
> classroom and I got my picture in the paper and full-page write-ups. I had no idea
> how this was affecting other teachers. Years later I discovered that the second
> grade teacher had fallen apart because she had been the principal's pet teacher for
> the last few years, and all of a sudden her very tightly controlled style was no
> longer in favor. In fact, the principal sent her into my classroom to observe my
> methods, and I was a first-year teacher in that school and she had been there for
> ten years! After that, she worked incredibly hard, but her way just wasn't what
> sold newspapers anymore. It was only after I left that school, and went to another
> school district where my style was no longer popular, that I learned how devastat-
> ing it can be when you have to prove constantly that you are competent, when that
> isn't taken for granted, and where the assumption is you are mediocre until you
> can prove otherwise. Of course, you become, at least I felt I was becoming,
> mediocre because I was so afraid to take chances for fear I would fail and prove
> them right.[17]

Administrators cite such "superteachers" not to encourage other teachers
to innovate within their own classrooms, but to limit the number of innovative teachers, requiring others to copy the method of the teacher currently in
favor or to encourage even the innovative teacher to hold on to a sure thing
else they disappoint, and jeopardize their favored status. The tendency of the

213

system thus is to encourage standardization, inevitably encouraging mediocrity and conformity as the general, and safer, way of continuing one's teaching career amid the many curricular changes demanded periodically of teachers.

> When I first started teaching 17 years ago, I believed in a very child-centered, developmental approach for kindergarten; I still do, but over the years my teaching style has changed because of feedback I've gotten from different principals, pushing me to rely more on workbooks and things like that which I never would have done on my own. When this new reading coordinator came in one day, I was working with a group of workbooks and my aid was working with another group in workbooks and everything was quiet, and we had exactly what my first principal would have loved. And she thought it was terrible. So what can I do? [she laughs] *Finally,* I accomplished what they wanted me to do, and it's hard to change tools. It's not that easy because they're habits you've formed over the years, and I got to like the other way because that's the way I've been doing it. I wouldn't mind going back, but I'm not sure that the reading coordinator will stay very long and I'm not sure that even that superintendent will stay very long.[18]

Even teachers deemed capable by one principal of developing curriculum may find that the next principal disagrees:

> There was one particular teacher who really was turned on to language experience teaching, a terrific teacher, so she set up a whole language experience program in her class. Well, we got a change of principals. Principals tend to be threatened by things they don't understand or can't control because they're more dependent upon the person, not a system. It's always easier to go by a traditional reading program. Well, she got a lot of flack from the principal. He completely belittled her efforts, even though her results, and the feel of her classroom, were fantastic. She withdrew, isolated herself. Her classroom was not exciting anymore. The kids were in straight rows. She does what she thinks is expected of her. She goes home at 3:30 and that's it. She's just waiting to retire.[19]

For a teacher to have influence outside her own classroom, the curriculum she has developed must be cleansed of any individualistic traits peculiar to the teacher originating it, making it a commodity suitable for sale outside the classroom.

> I think generally teachers would want to share with other teachers and feel good about it and do it. I think next door or even in another school somebody is doing something, and they become very excited about it and that excitement is transmitted to another person, and I think they're very apt to try it. My own feeling is that when I get a pile of things that somebody else has made it's lovely and I may use some of it, but it's not mine. But I think teachers resent that administrators who are supposed to be helping us come in and ask us to give them copies of things

we've done in our room. The administration's assumption is that now I'm going to be so committed to it — the whole curriculum — that you will go and you will sit and you will listen and you will learn and you will go back to your classroom and implement it.[20]

Researchers have been arguing for some time that teachers are subjected to such intrusions because they lack a shared body of professional knowledge. It is true that many teachers are not willing to lay down specific formulae for raising reading scores or teaching math facts or even lining children up to go out to recess. It does not necessarily follow that teachers lack concrete knowledge or that they have not demonstrated to themselves and other teachers the success of many techniques and strategies they have devised.

Teachers consistently report that their major and most reliable source of information inside the classroom is their personal interactions with their students, even if these interactions are not usually classified as part of the curriculum.

Discussion is not part of the core curriculum because it's not something you can write down and give back in a test. There's no way that you can empirically prove that a kid's attitude or opinion has developed and changed, except that the kid seems to be a different kid than he was before. We know he's changed because we can look at the kid and we can hear the way he communicates. We know that this is different. I think that teachers get so caught up with producing something that proves the kid scored one point on his reading test and that means he's now four months above his grade level — that type of thing. We have to have some way almost of justifying what we've been doing in our classrooms and talking about things. Somehow you can't justify an hour spent talking about why you feel the way you do because you can't empirically prove it later on a report card.[21]

Teachers also report that outside the classroom their most trusted source for new techniques and strategies, as well as feedback and confirmation, is the discussion they carry on with other teachers during break time between speakers at an in-service workshop, at crosstown meetings with teachers at the same grade level, or by a frank request for help in the teachers' room. The informal nature of these discussions, the low institutional and social status accorded the participants, the fact the issues are embedded in specific contextual situations, and the pressing need for immediate help, mask the fact that teachers do possess a great deal of knowledge and expertise about curricular as well as classroom management issues. An administrator or researcher, more comfortable with abstract and no-fault solutions, may not recognize these discussions as demonstrating knowledge or expertise but for the teacher the fact that someone who is really "in there" suggested these alternatives is the most solid reason for trying them out.

Teachers also know how mistakes and false judgments made in the past have led to present choices. But they also know they can never be sure, because this year's class is so different from last year's. Curriculum must respond to what the teacher experiences each year.

Perhaps if children's emotions could be easily defined, diagnosed, and treated, with the just the proper "treatment" given to each child — a treatment that had been agreed upon by experts on the basis of sample behaviors of children — then teachers could simply choose the right treatment, and the child would fall into line. Alas, or fortunately, that is not the case, as any one who has spent time actually working with children can tell you. Instead, teachers must, and good ones do, depend upon their empathy, their observation, their acceptance of each child as particular, when they teach them, talk to them, prepare them for the next grade level. The identification of good teaching with nurturing, while at the same time trivializing the importance of nurturing by categorizing it as a mindless, low-level skill, serves to restrict teachers to their classrooms by convincing them it is in their own and their pupils' best interests.

Creating a bureaucracy in schools does allow some people to distance themselves from students, teachers, and others — formalizing relationships and setting up specific times and timetables for when they will sit down and work with someone. That does not mean everyone in a school, however, has the luxury of such clear boundaries of time and emotions. Just as a husband can leave home and expect the wife to clear up any emotional loose ends that arise, some school people can set the rules while others are expected to continue the daily, intimate involvement that is required to put those or a reasonable facsimile of those rules into practice. It is easy for a principal to believe that it is the rules, and the clear expectations and boundaries that create adherence to them, that create school successes. That is because he does not see all the negotiating that makes them work (sometimes), all the recourse to individual ties that appear at a distance like standardized results.

Talk of "teacherproof" materials, for example, carries with it the assumption that if teachers are allowed to teach idiosyncratically and with a degree of emotional involvement, they will inevitably be led to make distinctions amongst their pupils, distinctions that would inhibit rather than enhance the equal opportunity, or simply the just rewards, of all. The belief that curriculum specialists and administrators, the great majority of whom are white males, are less prone to prejudice and stereotypes than classroom teachers, is fundamentally racist, classist, and sexist. Numerous examples of blatantly racist, sexist, and/or classist texts or curriculum packages that practice the benign neglect of simply projecting white middle-class values and experiences as national standards are found.

Today, a teacher who wishes a more active role in curriculum reform is forced to step out of the classroom and to become a specialist who devises curriculum for other people's classrooms. She cannot combine nurturing pupils, seen as essentially an idiosyncratic, personalized role, with the abstract analytic skills considered crucial to the development of curriculum. The oft heard remark, intended as a compliment, "What are you still doing in the classroom? You're so bright!" indicates the degree of popular contempt for the majority of teachers and the general unwillingness to believe that a large number of teachers could, and do — when given honest and sustained encouragement — create exciting curricula.

Removing curriculum reform from the individual classroom is doomed to failure. Teachers will resist such reform, either overtly or covertly, consciously or unconsciously; and so too will students, in an attempt to assert the significance of their own experience to what and how they want to learn. Good curriculum reform can come about only through a rethinking of the division between affect and cognition, between the heart and the mind, between the personalized and the abstract, between the public and the private. By analyzing how, and why, these divisions are embedded in our society, we can perhaps begin to understand what our society is trying to learn, and whether it is worth learning it.

Notes

1. Leonore Weitzman, *The Marriage Contract* (New York: Macmillian Company, 1981), p. 100.

2. Barbara Ehrenreich and Deirdre English, *For Her Own Good, 150 Years of the Experts' Advice to Women* (New York, Anchor Press, Doubleday, 1978), p. 9.

3. *Ibid.*, p. 9.

4. *Ibid.*, p. 9.

5. Nancy Cott, *The Bonds of Womanhood: "Woman's Sphere" in New England, 1780–1835* (New Haven, Conn.: Yale University Press, 1977), pp. 121-22.

6. Gerda Lerner, "The Lady and the Mill Girl: Changes in the Status of Women in the Age of Jackson, 1780–1840," in *A Heritage of One's Own*, Nancy F. Cott and Elizabeth H. Pleck, eds. (New York: Simon and Schuster, 1979), pp. 188–89.

7. Philip W. Jackson, *Life in Classrooms* (New York: Holt, Rinehart & Winston, 1969) p. 149.

8. Sara E. Freedman, Jane Jackson, and Katherine Boles, interview transcriptions from the research report, *The Effects of the Institutional Structure of Schools on Teachers* (Final report, NIE Grant No. NIE-G-81-0031, Boston Women's Teachers' Group, P.O. Box 169, W. Somerville, Mass. 02144, 1982).

9. *Ibid.*, p. 23.

10. *Ibid.*, p. 45.
11. *Ibid.*, p. 67.
12. *Ibid.*, p. 25.
13. *Ibid.*, p. 17.
14. *Ibid.*, p. 89.
15. *Ibid.*, p. 92.
16. *Ibid.*, p. 87.
17. Sara E. Freedman, *Personal Journal* (1979).
18. Freedman, Jackson, and Boles, *op. cit.*
19. *Ibid.*, p. 104.
20. *Ibid.*, p. 123.
21. *Ibid.*, p. 57.

TWELVE

Schooling for the Culture of Democracy

Landon E. Beyer

One of the central purposes of this volume is to document the wide array of issues and choices confronting teachers and others engaged in curricular activities and to broaden the parameters of such choices. The notion that teaching practices and curriculum deliberation can be carried on in a relatively isolated and technical way, separated from areas of discourse and action like those represented in the political, moral, and cultural domains of society, is effectively challenged and rejected by the contributors to this volume.

What must be stressed, of course, are the complicated, diverse, and often contradictory relations between curriculum matters and those larger arenas of discourse and action with which school practice is intertwined. And a good deal of recent scholarship has illuminated just such relations, highlighting in the process the inadequacy of the narrow, technical nature of much previous work in the curriculum field.[1] While this literature has added immeasurably to our understanding of what schools do socially and culturally, it has been less influential in outlining ways in which alternative practice may be constructed that alter current realities.

Part of the reason for this lies, paradoxically, at the center of the recent critical literature in curriculum studies, and the set of values it has advanced. The analysis of schools as agents of social maintenance and stability has primarily involved highlighting the sort of connections between curriculum and social life that the liberal tradition in education either ignored or discounted. For example, the notion that curriculum content formed an ideological bulwark that promoted race, gender, ethnic and social class inequalities was not one that could comfortably be accommodated within the prevailing meritocratic and individualistic orientations of liberal theory.[2] Thus, the aim of much critical curriculum scholarship was to reveal interconnections and patterns previously hidden; such critiques involved, as Maxine Greene said of other kinds of critical writing, "an interrogation of some surface reality. Each [critique] is a demystification, the object of which is to liberate — for praxis, for self-fulfillment, for awareness, and a degree of happiness."[3] In providing such a critical and emancipatory appraisal of schooling and curriculum matters, though, alternative visions and possibilities become less discussed and acted on.

In aligning this scholarship with certain traditions, moreover, we risk the tendency to overidentify with and attempt to legitimate certain essentially theoretical commitments. Such legitimation-oriented theory, while clearly important and useful, can also lead "to a series of self-alienating options in which our real political presence is as bystanders, historians or critics . . . with only marginal or rhetorical connections to the confused and frustrating politics of our own time and place."[4] When theories of social reproduction become examples of such marginal participation in the politics of our own time and place in education, even the most sophisticated analyses they provide will only accomplish part of what is now so urgently required: a recognition of "the 'material force of the idea': the production and the practice of possibility."[5]

This chapter focuses on the practice of possibility as it pertains to the idea of democratic participation in schooling and curriculum.[6] The practice of participatory democracy not only dovetails with a recurrent theme of this volume, it also resonates to a central value on which modern social systems have presumably been based. Within education, discussions regarding the possible role of U. S. schools in promoting a democratic social order are as old as attempts to establish a system of publicly supported education. Educational institutions have been both applauded and chastised for efforts to establish programs that will further particular democratic ideals and practices. From Thomas Jefferson's proposals for a system of schools in Virginia, to Horace Mann's call for school reform in the second quarter of the nineteenth century, to the recent report of the National Commission on Excellence in Education, America's schools have been called upon to advance a variety of purportedly democratic purposes.[7]

One problem that has repeatedly plagued such discussions is that the nature of democracy has itself undergone substantial, periodic revisions over the course of our history. This has resulted in schools that aim to fulfill a number of functions, related to one or another of the visions of democracy currently favored by other social institutions and practices.[8] Moreover, important conceptual and ideological variances exist among the interpretations of democracy that are presented. Each interpretation serves to support or subvert the interests of specific social groups. A fundamental problem facing schools in this regard is that these interests are themselves often contradictory, so that by supporting certain versions of democracy, other views may be neglected, even implicitly or explicitly opposed.[9] We cannot expect educational institutions uniformly to support a vision of democracy if, in fact, numerous visions comprise a constellation of competing interests and claims to social justice that do not allow for any straightforward synthesis.

Yet, the problems associated with schools as instruments of democratic ideals go even deeper than these conceptual and ideological differences. A key argument of this chapter is that our very conception of democracy has become so withered at its roots as to make doubtful the possibility that schools can assist in promoting the development of democracy. Not only do multiple realities surround conceptions of democracy, but the very conditions under which these realities might be clarified, debated, and acted on are increasingly difficult to locate. The reasons for this are complex, but basically reflect fragmentary, chaotic, and confused attempts to embed moral dialogue in current society. As long as moral discourse remains in this state, possible moral principles will remain obscure, with refuge increasingly sought in various forms of emotivism.[10] Second, the inability to provide a suitable context for the discussion of democratic ideas is also the result of a loss of communities within which such discourse can become meaningful and prompt the requisite social action.[11] Surrounded by larger institutional structures favoring technization, commodification, and the therapeutic privatization of social relations, we have all but lost a sense of the collective social good so necessary for discussion of democratic ideas.[12] Documenting the demise of moral discourse and genuine community participation, and their consequences for discussions concerning democracy, will occupy the first section of this chapter.

The second portion of this chapter will detail the relevance of education for rebuilding moral discourse and genuine communities. While the treatment of this issue will be necessarily suggestive rather than definitive, the outlines of an alternative approach to schooling that responds to the social trends identified in the first portion of this chapter will be offered here.[13] The basic argument is that we need to reconstitute democracy as a cultural form — one that helps further those moral and collective pursuits that are a central part of the now-required social transformation. As a part of this transformation, schools can play an important role in helping realize fully participatory democracy within U.S. society. This will go some way toward providing a set of ideas and values that go beyond analysis toward the positive construction of alternative practices, while respecting the need for the critical work that has been and will be undertaken in the curriculum field.

Given the confusion and contentiousness surrounding the concept of democratic participation, the view of democracy embraced in this chapter must be identified at the outset. While this characterization might well consume the whole of this chapter and a good deal more, the outlines of this view can be drawn briefly. First, democracy is intimately tied to a set of values regarding such issues as the nature of social justice, equality, freedom, and the like. To be engaged in democratic action is to guide one's actions in ways that are consistent with such values, principles, and commitments (begging the question, for the purposes of this discussion, of what these principles and commitments should be). Second, this view of democracy has an affinity with some of the recent literature concerning a reconstructed civic education.[14]

Recently, several critical analyses of the concept of *civic education* have appeared that suggest a new role for a *public philosophy*. These writers "look upon political philosophy as a form of civic educational *agency*, exploring its value as a moral and cognitive message system, judging it by its capacity to *inspire just action in daily life*."[15] (Emphasis added.) Insofar as democracy is more than an intellectual or cognitive matter, it has salience for the actions, positions, and commitments that form the heart of our common, daily interactions. Connecting this view with the previous point regarding the centrality of values within democracy, I agree that, "a value commitment involves a disposition to relevant action . . . and not simply the acceptance of various abstract propositions about democracy or the passive endorsement of a set of ideals."[16] Third, and building on this last point, rejuvenating the concept of democracy includes overcoming a number of dualisms that have become commonsensical: thought and feeling, theory and practice, idea and action, objective and subjective, rational and emotional, and so on. If the concept of democracy is to be a force for enlightened social action and reconstruction, the duplicity involved in such ideologically based antagonisms must be exposed and rejected.[17] Fourth, democracy must refer to a way of life, a cultural form, a world view that goes beyond political and civic affairs. It involves fundamentally a commitment to the broadest possible participation in decisionmaking by those whose interests are involved in the everyday workings of economic, familial, cultural, aesthetic, and educational arenas. In short, democracy is here conceived as a way of life that empowers people to act in those situations and institutions comprising the bulk of daily life, guided by a set of values and principles consistent with that vision of participation, and grounded in actions that overcome ideologically based dichotomies in the pursuit of socially just action.

Moral Disclosure and Community

Alasdair MacIntyre, in *After Virtue*, claims not only that moral theory has undergone a fundamental debasement in modern U. S. society, but that we have even lost the ability to use moral language sensibility. As MacIntyre expresses this,

> what we possess . . . are the fragments of a conceptual scheme, parts which now lack those contexts from which their significance derived. We possess indeed simulacra of morality, we continue to use many of the key expressions. But we have — very largely, if not entirely — lost our comprehension, both theoretical and practical, of morality.[18]

The collapse of genuine moral discourse and the concomitant demise of genuine communities have occurred for several reasons. In looking at some of the more theoretical or academic reasons for the former, as well as some of the more general social causes associated with the latter, I do not mean to imply a strict separation between these domains. Indeed, some of the most interesting questions surrounding the discourses on morality and community concern the interconnections between theoretical inquiry and patterns of social evolution. It is only for analytic purposes that such issues can be separated, with the hope that such an artificial distinction has some heuristic value.

Several elements within the traditions of academic theorizing have served to weaken the authenticity and potency of moral discourse. First, within the domain of philosophy, the widespread acceptance of investigations centering on ordinary language and conceptual analysis has supported the view that moral debate can be separated from social context. The usual way theoretical analysis of this sort proceeds is to identify "ideal types" that embody the essential elements of the concept under discussion: for example, that indicate what *autonomy, justice, freedom,* etc., properly mean as linguistic forms. Commonly, an initial appeal is made to the way such concepts are used in typical situations, in an attempt to clarify the meaning of these terms. Subsequently, these concepts may be analyzed for their possible internal contradictions, relations with other concepts and terms, implications for future analysis, and the like. The intent is to arrive at a more precise characterization of what a given concept entails, so that ambiguous or incorrect usages of language may be pinpointed and corrected.[19] As a result of this sort of abstracted and decontextualized treatment of concepts, philosophical clarity and the resolution of concrete dilemmas and problems may be perceived as separate, even antagonistic, endeavors. The view that too close an identification with concrete problems may obstruct conceptual clarity is not foreign to such ways of proceeding. Yet, in regarding conceptual sophistication as disconnected from any important social context, we tend to overlook the important political and ideological struggles that take place around these concepts and related ideas and that provide them with human significance. Walter Feinberg makes a similar point in his recent work, *Understanding Education:*

> Even though analytic philosophy has served to capture the meaning and use of concepts, it has failed to capture the significance of those concepts in a total system of practice. Conceptual analysis is limited because it can capture meaning and use but not significance. . . .
> The problem is . . . that [conceptual] analysis itself rests upon a sharp separation between conceptual adequacy and empirical truth . . . because it deals with crystallized concepts, it directs attention away from the struggles over meaning that occur prior to crystallization.[20]

While the crystallization of concepts that occurs within analytic philosophy may be advantageous for certain limited purposes, the separation of analytic clarity from empirical significance it encourages is especially detrimental to questions involving human values and decisions.[21] For in the process of resolving such issues, analytic philosophy that is abstracted in this way loses its point, with a corresponding gulf created between moral discourse and social action.[22]

This same sense of separation can be seen at another level of academic debate, one that has a longer tradition than ordinary language analysis. Since the writings of Plato, academics have commonly assumed what we might refer to as a position of epistemological and ontological dualism. That is, proper objects of knowledge, and those having a greater degree of permanency or authenticity, have been thought to be removed from the more variable, changing, and deceptive social and interpersonal contexts that comprise human existence. For Plato, the search was for those eternal and immutable Forms that, existing in a higher reality, give a limited legitimacy to objects and events of the physical world. Genuine knowledge and true understanding are to be found in other-worldly phenomena. Even though modern, secular philosophy has largely abandoned the search for such evanescent Forms, the commitment to certainty has continued, in part through the emphasis on conceptual clarity noted already. In addition, the epistemological legacy of Plato can be seen in our culture's reliance (until recently, at least) on positivism, especially in its enshrinement of empirical science that is allegedly objective, impersonal, value free, and atheoretical. Within such doctrines, knowledge is to be found precisely by separating our observations and analyses from that untrustworthy social context from which, as Plato surmised, only opinion can spring. Applied to questions of moral propriety, the epistemic dualism inherent in positivistic endeavors demeans the viability of moral judgments.[23]

A third factor that has promoted the dissolution of moral discourse relates more specifically to traditions of scholarship embodied in institutions of higher education in the United States. In the twentieth century, the image of the university as an association of scholars committed to the conservation, development, and dissemination of our cultural heritage was modified by an allegiance to research that had the potential to develop new products and commodities.[24] The modern university became more closely allied with social and governmental agencies, and responsive to the demands of the growing corporate sector.[25] As a result, university faculty became geared to the production of new knowledge. Such knowledge could be most productively pursued within increasingly narrow, specialized disciplinary and subdisciplinary boundaries, while moral questions became viewed as belonging properly to one particular discipline or subdiscipline within the academy. The result has been a further compartmentalization and erosion of moral debate.

These theoretical reasons for the rather unproductive and denuded forms of current moral discussion are complemented by various social events that were to have a correlative impact. These factors relate more directly to the loss of genuine community that has also compromised our ability to discuss sensibly the social meaning of democracy, as noted earlier.

As a society we have, to a very large degree, lost a sense of history. Not only is our understanding of previous events incomplete or even nonexistent, although this is surely a part of the problem, but we have also lost a sense of historical continuity — the notion that past, present, and future are not fragmented. This is as much a personal and local problem as it is a national one.[26] A part of the reason for this lack of historical perspective has to do with the incessant drive for novelty, future-oriented schemes of material reward, production, and distribution, and a certain fascination with the future generally.[27] As a culture, we emphasize goal-directedness and linear thinking, believing (or hoping) that the future will be an improvement upon the present. The fascination with a future more rewarding than the present is also furthered by the dismissal of authoritative traditions and the embrace of individualism:

> The American understanding of the autonomy of the self places the burden of one's own deepest self-definitions on one's own individual choice . . . the notion that one discovers one's deepest beliefs in, and through, tradition and community is not very congenial to Americans. Most of us imagine an autonomous self existing independently, entirely outside any tradition and community, and then perhaps choosing one.[28]

This negligence toward history and tradition has been accompanied by the drive for commodification and the massive production and consumption of nondurable goods.[29] Beginning with the rise of factory capitalism in the nineteenth century and increasing with the expansion of more corporate forms, the development of new markets for an expanded array of goods has typified our economic system. We are increasingly surrounded by "things" from which a large part of our identity is derived, as Lasch has recently commented:

> Both as a worker and as a consumer, the individual learns not merely to measure himself against others but to see himself through others' eyes. He learns the self-image he projects accounts for more than accumulated skills and experience. Since he will be judged, both by his colleagues and superiors at work and by the strangers he encounters on the street, according to his possessions, his clothes, and his 'personality' — not, as in the nineteenth century, by his 'character' — he adopts a theatrical view of his own 'performance' on and off the job ... the conditions of everyday social intercourse, in societies based on mass production and mass consumption, encourage an unprecedented attention to superficial impressions and images, to the point where the self becomes almost indistinguishable from its surface.[30]

Surrounded by nondurable objects from which our identity in no small way springs, goaded by images that promise health, happiness, sexuality, wealth, and social respectability virtually in an aerosol can, modern Americans have lost a sense of permanency and belonging. Everything becomes disposable — to be purchased, used, and discarded. Personal and social commitments, pursuit of nonemotivist principles, and political involvements alike become harder to understand, let alone justify. *Freedom,* in such a society, "comes down to the freedom to choose between Brand X and Brand Y, between interchangeable lovers, interchangeable jobs, interchangeable neighborhoods."[31] In a society enamored with the latest fads, "revolutionary" breakthroughs, and the dogged pursuit of commodity consumption through advertising, the larger historical context which might lend meaning to human life becomes obscured.

The lack of historical perspective may also be attributable in part to the contemporary forms of barbarism that virtually defy understanding and response. The horrors of the Holocaust, other genocidal practices in evidence during this and the preceding centuries, and the constant threat of total annihilation through nuclear attack or accident, present situations for which communal recognition and moral response seem equally implausible. The most that we seem able to do is promote various coping strategies that have survival as their ultimate end.[32] Given the unprecedented and all but incomprehensible atrocities of the past, we can understand how a society such as ours might be compelled to seek a more future-oriented perspective. Yet not only does ignorance of history condemn us to a repetition of past mistakes, it also makes the articulation and redevelopment of alternative futures more problematic. A society that denies historical continuity is one that also makes implausible a sense of genuine community.

The breakdown of moral discourse and the demise of genuine communities fostering visions of the social good, virtue, and commitments that are larger and more enduring than individuals, has resulted in the appearance of two distinctively American "character types" that, in social practice, subvert discussions of what is entailed by democracy. Generated by those processes detailed above, the therapist and the manager/administrator form a substantial part of our current cultural foci, as these embody perspectives and orientations that capture contemporary U. S. society.[33]

As a part of the larger bureaucratic structure of our economic and social worlds, the manager embodies those proclivities toward technical expediency that have come to dominate our world. As described by Bellah, *et al.*:

> The essence of the manager's task is to organize the human and non-human resources available to the organization that employs him so as to improve its position in the marketplace. His role is to persuade, inspire, manipulate, cajole, and intimidate those he manages so that his organization measures up to criteria of effectiveness shaped ultimately by the market. . . . The manager's view of things is akin to that of the technician of industrial society par excellence, the engineer.[34]

As the ultimate expression of what the authors call *utilitarian individualism*, the manager thus captures something of the essence of modern America's economic and social heart. It is important to see that, as character type, the manager has come to symbolize economic situations, and larger social and cultural patterns as well. Within education the contemporary trend toward deskilling of teaching and commodification of curricula are manifestations of this emphasis on management, technical control, and functional utility, as these values have infiltrated cultural institutions like schools.[35]

Importantly, this reliance on technical control means that moral discourse, religion, and art alike tend to be relegated to the sphere of the subjective, the relative, and the emotive, and to the domain of "the feminine" as well.[36] Again, as Bellah *et al.* document, "with the coming of the managerial society, the organization of work, place of residence, and social status came to be decided by criteria of economic effectiveness. . . . The older social and moral standards became in many ways less relevant to the lives of those Americans most directly caught up in the new system."[37] The manager symbolizes not only the ascendancy of the economic and the utilitarian in American life, but the near replacement of moral discourse by those more technical, consumptive, and bureaucratic work and lifestyles that accompanied the adoption of that character type.

The reaction to the dominance of the manager has taken several forms. The therapist, as the second of our American character types, captures our culture's fascination with psychologized life patterns and choices. In some ways the job of trying to reunite a self deluged with the demands of the managerial character has fallen to the therapist. Committed to "personal satisfaction," "self-actualization," "psychic wholeness," and the like, the therapist represents attempts to heal an assaulted psyche. Yet, "like the manager, the therapist takes the functional organization of industrial society for granted, as the unproblematical context of life."[38] Keyed to a notion of proper "adjustment" of individuals to a personal and social context that is regarded as largely immutable, the therapist seeks individualized accommodation of clients to those contexts. "Its genius is that it enables the individual to think of commitments — from marriage and work to political and religious involvement — as enhancements of the sense of individual well-being rather than as moral imperatives."[39] Like the manager whose work and social lives involve the furtherance of patterns that undermine moral discourse, the therapist — in individualizing people's choices, commitments, and actions — captures our culture's hostility to forms of moral and communal life.[40]

Given the cultural and social propensities outlined in this section, it is not surprising that our vision of democracy has often been clouded and confused. Unable to conceptualize moral commitment within a system continually denigrating — at both a theoretical and a more day-to-day level — historical tradition, extra-individualistic commitments, and communal involvements emphasizing the social good, democratic possibilities are short circuited. Because democratic possibilities and some set of value commitments are essentially conjoined, as indicated earlier, the former are theoretically clouded and all but impossible to put into practice because of our inability to engage in authentic, meaningful moral discourse. Within this context, it is not surprising that discussions of the possible role of educational institutions in fostering democracy have been accompanied by so much hesitancy and confusion. What, then, is to be done?

Schooling and the Culture of Democracy

In contrast to the development of what Bellah *et al.* refer to as *lifestyle enclaves* in which the manager and therapist take up an individualized residence (in their utilitarian and expressive guises, respectively), these authors pose the reestablishment of genuine communities — *communities of memory:*

> *Communities*, in the sense in which we are using the term, have a history—in an important sense they are constituted by their past—and for this reason we can speak of a real community as a 'community of memory', one that does not forget its past.
>
> ... The communities of memory that tie us to the past also turn us toward the future as communities of hope. They carry a context of meaning that can allow us to connect our aspirations for ourselves and those closest to us with the aspirations of a larger whole and see our own efforts as being, in part, contributions to the common good.[41]

One of the central functions of schooling, in helping rebuild those contexts within which discussions of democracy can be meaningfully instigated, must be the rebuilding of such communities of memory. At the same time, we must work to regain the authenticity of moral discourse and principles as they provide the grounding for the enactment of democratic participation.

These twin goals entail what I call the reconstitution of schooling for the culture of democracy. Before outlining some of the implications of this view for educational research and the work of teachers, some additional comments must be made about the notion of democracy.

With the renunciation of authentic moral discourse, the abandonment of communities in favor of lifestyle enclaves, and the emergence of the cults of managerial competence and therapeutic adjustment, democratic ideas have been relegated to smaller and less meaningful realms of life. To a large extent the meaning of democracy has been reduced to pulling the appropriate levers of a voting machine at designated intervals. And even this minimalist interpretation of what democracy means in civic affairs is being currently acted upon by fewer than one-half of the eligible participants. Two aspects of this situation are remarkable for our purposes. First, what constitutes *civic responsibility* and *democratic involvement* is becoming more and more narrowly circumscribed. The fact that some recent reports have concluded that a central problem of modern industrial nations is an excess of democratic participation perhaps epitomizes the conceptual and ideological confusion surrounding this term in contemporary culture.[42] At the same time, second, the cultural possibilities of participation have become increasingly restricted. As the cult of technical expertise has gained momentum in contemporary social life, the possibilities for active input and involvement in our daily work, recreation, and family lives have decreased. While the meaning of political democracy has been reduced, then, other social spaces for the inculcation of participatory possibilities have been precluded.

In rebuilding a commitment to democracy as a cultural form, the notion of participation becomes a key. In order for democracy to be a living, viable force in modern society, people must be provided opportunities—in their daily actions and involvements — to engage in genuinely participatory ventures. As Carole Pateman has argued, "for the operation of a democratic polity at national level, the necessary qualities in individuals can only be developed through the democratization of authority structures in all political systems."[43] Democracy as participation in life decisions, institutional configurations, and daily activities points to the need to see our commitment to democracy as a cultural force — one that has legitimacy within a wide range of settings.

The nature of participation in social settings is clearly central here. Pateman makes a distinction between full, partial, and pseudo-participation that is useful for this discussion. Pseudo-participation occurs in those cases when people are provided the *feeling* of participation without the reality, usually accompanied by various stylistic or human relations devices offered to help us feel soothed or placated. This is reminiscent of the therapeutic ethos of lifestyle enclaves as characterized by Bellah *et al.* Partial participation results when people are able to offer input into a course of action, but a power differential affects the ultimate resolution of the process. This is perhaps the typical mode of organization in work situations — even in those that purport to foster greater worker involvement. Full participation, on the other hand, is a "process where each individual member of a decisionmaking body has equal power to determine the outcome of decisions."[44] In working for democracy as a cultural form, it is the model of full participation that must guide our efforts.

One might object that such broadly defined participation is inconsistent with the development of communities of memory that emphasize tradition, collective consciousness, and principled action. For, it could be argued, to be "democratic" implies giving equal weight to all points of view, and disregarding traditions that are authoritative, resulting in intellectual relativism and social paralysis. Fully participatory democracy that emphasizes human agency on the basis of moral principles, certainly, is only possible within a context in which alternative, divergent perspectives may be articulated, expressed, and openly debated. Yet while allowing for the expression of divergent points of view, such a context must also include participants' challenging and defending their positions. In the process, judgments must necessarily be made about the range of alternative positions discussed, so that the possibility of enlightened action may be realized. Within these processes of expression, challenge, and defense of positions, the importance of communal traditions will be apparent, as tensions between stated positions and received traditions come to the fore. Such traditions are not to be uncritically superimposed, however. Rather, they are to be appropriated — as intimately connected with who we are as people, a culture, and a collective — reflectively, and examined and modified where necessary. Thus the development of authentic communities capable of genu-

230

ine moral discourse implies neither the acceptance of all viewpoints as equally valid (thereby disallowing judgment as to their suitability as a basis for action within that community), nor the potentially autocratic superimposition of traditions that are unreflectively internalized.

Within the context of education, democracy as a cultural form must include these elements: first, a commitment to moral discourse, and the development of moral principles, as guides for decisonmaking and action; second, the building of communities of memory that provide the social and historical context within which such discourse can be realized; and third, the enactment of full participation in a variety of settings, allowing morally principled, participatory agency to blossom as the key to democracy. Let us see how these elements would alter current forms of curriculum scholarship and teaching.

With respect to research on curriculum and teaching, we must reject both the amoral posturing that often accompanies traditional positivistic research, and the forms of more critically oriented research that side unreflectively with particular social groups. Within the former, a hallmark of "objectivity" and "certainty" in the research traditions we have inherited is their presumed value neutrality. It has been thought that legitimate educational research must be exclusively descriptive, focusing on the recording of facts apart from our evaluation of them. Two objections must be made to this picture of research.

On the one hand, the reliance on research that is purportedly objective, exclusively factual, and free of theory or value, is no longer tenable. Recent studies in epistemology, the philosophy of science, and social and political theory have demonstated conclusively that observations are always and necessarily value laden; they are accompanied by theoretical presuppositions that are in turn linked to larger questions regarding beliefs, attitudes, and ideologies. We must deconstruct the usual assumptions behind traditional educational research to discover the latent interests served by much educational research and analysis.[45] On the other hand, more critically oriented educational analysis, especially of a neo-Marxist and revisionist bent, has tended to side with those oppressed by current forms of educational and social policy. This has resulted in a celebration of various actions as forms of reputed "resistance," when it is not always clear that such a label is accurate or morally defensible.[46] The provision of moral principles, and the encouragement of moral dialogue as aspects of an expanded community of memory within education, are crucial if educational and social reforms are to be instituted that are genuinely emancipatory.

In addition, educational research within a community of memory must expand the membership of such a community.[47] Our research model has tended to be hierarchical and patriarchal, with university investigators carrying out research designs within a context where those studied have been left out of most conceptual and strategic decisions. This way of thinking about and conducting research has resulted in the maintenance of the schism between theory and practice, ideas and actions, and conception and execution. Parties on both sides of this chasm have suffered from this rift. Viewed as furthering the allegiance to community, full participation, and moral discourse, educational research must facilitate the expansion of communities to include teachers, administrators, students, parents, and others where appropriate. This does not mean, of course, that everyone involved in such an expanded research undertaking would bring to it the same set of assumptions and orientations. Indeed, part of the point of reorganizing the research community includes an obligation to express differences in outlook. Here, as elsewhere, conflict and disagreement can be productive.

With regard to the work of teachers, the sentiments embodied in this chapter also entail a reconstruction of classroom interactions and the workplace of teaching as well. Classrooms typically allow pseudo or partial participation, for both teachers and students. As the curriculum becomes increasingly standardized and centralized, the demands on teachers become more heavily weighted toward bureaucratic and administrative trivia, and teaching imbued generally with an ethos of technocratic rationality; in this situation the possibility of full participation is denied. Current proposals to identify "master teachers," increase teacher salaries while making them more highly correlated with student test scores, require competency measures at both the preservice level and later, foster a reliance on external sources for curricular and pedagogical guidance that are increasingly technicized, and so on, deny the legitimacy of a fully participatory environment for teachers.

At the same time, teaching continues to be an isolated, even lonely, profession, often characterized by an absence of cooperative ventures with other adults. Collegiality entailing collaborative efforts to construct curricula, develop materials and ideas, and share experiences, are something of a rarity. Yet these are the very activities from which could spring an identification with education as a communal, moral, and participatory undertaking. We must build into the school day, week, and year, such collaborative and collegial efforts, at the same time that we emphasize teachers' creative responsibilities.

These same values must be incorporated into the interactions among students, and between students and teacher. We have constructed most classrooms around principles that seek to divide, classify, and sort students rather than those that unite them into genuine communities. Ability grouping, further separation of "special," "normal," and "gifted and talented" students into separate programs and physical locations, undermine genuinely communal activities. So does a stress on competition for higher test scores, other forms of measured achievement, and a range of cultural practices in schools that foster differential status. We must work against such tendencies in the construction of fully participatory moral communities that schools can be. We must also provide opportunities for students to develop what Pateman calls "the sense of political efficacy and participation." We cannot reasonably expect American adults to exercise moral, political, and communal responsibility if these emphases are undervalued in our educational institutions. As she expresses this point, "there is something paradoxical in calling socialization inside existing organizations and associations, most of which, especially industrial ones, are oligarchical and hierarchical, a training explicitly in *democracy*."[48] If the schools are to play a central role in developing the culture of democracy, opportunities to realize the value and meaning of this culture must be provided in those institutions in which our children spend so large a portion of their lives.

The present volume is in many respects committed to morally and politically infused conceptions of democratic participation in education. This very commitment precludes the creation of detailed, specific, and elaborate proposals for the reform of teaching and curricula that can be authoritatively imposed on teachers, administrators, and students. Indeed, the very notion of education and educational inquiry as collaborative, participatory ventures prohibits such impositional activities on the part of researchers who are removed from the world of teaching and schooling. At the same time, of course, it is important that ideas and possibilities be articulated that are practicable; acknowledge the personal, moral, and political complexity of the situations now confronted by educators; and that resist the movement toward increased technization and hierarchical, patriarchal control in teaching and curriculum.[49] It is therefore more important than ever that we envision that "practice of possibility" Williams reminds us is so important, as we go beyond critique to explore the production of alternative educational and social worlds.

At base the conception of teaching and curricula outlined here seeks to reorient the daily activities of schooling and teaching. The direction of this movement toward schools as sites for the exploration of democracy as a cultural possibility is indicated by the changed role it conceives for teachers as curriculum designers, as politically and morally sensitive practitioners, and as people engaged in more collaborative, dialogical activities.[50] It requires that teachers be given far more academic freedom, including especially the opportunity to construct curricula with students, other teachers, administrators, and college and university educators. This entails in the long run, that local and state officials be less inclined to impose specific, detailed guidelines and requirements than is now the case. The current trend to specify curriculum content and form in greater detail is thus the very antithesis of what is needed to promote the growth of the culture of democracy in schools.

I noted at the outset of this chapter that recent critical inquiry in curriculum studies has documented the ways in which the formal content of the curriculum has helped promote and maintain a number of racial, gender, and social class inequalities. This can be seen in at least two ways. First, curricula in social studies, the language arts, science, and the arts often fail to recognize or value the contributions that women, members of minority communities, and others have made in these areas. Not only does this deny the legitimacy of these groups' efforts and achievements, it robs all of us of that "community of memory" that forms an essential component of genuine communities. Such communities generate a sensitivity to the common good and provide a sense of hope and possibility for the future. Thus, incorporating those now excluded from the formal curricula of schools not only promotes a more fair and honest view of the past and present, it helps orient us to a future world that may be itself more socially just and decent. Second, we have tended to convey to students the notion that a consensus has been reached on most issues and controversies, or that most questions have been or can be settled by applying rational criteria and thus are not really controversial at all. Not only is such a supposition often simply false, it presents a world more closed, predefined, and immutable than is permissible if we are to take seriously the idea that full participation in the public sphere is possible and desirable.

To counter these tendencies, those engaged in curriculum matters must redress the exclusion of women, Blacks, Hispanics, Native Americans, the working class, and so on, in our schools' curricula. Projects and classroom activities in which teachers, students, and community members cooperatively explore the histories of such groups as they contributed to the arts, literature, science, and so on, would be an important step in this direction. On the other hand, it is crucial that we recognize and even accentuate the reality of divergent, oppositional views as we move away from a consensual, positivistic outlook in the curriculum. This might involve exploring alternative explanations for events (e.g., the Civil War, the clash between business and government, the organization of labor, and the development of technological "advances") and appreciating the divergent positions people have taken with respect to a range of issues and questions. If our students are to become members of genuinely participatory and moral communities, they must learn to acknowledge a multiplicity of views, clarify the differences that account for such views, and develop positions that are appropriate and defensible. A part of this process must involve questioning the taken for granted and commonsensical, at all levels.

Like much of the recent literature in curriculum studies, the ideas outlined here have been developed to extend the critical tradition in our field and clarify what is at stake in thinking through issues related to schooling and teaching. In the end, our aim must always be the construction of better worlds for ourselves, our students, and our children. As people engaged in the phenomenon of world building, teachers are central actors in the construction of future communities that can embody a culture of democracy. There is no more important work to be done.

Notes

1. This literature is now rather vast, covering a multitude of subject areas and theoretical positions. See, for example, Samuel Bowles and Herbert Gintis, *Schooling in Capitalist America* (New York: Basic Books, 1976); Michael F. D. Young, *Knowledge and Control* (London: Collier-Macmillan, 1971); Michael W. Apple, *Ideology and Curriculum* (Boston: Routledge and Kegan Paul, 1979); Walter Feinberg, *Understanding Education* (New York: Cambridge University Press, 1983); and Michael W. Apple and Lois Weis, eds., *Ideology and Practice in Schooling* (Philadelphia: Temple University Press, 1983).

2. For important criticisms of this legacy of liberal theory, see, for example, Walter Feinberg, *Reason and Rhetoric* (New York: John Wiley & Sons, 1975); David Nasaw, *Schooled to Order* (New York: Oxford University Press, 1979); Clarence J. Karier, Paul Violas, and Joel Spring, *Roots of Crisis* (Chicago: Rand McNally, 1973); Joel Spring, *The Sorting Machine* (New York: Longman, 1976); and Michael W. Apple, *Education and Power* (Boston: Routledge & Kegan Paul, 1982).

3. Maxine Greene, *Landscapes of Learning* (New York: Teachers College Press, 1978), p. 54.

4. Raymond Williams, *Problems in Materialism and Culture* (London: Verso Editions and New Left Books, 1980), p. 238.

5. *Ibid.*, p. 273.

6. Some of the ideas in this chapter were originally discussed in Landon E. Beyer, "Schooling for Moral and Democratic Communities," *Issues in Education*, Vol. IV 1(Summer 1986).

7. See, for example, Gordon C. Lee, *Crusade Against Ignorance: Thomas Jefferson on Education* (New York: Teachers College Press, 1961); Lawrence A. Cremin, *The Republic and the School: Horace Mann on the Education of Free Men* (New York: Teachers College Press, 1957); and the National Commission on Excellence in Education, *A Nation at Risk: The Imperative for Education Reform* (Washington, D. C.: Government Printing Office, 1983).

8. Contemporary examples include desegregation efforts, a number of "compensatory education" efforts such as Head Start, and, more recently, the enlistment of schools in regaining lost economic and military ground. On this last point, see especially the National Commission on Excellence in Education, *op. cit.*

9. Consider this issue within the context of recent reform proposals. Again the National Commission on Excellence in Education provides an important parameter here. See also Mortimer Adler, *The Paideia Proposal* (New York: Macmillan Publishing Co., 1982), for an oppositional view of what democracy

might entail. Other contrasts can be found in the series entitled, "Educational Reform: A Dialogue," in *Curriculum Inquiry*, beginning with Vol. 15, No. 1, for which I served as special editor.

10. See Alasdair MacIntyre, *After Virtue: A Study in Moral Theory* (Notre Dame, Ind.: University of Notre Dame Press, 1984).

11. See Robert N. Bellah, Richard Madsen, William M. Sullivan, Ann Swidler, and Steven M. Tipton, *Habits of the Heart* (Berkeley, Calif.: University of California Press, 1985).

12. See Christopher Lasch, *The Minimal Self: Psychic Survival in Troubled Times* (New York: W. W. Norton & Company, 1984).

13. Also see Landon E. Beyer and George H. Wood, "Critical Inquiry and Moral Action in Education," *Educational Theory* Vol. 36, 1(Winter 1986).

14. See Barbara Finkelstein, "Thinking Publicly about Civic Learning: An Agenda for Education Reform in the '80's," in *Civic Learning for Teachers: Capstone for Educational Reform*, Alan H. Jones, Ed. (Ann Arbor, Mich.: Prakken Publications, 1985). For an analysis of the relationships among technicism, education, and community, see Manfred Stanley, *The Technological Conscience: Survival and Dignity in an Age of Expertise* (New York: Free Press, 1978), especially Part III, "Toward the Liberation of Practical Reason: The Problem of Countertechnicist Social Practice." See also Landon E. Beyer, "Beyond Elitism and Technicism: Teacher Education as Practical Philosophy," *Journal of Teacher Education* Vol. XXXVII, 1(March-April 1986).

15. Finkelstein, *op. cit.*, p. 15.

16. Richard L. Morrill, "Educating for Democratic Values," *Liberal Education* 68(1982) p. 367.

17. See Evelyn Fox Keller, *Reflections on Gender and Science* (New Haven, Conn.: Yale University Press, 1985)

18. MacIntyre, *op. cit.*, p. 2.

19. See, for example, Jonas Soltis, ed., *Philosophy and Education: Eightieth Yearbook of the National Society for the Study of Education* (Chicago: University of Chicago Press, 1981); and R. F. Dearden, *Theory and Practice in Education* (Boston: Routledge and Kegan Paul, 1984). More than other philosophers, however, Dearden is aware of some of the difficulties of ordinary language analysis I am pointing to here. See Landon E. Beyer, "The Practice of Philosophy," *The Review of Education* Vol. 11, 2(Spring 1985).

20. Walter Feinberg, *Understanding Education, op. cit.*, p. 114.

21. This separation may not be defensible in any areas of human investigation. See, for example, Richard J. Bernstein, *Beyond Objectivism and Relativism: Science, Hermeneutics, and Praxis* (Philadelphia: University of Pennsylvania Press, 1983); and Richard Rorty, *Philosophy and the Mirror of Nature* (Princeton, N.J.: Princeton University Presss, 1979).

22. This parallels the separation of art and social context implicit or explicit in a good deal of contemporary aesthetic theory. See Landon E. Beyer, "Aesthetic Theory and the Ideology of Educational Institutions," *Curriculum Inquiry* Vol. 9, 1(Spring 1979); and Landon E. Beyer, "Art and Society: Toward New

Directions in Aesthetic Education," *The Journal of Curriculum Theorizing*, Vol. 7, 2. The most insightful work currently being done that argues for the aesthetic as a productive, material force can be found in the writings of Raymond Williams. See, for example, *Marxism and Literature* (Oxford: Oxford University Press, 1977); and *The Long Revolution* (New York: Columbia University Press, 1961).

23. It is not at all clear that Plato would approve of the contemporary separation embedded here. While the centrality of Forms as embodying the most true and reliable objects of knowledge that exist in a separate universe is clear, his emphasis on the dialectic, his role as *mid-wife* in giving birth to knowledge that is recollected, and the like, emphasize the role of the Forms in providing authenticity to human exchange. Hence, our borrowing from Platonic theory may, as in other cases involving the appropriation of complex and intricate ideas, be rather selective.

24. I have elaborated on this in Beyer, "Beyond Elitism and Technicism: Teacher Education as Practical Philosophy," *op. cit.*

25. See Jacques Barzun, *The American University: How It Runs, Where It Is Going* (New York: Harper and Row, 1968).

26. There are, of course, counterexamples to this tendency toward ahistoricism. The success of *Roots* as a mass media production, the emphasis on local and oral history in some social studies programs, and the *Foxfire* and *Highlander* educational alternatives, provide some of the more well-known exceptions to our dominant orientation. We have much to learn from such efforts.

27. Many contradictions are involved here. To cite one irony, our fascination with the future is taking place at the same time that we are placing the survival of the human species and the planet itself in jeopardy. Our recent record in nuclear proliferation, contamination of ground water, destruction of wildlife habitat and numerous animal species, and a wide array of toxic waste and other pollution problems, provide disturbing evidence of our actual callousness toward the same future that we long for culturally.

28. Bellah *et al., op. cit.*, p. 65.

29. The classic essay on the subject of commodification of art is Walter Benjamin, "The Work of Art in the Age of Mechanical Reproduction," in his book, *Illuminations*, Harry Zohn, trans. (New York: Schocken Books, 1969).

30. Lasch, *op. cit.*, p. 30. There are important issues of gender in how people learn to see themselves through the eyes of others. See John Berger, *Ways of Seeing* (New York: Penguin Books, 1977).

31. Lasch, *op. cit.*, p. 38.

32. See *ibid.*, Chapter III, "The Discourse on Mass Death: 'Lessons' of the Holocaust."

33. Bellah, *et al., op. cit.*, p. 65.

34. *Ibid.*, p. 45.

35. See Apple and Weis, eds., *op. cit.*

36. For an interesting discussion of the extent to which *masculinity* is bound up with

objective, rational, and value-free inquiry associated with positivism, while subjective, emotional and caring relations have been equated with femininity, see Keller, *op. cit.*

37. Bellah, *et al.*, *op. cit.*, p. 46.

38. *Ibid.*, p. 47.

39. *Ibid.*, p. 47.

40. For a similarly psychologized view of art, see David Bleich, *Subjective Criticism* (Baltimore, Md.: Johns Hopkins University Press, 1978).

41. Bellah *et al.*, *op. cit.*, p. 153.

42. See Michael J. Crozier, Samuel P. Huntington, and Joji Watnauki, *The Crisis of Democracy: Report on the Governability of Democracies to the Trilateral Commission* (New York: New York University Press, 1975).

43. Carole Pateman, *Participation and Democratic Theory* (New York: Cambridge University Press, 1970), p. 35.

44. *Ibid.*, p. 71.

45. See Landon E. Beyer, "The Reconstruction of Knowledge and Educational Studies," *Journal of Education*, Vol. 168, 2(1986).

46. See Beyer and Wood, *op. cit.*

47. The general debt we owe to the work of John Dewey in this regard should be obvious. On the linkages between community, education, and communication, see *Democracy and Education: An Introduction to the Philosophy of Education* (New York: Free Press, 1916), especially Chapter I, "Education as a Necessity of Life." Numerous critics in the recent past have pointed to the evident shortcomings in Dewey's writings on democracy and their relationship to his faith in science, technology, and the development of meritocracy within the modern state. See, for example, Walter Feinberg, *Reason and Rhetoric*, *op. cit.* Important historical references for the view of democracy advocated here can be found in Jean Jacques Rousseau, *The Social Contract and Discourses*, G. D. H. Cole, trans. (New York: E. P. Dutton and Company, Inc., 1950); John Stuart Mill, *Considerations on Representative Government*, Currin V. Shields, ed. (New York: Liberal Arts Press, 1958); and G. D. H. Cole, *Social Theory* (New York: Frederick A. Stokes Company, 1920).

48. Pateman, *op. cit.*, p. 45.

49. Recently, an attempt has been made to strengthen the bureaucratic and technical control of curricula in an area where it might seem least likely to surface — art education. A number of researchers in this area are arguing for a curriculum in the arts that would be more formalized, commodified, and deskilled than has been the case. For a review of this literature and the dangers involved in this tendency, see Landon E. Beyer, "Art in Educational Reform: Toward What End?" *Journal of the Institute of Art Education*, Vol. 10, 3(1986).

50. These issues are developed further in Landon E. Beyer, *Knowing and Acting: Inquiry, Ideology, and Educational Studies* (London: Falmer Press, 1988).

V

Curriculum and Technology

THIRTEEN

Education, Technology, and the Military

Douglas D. Noble

Recent discussion about technology and American education is limited both by its ahistorical focus on recent microcomputer use in public schools and by its disregard for wider contexts, especially corporate and military. Rarely, for example, are connections drawn between the computer movement in education, on one hand, and, on the other hand, military developments in cognitive psychology and artificial intelligence, military and industrial training contexts from which computer-based instruction arose, and the militarized rhetoric of "task forces" bemoaning "a nation at risk" and mobilizing for "a nation prepared."[1] Connections are found among these developments, and their simultaneous emergence recommends both a wider perspective and a deeper appreciation of their interconnected history.

Scant attention has been paid to the broad preoccupation with "technology" — and to the historical dependence upon military technology — in the practice and collective ideology of schooling in America. In fact, the microcomputer phenomenon is simply the most visible and most recent instance of this preoccupation and dependence, which are reflected not so much in the latest "hardware" as in the ongoing technological reinterpretations of the *meaning* and the *practice* of education in a technological society.

The microcomputer phenomenon in education offers a handle for an exploration of these larger issues because it renders them visible, in two ways.

241

DOUGLAS D. NOBLE

First, its own history is saturated in military research and development in training and weapons systems; and, second, the abundant rhetoric accompanying the various computer-based educational agendas delineates rather nicely the larger discourse about education and technology which has remained largely unchanged since World War II.

Three Rationales

Three rationales exist, aside from administrative efficiency, for introducing computer technology into the educational process. The first focuses on the nature of *technological society:* the new "knowledge-based information age" requires new skills, including computer literacy and a general problem-solving ability, which are necessary for adaptation to constant technological and occupational change. A second rationale centers on a *technology of education:* computer-based instruction offers new, effective, and efficient ways to present material, to individualize instruction, and to motivate learners. The third rationale focuses on a *technology of mind:* interactions with computers enhance "cognitive skills," while offering the possibility for intellectual "mindstorms," expansive opportunities for intellectual discovery and amplification.

These three lines of justification are familiar to anyone who has been following the computer education movement over the past several years; certainly most discussion has turned on the validity and limitations of these three claims. My point in this chapter is not to contribute directly to these debates. What is needed instead, and what I want to begin here, is a study of the historical development of technological conceptions of *society,* of *education,* and of the *human mind* which these three rationales embody. They are deeply embedded not only in computer education but, more importantly, within a pervasive characterization of education as *a process, designed, through research and development (R and D), for the cultivation of productive and adaptive intellectual skills for a complex technological society.*

This characterization has its roots, to a large extent, in a highly militarized postwar scenario, within which much social policy and social science, including educational policy and research, relied for its models on military developments in information theory, cybernetics, computing, training psychology, operations research, and systems analysis. I hope to show that we are perhaps unwittingly trapped in our attempts to understand the current relation between technology and education by these invisible ideological constraints.

Due to space limitations, the following historical sketch focuses only on the first of the three principal themes, namely, on the military origins of a new technology of mind and on its implications for education. Throughout, how-

242

ever, I point to a broader discussion of the closely interwoven history of technology, education, and the military.

The Long History of Education and Technology

Although this chapter focuses on the decades after World War II, all three themes — technological conceptions of society, mind, and education — have a much longer history in American education. Questions about the changing nature of education in a *technological* — or industrial — *society* have been central to the national debate about educational policy since before the turn of the century and were of paramount importance to Dewey, Counts, and other progressives long before World War II.[2] Scientific inquiries into the nature of *mind* (specifically, of learning and intelligence) — and their relevance to the practice and theory of schooling — have an equally long and highly profiled history in American education, at least since the impact of World War I Army intelligence testing on educational practice. Finally, attempts to develop efficient, science-based *technologies of educational practice* predate the last half century as well. Technologies of school administration go back to the Taylorist "cult of efficiency" in the early decades of this century.[3] Technologies of instruction have been traced by some as far back as Abelard;[4] more recently, Pressey's first "teaching machines" in the late 1920s, which were intended to trigger a long-awaited "industrialization of education," are direct precursors of postwar instructional technologies.[5] Finally, the work of Bobbitt, Charters, and others in the first decades of this century constitutes early curriculum design technologies, which are often cited as the precursors of curriculum development during and after World War II.[6]

Despite these clear antecedent developments, my reason for focusing on the postwar decades is that the particular language of educational rhetoric in the 1980s — the discourse of cognition, of instructional design, and of the "information society" — first emerged in its present form during or soon after World War II. More importantly, new technology-based ideologies of education, society, and mind — ideologies embedded in practices and models of reality as well as in new terminology — first surfaced in the years immediately following the war, and they have remained the prevailing forms of educational practice and discourse into the 1980s.

An abundance of evidence suggests that the 1950s were watershed years in the formation of our current views of mind, society, and education. These were the "birth years," according to Daniel Bell, of the "postindustrial society," later renamed the *"information society".*[7] The founders of *cognitive science* cite the same years as the beginnings of the modelling of mind on information processing.[8] The early work in *artificial intelligence* and *systems analysis* research began at the same time,[9] followed by the systems approach to educational management.[10] The first major federal excursions in civilian scientific *research and development*, and, later, *educational research and development*, began in the postwar decade. Skinner's enormously influential first articles on the technology of teaching were published in 1954, and the Ford Fund for the Advancement of Education, a massive new funding source for the transformation of American education through technology, was founded the following year.

Finally, in the mid-1950s a "quantum leap" occurred in the development of *educational technology*,[11] most of it borne of military training research. Included among the military training technologies that eventually swept into the schools were educational television, educational film, teaching machines, language laboratories, simulations, overhead projectors, and computer-assisted instruction. Other military educational innovations included programmed instruction, instructional design, criterion-referenced instruction and measurement, and intensified use of task analysis, skill taxonomies, and behavioral objectives.

The postwar decade is clearly an appropriate focus for understanding the contemporary relationship between education and technology. I offer, therefore, a brief genealogy of several pivotal developments during these years.

Legacies of the War

Military Definition of Reality

Among the legacies of World War II was an "ideology of national preparedness,"[12] a "military definition of reality," which was used to mobilize the nation in preparation for "the next war." A "mobilized economy," according to Daniel Bell, leading exponent of postindustrial ideology, was a principal factor in the onset of the postindustrial society: "Once the fundamental policy decision was made to oppose the communist power, . . . technical decisions, based on military technology and strategic assessment, took on the highest importance."[13] This preparedness ideology soon filtered to educational policy, so that Walter Lippman could suggest (years before Sputnik): "We must measure our educational effort as we do our military effort. . . . For if, in the crucial years which are coming, our people remain as unprepared as they are for . . . their mission, . . . they may never have a second chance to try."[14]

Research and Development

A second legacy of World War II was a massive federal commitment to scientific research and development as a result of the new prestige and influence won by the scientists involved in the war. The result of their lobbying efforts was an array of military research institutions, including the Office of Naval Research, the Air Force Office of Scientific Research, the Army's Human Resources Research Office, and the Air Force's RAND ("R and D") Corporation. In 1950, the National Science Foundation was established; although nonmilitary, it was created and controlled by the leaders of the wartime science effort, among them Karl Compton and Vannevar Bush of the Massachusetts Institute of Technology and James B. Conant of Harvard University.[15]

New Theories of Man and Society

A third legacy of the war was a host of new technologies and theoretical constructions with powerful implications. Among the former were the atom bomb, radar, and the digital computer; included among the latter were information theory, cybernetics, and operations research. Almost immediately after the war, these theoretical formulations exploded into a host of fertile metaphors and analogies within an ever-widening array of disciplines, from biology to psychology to management forecasting. Information theory, shorn of its mathematical trappings, provided a new ontology: Everything — animal, vegetable, mineral — was now thought to be reducible to "information." Cybernetics offered the language of *feedback* to translate the purposive behaviors of organisms, including human beings, into automatic servomechanisms. Operations research, an amalgam of new mathematical techniques such as linear programming and queueing theory, was transformed into "management science," involving the formal modelling of management decisions. Eventually this methodology became *systems analysis*, the quintessential tool for managers of a new society at the "end of ideology."

Engineering Psychology

With the development during the war of radar, sonar, aircraft control devices, and other complex, high-speed weaponry, came an explosion of psychological research into the limitations and capacities of human perception, movement, and judgment. Psychologists were also enlisted to design and engineer machines — from radar screens to gunnery controls — which would better "fit" these human characteristics. A new discipline, *human engineering* or *psychotechnology*, emerged within military research. This work, in the Army Air Force Aviation Psychology Program and the Applied Psychology Panel, paralleled theoretical developments in information theory and cybernetics by wedding engineering and psychology into a study of "human factors" in machine design.[16]

Training Research and Technology

If "human factors" engineering was the design of machines to fit men, training was the design of men to fit machines. During the war, educators and experimental psychologists mounted a massive effort in training research and development, influenced heavily by behaviorist learning psychology, emerging technologies such as film and automatic instructional devices, and by the earlier curriculum work of Bobbitt and Charters. Although "no curriculum atom bombs"[17] emerged from wartime training research and practice, an enormous intensification of interest was seen in the use of behaviorally oriented instructional objectives, task analysis, training aids and simulation.

According to the reports of the Commission on the Curriculum Implications of Armed Services Education Programs, and the Conference on Planning Post-War Education, both established by the American Council on Education toward the war's end, the major contributions of wartime training included an emphasis on *objectives, change, realism* and *curriculum design*.[18] Wartime training involved developing specific objectives applicable to the performance of particular weapons or missions. These objectives were constantly modified as missions changed and weapons were modified, so adaptability to ongoing, rapid change became a crucial requisite of trainer and trainee alike. The realism of simulated military missions was a central ingredient in efficient training, as was the careful, sequential design of curriculum materials necessary for expedient production of trained personnel for new weapons and new missions.

Participants in this training effort included Robert Gagne, principal architect of instructional design; Fred Keller, author of the Keller Plan of Individual Prescribed Instruction; Robert Mager, industrial training giant and principal developer of criterion-referenced instruction; and Robert Glaser, key proselytizer for federal support of instructional technologies in public education.[19] B. F. Skinner, while not involved in wartime personnel training, was engaged in a military project called Project Pelican in which he trained pigeons as "organic" guidance systems for unmanned missiles; this involvement in what he called the "mass education" of pigeons had a "direct genetic connection"[20] with his seminal work on teaching machines and programmed instruction in the late 1950s.

Perhaps even more influential than the training concepts and technologies that emerged from the war effort were the institutions such as the Army's Human Resources Research Office (HumRRO), the Air Force Personnel and Training Center (AFPTRC), The American Institutes for Research (AIR), and the RAND Corporation offshoot, System Development Corporation. Within such institutions, military training technologies were further developed and were actively disseminated within an emerging federal effort to reform public education (itself orchestrated largely by foundation and university leaders who had played key roles in wartime military research). Because the above institutions were viewed by policymakers as the centers of research on learning and training in the decade after the war, the federal reform efforts begun in the late 1950s — to transform education through "innovation" — relied almost exclusively on these military contributions.

Weapon System as Metaphor For Mind and Society

In the early 1950s, the Air Force formalized the concept of the *weapon system*, which tied research agencies concerned with equipment components to those training and personnel agencies involved with what came to be called the *"human components."* With this step, the Air Force (and later the Navy and the Army as well) joined within a single "system" the twin halves of "psycho-technology": human factors engineering and training research (and eventually personnel management). In such military institutions as the Army's HumRRO and the AFPTRC, the new "doctrine of concurrency" dictated "that the human components and the remainder of the system must be programmed to arrive at a man-machine assembly point at the same moment in time."[21] Thus was developed a "new view of man":[22] one in which a person is regarded as a "human component" within the "personnel subsystem" of complex "man-machine systems" (i.e., weapon systems).

I focus here on one example of the pervasiveness of the man-machine concept: namely, how it provided the context for the reemergence of an emphasis on "mind" and thinking in American psychology, and how this context contributed to a new view of mind as information processing system, the centerpiece of cognitive psychology and artificial intelligence research.[23] This newly legitimated conception of mind came to be absorbed — through the work of Jerome Bruner and others — into an "intellectual" reform of American education, culminating in educators' recent fascination with the cognitive: problem-solving, thinking skills, and the microcomputer.

The Air Force's RAND Corporation was the center of the emerging man-machine systems concept in the early 1950s. The Systems Research Laboratory at RAND (which in 1957 became the Systems Development Corporation) was a "conceptual conglomerate"[24] of all the new theoretic advances emerging from the war. It was primarily involved with simulating an environment for an Air Defense Radar Center, in which the primary goal of the investigators was to conduct an analysis of the organizational behavior of teams of air controllers (the personnel subsystem) within the air defense system.[25]

In the early 1950s, the RAND Corporation was a paradise of well-funded, interdisciplinary research. One of the many beneficiaries of RAND's largesse was Herbert Simon, whose primary interest was in management decision-making in business organizations.[26] Simon was recruited by Allen Newell at the Systems Research Laboratory to study organizational decisionmaking within the team of air controllers. Many of the problems researched during the war had highlighted the central importance of human decisionmaking; studies in *signal detectability*, for example, had determined that the report of a faint blip on a radar screen involved as much an operator's decisionmaking as his perception. Borrowing from information theory, cybernetics, and human factors research, Newell and Simon began looking at decisionmaking as human information processing within the larger air defense simulation. Operators came to be seen as integral parts of an information system, as information receivers (of "blips"), information transmitters (through the controls), and information processors. In short, controllers were themselves information processing systems: "If one considers the organism to consist of effectors, receptors, and a control system for joining these, then," according to Simon, ours was "a theory of the control system."[27]

As human information processors, however, radar operators and air controllers were restricted by (among other factors) their limited "channel capacity" and decisonmaking capabilities. This limitation was viewed as a major bottleneck in overall system effectiveness, and Simon and Newell set about studying the limits of human information processing, both in order to improve upon and to circumvent its inherent limitations. Newell's use of RAND's digital computers to simulate radar "blips" (rather than to process numbers) led to Simon's and Newell's use of computers to manipulate other symbols, first of symbolic logic and then of chess. Within these symbolic environments, Newell and Simon attempted to simulate (and therefore to "understand") actual human thought processes involved in proving logical theorems and playing chess.[28]

These achievements were the beginning of the computer simulation of human decisionmaking (or "problem-solving"), presented by the investigators as "the next advance in operations research": "We are now poised for a great advance that will bring the digital computer and the tools of mathematics and the behavioral sciences to bear on the very core of managerial activity — on the exercise of judgment and intuition; on the processes of making complex decisions."[29] Thus, Simon's interest in management decisionmaking within business organizations, superimposed on an analysis of human "information processing" within a complex military man-machine system, gave birth to what was soon to be christened *artificial intelligence*.

The new field of cognitive psychology was also borne of this amalgam of management decision theory and military information processing. Simon was a zealous proselytizer of his ideas,[30] and by the mid-1950s, psychologists Carl

Hovland, Jerome Bruner, and George Miller were developing the information processing concept, intent on establishing a new "cognitive" psychology to replace a moribund behaviorism. They were beginning to reopen the "black box" of the mind after decades of neglect by behaviorist psychologists; inside the box, not surprisingly, Bruner and others found information processes, the new models for mind. With the assistance of their dean at Harvard, McGeorge Bundy, and with $250,000 from fellow psychologist John Gardner, then president of the Carnegie Corporation, Bruner and Miller founded the Center for Cognitive Studies at Harvard in 1960, an institutional turning point in the legitimation of the new cognitive approach to psychology.[31]

Just how independent of military projects like that of Simon and Newell was the simultaneous development of the information processing model of mind by these psychologists? Miller had been immersed in cybernetics and information theory at the Psychoacoustics Laboratory during and after the war.[32] Hovland arrived at the model from his work on mass media training and on the role of judgment in attitude formation, which was developed during his wartime tenure in the Research Branch of the Information and Education Division of the War Department.[33] Bruner, whose subsequent influence on American educational policy places him at the center of our larger story, claims to have arrived at the information processing model of mind by way of a theory of perception, but Bruner spent 1951 at the Institute for Advanced Studies at Princeton University within a strong information theory milieu,[34] and he cites information theory as a major source of his contribution to the "revival of mind" at mid-century.[35]

Bruner and Simon were aware of each other's work, and Bruner's explanation for the "turn to mind" in the 1950s clearly shows the mark of the management-military connection: "Develop a sufficiently complex technology and there is no alternative but to create cognitive principles in order to understand how people can manage it."[36] Bruner saw the "cognitive revolution" as "a response to the technological demands of the Post-Industrial revolution": "You cannot properly conceive of managing a complex world of information without a *workable* concept of mind."[37] Clearly, an important connection exists between the idea of a technocratic, "postindustrial" society and the development of the new "cognitive paradigm." Bruner fails to note, however, that both are products of wartime scientific theory and military technology. The information society and the human information processor are woven of the same cloth — the new irreducible of the man-machine system: information. In the words of Simon, information — symbols — had become "tangible" and the computer was the new "all-purpose lathe."[38]

The ideas of Bruner and Simon resemble each other most closely at this intersection of mind and society. An economist and management theorist, Simon wrote a paper in 1964 entitled "Decision-making As an Economic

Resource": "The bulk of the productive wealth consists of programs, corresponding to skills, stored in human minds," and "the principal under-utilized resources [are] . . . learning programs of the employed population," which represent "a huge reservoir of 'standby' learning capacity."[39] Decisionmaking had become, for Simon, the newest form of labor power – or, in management terms, the new human capital of the postindustrial society: ". . . all work [is] 'decision-making' except the actual, final application of physical energy"; and "the processes involved in the 'decision-making' of the worker on the assemblyline are not really very different from the decision-making processes of executives."[40] Human work and productivity were thus reduced to a finite set of (for Simon, quite simple) information processes – identical in human, animal, computer and machine.

In a similar vein, Bruner asserts, in an article called "On Teaching Thinking" (1985): "It is almost the essence of the post-industrial revolution to place a high premium on the skills of the generalist, the troubleshooter, the problem-solver. . . . Once 'mindful performance' becomes a practical necessity for the conduct of technology, the issue of mind and its status ceases to be governed by philosophical or religious debates."[41] In particular, according to Bruner, the issue of mind now becomes the urgent mandate to increase a person's capacity to adapt and to learn: "If we are to respond to accelerated change, we shall have to reduce the turn-around time in the system."[42] Thus, "the cognitive revolution . . . lies at the center of the post-industrial society, [and] the central premise of this society is that it is the generation and management of knowledge . . . which is the key to the industrial and social process. The new capital is know-how, forecast, intelligence. . . . The result has been not simply a renewal of interest in how the 'mind' works, but rather a new search for . . . how mindfulness is cultivated."[43]

One can see in such statements the long shadow of man-machine systems, where abstract mind, reduced to capacities for "troubleshooting" and "problem-solving" within a rapidly changing system, is now viewed as a "practical necessity" for the conduct of technology, a component in the "metamachine" called society. The wellspring of Mind, once a repository of mystery for philosophers and theologians, is thus filtered into strands of colorless, generic processes, diluted into an economic lubricant for a society composed of the same fluid material as itself: the flow of information.

One further link between Bruner's and Simon's approaches is the manner in which they both embed their theories of mind within a central notion of *evolution*. Simon speaks of "problem-solving as natural selection,"[44] meaning that acts of problem-solving are instances of adaptivity within an increasingly artificial world. Bruner sees an ongoing "perfectibility of the intellect" through such adaptation to technological change, and enjoins us to "do justice to our evolution" by transmitting through education the "acquired characteristics that amplify the mind": "Psychologists must re-enter the field of education in order to contribute to man's further evolution through social invention."[45]

This is the origin of Bruner's *evolutionary instrumentalism*, which, when articulated in his *Toward a Theory of Instruction*, exerted considerable influence on educational reformers in the 1960s, and which is enjoying renewed currency in computer education through the work of Bruner's former student, Roy D. Pea.[46] What is significant about this appeal to evolution in the work of both Bruner and Simon is its implicit disregard for the material, historical origins of their theories of mind. It is assumed that the theory of mind as information processor, rather than being the product of particular human factors problems in weapon system technologies, is instead simply the "next step" in human evolution, or, at least, a "natural" intellectual adaptation to a new technological order, itself an evolutionary advance (through scientific "progress"). What is lost in all of this is, of course, any consideration of the possibility that *things could have been different*—that our present "cognitive" understanding of mind, and of its role in society, is an historical invention whose hegemonic influence keeps us from considering alternative approaches to intellect, and (of particular interest here) to the meaning of intellectual development within education.

Bruner, of course, played a central role in technological reinterpretations of American public education, beginning in the early 1950s. Although Skinner is often regarded as the principal theoretician of educational technology, Bruner's (and, less visibly, Simon's) "cognitive revolution" had a far greater, albeit more subtle, influence on the marriage of education and technology in postwar America, transforming the "process" of education into the cultivation of cognitive resources for a postindustrial society.

In fact, several strands in the story of the realignment of public education in postwar technology-based reform appear, although their stories cannot be told here. Among them was the development of the new field of *educational technology*, an amalgam of military training technologies, behaviorist learning theory, instructional design, systems concepts, and audiovisual instruction. A second development in the 1950s was the emergence of a curriculum reform effort engineered by an enormously influential group of scientists and university educators variously referred to as the "New Education Establishment"[47] and the "New Foundation/Academic Network".[48] This group emphasized the emerging concepts of cognition discussed above, focusing on the development of intellect and on the underlying deep structures of subject matter, especially in the sciences and mathematics.

The early 1950s saw a call from many quarters for a renewal of "intellectual rigor" in public education, partly as a response to the weak *Life Adjustment* curriculum that had established itself in the schools at mid-century. This

251

created an educational policy vacuum that was quickly filled by promoters of new educational solutions based on military technologies. Their solutions emphasized one or the other half of this demand for "intellectual rigor": The educational technologists' solution emphasized "rigor," in the form of new, allegedly foolproof training techniques and gadgetry. The New Foundation/ Academic Network, a new breed of cognitivist progressives, focused, on the other hand, on the "intellectual" character of the new demand. They looked inside the "black box" of the mind at the "control system" of the human component, and on the deep structures and patterns of scientific disciplines.

These two groups managed to ride, and in some cases steer, massive new federal educational initiatives into the nation's public schools, culminating in major educational innovations that constitute a postwar legacy of the relation between education and technology. Computer education, and the other recent "high" technologies of education, can only be understood through a more complete understanding of this legacy. They are nothing but its latest incarnations.

Education and Technology in the 1980s

In order to show the relevance of this discussion to present concerns in education, I return to my earlier discussion of the three principal justifications for computer education in the 1980s: the effectiveness of computer-based instruction, the need for "computer literacy" in an "information society," and the enhancement of logical thinking and creative problem-solving through interaction with the computer. None of these justifications was born overnight; in fact, all three can be traced, along with the development of the computer itself, back to the weapons system scenario outlined above.

Computer-Based Instruction

The first computer-based instructional systems were developed to meet the training needs within the Air Force's Semi-Automatic Ground Environment (Project SAGE), precisely the air defense system at RAND's Systems Research Laboratory discussed earlier.[49] The latest concept in computer-based instruction, "intelligent computer-assisted instruction" (ICAI), which includes attempts to incorporate motivational and other affective components (known in the trade as "hot cognition"[50]) into computer programs, was first supported within the Air Force Human Resources Laboratory,[51] and is still being developed, by John Seeley-Brown and others, largely under the auspices of the Defense Advanced Research Projects Agency (DARPA), a post-Sputnik military funding agency for promising technological fantasies in weapon system design.[52]

The principal contribution of DARPA is considered by some to be its support of Project PLATO, developed from 1957 as a joint venture of the Army Signal Corps, the Office of Naval Research, and the Air Force Office of Scientific Research.[53] PLATO, now the linchpin of William Norris's Control Data Corporation, is widely considered to be the world's most sophisticated computer-based instructional system. (It is interesting that the acronym SAGE falsely encourages a reference to human intelligence and wisdom, as does the acronym PLATO, whose full rendering, Programmed Logic for Automatic Teaching Operations, belies any lineage to Socrates' pupil.)

Computer Literacy

One of the principal architects of "computer literacy" was J. C. R. Lick-lider, a prominent wartime "human factors" researcher in the Psychoacoustics Lab who, as a director of the Information Processing Techniques Office of DARPA (then just ARPA) in the sixties, engineered the introduction of "time-sharing" based on his concept of "man-computer symbiosis," which he considered "a subclass of man-machine systems."[54] This concept is the direct precursor of the endless references to the computer's *interactivity* born of the military need for "real time" man-computer decisionmaking in complex weapon systems. The concept is also behind the idea of *computer literacy*, which is simply the human side of the *symbiosis:* "We have retooled society; it is now time to retool ourselves."[55] Interestingly, Licklider, writing in 1960, saw the "man-computer symbiosis" concept as an interim measure, needed only until machines could do *all* the thinking that was required (1980 was Licklider's forecast).[56] (This raises the troubling question whether the perceived importance of "cognitive resources" to economic productivity, so common today, is focused on *human* intellectual resources only until such time as the cognitive terrain is sufficiently mapped (via "expert systems" and the like) to allow the elimination of human participation altogether.)

Logical Thinking and Problem-Solving

The most visible exponent of the third justification is Seymour Papert, creator of LOGO and promoter of children's "mindstorms" — explosive new intellectual powers — through LOGO programming. Papert was involved in the early RAND work on artificial intelligence, and in the sixties he was codirector, with Marvin Minsky, of the M.I.T. Artificial Intelligence Laboratory. His original development of LOGO emerged out of a conviction, resulting from frustrated attempts at simulating adult cognitive performance, that "one cannot expect machines to perform like adults unless they are first taught; . . . what is needed is a machine with the child's ability to learn."[57]

Papert's notion of LOGO "microworlds" was also a product of difficulties: artificial intelligence researchers at M.I.T. were forced to minimize the knowledge "environment" or "world" of the computer in order to arrive at human tasks simple enough to simulate. Ironically, we now find children's worlds reduced to "LOGO microworlds," as research in computer "learning" steadily determines new paradigms for children's learning. A similar twist has occurred in Simon's work in cognitive simulation: originally modelled after human protocols of thinking, cognitive models embodied in computer programs are now themselves offered as appropriate strategies for teaching thinking and problem-solving "skills" to school students.[58]

Conclusion

This chapter situates a discussion of the relationship between educaton and technology within an historical context that, it turns out, has been saturated by decades of military influence. (I had not set out to look for it.) This influence continues, in part because the Armed Forces continue to struggle with the difficulties of selecting and training personnel for increasingly "higher-order thinking" and problem-solving skills needed for overwhelmingly complex new weapon systems.[59] This present influence is evident in the ongoing Air Force, Navy, and DARPA sponsorship of cognitive science and artificial intelligence research related to issues of instruction and learning. These include learning strategies research and cognitive process instruction—especially in math and sciences[60]—as well as a resurgence of research on intelligence, aptitude, and human performance.[61] This new body of research is being welcomed by many leaders in public education, not least because it promises the expert knowledge and "effective" technique necessary for transforming teaching into a "profession."

During the last few years in American education reform, a confluence of the agendas of educational technology and cognitivism has occurred, as the goal of education has become, for many, the production of a population of "knowledge workers" who "think for a living."[62] A competitive high-technology society, we are told, requires above all else the cultivation of cognitive resources—the production of "higher-order thinking and problem-solving skills." The recent outpouring of studies on expert human performance, and the "cognitive processes" underlying learning and teaching strategies, are part of this general effort to gather data in order to "design" and mold intelligence for continual adaptation to the complexities of a new age. This steady transformation of the goal of education into the training of complex mental performance is the latest caricature of "intellectual rigor" in public education; its influence on educational practice is just beginning to be felt, not least through the increased use of computers in schools, and through the cognitivist educational discourse accompanying them.

The transformation I have begun to describe in this chapter is a subtle one, one that is practically invisible. This is because our best teachers have always told us that they want to teach their students how to think, how to learn, and how to develop their intelligence and potential. Many involved in the latest wedding of education and technology believe that they are contributing precisely toward this end. Therefore, we must understand the history of what they are doing and begin to articulate what is being lost in the process.

Notes

1. Examples abound. The most recent include the Committee for economic Development, *Investing in Our Children* (New York: Committee for Economic Development, 1986); Carnegie Forum on Education and the Economy, *A Nation Prepared: Teachers for the 21st Century* (Washington, D. C.: Carnegie Forum on Education and the Economy), which was signed by the presidents of both teachers unions; and U. S. Department of Education, *Transforming American Education: Reducing the Risk to the Nation* (Washington, D. C.: U. S. Department of Education, 1986). The *titles* alone of these reports from business, foundation, labor and the federal government suggest a view of education as a human capital development for a mobilized economy.

2. See, for example, George S. Counts, *Secondary Education and Industrialism* (Cambridge, Mass.: Harvard University Press, 1929); and Arthur G. Wirth, *Education in the Technological Society* (Scranton, Penn.: Intext Educational Publishers, 1972).

3. Raymond E. Callahan, *Education and the Cult of Efficiency* (Chicago: University of Chicago Press, 1962).

4. Paul Saettler, *A History of Instructional Technology* (Washington, D.C.: National Education Association, 1968), p. 18-20.

5. Among these are Sidney Pressey, "A Simple Apparatus Which Gives Tests and Scores — and Even Teaches," and "A Third and Fourth Contribution to the Coming 'Industrial Revolution' in Education." These can both be found in Robert Glaser and A. A. Lumsdaine, *Teaching Machines and Programmed Learning* (Washington, D. C.: NEA-DAVI, 1960) pp. 35-52.

6. James D. Finn, *Extending Education Through Technology* (Washington, D. C.: AECT, 1972) pp. 14, 72.

7. Daniel Bell, "The Post-Industrial Society: A Speculative View," in Edward Hutchings, *Scientific Progess and Human Values* (New York: American Elsevier Publishing Co., 1967) p. 158.

8. See Jerome S. Bruner, *In Search of Mind: Essays in Autobiography* (New York: Harper and Row, 1983); see also the historical addendum in Herbert A. Simon and Allen Newell, *Human Problem Solving* (Englewood Cliffs, N. J.: Prentice-Hall, 1972).

9. See Newell and Simon, *op. cit.;* pp. 869-889.

10. Paul N. Edwards, *Technologies of the Mind* (Silicon Valley Research Group, University of California, Santa Cruz, 1985), p. 72.

11. Finn, *op. cit.*, p. 275.

12. See Michael Sherry, *Preparing for the Next War* (New Haven, Conn.: Yale University Press, 1977).

13. Bell, *op. cit.*, p. 169.

14. Walter Lippman, "The Shortage in Education," *The Atlantic Monthly*, Vol. 193, 5(May 1954), p. 38.

15. See Daniel S. Greenberg, *The Politics of Pure Science* (New York: New Merican Library, 1967).

16. See Arthur W. Melton, "Military Psychology in the United States of America," and Franklin V. Taylor, "Psychology and the Design of Machines," both in *American Psychologist*, Vol. 12 (1957); and Robert Glaser, "Implications of Training Research for Education," in *Theories of Learning and Instruction*, NSSE Yearbook (1964), pp. 153-172. For primary sources, see Charles W. Bray, *Psychology and Military Proficiency* (Princeton, N. J.: Princeton University Press, 1948); and John C. Flanagan, *Aviation Psychology Program in the Army Air Force* (Washington, D. C.: Government Printing Office, 1948), Vol. 1.

17. See Samuel M. Goodman, *Curriculum Implications of Armed Services Educational Programs* (Washington, D. C.: American Council on Education, 1947), p. vii.

18. *Ibid.*, p. vii.

19. See a discussion of the military training work of Glaser, Gagne and Mager in Glaser, *op. cit.* Keller was a project director of radio code operators during World War II and developed an automatic Morse code teaching device (see Bray, *op. cit.*).

20. B. F. Skinner, "Pigeons in a Pelican," *American Psychologist*, Vol. 15 (1960) pp. 36, 37.

21. See Forward by Arthur W. Melton in Robert M. Gagne, *Psychological Principles in System Development* (New York: Holt, Rinehart, and Winston, 1962), p. viii.

22. Roy Lachman *et. al.*, *Cognitive Psychology and Information Processing* (Hillsdale, N. J.: Lawrence Erlbaum Associates, 1979), p. 57.

23. See Edwards, *op. cit.*

24. Newell and Simon, *op. cit.*, p. 882.

25. Robert L. Chapman and John L. Kennedy, "The Background and Implications of the Systems Research Laboratory Studies," in *Symposium on Air Force Human Engineering, Personnel and Training Research* (Washington, D. C.: National Academy of Sciences/National Research Council, 1956).

26. Simon's best known early work in management theory is his *Administrative Behavior* (New York: Macmillan Company, 1947). In an autobiographical essay, Simon later stated the essence of his entire work: "Two interrelated ideas . . . have formed the core of my whole intellectual activity: (1) that human beings are able to achieve only a very bounded rationality; (2) that, as one consequence of their cognitive limitations, they are prone to identifying with *subgoals*. I

would not object to having my whole scientific output described as largely a gloss . . . on the pages of *Administrative Behavior* where these ideas are first set forth"; Gardner Lindzey, ec., *A History of Psychology in Autobiography* (New York: W. H. Freeman, 1980). In 1978, Simon won the Nobel Prize in economics for his theory of "bounded rationality" which is most recently set forth in his *Reason in Human Affairs* (Stanford, Calif.: Stanford University Press, 1983).

27. Allen Newell, J. C. Shaw, and Herbert A. Simon, "Elements of a Theory of Human Problem Solving," *Psychological Review*, Vol. 65, 3(1958) 151.

28. For a full discussion of these developments, see the historical addendum in Simon and Newell, *op. cit.*

29. Herbert A. Simon and Allen Newell, "Heuristic Problem Solving: The Next Advance in Operations Research," *Operations Research*, January-February 1958, p. 3.

30. See Hubert Dreyfus, *What Computers Can't Do* (New York: Harper and Row, 1972), p. 76; and Simon's autobiography in Lindzey, *op. cit.*, p. 465.

31. Bruner, *op. cit.*, p. 126.

32. Edwards, *op. cit.*, pp. 76-84.

33. Carl E. Hovland and Muzafer Sherif, *Social Judgment* (New Haven, Conn.: Yale University Press, 1961), p. v-viii.

34. Jerome S. Bruner, *et al.*, *A Study of Thinking* (New York: John Wiley & Sons, 1956), pp. viii, ix.

35. Bruner, *In Search of Mind, op. cit.*, p. 62.

36. *Ibid.*, p. 62.

37. *Ibid.*, p. 63.

38. Simon and Newell, *op. cit.*, p. 878.

39. Herbert A. Simon, "Decision-Making as an Economic Resource," in Lawrence H. Seltzer, ed., *New Horizons of Economic Progress* (Detroit: Wayne State University Press, 1964), pp. 81-83.

40. *Ibid.*, p. 74.

41. Jerome S. Bruner, "On Teaching Thinking," in Susan F. Chipman and Robert Glaser, *Thinking and Learning Skills*, Vol. 2 (Pittsburgh: University of Pittsburgh Learning Research and Development Center, 1985), p. 599.

42. Jerome S. Bruner, *Toward a Theory of Instruction* (Cambridge, Mass.: Harvard University Press, 1966), p. 37.

43. Bruner, *In Search of Mind, op. cit.*, p. 274.

44. Herbert A. Simon, *The Sciences of the Artificial* (Cambridge, Mass.: MIT Press, 1969), p. 95.

45. Bruner, *Toward a Theory of Instruction, op. cit.*, p. 38.

46. Roy D. Pea, "Prospects and Challenges for Using Microcomputers in Schools," unpublished paper, 1983.

47. Finn, *op. cit.*, pp. 239-90.

48. Richard A. Dershimer, *The Federal Government and Educational Research and Development* (Lexington, Mass.: D. C. Heath, 1976), pp. 17ff.

49. John A. Ellis, ed., *Military Contributions to Instructional Technology* (New York: Praeger Publishers, 1986), pp. 175-78.

50. Robert Glaser, "A Letter in a Time Capsule," in Chipman and Glaser, *op. cit.*, p. 612.

51. Ellis, *op. cit.*, p. 181.

52. *Ibid.*, pp. 206-08.

53. *Ibid.*, pp. 208-12.

54. J. C. R. Licklider, "Man-Computer Symbiosis," IRE Transactions on Human Factors in Electronics, HFE-1 (March 1960), p. 4.

55. J. C. R. Licklider, "National Goals for Computer Literacy," in Seidel, *op. cit.*, p. 282.

56. Licklider, "Man-Computer Symbiosis," *op. cit.*, p. 5.

57. Dreyfus, *op. cit.*, p. 21.

58. See, for example, Deanna Kuhn, "Education for Thinking," *Teachers College Record*, Vol. 87, 4(Summer 1986); see also the sections "Teaching and Thinking" and "Decision Making: A New Paradigm for Education," both in a special issue on "Thinking," *Educational Leadership* (May 1986).

59. See Martin Binkin, *Military Technology and Defense Manpower* (Washington, D. C.: The Brookings Institution, 1986); and John A. Ellis, ed., *Military Contributions to Instructional Technology* (New York: Praeger Publishers, 1986).

60. See, for example, Richard E. Snow *et al.*, *Aptitude, Learning and Instruction* (Hillsdale, N. J.: Lawrence Erlbaum Associates, 1980), 2 vols.

61. See, for example, Robert J. Sternberg, *Human Abilities: An Information Processing Approach* (New York: W. H. Freeman and Co., 1985).

62. Carnegie Forum on Education and the Economy, *op. cit.*

FOURTEEN

A Critical Analysis of Three Approaches to the Use of Computers in Education

Michael J. Streibel

W e are currently in the process of introducing microcomputers into our public and private schools at an exponential rate.[1] We are doing this at a time when many are calling for a return to basics in education and for an increase in the productivity of students, teachers, and administrators.[2] These two phenomena are not unrelated because microcomputers are seen as an answer to the "productivity crises" in education.[3]

With respect to the content and outcome of education, however, microcomputers are not just another neutral "delivery system." Microcomputers are environments within which certain values, biases, and characteristics are played out; for example, calculation and logical operations are central within a computer-based environment. We therefore need to examine the way computers are used in education and the implications of this for the future of education.[4]

The three major approaches to using computers in education are: drill-and-practice, computer tutoring, and simulation and programming. Each of these approaches is analyzed in the following. Although each has some unique characteristics and a set of accompanying assumptions, a common conceptual framework, which is described throughout the remainder of the chapter, binds them all together.

MICHAEL J. STREIBEL

The investigation into the approaches of microcomputer use is shaped by three questions. First, what kind of logic is embedded in each approach and how does this logic express itself in a learning situation. Second, how do the various approaches treat the human learner and what are the consequences. Third, how does the "intellectual tool" use of computers help or hinder us in formulating, understanding, and solving problems.

The answers to these questions form the body of this chapter. They reveal, for example, that computerized drill-and-practice is designed to produce predictable learning performance. The logic used, however, runs counter to the dialectics of learning. Also, all of the approaches view the learner as a generic information-processor. Ultimately, this indicates that a learner's intellectual agency is *decreased* rather than increased in the case of computerized tutorials even though the rhetoric promises the exact opposite.

The other major influences on the body of the text are my own values and assumptions. My background is as a teacher, teacher educator, and scholar in the area of educational technology. I am motivated by a desire to teach others *how* to think about media and computers, and how to become empowered, lifelong learners. In my view, derived from critical theory, knowledge and learning are the result of a social construction of reality.[5] That is, what we *know* to be real is the result of historical and social processes of meaning-making, language-making, and symbol-system-making.[6] This social construction of reality applies to our knowledge of physical reality (i.e., scientific and technological knowledge), as well as to our knowledge of social reality (i.e., what we know about ourselves and others).[7] Both entail a process of human collaboration and dialogic engagement within interpretive communities. This collaboration and engagement creates a "public space" in the minds of the people involved that then leads to the further evolution of shared meanings and shared symbol systems. In a sense, collaboration and engagement within interpretive communities defines our very humanity because we are participating in the creation of our history, our language, and our values.[8]

Formal education is a social process of nurturing cognitive, affective, physical, aesthetic, and moral growth and diversity in children. The latter are dimensions of "meaning-making" and therefore can only happen within community. The arguments developed below are therefore based on my belief that acquisition of factual knowledge and skills are important but always subordinate to personal and communal growth and development. A simple way of stating this is to say that dialogue is at the heart of education.[9]

Furthermore, learning is as much a process of accommodation as assimilation.[10] *Accommodation* requires the active creation of new meanings and the active construction of new symbol systems to give expression to these meanings. This clearly requires dialogic engagement with an interpretive community. Although *assimilation* may at first sight seem like an individual psycho-

260

logical activity, it is also an intentional and constructive act. My reason for believing the latter derives from an ontology which views *all* events—both physical and social—as unique, historical, and irreversible.[11] Students who are learning facts or skills are not incorporating meaningless pieces of information or manipulating meaningless puzzles. They are expanding some part of how they make sense of the world. Humans are, in other words, *always* intentional agents and education must respect and foster this agency.

I also believe that our knowledge encompasses more than discrete, objective, rational symbolic representations, and that cognition entails more than formal operations that operate on explicit knowledge structures. An individual's cognitive processes are always subordinate to meaning-making, and, therefore, are always open to the future and new ways of representing meaning. Even quasiformal systems are never complete.[12]

Formal education is more than a "rationally managed process." Schooling should not be modelled on an industrial assembly line because schooling deals with "meaning-making" (and ultimately with "people-making") and not with widget production.[13] Predictability and control are appropriate concepts for the efficient production of identical products but human beings are never identical products and should not be treated as such.

In my view, a teacher is a central agent in a dialectical community of learning and one who forms a triadic relationship with the learner and the subject matter. This maintains a learning community that extends backward and forward in time. Teaching is seen as having a craft status—a status that is particularly important today because a technological environment tends to leave most people "powerless" and inarticulate about their state of being.[14]

Finally, a teacher nurtures various types of intelligence in students and facilitates the conception and execution of learning. A teacher is not someone who adopts a theoretical stance towards the learner as does a researcher. Rather, a teacher is a lifelong learner who engages and guides others along a similar path.

I value individual and cultural uniqueness and diversity as well as the knowledge and skills that contribute to the social construction of reality. Maintaining a balance between uniqueness and uniformity (of person, culture, knowledge, and skills) is a daily struggle for a teacher that will be profoundly affected by the computer.[15]

Drill-and-Practice Computer Programs

Introduction to Drill-and-Practice Courseware

Drill-and-practice courseware programs (i.e., computer programs that guide learning with a drill-and-practice instructional strategy) are the domi-

261

nant use of computers in education today.[16] They currently run on time-sharing computers and microcomputers. As described below, the characteristics of the drill-and-practice approach legitimize behavioral performances over other types of educational goals. Ironically, behaviorally oriented learning cultures must still be created, mediated, and sustained by interpersonal interactions that have the potential for forming alternate cultures (and thereby alternate types of educational goals). Drill-and-practice courseware programs, however, do not permit these alternate goals to develop.

Description and Analysis of Drill-and-Practice Courseware

Drill-and-practice courseware programs make a number of assumptions about instruction:[17]

1. Previous instruction in the concept or skill has already occurred.
2. Regular instruction is only being supplemented and not replaced.
3. Instruction is to follow a controlled, step-by-step linear sequence of subskills according to an algorithm embedded in the computer program. This algorithm does *not* constitute a model of a student or an expert but constitutes a model of:
   a. rote skill-building in the case of drill; and,
   b. patterned skill-building according to the logic of the content and an instructional theory in the case of practice.[18]
4. A right/wrong answer dichotomy exists in the logic of the content.
5. The basic unit of instructional interaction is a question/answer-branch episode.[19] Continuous learner responses in the form of correct answers are therefore expected.
6. The best feedback by the program from an instructional point of view is an immediate check on a student's responses according to the logic of the content:
   a. positive feedback when the answer is correct; and,
   b. corrective (rather than judgmental) feedback when the answer is incorrect.

The characteristics described above make several things clear: drill-and-practice courseware programs are designed to provide immediate corrective interventions in the learning process when continuously monitored performance-measures indicate incorrect responses. The learner is viewed as a "black box" and his or her behaviors are shaped by an external, mechanical process (i.e., by an instructional algorithm that uses feedback mechanisms to guide the learner toward a prespecified behavioral goal). Drill-and-practice courseware programs therefore constitute a deterministic form of behavioral technology.[20] This may be adequate for beginning skill-building but may mitigate against higher levels of learning.[21] To understand why, we must examine the concepts of mastery learning, individualized learning, and educational work.

Mastery Learning and Drill-and-Practice Courseware

The mastery-learning paradigm assumes that most students can learn most things to a specific level of competence in varying amounts of time.[22] It therefore associates differences in the *amount* of learner-performances at any point in time with differences in the *rates of learning*. Second, the mastery-learning paradigm assumes that instruction can be consciously designed to guarantee specific outcomes. It therefore places a heavy emphasis on the *quality of instructional materials*. Finally, the mastery-learning approach uses criterion-referenced tests that restrict themselves to the level of the objective in order to decide whether a student has met the criterion of success. Success is *not* defined with reference to a higher-level objective.

One can see from this description that the mastery-learning paradigm closely resembles a rationally managed input/output model of educational performance. It therefore makes a number of assumptions about the (1) pedagogical principles, (2) classroom practices, and (3) instructional arrangements involved.[23] These assumptions elaborate the input/output model:

1. Pedagogical Principles

The mastery-learning paradigm assumes that students vary in their aptitude, ability to understand instruction, motivation, and perseverance. These factors are only considered in so far as they affect educational performance. They are not, for example, considered in terms of their contribution to nonperformance educational goals (e.g., growth in consciousness, growth in aesthetic appreciation, moral growth, etc.). Finally, the mastery-learning paradigm assumes that all students are able to achieve mastery *given enough time*.

This pedagogical assumption treats learning as a rationally managed process because sufficient time and resources will guarantee predictable performance. Considerations such as the dialectics of learning, accommodation to individual uniqueness, and the possibility of emergent goals have been factored out of the process. Yet these considerations are essential for learning — even at the level of simple skills.

2. Classroom and School Practices

The mastery-learning paradigm manipulates the *time* allowed for learning and the *quality of instructional stimuli* to help students achieve mastery. It therefore entails the rational planning of classroom time, schedules, organization, and conditions of instruction, as well as the rational design of instructional materials.[24] Such design and planning activities are only called rational to the extent that they are guided by the pragmatics of instructional and organizational theories. They are *not* guided by the pragmatics of classroom teaching.[25] For example, predictability and manageability of process and product are prime considerations, not whether some unique classroom event becomes an occasion for further learning. Hence, the *conception* of instructional events is separate from and directs the *execution* of such events.[26] In this scheme of things, we would expect to evaluate teacher performance (and ultimately administrator and even system performance) in terms of student performance because correct student behavior is the ultimate product. However, I will show later that this in fact serves the system's needs more than the learner's needs.

3. *Instructional Arrangements*

The mastery-learning paradigm follows a number of procedures to guarantee that students will perform at prespecified levels:[27]

a. preinstructional assessment procedures are used to measure the presence or absence of prerequisite knowledge in the learner;
b. initial teaching methods are used to inform the learner of the objectives and prerequisite knowledge;
c. training procedures are used to help the learner acquire the appropriate knowledge and skills;
d. continual assessment procedures are used to ensure the presence or absence of subskills;
e. immediate remediation procedures are used if the subskills are not present; and
f. certification of mastery is added when some predetermined criterion performance is reached by the learner.

One can see from all these techniques that the mastery-learning paradigm conceptualizes the instructional process in quality-control terms. Each step in the paradigm is expressed as a procedure and all instruction is arranged to maximize output. Knowledge is categorized as a hierarchy of prerequisite knowledge such that it becomes illogical to focus on higher-level skills before lower-level skills, and such that higher-level skills are somehow the *sum* of component subskills.

The mastery-learning paradigm described above therefore specifies *what kinds* of things are to be achieved (i.e., measurable performance gains) and *how* these things are to be achieved (i.e., through the manipulation of time and instructional stimuli). Drill-and-practice courseware functions as the training and remediation component within this framework. Although group

[handwritten marginalia: Drill & practice or training or remediation; framework; tends to individualize]

work is permissable within the mastery paradigm, drill-and-practice courseware is usually individualized.

Individualization and Drill-and-Practice Courseware

Individualization can mean many things: e.g., independent study, individual pacing, individual diagnosis, individual educational outcomes.[28] It arises out of the larger recognition that individuals differ from each other.[29] Within computer-based forms of individualized learning, however, it refers to generic outcomes for generic individuals rather than to personal goals for unique individuals.

[handwritten marginalia: define indiv. w/ microcomp]

The philosophy of individualization contains a number of specific assumptions:[30]

1. A belief that each person has a unique set of characteristics or aptitudes that ultimately influence the *rate* at which competent performance in a particular skill is achieved.
2. A belief that a well-defined and well-structured sequence of instructional events will facilitate progress toward preplanned outcomes.
3. A belief that time and quality of instructional materials will influence successful completion of an objective.
4. A belief that student "needs" and characteristics can indicate a readiness for the objectives by the learner.
5. A belief that an evaluation mechanism can be found for *constantly* monitoring the student's progress toward a preplanned outcome (thereby providing data for the instructional system's performance).
6. A shift in the role of the teacher *from* a pedagogical one *toward* an instructional decisionmaking one (e.g., placement of students; selection, use, and allocation of space, time, and materials; data collection and report writing).

[handwritten marginalia: no gradual interaction]

In some systems of individualized learning such as the Keller Plan, students have a great amount of flexibility in setting schedules, getting help from student tutors, and following any number of paths toward a predefined goal.[31] Each of these factors is adjusted for the sake of individual rates of learning. In the Skinnerian version of the philosophy of individualization, on the other hand, instruction is broken down into much smaller units, and instructional events are more controlled and automated.[32]

It is this latter version that is most often seen in drill-and-practice courseware, which overwhelmingly uses rate-of-progress as their major dimension of individualization although they sometimes include level of difficulty. Other dimensions such as cognitive style are often called for but rarely implemented because of the computational complexity involved.[33]

Drill-and-practice courseware programs also break the instructional process into very small steps. They then assess each learner's response and specify a finite number of paths for the learner to follow. They are therefore "individualized" in the narrow sense of allowing individual rates of progress along finite, forced-choice paths that lead to prespecified, measurable outcomes. Because they control both the *presentation of information* as well as the learner's *interactions with that information,* they control the individual's total attention during the time that they are used.

Finally, drill-and-practice courseware programs relegate the teacher to a resource manager or exception handler.[34] This is not to suggest that a teacher is forced by the computer to organize the classroom according to the Skinnerian philosophy of individualization, only that drill-and-practice courseware programs are biased toward such an orientation. In many schools, the shift toward teacher-as-manager has already taken place without the computer.[35]

In many ways, the philosophy of drill-and-practice courseware is consistent with the movement in the curriculum field towards the "technical control" of learning.[36] I will describe this notion under the rubric of the *technological framework* throughout the rest of this chapter. For now, the concept of replicated work will help us begin to understand the concept of *technical control* in courseware.

Courseware as Replicated Work

Victor Bunderson has developed one of the most thorough analyses of the concept of courseware as replicated work.[37] The following discussion expands his analysis.

Computer courseware, he argues, has both a product and a process dimension. As a *product,* courseware consists of the "consumable [materials of instruction] that operate on and with a technologically mediated instructional delivery system." As a *process,* courseware constitutes an "economically replicable and easily portable package that, when used in combination with a technologically mediated insructional delivery system, is capable of performing work related to training and performance improvement."

The instructional delivery system consists of both *the physical objects and structures* "designed to perform or facilitate the work necessary to achieve educational and training goals," and a *human culture* of "traditions, values, and habits that inform and constrain the use of the physical artifacts." All components of the ensemble therefore derive their meaning from the instructional delivery system.

We can see from the description above that the technical structure of the delivery system shapes the form and function of the human culture and the physical artifacts. The technical structure also orients these components towards some external goal (i.e., educational performance) and then tries to maximize the levels of this goal. A technological delivery system will therefore ultimately influence the nature of the classroom culture — unless, of course, the classroom is already organized as a work culture.

The technical structure imposed by courseware allows students only pseudocontrol because they can only choose from a finite number of paths toward a predetermined goal. Bunderson acknowledges this somewhat by saying that "learner-centered will emphasize learner productivity, not necessarily learner control." This restricts the meaning of "individualized learning" to that of "individualized productivity level."

Bunderson continues his discussion of educational work by criticizing the inability of current teacher-centered delivery systems to be more "productive." The teacher-centered culture, he argues, has reached the "limits of [its] improvability." His solution is a technological one: "when education is analyzed into the work that is required, technology is seen as the *only* way to make a fundamental difference." Bunderson's argument is very general and even applies to book-based technology (i.e., a teacher with books can accomplish more than a teacher without books).

By conceiving of the classroom as an instructional delivery system (rather than, say, an instructional setting for the dialectical encounter of mutually respected and unique individuals), Bunderson narrows the debate about what can happen in such a setting. The classroom, in effect, becomes a place for training and development. I mentioned earlier that the mastery-learning paradigm turned the classroom into a work place for both teachers and students. The concept of the classroom as a work place is further compounded by highlighting the work potential of classroom technologies.

When teacher-delivered instruction and technology-delivered instruction are conceptualized in similar terms, computer courseware is then seen as a more efficient mechanism. Observation of certain classrooms containing hierarchical authority, rigid schedules, and mindless workbooks may support Bunderson. But even in such classrooms, students still have some opportunity for personal integration of experiences and skills. They can still integrate their drill-and-practice activities with exploration, planning, negotiation, and collaboration — even if it is done as a subterfuge. These latter characteristics are essential for education.[38] In individualized drill-and-practice courseware, on the other hand, where a student's total time, attention, and interactions are controlled by the computer, such integrations are no longer possible.[39] Is this loss worth the price — even for low levels of learning where only the acquisition of procedural rules is involved?

When we examine the actual characteristics of Bunderson's concept of educational work, we find that they all embody the *extensional* side of education (i.e., the measurable and procedural). According to Bunderson, a teacher

267

presents information, models processes, provides students with trials and feedback, discusses "individual needs" with students, uses affective appeals to motivate learning, trains students how to use the delivery system, assesses student performance, manages the assessed information, and manages classroom interactions. Where, within this analysis, is a teacher's affective and semantic engagement with students beyond maximizing performance gains? All that Bunderson describes are procedural skills and information-processing functions: such functions *can* be carried out more efficiently and effectively by technology (e.g., video, microcomputer, etc.). Efficiency here means maximizing educational productivity at the lowest financial cost. Effectiveness means reliably reproducing the process and the product.[40] In effect, these things are no longer subject to the qualitative criteria of excellence and expertise within a particular subject area but to the quantitative criteria of economics.[41] No wonder teachers cannot compete!

Bunderson's point of view has a fundamental contradiction, however. The rhetoric stresses the "needs" of the individual but the terms of the debate emphasize instructional systems concerns. By shifting the educational interactions away from the intensional logic of interpersonal interactions and toward the extensional logic of procedural skills and information-processing functions, the following criteria are emphasized:

1. *systems efficiency*, maximizing the throughput of students for the time and resources invested rather than developing individual talents;

2. *systems reliability*, emphasizing quality control and replicability of output rather than individual, communal, or cultural diversity; and

3. *systems economy*, "more scholar for the dollar" rather than personally determined pursuit of excellence.

Hence, *only those "individual needs" amenable to systems' logic are served.*

Bunderson's concept of educational work has another contradiction. The very work culture that has to exist in a classroom for a technological instructional system to operate can only come about from intentional human engagement, negotiation, and interaction. Students and teachers are therefore essential and continuous agents in the creation of a classroom work culture.[42] However, the very processes that are required to *produce* the work culture then have to be *denied* because they contradict the technological framework. This is the case because an instructional delivery system embodies a technological culture that tries to shape the human culture to its own ends, whereas human cultures shape their own ends.[43]

This can be seen in the teacher roles that Bunderson believes will predominate in a technological environment: corrector of imperfect and outdated information, illustrator and augmenter of delivered instruction, illustrator and augmenter of the expert algorithms embodied in the instructional system, creator of a technologically acceptable setting, and interpreter of automatically tested and recorded results. Each of these requires insight, understanding, and interpretation on the part of the teacher; yet each reinforces the technological delivery system as the central organizing factor in the classroom. The classroom has thereby been structured as a work place by someone other than the teacher while at the same time requiring the teacher's unacknowledged labor.[44] A simple drill-and-practice courseware program is therefore not all that innocent an aid to teaching in a classroom community.[45] In fact, such programs may ultimately conflict with the nature of teaching because teaching is *more* than a highly rational, decisionmaking affair.[46]

Summary of Drill-and-Practice Courseware

Drill-and-practice courseware programs embody narrow aspects of the mastery-learning paradigm, the philosophy of individualization, and the concepts of educational work and efficiency. They convert the learning process into a form of work that tries to maximize performance-gains, and they restrict the meaning of individualization to rate-of-progress and level-of-difficulty (and ultimately to individualized levels of productivity). Drill-and-practice courseware programs restrict the type of interaction of learner and computer to a decontextualized performance-domain and diminish integration of subskills with higher-level skills. Thus, even though they maximize performance, they may *not* be the best instructional supplement. Finally, drill-and-practice courseware programs are part of a behavioral learning culture that mitigates against nonbehavioral goals. Hence, such programs do not lead to critical thinking or personal empowerment. The question therefore arises whether computer-based *tutorials* have such a potential or whether they simply develop the behaviorally oriented learning philosophy in a more sophisticated way. Many authors have argued that computer-based tutorials do in fact solve some of the limitations of drill-and-practice programs.[47]

Tutorial Computer Programs

Introduction to Tutorial Courseware

Tutorial courseware programs go beyond drill-and-practice approaches in that they are *designed* to "take total responsiblity for instruction" and to contain a "mixed-initiative dialogue."[48] These terms are examined in depth later. Analyzing the nature of "dialogue" in human-computer interactions is a way of analyzing the nature of tutorial programs, because dialogue is often seen as the basic building block for higher levels of learning.[49] Another critical element to be examined is the *type* of "quality-control" procedures used in computer-based tutorials. Other themes uncovered in my analysis of computerized drill-and-practice reemerge in computerized tutorials in a more sophisticated form. This will stand in sharp contrast to the rhetoric about tutorial courseware programs, which claims that such tutorials resemble real conversations and real teaching.[50]

Description and Analysis of Tutorial Courseware

The various types of human-computer interactions in tutorial courseware programs are on-line tests, remedial dialogues, and interactive proofs.

On-line tests are initiated by a computer as part of the tutorial interaction. They compare a model of student performance with a model of expert performance. In simpler tutorials, on-line tests only involve a comparison between student performances and prespecified, content-determined performance-levels.[51] In both cases, on-line tests provide continual diagnoses of students' performances.

An immediate consequence of having on-line tests in computerized tutorials is that the learner is subject to constant quality control. This does not seem unreasonable because, in interpersonal interactions, humans also check out their inferences about each other.[52] Why should a computer not do the same? Yet, in interpersonal dialogues, such monitoring takes place in the context of semantic engagement and conjoint intentions; in human-computer interactions, such monitoring is guided by an external agent's (i.e., author, instructional designer, or programmer) intentions, which are fixed *for the duration of the interaction.* These external intentions establish preset, non-negotiable, and measurable performance outcomes *for the learner.* Constant monitoring is therefore not intended to understand the learner and his or her messages (as in interpersonal dialogue) but rather intended to guarantee a behavioral outcome. In drill-and-practice courseware, this was rather obvious. In "mixed-initiative" computer "dialogues," this is not always so evident.

The constancy and immediacy of diagnosis and feedback in on-line tests has several other consequences:

1. It emphasizes accretion learning because the computer is looking for evidence of normal progress towards a prespecified goal. This discourages "messing around" with the subject matter: "messing around behavior" is not evidence that a learner is building towards a quantum leap of understanding.[53]

2. It tends to focus learning on *generic* means in spite of the fact that tutorials are individualized. The computer, in effect, *controls the means as well as the ends* and constitutes a powerful "other" that structures and dominates the entire interaction.[54]

   In interpersonal interactions, learning tends to focus on the ends-in-view and not on the means.[55] Learning here incorporates personally constructed means and meanings, something preempted in on-line tests. This is not to suggest that human teachers cannot dominate an interaction with a learner but only that learners have the opportunity to develop personal ways to reach a particular goal.

3. It tends to accelerate the learning process because it creates a set of temporal expectations where rate-of-learning is the major dimension of individualization, and faster rates increase the efficiency of the system. This, in turn, biases the tutorial interaction *against* reflectiveness and critical thinking.[56] Some courseware authors have suggested that this bias can be countered by using "individualized" wait loops in the programs.[57] However, reflectiveness is *not* a matter of waiting longer.

Remedial dialogues are initiated by the computer when the learner's performance does not match some prespecified performance-criteria.[58] They assume that the student already knows the area and can work with the information presented. This also parallels what happens in interpersonal dialogues but with some very important distinctions:

1. In interpersonal tutorials, remedial dialogues are initiated by a teacher on the basis of his or her tacit knowledge about the unique characteristics of the learner. The teacher tries to understand the learner's state of mind by "thinking like the student" in order to unravel the student's conceptual bind or misunderstanding. This is a unique, constructive, and intentional act of empathy and engagement by the teacher and *only nominally entails the student's behaviors.*

2. In human-computer tutorials, remedial "dialogues" are initiated on the basis of a set of explicit and procedural models (expert or content-related algorithms).[59] The tutorial courseware program, in effect, constitutes a generic, rule-driven process that engages an internal, *generic* model of the learner. The actual human agent (i.e., student) in this "dialogue" only provides the data for the computer's formal, generic model of the learner. Remedial "dialogues" therefore do not involve *this* student but rather this *type* of student.

Interactive proofs are a type of computer-based tutorial that permit the learner to make decisions beyond a predefined set of choices.[60] Hence, students can ask for information, work through a variety of examples that embody some concept, and even construct their own models of the problem. However, the very nature of the computing environment still constrains the terms of the debate. The best examples of interactive proofs usually come from mathematics and science where the nature of the content parallels the nature of the computing environment. Of course, even nonmathematical

271

subject areas can be reformulated to be amenable to interactive proofs. Hence, the socio-political problem of hunger can be recast into economic terms and then reduced to a set of formulae that relate an arbitrarily chosen set of variables. The interactive "proof" then proceeds *as if* it were a mathematical problem, treating a problem such as hunger as if it were a computerized numbers game or an "artificial" reality.

Human-Computer "Dialogues" in Tutorial Courseware

The central assumption of computer-based tutorials is that human-computer "dialogues" should resemble interpersonal conversations. Bork has modified this claim somewhat by saying that the student is really conducting a dialogue with the author of the computer tutorial rather than with the computer itself, but this is a facile reformulation. Bork also admits that the author of a computer tutorial is trying to manipulate the student by "stimulat[ing] meaningful responses which contribute to learning."[61] Hence, human-computer "dialogues" are a form of behavioral technology where dialogic interactions are controlled by an author who is *not part of the actual interaction*. Student responses are only meaningful in light of their contribution to educational performance. The actual confrontations between humans and computers are, therefore, one-sided affairs because the computers have fixed-goal structures, interactive strategies, and deductive capabilities.

What *should* human-computer interactions in a tutorial be called? To answer this, we must compare them with interpersonal interactions. Interpersonal dialogues contain an essential component of *conjoint control* (in spite of the power differentials that may exist between students and teachers). In human-computer "dialogues," however, students only control the *rate* (i.e., pacing of predefined sequences), *route* (i.e., any one of a finite number of predefined, or algorithmically-constrained, paths towards a predefined goal), and *timing* (i.e., speed of individual responses). All other control resides in the courseware program, leaving students with a form of pseudocontrol because the actual interaction follows a preplanned, goal-oriented, procedural network. Hence, human-computer tutorial interactions are best called *"utilogs"* rather than "dialogues."[62] Of course, utility here is defined by a courseware author who in turn is restricted to certain categories within the technological framework.[63]

The deeper implications of having interactions in a computer tutorial shaped by the external intentions of an author are summarized below.

1. Humans Are Treated as Data-Based, Rule-Following, Symbol-Manipulating Information-Processors

This implication emerges from the nature of the computer technology used to carry out the actual tutorial interactions. Machine processes can only

272

operate on explicit information according to algorithmic rules. Computers cannot semantically or affectively engage human beings. Humans therefore have to adapt to the *nature* of the computational environment, although within that framework, computer processes can be designed to adapt to the "individual differences" of humans.

Recall that computers only engage *data* from an individual, not the actual person. This data is organized by the program into a model of the learner (in simpler programs, this is merely a data-base of variables and values). The particular model of an individual that the program contains (or builds up) always remains a formal and abstract *type*. Furthermore, this model is a *means* for the computer to carry out the interaction. The human is therefore treated by the computer as a *generic type* and a *means* to an end. This has serious implications for education.

Because human beings develop personal intellectual agency through dialogic interactions,[64] the learner in computer-based tutorial interactions can *never* develop such agency. Furthermore, human beings tend to model the "other" in dialogic interactions,[65] so that computer-based tutorials may actually teach students to treat other dialogic partners as *anthropomorphized processes* and *means* rather than as ends.

In interpersonal dialogic interactions, on the other hand, persons encounter, confront, accept (to a greater or lesser degree), and engage each other as unique individuals. The person in interpersonal dialogues is therefore a *unique ontological entity* (rather than a generic type) and an *end* (rather than a means). This sets the stage for personal agency in learning. Interpersonal dialogue can, of course, become mechanical if the humans involved act on the basis of some stereotypical image about each other. However, the potential for true discourse is *always* present in interpersonal interactions. This potential can *never* exist in human-computer interactions.[66]

Viewing humans as rule-following information-processors (as opposed to individuals with unique intentionalities) legitimizes uniform educational goals, methods, and outcomes. Uniformity in education is enforced not only because the instructional systems attempt to shape a uniform product (i.e., prespecified learning outcomes) but also because the very conceptualization of the individual places "semantic and syntactical constraints on acceptable language for the discussion of human beings."[67] This, in turn, makes expressing and legitimizing other conceptions of human beings, educational goals, and methods outside of the technological framework impossible.[68] A simple example of an alternative framework can make this clear.

In order to create a community and carry out community action, we must:[69] (a) unconditionally accept individual uniqueness and diversity; (b) carry out an on-going dialectical synthesis of opposing viewpoints with the actual members of the community; and, (c) respect emergent community goals. The technological framework, on the other hand, builds on the generic characteristics of individuals, a means-ends rationality, and a predetermined set of performance goals. The two opposing sets of assumptions cannot be balanced.

2. Machine Processes Will Eventually Match Human Processes

This second implication derives from the first implication: if humans are ultimately rule-following information-processors, then computers will eventually do everything that humans can do. Human-computer interactions will then in fact become dialogues because both sides of the interaction will have identical ontological status.

This statement has some serious implications for education, even if we only restrict ourselves to the cognitive domain. If we as educators accept the responsibility for the growth of young minds, then we are obligated to ask how such minds do in fact grow. Furthermore, if we find that mental development at all levels requires a dialectical synthesis of personally and socially constructed meanings, then we can see that the very ontology of the technological framework (i.e., the world is made up of specifiable and controllable processes) is inadequate for the whole domain of intentions and interpersonal meanings. *Machine processes*, in this case, *will never replace interpersonal interactions!*

Finally, if we find that human skills and knowledge are ultimately based on tacit beliefs and judgments that cannot be analyzed into components, then computational processes (which by their nature reduce similarity *judgments* to computable comparisons of component identities) will never match human processes.[70]

3. Education Will Be Viewed as a Form of Training and Be Subject to Explicit, Extensional Logic

Having an expert author design the goals, rules, and messages for a human-computer interaction means that the logic of prediction and control (the technological framework) is applied to developing preplanned performance outcomes. The whole educational enterprise is then reduced to a means-ends rationality because the ends are specified first and then the most efficient means are employed to guarantee a quality product. The resulting mechanization of interaction is sometimes hard to see when computers carry out the actual interaction because of the sophistication, speed, and variety of media involved. But we should never confuse sophisticated technique with sophisticated instruction.[71] Technique does not have a tacit dimension whereas all human knowledge and learning does.[72] Technique is solely subject to extensional logic whereas knowledge is subject to *both* intentional and extensional logic.

We can see the implications of computer-based tutorial interactions for

274

education most clearly when we examine the nature of experiential learning within the technological and nontechnological frameworks[73] This statement can be explored by comparing the following notions: the nature of experience, events, and activities; the concept of individual; the methods of knowledge; and, the types of thinking involved.

When restricted to a computational environment, "experiences" take on the form of puzzles *of the same type* (i.e., declarative, quantifiable, procedural). Events are nonhistorical because they are reversible and activities are restricted to a nondialectical logic (i.e., formal operations).[74] Furthermore, an individual is only trivially unique (i.e., the variables of a student model in the computer are generic, only the *values* of the variables are unique). Finally, an individual only needs the ability to decode abstract symbols because the "text" and "context" are predetermined by an external agent, and because knowledge is expressed in an explicit, abstract form. Critical and dialectical thinking are not needed because they make too many things problematical, ambiguous, and noncontrollable.

In a natural environment, on the other hand, "experiences" are made up of indefinite *types*. Events are ambiguous, historical, and irreversible.[75] Activity involves a confrontation between persons and events, and meanings are personally and interpersonally constructed. Experiences and actions are dialectical and historical. Furthermore, natural experiences entail an accommodation to, and assimilation of, an indefinite variety of uniqueness in persons, ideas, and events. These, in turn, become the experiential basis for further critical and dialectical thinking. Finally, individuals need interpretive as well as decoding skills because they are forced to construct as well as deconstruct the meanings-in-use of others.[76] Interpersonal dialogue plays a central role here because knowledge is dialectical, historical, and subject to transformation.

In brief, the technological framework places tremendous restrictions on the variety of educational experiences. Computer-based tutorials therefore seem to rule out everything that is of value in the natural and social worlds.

Summary of Tutorial Courseware Programs

Tutorial courseware does go beyond drill-and-practice because it is a more sophisticated form of interaction, but it also stays well within the bounds of the behavioral and technological framework. Behavioral outcomes are still prespecified by expert agents outside of the actual interaction, quality-control procedures are still used to guarantee that the learner will reach the intended outcomes, and learners are still only given a form of pseudo-control (i.e., rate, route, and timing). Furthermore, though the interaction is less rigid, it is still constrained by an explicit algorithm, is still focused on maximizing educational performance-gains, and still treats the learner as a means toward someone else's end. Computer-based tutorial interactions, therefore, provide an artificial "other" that preempts personal intellectual agency and ultimately inner-directed learning. Computer-based tutorials are also biased against experiential learning outside of the technological framework, quantum leaps in learning, and reflective thinking. Their value in education is therefore very limited.

A question now arises about using computers as "intellectual tools." Does *this* use of computers go beyond the limitations discussed so far? On first reflection, personal intellectual agency seems to be a natural concomitant of the "tool" use of computers, but this conclusion requires a careful analysis.

Computers as Intellectual Tools

Introduction to the Intellectual Dimension of Computers

What are the intellectual dimensions, if any, of computers? To answer this question, we must not focus on the computer as a personal productivity tool (e.g., word processor) but rather as an "object to think with."[77] This brings me into the realm of computer languages and simulations.

Thus far, I have described the way drill-and-practice and tutorial courseware programs introduce a means-end rationality into the learning process. Knowledge acquisition and skill building (the terms themselves are revealing) become subject to efficiency and performance criteria, and learning becomes a systematically designed and rationally managed process. Does such a situation apply to the case where the learner programs his or her own solutions to problems?[78] Surely here we will not see the means-ends rationality of an external agent conceptualizing, designing, and managing the learning process. After all, the *learner* is now in control of the whole process!

Can the student who controls the computer go beyond the technological framework of the computer (the values associated with the computer and the symbol systems that can be manipulated by the computer)? Tools tend to insist that they be used in certain ways and intellectual tools tend to define the user's mental landscape.[79] Computational intellectual tools (i.e., computer programming and simulations) therefore bias our ways of knowing toward the quantitative, declarative, and procedural kinds of knowledge, hiding other kinds of knowledge.

The Computer as an Intellectual Problem-Solving Tool

A computer is basically a box that manipulates symbols (and information) according to a plan. When someone else writes the plan, we are forced to follow his or her set of procedures. When we write the plan, we are forced to use the computer's language. In both cases, we are confronted with a question about the nature of the plans and the types of symbols that the computer can manipulate. We therefore need to explore how programming a problem in a computer language helps us learn and think about that problem.

The symbols a computer manipulates are actually only energy states in an electronic machine which are transformed according to formal, algorithmic rules. Even if a computer manipulates two high-level representational constructs such as "All men are mortal," plus "Socrates is a man," and ends up with, "Therefore Socrates is a mortal," it only manipulates semantically empty energy states (which we call input or data or symbols) according to syntactical rules — regardless how high-level those rules. It is *we* who actively construct and ascribe meaning. A computer language is therefore *not* a language in the traditional sense of the term (i.e., expressive, intentional, and connotative as well as denotative and based on qualitative knowing) but rather a set of syntactical notations to control computer operations.[80] Hence, *a computer's expressive potential only extends over the syntactical dimension of its formal operations.* Of course, for those who equate cognition with computation, the expressive potential of computer languages extends into the semantic domain because "all relevant semantic distinctions [are] mirrored by syntactic distinctions."[81]

Clearly, if humans are going to use computers as intellectual tools, then they must work within the epistemological limitations of these tools.[82] Because computers can only manipulate explicit data and symbols according to formal, syntactical rules, they tend to legitimize those types of knowledge that fit into their framework and delegitimize other types of knowledge.[83]

Hence, computers tend to *legitimize* the following characteristics of knowledge:[84] rule-governed order, objective systematicity, explicit clarity, nonambiguity, nonredundancy, internal consistency, noncontradiction (i.e., logic of the excluded middle), and quantitative aspects. They also tend to legitimize deduction and induction as the only acceptable epistemological methods.

By way of contrast, computers tend to *delegitimize* the following characteristics of knowledge: emergent goals, self-constructed order, organic systematicity, connotation and tacitness, ambiguity, redundancy, dialectical rationality, simultaneity of multiple logics, and qualitative aspects. Finally, they tend to delegitimize the following epistemological methods: abduction, interpretation, intuition, introspection, and dialectical synthesis of multiple and contradictory realities.

The more computers are used as intellectual tools, therefore, the more we rely on the formal characteristics of knowledge and the less we rely on the tacit and interpretative dimensions of knowledge. It is almost as if the technological framework is not only incompatible with other ways of knowing, but inevitably excludes them from our mental landscape as well. Of course, the formal and the tacit dimensions of knowledge can never be separated from each other.[85] The tacit dimension can only become hidden.

Thus, we return to an earlier conclusion: computers force us to act *as if* we were rule-governed information-processors. They also force us to construe thinking as "'cognitive problem-solving' where the 'solutions' are arrived at by formal calculation, computation, and rational analysis."[86] Even if we are active and constructive and intuitive in our approach to the world, we must still analyze and reduce problems into explicit and procedural terms. The concept of the computer as an intellectual tool is therefore *not* a neutral formulation because it forces us to objectify ourselves as agents of prediction, calculation, and control. Personal intellectual agency has thereby been limited to the technological framework.

Computer Programming and Computer Simulations

We can easily see how programming is a paradigm of *thinking* in the context of the tool use of computers. If the only legitimate knowledge entails objective facts, explicit representations of facts as data, and formal operations on these representations, then programming is the ideal way to process such knowledge. The same can be said of programming as a paradigm for *learning*. If the only way to think about things is through analysis and procedural debugging, then programming is also the ideal way to *learn* how to deal with the world. After all, we are not just learning to act *as if* we were computers, we are developing operational and representational cognitive structures to deal with *any* aspect of the world! Gone are aesthetic, metaphoric, artistic, affective, interpretive, and moral structures for dealing with the world!

We can, therefore, understand how many of the chief advocates of the tool use of computers see computer literacy as the ability to "do computing"[87] and see computer programming as the best way to shape a child's cognitive development.[88] However, in this scheme of things, we can also see that our rational life is thereby reduced to a set of operational, problem-solving skills—to say nothing about our emotional life.

Is there anything positive to be gained from programming aside from the actual technical skills? In several studies, very little positive transfer was found from programming to other domains of cognitive problem-solving.[89] However, this conclusion is only tentative because the field is still new.[90] We must therefore fall back on an analysis of the nature of programming in order to see what is possible with this approach.

Computing, as Arthur Luehrmann, one of the chief advocates of programming, argues,

> belongs as a regular school subject for the same reason as reading, writing, and mathematics. Each gives the student a basic intellectual tool with wide areas of

application. Each gives the student a distinctive means of thinking about and representing a problem, of writing his or her thoughts down, of studying and criticizing the thoughts of others, whether they are embodied in a paragraph of English, a set of mathematical equations, or a computer program. Students need practice and instruction in all these basic modes of expressing and communicating ideas.[91]

This certainly is an admirable statement because it integrates computing (algorithmic, procedural thinking) into the other "basics" of education (i.e., reading, writing, and arithmetic). Luehrmann's argument also casts programming as an aid to understanding.

What grounds exist for objecting to programming as a school subject? The answer applies to other "distinctive means of thinking and representing a problem": whenever technique is emphasized over grappling with content, then the innermost principles of that content are lost.[92] This is especially true for computer programming because the computer is an instrument of technique *par excellence*. It can *only* manipulate content-free symbols according to formal procedures. Hence, although computer programming may force one to structure *information* in precise and systematic ways and carry out *logical operations* on abstract representations of that information, it tells us *nothing* about *what* information should be treated in this way nor about the *nature* of the real world. A simple computer-simulation example should make this clear. The same argument applies to programming the simulation.

Oregon Trail is a popular computer simulation that records the problems faced by pioneers crossing the American frontier.[93] It provides a simplified environment for elementary school children where they can make decisions and watch the consequences of their "actions." For example, forgetting to "buy" enough bullets leads to the "death" of the settlers. A student can "win" if he or she keeps a careful record of the "purchases" and analyzes the relationships between events, supplies, and mileage. Yet this is a quantitative, artificial reality with no hint of the lived reality. The simulation, in fact, represents an abstract world of algorithmic logic. Historical logic is incapable of being represented. It would be more justifiable to say that winning here (i.e., solving the problem) is more the result of looking for patterns among the numbers than developing a sense of history. *The simulation is simply a well-disguised numbers game.*

One might object to the foregoing discussion on a number of grounds:

1. The algorithmic logic of simulations does in fact parallel a similar logic in *some* content areas (such as mathematics) so that computer simulations have a place in education.
2. All learning proceeds from the known to the unknown (and from the simple to the complex) so that simulations are a stepping stone to life.

279

3. Persons can learn to become autonomous inquirers within the limitations of a safe and simple artificial reality—a skill that they can later use in real life.

Each of these objections has an intuitive appeal and therefore warrants our attention.

The first objection is easy to handle. It is certainly the case that many real-world activities contain the same logical and procedural structure that is found in the realm of computation. Learning to subtract can be modelled in a computer program because procedural rules are all there is to the *process* of subtraction. But does it tell you about the *reasons* for subtracting?

Brown and Burton have developed an "intelligent" computer tutor that recognizes more than 90 ways to make a mistake during subtraction.[94] This is certainly a very sophisticated approach and may be very useful in some cases. However, it only elaborates the procedures surrounding subtraction. A logical positivist would say: fine, that's all there is to subtraction. A trainer might also say: fine, this will help establish the automaticity of the subtraction skill more efficiently. But an educator would say: wait a minute—subtraction is not an isolated, decontextualized skill. At a minimum, it should lead to competence in *using* subtraction with real-world problems. At a maximum, it should lead to mathematical understanding. In both cases, it should be connected to experiences that ultimately generate personal expertise, involving judgments as well as calculations. As Dreyfus and Dreyfus conclude,

> at the higher stages of skill acquisition, even if there are rules underlying expertise, the rules that the expert has access to are not the rules that generate his expertise . . . [Hence], trying to find rules or procedures in a domain often stands in the way of learning *even at the earliest stages.*[95] (Emphasis added.)

Developing procedure-following skills, therefore, does *not* facilitate broader learning. This argument applies even more for nonprocedural kinds of expertise and understanding (e.g., historical expertise and understanding).

The second objection is more difficult to handle: all learning proceeds from the known to the unknown and from the simple to the complex. But we have to define simple in a way that does not prejudge the *nature* of the complex. This problem is a perennial concern in the philosophy of science: should we base our scientific concepts on our intuitions and lived experiences, or should we base them on counterintuitive conceptual constructions that happen to fit empirical facts?[96] This problem emerges in education in a number of forms. For example, in science education, should we teach young children to be Aristotelians before Newtonians—let alone, before Einsteinians?[97]

In the context of this discussion, is a simple, context-free, quantitative, and procedural simulation *ever* an adequate preparation for a complex, contextual, qualitative, and nonprocedural lived-experience?[98] If we wanted to prepare children to understand and deal with the real world, should we not develop simple learning situations *of the same kind* as those they will later encounter in a more complex form? Is not problem-solving, in fact, domain-specific regardless how high-level the activity?[99] Using computers to develop problem-solving skills, however, establishes a dichotomy between "*simple* artificial reality" and "*complex* natural reality." Notice that the *artificial-natural* dimension of the above dichotomy is usually hidden in the debate on the matter.[100] Learning to program the computer may therefore *not* be the best way to prepare children for real life.

The final objection is the most difficult to answer: can persons develop analytical and inquiry skills within the limitations of a computational environment that can then be used in real life? After all, analytical and inquiry skills are very general and more like "frames of mind" than simple procedures.[101] The question can be reformulated, however, to reveal what has been hidden: are the analytical and inquiry skills developed within a noncontextual, nondialectical, and judgment-free computational environment useful within a lived environment that requires tolerance for ambiguity, interpersonal construction of new meanings, dialectical thinking, the acceptability of incomplete solutions, and judgment-based actions? A positive answer is now doubtful. The reason is twofold: the computer embodies a technological framework that crowds out other forms of conceptualizing and understanding problems; yet thinking is only ever thinking *about* something. Hence, mature analysis and inquiry can only be the result of a history of dealing with similar *kinds* of things. Flight simulators work so well for this reason — both the simulation and the real-world event are controlled by the same kinds of procedures.

A final answer to the third objection remains to be seen. It does seem, however, that the computer restricts our rational life to utilitarian, problem-solving skills. Although such skills are under our control, they have delegitimized other ways of knowing. Saying that such skills display "intelligence" does not help either because intelligence itself has been redefined in a restricted manner. As Broughton laments,

one can measure the educational impact of computers, and particularly of learning to program them, in terms of what is lost in the process. To the curriculum is lost the arts and the humanities. To pedagogy is lost the hermeneutic art and language that allows us to ask about the meaning of things and of life, to interpret them in their many and various cultural horizons. To both is lost the self and the autonomous capacity to examine critically what we interpret.[102]

Hence, although problem-solving with a computer appears more desirable and high-level than computerized drill-and-practice, programming still limits us to the technological framework. It is, therefore, a more subtle form of behavioral learning technology, done with the active consent and participation of the learner. It represents, as one author has called it, the "industrialization of intellectual work."[103] This is particularly disturbing because programming (as well as drill-and-practice and tutorial courseware) is being introduced to children in their most plastic and formative years.[104]

Summary of Computers as Intellectual Tools

Computers do help us develop a limited personal intellectual agency by forcing us to structure information in precise, systematic ways and specify logical operations for that information. However, this agency only develops within the computational domain. Hence, we are left with an underdeveloped intellectual agency within the qualitative, dialectical, and experiential domain of natural and social events. Learning to program is therefore only a good way to learn and think about procedural problems — although even here there are some limitations.

The root of the difficulty seems to reside in the nature of computer languages: the expressive potential of computer languages only extends over the syntactical dimension of computer operations. This contrasts sharply with the expressive potential of natural languages which extend over the aesthetic, metaphoric, artistic, affective, and moral domains. Why cannot these various languages coexist? The answer boils down to this: computer languages are part of a technological framework that, when applied to a number of problems, delegitimizes other frameworks. We are then left with a very restricted mental landscape.

Conclusion

Each of the three major approaches to the use of computers in education has serious limitations. The drill-and-practice approach was shown to embody a deterministic, behavioral technology that turned learning into a systematically designed and quality controlled form of work. Although intended only to supplement instruction, they, in fact, introduced a technological framework into the classroom culture that mitigated against nonbehavioral educational goals. Computerized tutorial programs were shown to extend these limitations. That is, interactions in tutorial courseware programs are still shaped by an external agent's intentions and still constrained by computable algorithms. Furthermore, the human learner is treated as a means towards someone else's ends and only given a form of pseudocontrol in the interaction. Most seriously, computerized tutorial interactions preempted personal intellectual agency and ultimately inner-directed learning. Finally, the use of computer programming and simulations in education was shown to limit the learner's mental landscape to objective, quantitative, declarative, and procedural intellectual tools. This left the learner with an underdeveloped intellectual agency within the qualitative, dialectical, and experiential domains of natural and social events.

Each of the approaches described above may have some short-term benefits associated with it. Taken together, however, they represent a shift towards technologizing education. Drill-and-practice courseware programs alter the nature of subskill acquisition, tutorial courseware programs restrict the full range of personal intellectual agency, and computer programming and simulations delegitimize nontechnological ways of learning and thinking about problems. Is this worth the price?

Notes

1. Henry J. Becker, *School Uses of Microcomputers: Reports from a National Survey* (Baltimore, Md.: Center for Social Organization of Schools, Johns Hopkins University, 1983, 1985).

2. Michael W. Apple, *Education and Power* (Boston: Routledge & Kegan Paul, 1982).

3. Andrew R. Molnar, "The Next Great Crisis in American Education: Computer Literacy," *Journal of Educational Technology Systems*, Vol. 7 (1972).

4. Douglas Sloan, "On Raising Critical Questions About the Computer in Education," *Teachers College Record*, Vol. 85, 4(1984).

5. Jurgen Habermas, *The Theory of Communicative Action. Vol. 1. Reason and the Rationalization of Society* (Boston: Beacon Press, 1984).

6. Walter J. Ong, *Orality and Literacy: The Technologizing of the Word* (New York: Methuen, 1982).

7. Peter L. Berger and Thomas Luckmann, *The Social Construction of Reality* (New York: Doubleday, 1966).

8. Maxine Greene, "Literacy for What?" *Phi Delta Kappan*, Vol. 63, 5(1982).

9. Theodore Roszak, *The Cult of Information* (New York: Pantheon, 1986).

10. Hans G. Furth, *Piaget and Knowledge: Theoretical Foundations* (Englewood Cliffs, N. J.: Prentice-Hall, 1969).

11. Alfred North Whitehead, *The Aims of Education and Other Essays* (New York: Free Press, 1967).

12. Kurt Godel, *On Formally Undecidable Propositions in "Principia Mathematica" and Related Systems*, R. B. Braithwaite, ed., B. Meltzer, trans. (New York: Basic Books, 1962).

13. Michael W. Apple, "The Adequacy of Systems Management Procedures in Education," in Ralph A. Smith, ed., *Regaining Educational Leadership* (New York: John Wiley & Sons, 1975).

14. Jacques Ellul, "The Power of Technique and the Ethics of Non-Power," in Kathleen Woodward, ed., *The Myths of Information* (Madison, Wisc.: Coda Press, 1980).

15. Ann Berlak and Harold Berlak, *The Dilemmas of Schooling* (New York: Methuen, 1981).

16. Patrick Suppes, "The Uses of Computers in Education," *Scientific American*, Vol. 215, 3(1966).

17. David F. Salisbury, "Cognitive Psychology and Its Implications for Designing Drill-and-Practice Programs for Computers," presented at the annual meeting of the *American Educational Research Association*, New Orleans, April 1984.

18. Robert M. Gagne, Walter Wagner, and A. Rojas, "Planning and Authorizing Computer-Assisted Instruction Lessons," *Educational Technology*, Vol. 21 (1981).

19. J. Richard Dennis, "The Question-Episode: Building Block of Teaching with a Computer," *The Illinois Series on Educational Applications of Computers*, Vol. 4e (Urbana, Ill.: College of Education, The University of Illinois, 1979).

20. B. F. Skinner, *The Technology of Teaching* (Englewood Cliffs, N. J.: Prentice-Hall, 1968).

21. Hubert L. Dreyfus and Stuart E. Dreyfus, "Putting Computers in Their Proper Place: Intuition in the Classroom," *Teachers College Record*, Vol. 85, 4(1984).

22. Benjamin S. Bloom, *Human Characteristics and School Learning* (New York: McGraw-Hill, 1976).

23. Robert Barr and Robert Dreeben, "Instruction in Classrooms," in Lee Shulman, ed., *Review of Research in Education*, Vol. 5 (Ithaca, Ill.: F. E. Peacock, 1978).

24. Ted Nunan, *Countering Educational Design* (New York: Nichols Publishing, 1983).

25. Harry F. Wolcott, *Teachers Versus Technocrats* (Eugene, Ore.: University of Oregon Press, 1977).

26. Apple, *Education and Power, op. cit.*

27. Bloom, *op. cit.*

28. J. O. Bolvin, "Classroom Organization," in Harold E. Mitzel, ed., *Encyclopedia of Educational Research*, 5th Edition, Vol. 1 (New York: Macmillan, 1982).

29. Lee J. Cronbach and Richard E. Snow, *Aptitudes and Instructional Methods* (New York: Irvington, 1977).

30. Steven Lukes, *Individualism* (Oxford: Basil Blackwell, 1973).

31. Fred S. Keller, "Goodbye, Teacher," *Journal of Applied Behavior Analysis*, Vol. 1, 1(1968).

32. Skinner, *op. cit.*

33. Michael Scriven, "Problems and Prospects for Individualization," in Harriet Talmadge, ed., *Systems of Individualized Education* (Berkeley, Calif.: McCutchan Publishing Corporation, 1975).

34. G. M. Boyd, "Four Ways of Providing Computer-Assisted Learning and Their Probable Impacts,"*Computers and Education*, Vol. 6 (1983).

35. Raymond E. Callahan, *Education and The Cult of Efficiency* (Chicago: University of Chicago Press, 1962).

36. Dennis L. Carlson, "'Updating' Individualism and the Work Ethic: Corporate Logic in the Classroom," *Curriculum Inquiry*, Vo. 12, 2(1982).

37. Victor Bunderson, "Courseware," in Harold F. O'Neil Jr., ed., *Computer-Based Instruction: A State of the Art Assessment* (New York: Academic Press, 1981).

38. David A. Kolb, *Experiental Learning: Experience As the Source of Learning and Development* (Englewood Cliffs, N. J.: Prentice-Hall, 1984).

39. Dreyfus and Dreyfus, *op. cit.*

40. Bunderson, *op. cit.*

41. Elliot W. Eisner, *The Educational Imagination* (New York: Macmillan, 1979).

42. Seymour B. Sarason, *The Culture of the School and the Problem of Change*, second edition (Boston: Allyn and Bacon, 1982).

43. Nunan, *op. cit.*

44. Wolcott, *op. cit.*

45. Kenneth D. Benne,"Technology and Community: Conflicting Bases of Educational Authority," in Walter Feinberg and Henry Rosemont, Jr., eds., *Work, Technology, and Education* (Urbana, Ill.: University of Illinois Press, 1975).

46. Philip W. Jackson, *Life in Classrooms* (New York: Holt, Rinehart, & Winston, 1968).

47. Harold F. O'Neil Jr., and J. Paris, "Introduction and Overview of Computer-Based Instruction," in O'Neil, *op. cit.*

48. Alfred Bork, "Interactive Learning," in Robert Taylor, ed., *The Computer in the School* (New York: Teachers College Press, 1980).

49. Paulo Freire, *Education for Critical Consciousness* (New York: Seabury Press, 1973).

50. Alfred Bork, "Preparing Student-Computer Dialogs: Advice to Teachers," in Taylor, *op. cit.*

51. Tim O'Shea and John Self, *Learning and Teaching with Computers* (Englewood Cliffs, N. J.: Prentice-Hall, 1983).

52. Richard Nisbett and Lee Ross, *Human Inference: Strategies and Shortcomings of Social Judgement.* (Englewood Cliffs, N. J.: Prentice-Hall, 1980).

53. David Hawkins, *The Informed Vision* (New York: Agathon Press, 1974).

54. Sherry Turkle, *The Second Self* (New York: Simon and Schuster, 1984).

55. Maxine Greene, *Landscapes of Learning* (New York: Teachers College Press, 1978).

56. Ira Shor, *Critical Teaching and Everyday Life* (Boston: South End Press, 1980).

57. Ben Shneiderman, *Software Psychology* (Cambridge, Mass.: Winthrop, 1980).

58. Bork, "Preparing Student-Computer Dialogs," *op. cit.*

59. O'Shea and Self, *op. cit.*

60. Bork, "Preparing Student-Computer Dialogs," *op. cit.*

61. *Ibid.*

62. Shneiderman, *op. cit.*

63. Jacques Ellul, *The Technological System* (New York: Continuum, 1980).

64. Maxine Greene, "The Literacy that Liberates," Tape No. 612–20312. *Association for Supervision and Curriculum Development* (Alexandria, Va.: 1983).

65. Karl E. Scheibe and Margaret Erwin, "The Computer as Alter," *Journal of Social Psychology*, Vol. 108 (1979).

66. Joseph Weizenbaum, *Computer Power and Human Reason* (San Francisco: W. H. Freeman, 1976).

67. Kenneth A. Strike, "On the Expressive Potential of Behaviorist Langauge," *American Educational Research Journal*, Vol. 11, 2(1974).

68. Ellul, *The Technological System, op. cit.*

69. Fred Newmann and Donald Oliver, "Education and Community," *Harvard Educational Review*, Vol. 37, 1(1967).

70. Hubert L. Dreyfus, *What Computers Can't Do*, second edition (New York: Harper & Row, 1979).

71. Marianne Amarel, "The Classroom: An Instructional Setting for Teachers, Students, and the Computer," in Alex C. Wilkinson, ed., *Classroom Computers and Cognitive Science* (New York: Academic Press, 1983).

72. Michael Polanyi, *The Tacit Dimension* (Garden City, N.J.: Doubleday, 1966).

73. Kolb, *op. cit.*

74. Myron Krueger, *Artificial Reality* (Reading, Mass.: Addison-Wesley, 1983).

75. Whitehead, *op. cit.*

76. Greene, *Landscapes of Learning, op. cit.*

77. Seymour Papert, *Mindstorms* (New York: Basic Books, 1980).

78. Margot Critchfield, "Beyond CAI: Computers as Personal Intellectual Tools," *Educational Technology*, Vol. 19, 10(1979).

79. Jerome S. Bruner, "Language As an Instrument of Thought," in Alan Davies, ed., *Problems of Language and Learning* (London: Heineman, 1975).

80. K. Iverson, "Notation as a Tool for Thought," *Communications of the ACM*, 23 (1980).

81. Zenon W. Pylyshyn, *Computation and Cognition* (Cambridge, Mass.: M.I.T. Press, 1984).

82. Abbe Mowshowitz, *The Conquest of Will* (Reading, Mass.: Addison-Wesley, 1976).

83. Strike, *op. cit.*

84.. James M. Broughton, "Computer Literacy as Political Socialization," presented at the annual meeting of the American Educational Research Association, New Orleans, April, 1984.

85. Polanyi, *op. cit.*

86.. Broughton, *op. cit.*

87. Arthur Luehrmann, "Computer Literacy: What Should It Be?" *Mathematics Teacher*, Vol. 74, 9(1981).

88. Papert, *op. cit.*

89. R. D. Pea and D. M. Kurland, "On the Cognitive Effects of Learning Computer Programming," *Bank Street Technical Report #18* (New York: Bank Street College, 1983).

90. Marion C. Linn, "The Cognitive Consequences of Programming Instruction in Classrooms," *Educational Researcher*, Vol. 14, 5(1985).

91. Luehrmann, *op. cit.*

92. A. P. Ershov, "Aesthetics and the Human Factor in Programming," *Datamation*, Vol. 18, 9(1981).

93. David Grady, "What Every Teacher Should Know About Computer Simulations," *Learning*, Vol. 11, 8(1983).

94. John S. Brown and Richard S. Burton, "Diagnostic Model for Procedural Bugs in Basic Mathematical Skills," *Cognitive Science*, Vol. 2 (1979).

95. Dreyfus and Dreyfus, *op. cit.*

96. Thomas S. Kuhn, *The Structure of Scientific Revolutions* (Chicago: University of Chicago Press, 1962).

97. A. DiSessa, "Unlearning Aristotelian Physics: A Study of Knowledge-Based Learning," *Cognitive Science*, Vol. 6, 1(1982).

98. Jacquetta Megarry, "Thinking, Learning, and Educating: The Role of the Computer," in Jacquetta Megarry *et al.*, *World Yearbook of Education, 1982/83: Computers and Education* (New York: Kogan Page, 1983).

99. Allen Newell and Herbert A. Simon, *Human Problem Solving* (Englewood Cliffs, N. J.: Prentice-Hall, 1972).

100. Douglas D. Noble, "Computer Literacy and Ideology," *Teachers College Record*, Vol. 85, 4(1984).

101. Michael J. Streibel, "Beyond Computer Literacy: Analytical Skills, Inquiry Skills, and Personal Empowerment," *T.H.E. Journal*, June 1985.

102. Broughton, *op. cit.*

103. Ershov, *op. cit.*

104. Harriet K. Cuffaro, "Microcomputers in the Classroom: Why Is Earlier Better?" *Teachers College Record*, Vol. 85, 4(1985).

FIFTEEN

Teaching and Technology: The Hidden Effects of Computers on Teachers and Students

Michael W. Apple

M any of the western industrialized nations are facing extensive structural crises in the economy, in authority relations, in values. The symptoms are visible everywhere – in the very high under- and unemployment rates now plaguing us, in the fear that the United States, for example, is losing its edge in international competition, in the calls for sacrifices by labor and for greater work discipline, and in the seemingly widespread belief that "our" standards are falling. The analyses of these crises have not been limited just to our economic institutions. Commentators and critics have spent a good deal of time focusing on the family and especially on the school. Economically and politically powerful groups have, in fact, been relatively successful in shifting the blame for all of the above-mentioned problems *from* the economy *to* institutions such as schools. That is where the real problem lies or so it is said. Thus, if we could solve the problems of education, we could solve these other problems as well. Change the "competencies" of our teachers and students, and all else will tend to fall into place naturally.

Documents such as *A Nation at Risk* and others have pointed to a crisis in teaching and in education in general. Among the many recommendations these reports make is greater stress on the "new technology." The crisis in schools and teaching, they admit, is complicated and widespread, but one step

289

toward a solution is the rapid introduction of computers into schools. The emphasis on computers is quite strong. It is singled out for special attention in nearly all of the national documents, especially those that are responding to the larger social and economic problems we are now experiencing. This will give our students new skills, skills that are necessary in the international competition for markets and jobs. It will also necessitate and create a more technically knowledgeable teaching force (hence the proposals in many states to mandate computer literacy for all students now in teacher education programs). It will also eliminate much of the drudgery of teaching and make the tasks of teaching more interesting and creative. Will it?

The Politics of Technology

In our society, technology is seen as an autonomous process. It is set apart and viewed as if it had a life of its own, independent of social intentions, power, and privilege. We examine technology as if it was something constantly changing and as something that is constantly altering our lives in schools and elsewhere. This is partly true, of course, and is fine as far as it goes. However, by focusing on what is changing and being changed, we may neglect to ask what relationships are remaining the same. Among the most important of these are the sets of cultural and economic inequalities that dominate even societies like our own.[1]

By thinking of technology in this way, by closely examining whether the changes associated with "technological progress" are really changes in certain relationships after all, we can begin to ask political questions about their causes and especially their multitudinous effects. Whose idea of progress? Progress for what? And fundamentally, who benefits?[2] These questions may seem rather weighty ones to be asking about schools and the curricular and teaching practices that now go on in them or are being proposed. Yet, we are in the midst of one of those many educational bandwagons that governments, industry, and others so like to ride. This wagon is pulled in the direction of a technological workplace, and carries a heavy load of computers as its cargo.

The growth of the new technology in schools is definitely not what one would call a slow movement. In one recent year, a 56 percent increase was reported in the use of computers in schools in the United States and even this may be a conservative estimate. Of the 25,642 schools surveyed, more than 15,000 schools reported some computer usage.[3] In the United States alone, it is estimated that in excess of 350,000 microcomputers have been introduced into the public schools in the past four years.[4] This is a trend that shows no sign of abating. Nor is this phenomenon only limited to the United States. France, Canada, England, Australia, and many other countries have "recognized the future." At its center seems to sit a machine with a keyboard and a screen.

I say "at its center," because in both government agencies and in schools themselves the computer and the new technology have been seen as something of a savior economically and pedagogically. "High tech" will save declining economies and will save our students and teachers in schools. In the latter, it is truly remarkable how wide a path the computer is now cutting.

The expansion of its use, the tendency to see all areas of education as a unified terrain for the growth in use of new technologies, can be seen in a two-day workshop on integrating the microcomputer into the classroom held at my own university, The University of Wisconsin. Among the topics covered were computer applications in writing instruction, in music education, in secondary science and mathematics, in primary language arts, for the handicapped, for teacher recordkeeping and management, in business education, in health occupation training programs, in art, and in social studies. To this is added a series of sessions on the "electronic office," how technology and automation are helping industry, and how we all can "transcend the terror" of technology.[5]

Two things are evident from this list. First, vast areas of school life are now seen to be within the legitimate purview of technological restructuring. Second, a partly hidden but exceptionally close linkage is seen between computers in schools and the needs of management for automated industries, electronic offices, and "skilled" personnel. Thus, recognizing both what is happening inside and outside of schools and the connections between these areas is critical to any understanding of what is likely to happen with the new technologies, especially the computer, in education.

As I have argued elsewhere, all too often educational debates are increasingly limited to technical issues. Questions of "how to" have replaced questions of "why."[6] In this chapter, I want to reverse this tendency. Rather than dealing with what the best way might be to establish closer ties between the technological requirements of the larger society and our formal institutions of education, I want to step back and raise a different set of questions. I want us to consider a number of rather difficult political, economic, and ethical issues about some of the tendencies in schools and the larger society that may make us want to be very cautious about the current technological bandwagon in education. In so doing, a range of areas must be examined: Behind the slogans of technological progress and high-tech industry, what are some of the real effects of the new technology on the future labor market? What may happen to teaching and curriculum if we do not think carefully about the new technology's place in the classroom? Will the growing focus on technological expertise, particularly computer literacy, equalize or further exacerbate the lack of social opportunities for our most disadvantaged students?

At root, my claim will be that the debate about the role of the new technology in society and in schools is not and must not be just about the technical correctness of what computers can and cannot do. These may be the least important kinds of questions, in fact. At the very core of the debate instead are the ideological and ethical issues concerning what schools should be about and whose interests they should serve.[7] The question of interests is very important in contemporary society because, due to the severe problems currently besetting economies like our own, a restructuring of what schools are *for* has reached a rather advanced stage.

Thus, while a relatively close connection has always existed between the two, an even closer relationship now exists between the curriculum in our schools and corporate needs.[8] In a number of countries, educational officials and policymakers, legislators, curriculum workers, and others have been subject to immense pressure to make the "needs" of business and industry the primary goals of the school system. Economic and ideological pressures have become rather intense and often very overt. The language of efficiency, production, standards, cost effectiveness, job skills, work discipline, and so on – all defined by powerful groups and always threatening to become the dominant way we think about schooling[9] – has begun to push aside concerns for a democratic curriculum, teacher autonomy, and class, gender, and race equality. Yet, we cannot fully understand the implications of the new technology in this restructuring unless we gain a more complete idea of what industry is now doing not only in the schools but in the economy as well.

Technological Myths and Economic Realities

Let us look at the larger society first. Some claim that the technological needs of the economy are such that unless we have a technologically literate labor force we will ultimately become outmoded economically. But what will this labor force actually look like?

A helpful way of thinking about this is to use the concepts of increasing *proletarianization* and *deskilling* of jobs. These concepts signify a complex historical process in which the control of labor has altered, one in which the skills workers have developed over many years are broken down and reduced to their atomistic units, automated, and redefined by management to enhance profit levels, efficiency, and control. In the process, the employee's control of timing, over defining the most appropriate way to do a task, and over criteria that establish acceptable performance are slowly taken over as the prerogatives of management personnel who are usually divorced from the place where the actual labor is performed. Loss of control by the worker is almost always the result. Pay is often lowered. And the job itself becomes routinized, boring, and alienating as conception is separated from execution and more and more aspects of jobs are rationalized to bring them into line with management's need for a tighter economic and ideological ship.[10] Finally, and very importantly, many of these jobs may simply disappear.

Undoubtedly, the rapid developments in, say, microelectronics, genetic engineering and associated "biological technologies," and other high-tech areas are in fact partly transforming work in a large number of sectors in the economy. This may lead to economic prosperity in certain sections of our population, but its other effects may be devastating. Thus, as the authors of a recent study that examined the impact of new technologies on the future labor market demonstrate:

> This transformation . . . may stimulate economic growth and competition in the world marketplace, but it will displace thousands of workers and could sustain high unemployment for many years. It may provide increased job opportunities for engineers, computer operators, and robot technicians, but it also promises to generate an even greater number of low level, service jobs such as those of janitors, cashiers, clericals, and food service workers. And while many more workers will be using computers, automated office equipment, and other sophisticated technical devices in their jobs, the increased use of technology may actually reduce the skills and discretion required to perform many jobs.[11]

Let us examine this scenario in greater detail.

Rumberger and Levin make a very useful distinction for this discussion. They differentiate between high-tech industries and high-tech occupations — in essence between what is made and the kinds of jobs these goods require. High-tech industries that manufacture technical devices such as computers, electronic components, and the like currently employ fewer than 15 percent of the paid work force in the United States and other industrialized nations. Just as importantly, a substantial knowledge of technology is required by *fewer than one-fourth of* all occupations within these industries. On the contrary, the largest share of jobs created by high-tech industries are in areas such as clerical and office work or in production and assembly. These actually pay below-average wages.[12] Yet this is not all. High-tech occupations that do require considerable skill — such as computer specialists and engineers — may indeed expand. However, most of these occupations actually "employ relatively few workers compared to many traditional clerical and service fields."[13] Rumberger and Levin summarize a number of these points by stating that "although the percentage growth rate of occupational employment in such high technology fields as engineering and computer programming was higher than the overall growth rate of jobs, far more jobs would be created in low-skilled clerical and service occupations than in high technology ones."[14]

Michael W. Apple

Some of these claims are supported by the following data. It is estimated that even being generous in one's projections, only 17 percent of new jobs that will be created between now and 1995 will be in high-tech industries. (Less generous and more restrictive projections argue that only 3 to 8 percent of future jobs will be in such industries.[15]) As I noted, though, such jobs will not all be equal. Clerical workers, secretaries, assemblers, warehouse personnel, etc., will comprise the largest percentage of occupations within the industry. If we take the electronic components industry as an example here, this is made much clearer. Engineering, science, and computing occupations constituted approximately 15 percent of all workers in this industry. The majority of the rest of the workers were engaged in low-wage assembly work. Thus, in the late 1970s, nearly two-thirds of all workers in the electronic components industry took home hourly wages "that placed them in the bottom third of the national distribution."[16] If we take the archetypical high-tech industry — computer and data processing — and analyze its labor market, we get similar results. In 1980, technologically oriented and skilled jobs accounted for only 26 percent of the total.[17]

These figures have considerable weight, but they are made even more significant by the fact that many of those 26 percent may themselves experience a deskilling process in the near future. That is, the reduction of jobs to simpler, atomistic components, the separation of conception from execution, and so on — processes that have had such a major impact on the labor process of blue, pink, and white color workers in so many other areas — are now advancing into high technology jobs as well. Computer programming provides an excellent example. New developments in software packages and machine language and design have meant that a considerable portion of the job of programming now requires little more than performing "standard, routine, machine-like tasks that require little in-depth knowledge."[18]

What does this mean for the activities of schooling and the seemingly widespread belief that the future world of work will require increasing technical competence on the part of all students? Consider the occupations that will contribute the most number of jobs not just in high-tech industries but throughout the society by 1995. Economic forecasts indicate that these will include building custodians, cashiers, secretaries, office clerks, nurses, waiters and waitresses, elementary school teachers, truck drivers, and other health care workers such as nurses aides and orderlies.[19] None of these are directly related to high technology. Excluding teachers and nurses, none of them require any post-secondary education. (Their earnings will be approximately 30 percent below the current average earnings of workers, as well.[20]) If we go further than this and examine an even larger segment of expected new jobs by including the 40 job categories that will probably account for about one-half

294

of all the jobs that will be created, only about 25 percent will require people with a college degree.[21]

In many ways, this is strongly related to the effects of the new technology on the job market and the labor process in general. Skill levels will be raised in some areas, but will decline in many others, as will jobs themselves decline. For instance, "a recent study of robotics in the United States suggests that robots will eliminate 100,000 to 200,000 jobs by 1990, while creating 32,000 to 64,000 jobs."[22] My point about declining skill requirements is made nicely by Rumberger and Levin. As they suggest, while it is usually assumed that workers will need computer programming and other sophisticated skills because of the greater use of technology such as computers in their jobs, the ultimate effect of such technology may be somewhat different. "A variety of evidence suggests just the opposite: as machines become more sophisticated, with expanded memories, more computational ability, and sensory capabilities, the knowledge required to use the devices declines."[23] The effect of these trends on the division of labor will be felt for decades. But it will be in the sexual division of labor where it will be even more extreme. Historically, *women's work* has been subject to these processes in very powerful ways; consequently, we will see increased proletarianization and deskilling of women's labor and, undoubtedly, a further increase in the feminization of poverty.[24]

These points clearly have implications for our educational programs. We need to think much more rigorously about what they mean for our transition from school to work programs, especially because many of the "skills" that schools are currently teaching are transitory because the jobs themselves are being transformed (or lost) by new technological developments and new management offensives.

Take office work, for example. In offices, the bulk of the new technology has not been designed to enhance the quality of the job for the largest portion of the employees (usually women clerical workers). Rather, it has usually been designed and implemented in such a way that exactly the opposite will result. Instead of generating work that is stimulating and satisfying, the technology is there to make managers' jobs "easier," to eliminate jobs and cut costs, to divide work into routine and atomized tasks, and to more easily accomplish administrative control.[25] The vision of the future society seen in the microcosm of the office is inherently undemocratic and perhaps increasingly authoritarian. Is this what we wish to prepare our students for? Surely, our task as educators is neither to accept such a future labor market and labor process uncritically nor to have our students accept such practices uncritically as well. To do so is simply to allow the values of a limited but powerful segment of the population to work through us. It may be good business but I have my doubts

deskilling + reskilling work
b + m jobs
less jobs

about whether it is ethically correct educational policy.

In summary, then, what we will witness is the creation of enhanced jobs for a relative few and deskilled and boring work for the majority. Furthermore, even those boring and deskilled jobs will be increasingly hard to find. Take office work, again, an area that is rapidly being transformed by the new technology. It is estimated that between one and five jobs will be lost for every new computer terminal that is introduced.[26] Yet this situation will not be limited to office work. Even those low-paying assembly positions noted earlier will not necessarily be found in the industrialized nations with their increasingly service oriented economies. Given the international division of labor, and what is called "capital flight," a large portion of these jobs will be moved to countries such as the Philippines and Indonesia.[27]

This is exacerbated considerably by the fact that many governments now find "acceptable" those levels of unemployment that would have been considered a crisis a decade ago. "Full employment" in the United States is now often seen as between 7 and 8 percent *measured* unemployment. (The actual figures are much higher, of course, especially among minority groups and workers who can only get part time jobs.) This is a figure that is *double* that of previous economic periods. Even higher rates are now seen as "normal" in other countries. The trend is clear. The future will see fewer jobs. Many of those that are created will not be fulfilling, nor will they pay well. Finally, the level of technical skill will continue to be lowered for a large portion of them.[28]

Because of this, we need convincing answers to some very important questions about our future society and the economy before we turn our schools into the "production plants" for creating new workers. *Where* will these new jobs be? *How many* will be created? Will they *equal* the number of positions lost in offices, factories, and service jobs in retailing, banks, telecommunications, and elsewhere? Are the bulk of the jobs that will be created relatively unskilled, less than meaningful, and themselves subject to the inexorable logics of management so that they too will probably be automated out of existence?[29]

These are not inconsequential questions. Before we give the schools over to the requirements of the new technology and the corporation, we must be very certain that it will benefit all of us, not mostly those who already possess economic and cultural power. This requires continued democratic discussion, not a quick decision based on the economic and political pressure now being placed on schools.

Much more could be said about the future labor market. I urge the interested reader to pursue it in greater depth because it will have a profound impact on our school policies and programs, especially in vocational areas, in working-class schools, and among programs for young women. The difficulties with the high-tech vision that permeates the beliefs of the proponents of a technological solution will not remain outside the school door, however. Similar disproportionate benefits and dangers await us inside our educational institutions as well and it is to this that I now turn.

Inequality and the Technological Classroom

Once we go inside the school, a set of questions concerning "who benefits?" also arises. We need to ask about what may be happening to teachers and students given the emphasis now being placed on computers in schools. I will not talk about the individual teacher or student here. Obviously, some teachers will find their jobs enriched by the new technology and some students will find hidden talents and will excell in a computer-oriented classroom. What we need to ask instead (or at least before we deal with the individual) is what may happen to classrooms, teachers, and students differentially. Once again, I seek to raise a set of issues that may not be easy to solve, but cannot be ignored if we are to have a truly democratic educational system in more than name only.

While I have dealt with this in greater detail in *Ideology and Curriculum* and *Education and Power*,[30] let me briefly situate the growth of the technologized classroom into what seems to be occurring to teaching and curriculum in general. Currently, considerable pressure is building to have teaching and school curricula be totally prespecified and tightly controlled for the purposes of "efficiency," "cost effectiveness," and "accountability." In many ways, the deskilling that is affecting jobs in general is now having an impact on teachers as more and more decisions are moving out of their hands and as their jobs become even more difficult to do. This is more advanced in some countries than others, but it is clear that the movement to rationalize and control the act of teaching and the content and evaluation of the curriculum is very real.[31] Even in those countries that have made strides away from centralized examination systems, powerful inspectorates and supervisors, and tightly controlled curricula, an identifiable tendency is found to move back toward state control. Many reforms have only a very tenuous hold currently. This is in part due to economic difficulties and partly due as well to the importing of American styles and techniques of educational management, styles and techniques that have their roots in industrial bureaucracies and have almost never had democratic aims.[32] Even though a number of teachers may support computer-oriented curricula, an emphasis on the new technology needs to be seen in this context of the rationalization of teaching and curricula in general.

Given these pressures, what will happen to teachers if the new technology is accepted uncritically? One of the major effects of the current (over)emphasis on computers in the classroom may be the deskilling and depowering of a considerable number of teachers. Given the already heavy work load of planning, teaching, participating in meetings, and completing paperwork for most teachers, and given the expense, it is probably wise to assume that the largest proportion of teachers will not be given more than a very small amount of training in computers, their social effects, programming, and so on. This will be the case especially at the primary and elementary school level where most teachers are already teaching a wide array of subject areas. Research indicates, in fact, that few teachers in any district are actually given substantial information before computer curricula are implemented. Often only one or two teachers are the "resident experts."[33] Because of this, most teachers have to rely on prepackaged sets of material, existing software, and specially purchased material from any of the scores of software manufacturing firms that are springing up in a largely unregulated way.

The impact of this can be striking. What is happening is the exacerbation of trends we have begun to see in a number of nations. Rather than teachers having the time and the skill to do their own curriculum planning and deliberation, they become isolated executors of someone else's plans, procedures, and evaluation mechanisms. In industrial terms, this is very close to what I noted in my previous discussion of the labor process (the separation of conception from execution.[34]

The question of time looms larger here, especially in gender terms. Because of the large amount of time it takes to become a "computer expert" and because of the patriarchal relations that still dominate many families, *men teachers* will often be able to use "computer literacy" to advance their own careers while women teachers will tend to remain the recipients of prepackaged units on computers or "canned" programs over which they have little control.

In her excellent ethnographic study of the effects of the introduction of a district wide computer literacy program on the lives of teachers, Susan Jungck makes exactly this point about what happened in one middle school.

> The condition of time [needs to] be examined in terms of gender differences because it was the women teachers, not the men, in the Math Department who were unprepared to teach about computers and they were the ones most dependent on the availability of the [canned] Unit. Typically, the source of computer literacy for in-service teachers is either college or university courses, school district courses or independent study, all options that take considerable time outside of school. Both [male teachers] had taken a substantial number of university courses on computers in education. Many [of the] women, [because of] child care and household responsibilities . . . , or women who are single parents . . . , have relatively less out of school time to take additional coursework and prepare

new curricula. Therefore, when a new curriculum such as computer literacy is required, women teachers may be more dependent on using the ready-made curriculum materials than most men teachers.[35]

The reliance on prepackaged software can have a number of long-term effects. First, it can cause a decided loss of important skills and dispositions on the part of teachers. When the skills of local curriculum planning, individual evaluation, and so on are not used, they atrophy. The tendency to look outside of one's own or one's colleagues' historical experience about curriculum and teaching is lessened as considerably more of the curriculum, and the teaching and evaluative practices that surround it, are viewed as something one purchases. In the process — and this is very important — the school itself is transformed into a lucrative market. The industrialization of the school I talked of previously is complemented, then, by further opening up the classroom to the mass-produced commodities of industry. In many ways, it will be a publisher's and salesperson's delight. Whether students' educational experiences will markedly improve is open to question.

The issue of the relationship of purchased software and hardware to the possible deskilling and depowering of teachers does not end here, though. The problem is made even more difficult by the rapidity with which software developers have constructed and marketed their products. There is no guarantee that the mass of such material has any major educational value. Exactly the opposite is often the case. One of the most knowledgeable government officials has put it this way. "High-quality educational software is almost nonexistent in our elementary and secondary schools."[36] While perhaps overstating his case to emphasize his points, the director of software evaluation for one of the largest school systems in the United States has concluded that of the more than 10,000 programs currently available, approximately 200 are educationally significant.[37]

To their credit, the fact that this is a serious problem is recognized by most computer enthusiasts, and reviews and journals have attempted to deal with it. However, the sheer volume of material, the massive amounts of money spent on advertising software in professional publications, at teachers' and administrators' meetings, and so on, the utter "puffery" of the claims made about much of this material, and the constant pressure by industry, government, parents, some school personnel, and others to institute computer programs in schools *immediately*, all of this makes it nearly impossible to do more than make a small dent in the problem. As one educator put it, "There's a lot of junk out there."[38] The situation is not made any easier by the fact that teachers simply do not now have the time to evaluate thoroughly the educational strengths and weaknesses of a considerable portion of the *existing* curricular material and texts before they are used. Adding one more element, and a sizeable one at that, to be evaluated only increases the load. Teachers' work is increasingly becoming what students of the labor process call *intensified*. More and more needs to be done; less and less time is available to do it.³⁹ Thus, one has little choice but to simply buy ready-made material, in this way continuing a trend in which all of the important curricular elements are not locally produced but purchased from commercial sources whose major aim may be profit, not necessarily educational merit.⁴⁰

There is a key concept found in Jungck's argument above that is essential here, that of gender. As I have demonstrated in considerable detail in *Teachers and Texts*,⁴¹ teaching — especially at the elementary school level — has been defined as "women's work." We cannot ignore the fact that 87 percent of elementary teachers and 67 percent of teachers overall *are* women. Historically, the introduction of prepackaged or standardized curricula and teaching strategies has often been related to the rationalization and attempt to gain external control of the labor process of women workers. Hence, we cannot completely understand what is happening to teachers — the deskilling, the intensification, the separation of conception from execution, the loss of control, and so on — unless we situate these tendencies into this longer history of what has often happened to occupations that primarily comprise women.⁴² Needless to say, this is a critically important point, for only by raising the question of *who* is most often doing the teaching in many of these schools now introducing prepackaged software can we see the connections between the effects of the curricula and the gendered compostion of the teaching force.

A significant consideration here, besides the loss of skill and control, is expense. This is at least a three-pronged issue. First, we must recognize that we may be dealing with something of a "zero-sum game." While dropping, the cost of computers is still comparatively high, although some manufacturers may keep purchase costs relatively low, knowing that a good deal of their profits may come from the purchase of software later on or through a home/school connection, something I discuss shortly. This money for the new technology *must come from somewhere*. This is an obvious point but one that is very consequential. In a time of fiscal crisis, where funds are already spread too thinly and necessary programs are being starved in many areas, the addition of computer curricula most often means that money must be drained from one area and given to another. What will be sacrificed? If history is any indication, it may be programs that have benefitted the least advantaged. Little serious attention has been paid to this, but it will become an increasingly serious dilemma.

A second issue of expense concerns staffing patterns, for it is not just the content of teachers' work and the growth of purchased materials that are at stake. Teachers' jobs themselves are on the line here. At a secondary school level in many nations, for example, layoffs of teachers have not been unusual as funding for education is cut. Declining enrollment in some regions has meant a loss of positions as well. This has caused intense competition over students within the school itself. Social studies, art, music, and other subjects must fight it out with newer, more "glamorous" subject areas. To lose the student numbers game for too long is to lose a job. The effect of the computer in this situation has been to increase competitiveness among staff, often to replace substance with both gloss and attractive packaging of courses, and to threaten many teachers with the loss of their livelihood.[43] Is it really an educationally or socially wise decision to tacitly eliminate a good deal of the choices in these other fields so that we can support the "glamor" of a computer future? These are not only financial decisions, but are ethical decisions about teachers' lives and what our students are to be educated about. Given the future labor market, do we really want to claim that computers will be more important than further work in humanities and social sciences or, perhaps even more significantly in working-class and ethnically diverse areas, in the students' own cultural, historical, and political heritage and struggles? Such decisions must not be made by only looking at the accountant's bottom line. These too need to be arrived at by the lengthy democratic deliberation of all parties, including the teachers who will be most affected.

Third, given the expense of microcomputers and software in schools, the pressure to introduce such technology may increase the already wide social imbalances that now exist. Private schools to which the affluent send their children and publicly funded schools in more affluent areas will have more ready access to the technology itself.[44] Schools in inner city, rural, and poor areas will be largely priced out of the market, even if the cost of "hardware" continues to decline. After all, in these poorer areas and in many public school systems in general in a number of countries, it is already difficult to generate enough money to purchase new textbooks and to cover the costs of teachers' salaries. Thus, the computer and literacy debates and resolutions will "naturally" generate further inequalities. Because, by and large, it will be the top 20 percent of the population that will have computers in their homes[45] and many of the jobs and institutions of higher education their children will be applying for will either ask for or assume "computer skills" as keys of entry or advancement, the impact can be enormous in the long run.

The role of the relatively affluent parent in this situation does not go unrecognized by computer manufacturers.

> Computer companies . . . gear much of their advertising to the educational possibilities of computers. The drive to link particular computers to schools is a frantic competition. Apple, for example, in a highly touted scheme proposed to "donate" an Apple to every school in America. Issues of philanthropy and intent aside, the clear market strategy is to couple particular computer usages to schools

where parents — especially middle-class parents with the economic wherewithal and keen motivation [to ensure mobility] — purchase machines compatible with those in schools. The potentially most lucrative part of such a scheme, however, is not in the purchase of hardware (although this is also substantial) but in the sale of proprietary software.[46]

This very coupling of school and home markets, then, cannot fail to further disadvantage large groups of students. Those students who already have computer backgrounds — be it because of their schools or their homes or both — will proceed more rapidly. The social stratification of life chances will increase. These students' original advantage — one *not* due to "natural ability," but to *wealth* — will be heightened.[47]

We should not be surprised by this, nor should we think it odd that many parents, especially middle-class parents, will pursue a computer future. Computer skills and "literacy" are, in part, strategies for the maintenance of middle-class mobility patterns.[48] Having such expertise in a time of fiscal and economic crisis, is similar to having an insurance policy. It partly guarantees that certain doors remain open in a rapidly changing labor market. In a time of credential inflation, more credentials mean less closed doors.[49]

The credential factor here is of considerable moment. In the past, as gains were made by ethnically different people, working-class groups, women, and others in schooling, one of the latent effects was to raise the credentials required by entire sectors of jobs. Thus, class, race, and gender barriers were partly maintained by an ever-increasing credential inflation. Although this was more of a structural than a conscious process, the effect over time has often been to again disqualify entire segments of a population from jobs, resources, and power. This too may be a latent outcome of the computerization of the school curriculum. Even though, as I have shown, the bulk of new jobs will not require "computer literacy," establishing computer requirements and mandated programs in schools will condemn many people to even greater economic disenfranchisement. Because the requirements are, in many ways, artificial — computer knowledge will not be so very necessary and the number of jobs requiring high levels of expertise will be relatively small — we will simply be affixing one more label to these students. "Functional illiteracy" will simply be broadened to include computers.[50]

Thus, rather than blaming an unequal economy and a situation in which meaningful and fulfilling work is not made available, rather than seeing how the new technology for all its benefits is "creating a growing underclass of displaced and marginal workers," the lack is personalized. It becomes the students' or workers' fault for not being computer literate. One significant social and ideological outcome of computer requirements in schools, then, is that they can serve as a means "to justify those lost lives by a process of mass disqualification, which throws the blame for disenfranchisement in education and employment back on the victims themselves."[51]

Of course, this process may not be visible to many parents of individual children. However, the point does not revolve around the question of individual mobility, but large scale effects. Parents may see such programs as offering important paths to advancement and some will be correct. However, in a time of severe economic problems, parents tend to overestimate what schools can do for their children.[52] As I documented earlier, there simply will not be sufficient jobs and competition will be intense. The uncritical introduction of and investment in hardware and software will, by and large, hide the reality of the transformation of the labor market and will support those who are already advantaged unless thought is given to these implications now.

Let us suppose, however, that it was important that everyone become computer literate and that these large investments in time, money, and personnel were indeed so necessary for our economic and educational future. Given all this, what is currently happening in schools? Is inequality in access and outcome now being produced? While many educators are continually struggling against these effects, we are already seeing signs of this disadvantagement being created.

There is evidence of class, race, and gender-based differences in computer use. In middle-class schools, for example, the number of computers is considerably more than in working-class or inner city schools populated by children of color. The ratio of computers to children is also much higher. This in itself is an unfortunate finding. However, something else must be added here. These more economically advantaged schools not only have more contact hours and more technical and teacher support, but the very manner in which the computer is used is often different than what would be generally found in schools in less advantaged areas. Programming skills, generalizability, a sense of the multitudinous things one can do with computers both within and across academic areas, these tend to be stressed more[53] (although simply drill-and-practice uses are still widespread even here).[54] Compare this to the rote, mechanistic, and relatively low level uses that tend to dominate the working-class school.[55] These differences are not unimportant, for they signify a ratification of class divisions.

Further evidence to support these claims is now becoming more readily available as researchers dig beneath the glowing claims of a computer future for all children. The differential impact is made clearer in the following figures. In the United States, while more than two-thirds of the schools in affluent areas have computers, only approximately 41 percent of the poorer public schools have them. What one does with the machine is just as important as having one, of course, and here the differences are again very real. One study of poorer elementary schools found that white children were four times more likely than black children to use computers for programming. Another found that the children of professionals employed computers for programming and for other "creative" uses. Children of nonprofessionals were more apt to use them for drill-and-practice in mathematics and reading, and for "vocational" work. In general, in fact, "programming has been seen as the purview of the gifted and talented" and of those students who are more affluent. Less affluent students seem to find that the computer is only a tool for drill- and practice-sessions.[56]

Gender differences are also very visible. Two out of every three students currently learning about computers are boys. Even here these data are deceptive because girls "tend to be clustered in the general introductory courses," not the more advanced level ones.[57] One current analyst summarizes the situation in a very clear manner.

> While stories abound about students who will do just about anything to increase their access to computers, most youngsters working with school computers are [economically advantaged,] white, and male. The ever-growing number of private computer camps, after-school and weekend programs serve middle-class white boys. Most minority [and poor] parents just can't afford to send their children to participate in these programs.[58]

This class, race, and gendered impact will also occur because of traditional school practices such as tracking or streaming. Thus, vocational and business tracks will learn operating skills for word processing and will be primarily filled with (working-class) young women.[59] Academic tracks will stress more general programming abilities and uses and will be disproportionately male.[60] Because computer programs usually have their home bases in mathematics and science in most schools, gender differences can be heightened even more given the often differential treatment of girls in these classes and the ways in which mathematics and science curricula already fulfill "the selective function of the school and contribute to the reproduction of gender differences."[61] While many teachers and curriculum workers have devoted considerable time and effort to equalize both the opportunities and outcomes of female students in mathematics and science (and such efforts are important), the problem still remains a substantive one. It can be worsened by the computerization of these subjects in much the same way as it may have a gendered impact on the teachers themselves.

Toward Social Literacy

We have seen some of the possible negative consequences of the new technology in education, including the deskilling and depowering of teachers and the creation of inequalities through expense, credential inflation, and limitations on access. Yet, the issues surrounding the deskilling process are not limited to teachers. They include the very ways students themselves are taught to think about their education, their future roles in society, and the place of technology in that society. Let me explain what I mean by this.

The new technology is not just an assemblage of machines and their accompanying software. It embodies a *form of thinking* that orients a person to approach the world in a particular way. Computers involve ways of thinking that under current educational conditions are primarily *technical.*[62] The more the new technology transforms the classroom into its own image, the more a technical logic will replace critical political and ethical understanding. The discourse of the classroom will center on technique, and less on substance. Once again "how to" will replace "why," but this time at the level of the student. This situation requires what I call *social,* not *technical,* literacy for all students.

Even if computers make sense technically in all curricular areas and even if all students, not mainly affluent white males, become technically proficient in their use, critical questions of politics and ethics remain to be dealt with in the curriculum. Thus, it is crucial that whenever the new technology is introduced into schools students have a serious understanding of the issues surrounding their larger social effects, many of which I raised earlier.

Unfortunately, this is not often the case. When the social and ethical impacts of computers are dealt with, they are usually addressed in a manner that is less than powerful. One example is provided by a recent proposal for a statewide computer curriculum in one of the larger states in the United States. The objectives that dealt with social questions in the curriculum centered around one particular set of issues. The curriculum states that "the student will be aware of some of the major uses of computers in modern society . . . and the student will be aware of career opportunities related to computers."[63] In most curricula, the technical components of the new technology are stressed. Brief glances are given to the history of computers (occasionally mentioning the role of women in their development, which is at least one positive sign). Yet in this history, the close relationship between military use and computer development is largely absent. "Benign" uses are pointed to, coupled with a less than realistic description of the content and possibility of computer careers and what Douglas D. Noble has called "a gee-whiz glance at the marvels of the future." What is almost never mentioned is job loss or social disenfranchizement. The very real destruction of the lives of unemployed autoworkers, assemblers or clerical workers is marginalized.[64] The ethical dilemmas involved when we choose between, say, "efficiency" and the quality of the work people experience, between profit and someone's job — these too are made invisible.

How would we counterbalance this? By making it clear from the outset that knowledge about the new technology that is necessary for students to know goes well beyond what we now too easily take for granted. A considerable portion of the curriculum would be organized around questions concerned with social literacy. "Where are computers used? What are they used to do? What do people *actually* need to know in order to use them? Does the computer enhance anyone's life? Whose? Does it hurt anyone's life? Whose? Who decides when and where computers will be used?"[65] Unless these are *fully* integrated in a school program at *all* levels, I hesitate advocating the use of the new technology in the curriculum. Raising questions of this type is not just important in our elementary and secondary schools. It is even more essential that they be dealt with in a serious way with teachers both in their own undergraduate teacher education programs where courses in educational computing are more and more being mandated and in the many in-service workshops now springing up throughout the country as school districts frantically seek to keep up with the "computer revolution." To do less makes it much more difficult for teachers and students to think critically and independently about the place the new technology does and should have in the lives of the majority of people in our society. Our job as educators involves skilling, not deskilling. Unless teachers and students are able to deal honestly and critically with these complex ethical and social issues, only those now with the power to control technology's uses will have the capacity to act. We cannot afford to let this happen.

Conclusion

I realize that a number of my points in this essay may prove to be rather contentious. Stressing the negative side, however, can serve to highlight many of the critical issues that are too easy to put off, given the immense amount of work for which school personnel are already responsible. Decisions are often made too quickly, only to be regretted later on when forces are set in motion that could have been avoided if the implications of one's actions had been thought through more fully.

As I noted at the outset of this chapter, there is now something of a mad scramble to employ the computer in every content area. In fact, it is nearly impossible to find a subject that is not being "computerized." Although mathematics and science (and some parts of vocational education) remain the home base for a large portion of proposed computer curricula, other areas are not far behind. If it can be packaged to fit computerized instruction, it will be, even if it is inappropriate, less effective than the methods that teachers have developed after years of hard practical work, or less than sound educationally or economically. Rather than the machine fitting the educational needs and visions of the teacher, students, and community, all too often these needs and visions are made to fit the technology itself.

Yet, as I have shown, the new technology does not stand alone. It is linked to transformations in real groups of people's lives, jobs, hopes, and dreams. For some of these groups, those lives will be enhanced. For others, the dreams will be shattered. Wise choices about the appropriate place of the new technology in education, then, are not only educational decisions. They are fundamentally choices about the kind of society we shall have, about the social and ethical responsiveness of our institutions to the majority of our future citizens, and to the teachers who now work in our schools. To understand teaching in this situation requires us to situate it into a more complicated nexus of relationships. Only then can choices be made in an ethically justified way.

In the current difficult social and economic situation, it is exceptionally important that educators not allow powerful groups to export their crisis onto the schools. By redefining the serious dilemmas this society faces as being primarily those of the school, and by then convincing the public that many of these problems can simply be solved by an infusion of computers and computer literacy into our educational institutions, dominant groups may create a climate in which the public continues to blame the already hard-working teachers and administrators for economic conditions over which they may have little control. This would be extremely unfortunate, because as many researchers have shown, the crisis is more widespread, more related to inequalities in the economy and in political representation, than could be accounted for by continually blaming the school.[66]

My discussion here has not been aimed at making us all neo-Luddites, people who go out and smash the machines that threaten our jobs or our children. The new technology is here. It will not go away. Our task as educators is to make sure that when it enters the classroom it is there for politically, economically, and educationally wise reasons, not because powerful groups may be redefining our major educational goals in their own image. We should be very clear about whether the future it promises to our teachers and students is real, not fictitious. We need to be certain that it is a future in which *all* of our students can share, not just a select few. After all, the new technology is expensive and will require a good deal of our time and that of our teachers, administrators, and students. It is more than a little important that we question whether the wagon we have been asked to ride on is going in the right direction. It's a long walk back.

Notes

This article is based on a more extensive analysis in Michael W. Apple, *Teachers and Texts: A Political Economy of Class and Gender Relations in Education* (New York: Routledge and Kegan Paul, 1987).

1. David Noble, *Forces of Production: A Social History of Industrial Automation* (New York: Alfred A. Knopf, 1984), pp. xi-xii. For a more general argument about the relationship between technology and human progress, see Nicholas Rescher, *Unpopular Essays on Technological Progress* (Pittsburgh: University of Pittsburgh Press, 1980).

2. *Ibid.*, p. xv.

3. Paul Olson, "Who Computes? The Politics of Literacy," unpublished paper, Ontario Institute for Studies in Education, Toronto, 1985, p. 6.

4. Patricia B. Campbell, "The Computer Revolution: Guess Who's Left Out?," *Interracial Books for Children Bulletin* 15 3(1984), p. 3.

5. "Instructional Strategies for Integrating the Microcomputer Into the Classroom," The Vocational Studies Center, University of Wisconsin-Madison, 1985.

6. Michael W. Apple, *Ideology and Curriculum* (Boston: Routledge and Kegan Paul, 1979).

7. Olson, *op. cit.*, p. 5.

8. See Michael W. Apple, *Education and Power* (Boston: Routledge and Kegan Paul, 1982).

9. For further discussion of this, see Apple, *Ideology and Curriculum, op. cit.*; Apple, *Education and Power, op. cit.*; and Ira Shor, *Culture Wars* (Boston: Routledge and Kegan Paul, 1986).

10. This is treated in greater detail in Richard Edwards, *Contested Terrain* (New York: Basic Books, 1979). See also the more extensive discussion of the effect these tendencies are having in education in Apple, *Education and Power, op. cit.*

11. Russell W. Rumberger and Henry M. Levin, "Forcasting the Impact of New Technologies on the Future Job Market," Project Report No. 84–A4, Institute for Research on Educational Finance and Government, School of Education, Stanford University, February 1984, p. 1.

12. *Ibid.*, p. 2.

13. *Ibid.*, p. 3.

14. *Ibid.*, p. 4.

15. *Ibid.*, p. 18.

16. *Ibid.*, p. 18.

17. *Ibid.*, p. 19.

18. *Ibid.*, pp. 19–20.

19. *Ibid.*, p. 31.

20. *Ibid.*, p. 21.

21. *Ibid.*, p. 21.

22. *Ibid.*, p. 25.

23. *Ibid.*, p. 25.

24. The effects of proletarianization and deskilling on women's labor is analyzed in more detail in Michael W. Apple, "Work, Gender and Teaching," *Teachers College Record* 84(Spring 1983)611–28 and Michael W. Apple "Teaching and 'Woman's Work': A Comparative Historical and Ideological Analysis," *Teachers College Record* 86(Spring 1985). On the history of women's struggles against proletarianization, see Alice Kessler-Harris, *Out to Work* (New York: Oxford University Press, 1982).

25. Ian Reinecke, *Electronic Illusion* (New York: Penguin Books, 1984), p. 156.

26. See the further discusison of the loss of office jobs and the deskilling of many of those that remain in *Ibid.*, pp. 136–58. The very same process could be a threat to middle- and low-level management positions as well. After all, if control is further automated, why does one need as many supervisory positions? The implications of this latter point need to be given much more consideration by many middle-class proponents of technology because their jobs may soon be at risk, too.

27. Peter Dwyer, Bruce Wilson, and Roger Woock, *Confronting School and Work* (Boston: George Allen and Unwin, 1984), pp. 105–6.

28. The paradigm case is given by the fact that three times as many people now work in low-paying positions for MacDonalds as for U. S. Steel. See Martin Carnoy, Derek Shearer, and Russell Rumberger, *A New Social Contract* (New York: Harper and Row, 1983), p. 71. As I have argued at greater length elsewhere, however, it may not be important to our economy if all students and workers are made technically knowledgeable by schools. What is just as important is the production of economically useful knowledge (technical/administrative knowledge) that can be used by corporations to enhance profits, control labor, and increase efficiency. See Apple, *Education and Power, op. cit.*, especially Chapter 2.

29. Reinecke, *Electronic Illusions*, p. 234. For further analysis of the economic data and the effects on education, see W. Norton Grubb, "The Bandwagon Once More: Vocational Preparation for High-Tech Occupations," *Harvard Educational Review* 54(November 1984)429–51.

30. Apple, *Ideology and Curriculum, op. cit.*, and Apple, *Education and Power, op. cit.* See also Michael W. Apple and Lois Weis, eds., *Ideology and Practice in Schooling* (Philadelphia: Temple University Press, 1983).

31. *Ibid.* See also Arthur Wise, *Legislated Learning: The Bureaucratization of the American Classrom* (Berkeley: University of California Press, 1979).

32. Apple, *Ideology and Curriculum, op. cit.*, and Apple, *Education and Power, op. cit.* On the general history of the growth of management techniques, see Edwards, *op. cit.*

33. Douglas D. Noble, "The Underside of Computer Literacy," *Raritan* 3(Spring 1984)45.

34. See the discussion of this in Apple, *Education and Power*, *op. cit.*, especially Chapter 5.

35. Susan Jungck, "Doing Computer Literacy," unpublished Ph.D. dissertation, University of Wisconsin, Madison, 1985, pp 236–37.

36. Douglas Noble, "Jumping Off the Computer Bandwagon," *Education Week*, October 3, 1984, p. 24.

37. *Ibid.*, p. 24.

38. *Ibid.* See also, Noble, "The Underside of Computer Literacy," *op. cit.*, p. 45.

39. For further discussion of the intensification of teachers' work, see Apple, "Work, Gender and Teaching," *op. cit.*

40. Apple, *Education and Power*, *op. cit.* For further analysis of the textbook publishing industry, see Michael W. Apple, "The Culture and Commerce of the Textbook," *Journal of Curriculum Studies* Vol. 17 1(1985).

41. Michael W. Apple, *Teachers and Texts: A Political Economy of Class and Gender Relations in Education* (New York: Routledge and Kegan Paul, 1987).

42. *Ibid.*

43. I am indebted to Susan Jungck for this point. See Jungck, "Doing Computer Literacy," *op. cit.*

44. Reinecke, *Electronic Illusions*, *op. cit.*, p. 176.

45. *Ibid.*, p. 169.

46. Olson, *op. cit.*, p. 23.

47. *Ibid.*, p. 31. Thus, students' familiarity and comfort with computers becomes a form of what has been called the "cultural capital" of advantaged groups. For further analysis of the dynamics of cultural capital, see Apple, *Education and Power*, *op. cit.*, and Pierre Bourdieu and Jean-Claude Passeron, *Reproduction in Education, Society and Culture* (Beverly Hills, Calif.: Sage Publications, 1977).

48. *Ibid.*, p. 23. See also the discussion of interclass competition over academic qualifications in Pierre Bourdieu, *Distinction* (Cambridge, Mass.: Harvard University Press, 1984), pp. 133–68.

49. Once again, I am indebted to Susan Jungck for this argument.

50. Noble, "The Underside of Computer Literacy," *op. cit.*, p. 54.

51. Douglas D. Noble, "Computer Literacy and Ideology," *Teachers College Record* 85(Summer 1984), p. 611. This process of "blaming the victim" has a long history in education. See Apple, *Ideology and Curriculum*, *op. cit.*, especially Chapter 7.

52. R. W. Connell, *Teachers' Work* (Boston: George Allen and Unwin, 1985), p. 142.

53. Olson, *op. cit.*, p. 22.

54. For an analysis of the emphasis on and pedagogic problems with such limited uses of computers, see Michael J. Streibel, "A Critical Analysis of the Use of Computers in Education," unpublished paper, University of Wisconsin, Madison, 1984, and the chapter by Streibel herein.

55. Olson, *op cit.*, p. 22.

56. Campbell, *op. cit.*, p. 3. Many computer experts, however, are highly critical of the fact that students are primarily taught to program in BASIC, a less than appropriate language for later advanced computer work. Michael Streibel, personal communication.

57. *Ibid.*

58. *Ibid.*

59. An interesting analysis of what happens to young women in such business programs and how they respond to both the curricula and their later work experiences can be found in Linda Valli, "Becoming Clerical Workers: Business Education and the Culture of Femininity," in Apple and Weis, *op. cit.*, pp. 213-234. See also her more extensive treatment in Linda Valli, *Becoming Clerical Workers* (Boston: Routledge and Kegan Paul, 1986).

60. Jane Gaskell in Olson, *op. cit.*, "Who Computes?," p. 33.

61. Feodora Fomin, "The Best and the Brightest: The Selective Function of Mathematics in the School Curriculum," in Lesley Johnson and Deborah Tyler, eds., *Cultural Politics: Papers in Contemporary Australian Education, Culture and Politics* (Melbourne: University of Melbourne, Sociology Research Group in Cultural and Educational Studies, 1984), p. 220.

62. Michael J. Streibel's work on the models of thinking usually incorporated within computers in education is helpful in this regard. See Streibel, "A Critical Analysis of the Use of Computers in Education," *op. cit.*, and his chapter in this volume. The more general issue of the relationship between technology and the control of culture is important here. A useful overview of this can be found in Kathleen Woodward, ed., *The Myths of Information: Technology and Postindustrial Culture* (Madison: Coda Press, 1980).

63. Quoted in Noble, "The Underside of Computer Literacy," *op. cit.*, p. 56.

64. *Ibid.*, p. 57. An interesting, but little known fact is that the largest proportion of computer programmers actually work for the military. See Joseph Weizenbaum, "Thie Computer in Your Future," *The New York Review of Books*, October 27, 1983, pp. 58–62.

65. Noble, "The Underside of Computer Literacy," *op. cit.*, p. 40. For students in vocational curricula especially, these questions would be given more power if they were developed within a larger program that would seek to provide these young women and men with extensive experience in and understanding of *all* aspects of operating an entire industry, not simply those "skills" that reproduce workplace stratification. See Center for Law and Education, "Key Provisions in New Law Reforms Vocational Education: Focus is on Broader Knowledge and Experience for Students/Workers," *Center for Law and Education, Inc. D.C. Report*, December 28, 1984, 1–6.

66. See, especially, Marcus Raskin, *The Common Good* (New York: Routledge and Kegan Paul, 1987). This does not mean that schools have no place in helping to solve these problems, simply that: (1) it is insufficient and naive to search for mostly educational solutions; and (2) that the solutions must be considerably more democratic in process *and* effects than those being proposed currently.

VI
Curriculum and Evaluation

SIXTEEN

The Human Problems and Possibilities of Curriculum Evaluation

George Willis

If we are fortunate, at some time in the distant future, historians will be able to look back at the twentieth century and see it clearly as a major turning point in Western educational thought and practice, as an ever chaotic but always interesting period of transition from the major assumptions and ideologies which had guided education until well into the nineteenth century to those which then guided it in the twenty-first century and beyond. If we are to be so fortunate, then the chaos of our century will have proved fertile and the educational practices of the future — including curriculum evaluation — will surely embody a fuller, more comprehensive vision of humanness than those of the present. If so, then the basic problems of curriculum evaluation will come to be seen neither as essentially metaphysical (as they have been seen in the past), nor as essentially technical (as they are usually seen in the present), but as essentially the problems of human possibility they are. Human problems, of course, are subject to multiplicity of perspectives, personal decisions, and inconclusive testing of alternative actions in ways that other kinds of problems are not. How, then, do different orientations to curriculum evaluation embody different presuppositions about how evaluee, evaluator, and audience of evaluation (whether these be different persons or one in the same) actually make decisions or, in a larger sense, actually live their lives?

This chapter will not attempt to provide closure on such broad questions. Its purpose is simply to outline briefly some different possibilities between the messy human approach to curriculum evaluation which may characterize our future and the neater technical approach which now, in the latter one-half of the twentieth century, dominates curriculum evaluation in the United States. In keeping with this purpose, it will not attempt precisely to define or to delineate the two approaches, for neither can be completely characterized by reference to methodology, procedures, or anything else which is invariant. More properly, therefore, each approach should be seen as a general orientation specifically toward the tasks of curriculum evaluation, but in a broader sense toward life itself. What are the beliefs and intentions of evaluators? Why have they chosen certain procedures? What do they expect to accomplish by casting their findings in certain forms? How do they perceive other people? What do they think about themselves? While orientations differ from one another, they are still broad and flexible enough to admit of some change and some overlap. Thus, although statistically derived generalizations are commonly used in the technical approach, a humanly oriented evaluator may sometimes find ways of using such generalizations to inform the autonomous actions of students and teachers. Although case studies of specific individuals and situations are commonly used in the human approach, a technically oriented evaluator may believe such studies represent universal truths from which desirable courses of action for all students and teachers can always be derived and warranted. Rather than provide definitions, this essay will attempt to gradually build up portraits of the two approaches.

What Is Being Evaluated?

In general, a curriculum can be considered in one of two ways. Perhaps the more common way is to define a curriculum as a course of study, an arrangement of subject matter or a plan of what is to happen in school. The technical approach to curriculum evaluation usually views curricula in this way and is based on the assumption that a curriculum can best be evaluated by determining its results. For instance, one assumes that if students learn more when subject matter is arranged the first way than the second way, then the first arrangement is a more desirable curriculum than the second. Evaluation becomes the search — usually "objective" or "scientific" — for results, usually those prespecified as "goals." On its surface this assumption is straightforward and commonsensical; evidence of success is hard to argue with, especially if it is gathered in an open and aboveboard way. At the very least, however, the technical approach leaves the term *curriculum evaluation* as a misnomer.

In the first place, this approach begs the question of the desirability of the curriculum; hence, it is not really evaluation at all. Because students learned the chosen subject matter does not mean that subject matter was worth learning. Why was that subject matter chosen? Why is it more worthwhile than some other subject matter? Any complete vision of curriculum evaluation must include the human application of values to competing states of affairs (i.e., proposed curricula) in order to determine their desirability. Questions of value require direct analysis of the curriculum itself and cannot be answered simply by appeal to results. Direct analysis begins with such fundamental questions as: How adequately does proposed subject matter represent reality? How logically is subject matter arranged? These questions are essentially metaphysical, and the evaluator may believe that the most desirable state of affairs is the one which most accurately reflects the underlying reality of the universe. Surely a course of study that accurately and coherently reflects reality is more intrinsically worthwhile than one that does not and is also more likely — even if incidentally — to yield desirable utilitarian results. Beginning with metaphysical questions precludes consideration of neither human problems nor utilitarian ends. However, it is a reminder that when curriculum is considered as the course of study, curriculum evaluation must include direct analysis of the subject matter itself and some search for how its intrinsic characteristics can be valued in human terms. In general, the technical approach fails to undertake these tasks, for in reducing its focus to the search for specific results, it assumes that subject matter has no intrinsic value, that it can be valued only as it contributes to certain extrinsic goals, that, in effect, curricular means are justified only by their utilitarian ends. This is not to evaluate the curriculum itself.

In the second place, the technical approach always involves a leap of faith: the evaluator assumes, but can never be sure, that any results discerned are actually the results of the course of study. Hence, what the evaluator investigates may have nothing to do with the curriculum at all. In the natural sciences, which the technical approach takes as its model, the search is for unambiguous causal relationships. When these always apply under the same conditions they can be stated as causal laws; thus, in the natural sciences leaps of faith are minimized or avoided altogether. But the human sciences are different. Human sciences deal with individual human beings as autonomous moral agents living under a myriad of constantly changing circumstances that can never be exactly repeated. Although influenced by their environments, autonomous human beings work out their own values and take their own actions. Therefore, in human affairs causal laws never apply. What the technical approach offers as the results of the curriculum are only a few of the many things that may be influenced by it, but even these have been highly mediated by numerous intervening human decisions (mostly by teachers and students) and by the complex social context in which they take place. Such considerations are what make the study of schooling at once immensely complicated and immensely fascinating. The technical approach usually attempts to deal with these difficulties by focusing only on prespecified goals and by using statistical procedures to derive generalizations about the fit between goals and selected evidence. While such generalizations are sometimes useful, they reduce live human beings and their problems to abstractions and illicitly suggest that causal relationships can be established in human affairs. Evidence of presumed results of a course of study can never avoid the leap of faith and can never settle questions of value. In education, as in all human affairs, good means can exist simultaneously with bad ends and vice-versa, and causal connections are at best tenuous. The notorious truth about schooling is that what students learn depends on a lot more than the formal course of study.

A curriculum can be considered in a second general way, however: not as the course of study or a plan, but as what actually happens to the student. The technical approach seldom views a curriculum in this way (and when it does so it begins to blend off into the human approach to curriculum evaluation). This second view obviates some major difficulties of the first but opens up some new complexities. Because evidence of "what actually happens" is considered a manifestation of a curriculum itself, the evaluator need not attempt to establish connections between evidence and something more remote. Classroom life itself is thrust to the forefront of evaluation, becoming both means and ends simultaneously; therefore, a leap of faith is unnecessary. Furthermore, although the central task of evaluating can still be evaded by whoever refuses to apply values and insists on collecting evidence only (leaving the term *curriculum evaluation* a misnomer), this evasion becomes less likely. Because the curriculum is viewed as immediate instead of remote, it can also be analyzed and valued immediately, in terms of both its intrinsic and extrinsic characteristics. No longer bound by prespecified goals, the evaluator is free to ponder the desirability of what happens in a variety of ways, both before and after the fact. For instance, the evaluator may decide that what happened was different from but more desirable than what was anticipated.

In this second view of curriculum, the "what actually happens" can itself be considered in a variety of ways ranging from the narrow notion that what happens to the student is the same as what the student is exposed to (leaving this view little different from the first view), to the broader notion that what happens is what the student does, to the broadest possible notion that what happens is what the student experiences. The idea of experiencing is itself subject to a variety of interpretations. In general, the human approach to curriculum evaluation considers the curriculum as experience in the broadest possible sense, as the complex array of thoughts, feelings, and actions that individual students undergo and undertake in living their lives in schools. In this sense, evaluating the curriculum is not much different from evaluating living in general. The same problems of human possibility obtrude whenever one attempts to assess the quality of experiencing or living. In weighing alternative values and alternative courses of action, the same complexity obtains. In the human approach, the course of study is viewed as one of many things that influences the curriculum, the experience of individual students, but investigation focuses on the quality of experiencing itself. Thus, the second general view of curriculum, as what actually happens to students (unless the "what actually happens" is itself defined extremely narrowly), opens up a wide variety of tasks to the evaluator. These may include analysis of the course of study and investigation of how parts of the environment influence students, but they also include the weighing of how autonomous individuals choose to live their lives.

A Little History

Until well into and perhaps even throughout the nineteenth century, the course of study in most American schools was more classical than utilitarian. American schools largely embodied the time-honored Western belief that a relatively few, well-ordered, academic subjects were repositories of the highest knowledge and led to understanding, virtue, and godliness, the proper condition of cultivated human beings. There were a few protests, such as Benjamin Franklin's proposal for a practical course of study for the youth of Pennsylvania, and, of course, the study of such classical subjects as mathematics did yield utilitarian benefits. But in a sparsely settled, agrarian country, few Americans received more than a rudimentary formal education, and practical pursuits were learned in the home, through apprenticeships, and through the activities of daily living.

The prevailing ideology was culturally conservative. The aim of schooling was to preserve the culture by immersing students in it. The mass of students whose brief immersion led to little more than basic skills in reading, writing, and mathematics could at least take their appropriate places in the American social order. The few who were cultivated by any higher knowledge could become the leaders of society. The major difference between American ideology and that which usually prevailed elsewhere in Western civilization lay in the growing American impulse toward egalitarianism and democracy. This impulse provided the ethical basis for the expanded schooling made available to increasing numbers of students, though expanded schooling soon became justified in utilitarian terms. At the beginning of the nineteenth century, most Americans probably believed that everyone deserved a little formal education but only a few people would actually benefit from a lot; by the beginning of the twentieth century, most seemed to believe that almost everyone could benefit materially from extended formal education.

As long as the older order prevailed, however, curriculum evaluation was divorced from a search for practical results. The course of study was viewed as the curriculum, and asking about its metaphysical character was primary: How well did the time-honored academic subjects embody the underlying truths and order of the universe? Curriculum evaluation *was* this kind of analysis of subject matter. Although different arrangements of subject matter were advocated, few evaluators saw any reason to question the assumptions that the basic purpose of the curriculum was to reflect the metaphysical order and that classical subjects did so more directly than did utilitarian subjects. And if students failed to learn, these deficiencies were not attributable to the curriculum, but to deficiencies in the students themselves or in how they were instructed.

By the twentieth century, the older order was crumbling. Shifts from a rural-agrarian society to an urban-industrial one, massive waves of immigrants, the gradual expansion of schooling, and numerous other changes in American life helped create conditions under which the prevailing educational ideology in the United States had become essentially utilitarian. Although resisted by conservatives, emphasis increasingly fell on the practical and social ends of schooling. With the rise of progressive education, many educators came to believe that society itself could be improved either through the direct efforts of the school or as an indirect consequence of the individual development of large numbers of students. Education could begin with the individual interests of students, and the course of study could largely be determined by those activities which led to good consequences. As the leading spokesman for progressive education, John Dewey made clear that this kind of utilitarianism must not be construed too narrowly, that the enrichment of individual experience began in the cultivation of the student's intelligence and led to the individual's autonomous and humane participation in a democratic social order. However, despite Dewey's warnings, on a mass scale the utilitarian ideology was construed narrowly: many educators focused not on the development of intelligence but on the development of specific skills, not on autonomous participation in a democratically evolving society but on fitting into the existing society. The ethical basis for the ideology, fostering the fullest development of all students by treating them in individually appropriate ways, could be subverted when ends were chosen for students, conceived narrowly, or otherwise constrained.

Given the new ideology, how it was commonly interpreted, and the growing number and kinds of courses taught in American schools, the curriculum came to be regarded as something that should be evaluated primarily by its results. No longer could classical, academic, or any other subjects be regarded as intrinsically valuable; their value had to be demonstrated in terms of their usefulness. Further compounding the problem was the fact that the same subject could have different degrees of usefulness for different students or simply because of differences in how it was arranged or taught. Dewey in his own writings identified the curriculum with experience, but progressive education in general tended to emphasize the social side of experience more than the personal side. This emphasis tended to thrust back toward the older view of curriculum as subject matter, which was held by most socially conservative educators, whether they were old-line advocates of a classical, academic curriculum or newer advocates of a functional, well-ordered, efficient society. During the first one-half of the twentieth century the main educational and social currents in the United States were, therefore, more conducive to the development of the technical approach to curriculum evaluation than the human approach.

Illustrating the conflicting forces in curriculum evaluation during the first one-half of the century is the Eight-Year Study.[1] This study in some ways still represents the single most significant piece of curriculum research and evaluation ever undertaken. It compared students who attended progressive, experimental secondary schools with those who attended traditional schools, following them from 1932 to 1940, their eight high school and college years. Students from each of the two types of secondary schools were placed in 1,475 matched pairs on the basis of their background, academic aptitude, and other personal characteristics. Comparisons were made not only on their academic achievement, but also on such things as their intellectual and personal resourcefulness, particularly their ability to solve problems, meet new situations, and participate in a variety of activities. What the study seemed to demonstrate was that in general students from the experimental secondary schools did slightly better in college academically but were decidedly better off in their personal and social lives. It was widely interpreted as indicating the superiority of a progressive over a traditional arrangement of subject matter, especially one which left choices open to students.

As an outgrowth of progressive education, the Eight-Year Study accepted the utilitarian ideology but interpreted it more broadly and generously than any other large-scale evaluation study of the time. It served as an example in which what was seen as useful was not just academic achievement or specific skills, but a whole host of things that helped students live their lives well. Long-range, relatively intangible forms of growth were carefully considered. Particularly impressive were the many new techniques that the study pioneered for collecting information about thinking, interests, social adjustment, and so on. In thus evincing concern for the overall experience of students and how they managed their own development, it was consistent with the human approach to curriculum evaluation and can appropriately be seen as a forerunner of this approach. On the other hand, the study hinged on comparing two

321

alternative forms of education (largely defined by alternative arrangements of subject matter and their implementation) in terms of discernible results. In so doing it treated generalized results as more important in determining desirability than the immediate and specific qualities of classroom experience. What, for instance, did the study mean for those specific students in matched pairs in which results were mixed or the student from the traditional school seemed to develop more fully? Generalized results were not very helpful in understanding their specific situations. In creating new techniques for collecting information about developmental growth, the study also seemed to suggest that desirable experiencing could be inferred directly from evidence of growth and that all useful evidence could be somehow discerned objectively, without painstakingly sifting the divergent—and perhaps equally valuable—perspectives of different participants for their own insights. In so embodying a less than full notion of experiencing and a utilitarian means-ends rationale implicit in its search for objective results, the Eight-Year Study was thereby also consistent with the technical approach to curriculum evaluation. Certainly, it ran against the main currents of the time, proved instructive, and advanced some forms of progressive education that tended to open up human possibilities, but in the last analysis it embodied a mixed approach to evaluation that was perhaps as much technical as human.

Despite its example, in the second one-half of the century, educational and social currents have become even more conducive to the technical approach and the Eight-Year Study has been largely forgotten or ignored by curriculum evaluators. The prevailing educational ideology in the United States has become increasingly homogenized and more pointedly utilitarian, not in the relatively grotesque ways of the earlier social efficiency movements, which were easy to burlesque, but in more subtle and seductive ways. For example, the ethical impulse behind the national push toward egalitarianism and democracy was originally based on Enlightenment ideas about the value and the rights of individuals. It led in the nineteenth century toward the break up of the old, culturally conservative educational ideology and the demand for universal education, and in the first one-half of the twentieth century toward the development of a utilitarian ideology that could accommodate cultural change and the concomitant demand for education of sufficient quality and appropriateness to actualize the diverse individual potentials of all students. In the second one-half of the century, however, the ethical impulse has been transmuted as the utilitarian ideology has been interpreted more and more in strictly materialistic terms. Egalitarianism and democracy may no longer mean to most Americans that all individuals should have the same rights and opportunities to participate in a pluralistic society, but that all should receive the same tangible benefits from their participation. Therefore, schools have been seen as places that should homogenize society by guaranteeing that all students learn the same things. After all, countless students have been economically handicapped throughout their lives because they have not learned to read, or write, or perform simple mathematical calculations as well as their peers. Thoughtful critics have pointed out how schools, at times, have served to maintain social stratification. For these and many other reasons, schools have been seen increasingly as places that fulfill their ethical obligations primarily by bestowing the same tangible benefits and only secondarily by releasing diverse human potential. The egalitarian push has shifted in the direction of educational and social sameness; hence, the new utilitarian ideology has become culturally conservative once more. Under these circumstances, curriculum evaluation is itself pushed toward the search for discernible evidence of those useful results that society believes the schools should be achieving, and, particularly during the 1980s, usefulness has been seen by American society primarily in terms of specific skills and financial rewards.

This narrowing of America's ethical impulse and its collective interpretation of utilitarianism has been channelled by numerous cultural, economic, and political currents in the social mainstream. Among those most powerful in carrying forward the technical approach to curriculum evaluation have been certain well-intentioned actions of the federal government. Focused by the *Brown v. Board of Education of Topeka* decision of the Supreme Court in 1954, the federal government became increasingly concerned with the problem the Court called "equality of educational opportunity." Efforts to end segregation met opposition, of course, but left the government with no great psychic dilemma. But should the government attempt more directly to promote educational equality? And if so, on ethical or economic grounds? In *Brown*, the Court had held that both grounds are important, ruling that segregated education deprives students of constitutional rights *and* impedes learning. In the 1960s, the government answered these questions with the Great Society programs of the Johnson Administration, which stressed the economic value of education, particularly to poor or potentially poor people who, it claimed, could use education to lift themselves out of poverty. Clearly, however, the quality of education in the diverse public schools across the nation was highly uneven. The United States had achieved universal education, but not all schools achieved the same universally good results. The programs of the Johnson administration dealt with this problem by infusing into local schools large amounts of federal financial aid on an unprecedented scale. These programs did not equalize the quality of education across the country (though they did serve to distribute more equally some of its benefits), but they helped create a new set of national expectations and certainly created a new breed of educational evaluator.

Although the intentions of the Johnson Administration were in part shaped by ethical concerns for the individual, the effects of its programs were to help foster the beliefs that education can be judged by its tangible results and that tangible results should be equalized for all students, closely related to economic benefits, and created on a mass scale by appropriate strategies and actions. Such beliefs, of course, were instrumental in shifting educators' efforts from attempting to maximize each individual's development to attempting to equalize what each individual learned. Furthermore, in order to ensure that aid was being used in intended programs and to bring about intended results, most federal legislation soon required that 10 percent of the aid be used for "objective" evaluation of the programs. Prior to this period, most educational evaluation had been relatively small and informal. Districts or individual schools worked out their own principles and procedures. Where there was formal evaluation, it was often tied to classroom observations of supervisors aimed at helping teachers improve or to the districtwide administration of standardized achievement tests. It was obvious that across the nation few districts were prepared to provide the kind of evaluations that the federal government now demanded and that even those who could do so should not be entrusted with evaluating themselves. A lot was at stake. The curriculum to be evaluated was no longer just the course of study, it was the whole host of new, federally funded programs intended to solve the nation's most intractable educational and social problems. Determining results (and, by the 1970s, cost effectiveness) became a national priority. A vague, human approach would not satisfy the federal government, which now paid the evaluation piper; the technical approach quickly became the only called for tune in town.

Drawn into this vacuum created by federal expectations and money was the new breed of educational evaluator, which included people who could most convincingly lay claim to objectivity and technical expertise. With few exceptions, they were neither school people nor familiar with the Eight-Year Study; they were trained in the then-emerging techniques of social science research — measurement, statistical analysis, experimental design — which largely emulated the natural sciences. Many came from specialties outside of education, such as psychology and sociology, because familiarity with techniques was seen as necessary for evaluators, not familiarity with educational issues and settings. Use of social science techniques itself seemed important, whereas insight into education did not. Ability to distance oneself from the situation and to abstract data seemed to provide objectivity, whereas ability to immerse oneself in the situation and to interpret data in context did not. Perhaps drawn into this vacuum also was the nation at large, for it seemed willing to accept the specific assumptions and the overall ethos of the technical approach. Over the last two decades the new breed of evaluator has gradually learned some of the inherent limitations and difficulties of attempting to provide a warrant of success or failure for programs by abstracting selected evidence. For at least the first of these two decades, however, the technical approach completely dominated educational evaluation in the United States. Only since the late 1970s and early 1980s has the evaluation community formed by the vacuum of the 1960s grudgingly afforded any real legitimacy to procedures associated with the human approach (for example, use of participant observation and the case study format), and it still collectively persists in forcing even these into a technical framework. Progress toward a broadened view of evaluation has been exceedingly slow.

These developments, however, merely illustrate what is at the heart of the matter, the twentieth century shift in America's utilitarian educational ideology and in what the nation collectively believes the schools can and should accomplish. If usefulness is interpreted in the most narrowly practical way, then schools will have little more to do than teach specific skills useful in maintaining the existing society. If America's democratic impulses are continually compressed into a materialistic egalitarianism, then schools will not be encouraged to aim at maximizing diverse human potential but at teaching minimum competencies. There is a twofold problem with education that aims at providing everyone with similar results, particularly in a narrowly utilitarian, materialistic sense. First, as a practical matter, the aims cannot be realized. Individual people and their interests, aspirations, ideas, and skills are too diverse. Then, too, the health of a democracy and the enrichment of individual lives depend on this diversity. Second, as an ethical matter the aims themselves become a source of error, both because they encourage educators to claim they can produce results that they cannot (inevitably lacking certain knowledge of the relationship between means and ends, B. F. Skinner notwithstanding) and because they encourage educators to try in ways that treat students as less than fully human (not, for instance, as autonomous). The basic problem with the technical approach to curriculum evaluation is the same. In accepting the task of providing warrant for education defined in terms of results, it accepts a distorted and stereotypical vision of education, of human beings, and of the real human problems and possibilities in ethical living.

A Potential Ideology

What this chapter has thus far suggested is that under the twentieth century press toward social efficiency in the United States, the nation's educational ideology and ethical impulses have become unduly narrow, focusing less on individual development and democratic social change and more on specific functioning within the prevailing social framework. As education has become more narrowly utilitarian it has tended to treat individuals in technical, less than fully human terms. Therefore, what is needed is a new ideology within which the development of individual potential can be highly valued and a complete vision of humanness can emerge, one in which the individual is seen as an autonomous perceiver, meaning-maker, and world-builder. Within such an ideology the curriculum might come to be valued more for how it helps people become fully human and less for its purported technical results; hence, curriculum evaluation would itself be seen in light of human problems and possibilities. The precise form of such an ideology that might actually emerge in the twenty-first century is, of course, impossible to foresee, but James B. Macdonald has sketched a possible prototype in his essay "A Transcendental Developmental Ideology of Education."[2]

According to Macdonald, an ideology must account for the dialectic between the inner experience of individuals and the outer world in which they live. In his view, the four specific ideologies that have recently vied for currency in the United States do not adequately account for the dialectic. These are the romantic, developmental, cultural transmission, and radical ideologies. The romantic ideology deals with only one side of the dialectic. It locates knowledge and value solely in inner experience. Truth is self-knowledge, and value is derived from the unfolding or maturation of the individual. As long as individuals are free, they are essentially good unless somehow corrupted by society. The cultural transmission ideology deals only with the opposite side of the dialectic. It locates knowledge and value solely in the outer world. The individual is to learn about and to be shaped by the "objective" world and its truths, or at least by those cultural values for which there is a consensus. The developmental ideology locates knowledge and value in transactions between the inner self and the outer world. Truth is pragmatic in that it is what is useful in resolving relationships between the inner and the outer, but, as this ideology is interpreted by most adherents, values are based upon ethical universals that are derived rationally and serve developmental means and ends. Although the developmental ideology deals with both sides of the dialectic, it is weighted toward the side of inner experience in assuming that transactions can best be carried out only by individuals who have developed in terms of universal cognitive and moral structures, and it therefore assumes that inner experience should be fundamentally the same for all individuals. The radical ideology is similar to the developmental in locating knowledge and value in transactions, and viewing truth as pragmatic and values as rationally derived. Historically, however, radical ideology has so heavily emphasized the analysis of shortcomings in social reality that it is weighted toward the side of the outer world in assuming that analysis must be carried out in terms of external, environmental structures, and it therefore assumes that the outer world affects all individuals in fundamentally the same way.

The major shifts in America's educational ideology exemplify Macdonald's analysis. The prevailing ideology in the nineteenth century was that of cultural transmission, which emphasized the structures of the outer world and a pedagogy of efficient transmisson. The twentieth century shifts to a predominantly utilitarian ideology at first opened the possibility of a balanced dialectic between inner experience and outer world, but as even progressive education came to encourage socialization more than personal development, emphasis again fell on the outer world. Social adjustment could be facilitated by using principles from behavioral psychology, and even personal development came to be seen in terms of universal structures that could be sought out scientifically, encouraged efficiently, and evaluated technically. As utilitarianism became interpreted in more narrow and materialistic ways, the split between inner experience and outer world deepened and technical, socially efficient approaches to education, such as behaviorism, became thoroughly engrained. Radicalism might emphasize why democratic ideals have not been fully realized in American society, and romanticism the value of unrestrained personal development, but neither could establish a balanced dialectic. For instance, Macdonald sees considerable value in the radical critique of society but believes the radical ideology accepts too many of the same assumptions about the external world and rationality as do the cultural transmission and developmental ideologies to undermine the current utilitarianism.

The transcendental developmental ideology Macdonald advocates strikes a balance between inner experience and outer world and is meant to overcome misguided efforts to provide empirical grounding of developmental norms and benign control of developmental growth. Both efforts place undue limits on human potential and distort the nature of inner experience. The transcendental developmental ideology is based on a dual dialectical process. One dialectic exists between individuals and their outer worlds; another, within individuals themselves. The outer world consists not only of the immediate environment, situations, decisions, and acts of which the individual is aware, but also of all larger environmental structures which impinge on each situation. The outer dialectic exists as a reflective transaction between the outer world and the explicit awareness of the individual (the individual's explicit knowledge, beliefs, ideas, and wishes). The inner dialectic exists as an aesthetic transaction between explicit beliefs, ideas, and wishes and the individual's preconscious and unconscious functioning (the tacit knowledge, values, needs, and potentials that are the source and grounding of explicit beliefs). The outer dialectic is the source of utilitarian values as the individual intelligently reflects upon the consequences of human activities within objective and historical situational contexts. The inner dialectic is the source both of values beyond the utilitarian (such as personal and aesthetic) and of the validation of values as the individual encounters what it means to be a human being. For instance, one could not *decide* to act rationally without grounding

327

this decision in the tacit self. Thus, one literally feels one's way to being fully human by living values in addition to the utilitarian. The outer dialectic puts us in touch with the human problems and possibilities of acting rationally in the outer world; the inner dialectic, with the human problems and possibilities of being fully human. As Macdonald states:

> Values, I believe, are articulated in the lives of people by the dual dialectic of reflecting upon the consequences of an action and sounding the depths of our inner selves. Only a process something like this can explain why 'what works is not always good'. Some dual dialectic is also needed to explain the existence of reason, or aesthetic rationality, to counterbalance purely technological rationality.[3]

Given the dual dialectic, which balances outer worlds and inner experience, the general aim of education consistent with the transcendental developmental ideology is what Macdonald calls *centering*. Centering cannot be defined in specific terms. It is a search that is facilitated by a spiritual attitude, utilizes the full potential of each individual, and leads toward the creation of meaning and the awareness of wholeness as a person. It depends on knowledge of the outer world waiting to be discovered, but this knowledge must be personalized and validated within the idiosyncratic inner experience of each individual. But personal knowledge thrusts back toward the outer world because culture is created by the common set of personal constructs that individuals use to share their perceptions of what it means to be human; therefore, within this ideology, education may be culturally conservative yet still promote cultural change as centering grounds knowledge in the human base from which it grows.

Centering can be seen as the developmental goal of education, but being a process of releasing an almost infinite variety of human potential, it transcends the ordinary developmental goals that are empirically grounded in the outer world and that can, thus, be as limiting as liberating. The curriculum should not be seen, therefore, as a series of goals or results justified by their utility in the outer world but as a series of processes that include activities consonant with the process of centering itself, hence innately valuable in releasing potential. Macdonald suggests that many processes facilitate centering, among which are pattern making, playing, meditative thinking, imagining, educating awareness of aesthetic principles, educating awareness of the body and our biology, and educating perception. Clearly, activities embodying such processes traditionally have been absent or neglected within the curricula of American schools or rendered inconsonant with the aim of centering under the utilitarian press of the twentieth century. Macdonald also suggests the kinds of questions that can be asked about curricula in light of the transcendental developmental aim of centering:

1. What kinds of activity are encouraged that provide for opening up perceptual experiences?
2. What kinds of activity facilitate the process of sensitizing people to others, to inner vibrations?
3. What kinds of activity provide experiences for developing closeknit community relationships?
4. What kinds of activity encourage and facilitate religious experiences?
5. What kinds of activity facilitate the development of patterned meaning structures?
6. What ways can we organize knowledge to enlarge human potential through meaning?
7. How can we facilitate the development of inner strength and power in human beings?[4]

This list of questions is far from exhaustive of those that could be asked about curricula within a new and human ideology of the type Macdonald describes and that could guide American education in the twenty-first century. For the purposes of this chapter, it illustrates the kinds of questions about curricula that the technical approach to evaluation does not ask and the human approach does. Curriculum evaluation *can* focus on such human questions concerning centering and not merely on questions about utilitarian results. Even more important for the purposes of this chapter, the list illustrates the kinds of questions that can be asked about curriculum evaluation itself. Curriculum evaluation can be evaluated in terms of whether its assumptions and activities promote centering, for curriculum evaluators cannot suppress their inner dialectics and still hope to carry on adequate dialectics with the outer world.

The Perceptive and Reflective Evaluator

To be fully human, all people must engage in the dual dialectic. Hence, centering is the general transcendental aim of all education and all living, regardless of whatever smaller, more narrowly utilitarian goals may obtrude along the way. The point is not that such goals never serve certain limited developmental outcomes, but that they may interfere with the process of being fully human. At the close of his essay, Macdonald points out that in the ordinary developmental ideology the teacher stands back from the student in a judgmental stance. The teacher's knowledge of the student, the student's developmental status, and long-range developmental goals are explicitly cognitive. Despite any humane intentions, the teacher's predominant rationality is technical: planning, manipulating, calculating. In contrast, when teachers and students immerse themselves in the mutual process of centering, the predominant rationality becomes aesthetic, intuitive, and spontaneous. They become willing to "let go" of externally defined roles, to undertake a joint pilgrimage in creative human living, having faith that they themselves, others, and the culture in which they exist will become a medium for developing centering.

The same relationships can exist between evaluators and evaluees. Evaluators may distance themselves from specific situations, adopt a technical rationality, attempt to obtain objectified evidence, and make judgments in terms of utilitarian goals for "the good of" evaluees or the external society. In contrast, they may immerse themselves in specific situations with evaluees, carry on a dual dialectic, respond aesthetically and intuitively to the lived situations, and make judgments in terms of how this joint living contributes to the mutual aim of centering. In the former case, good evaluation is seen as skillful use of techniques that reify the situation, the evaluator's dialectic is solely outer, and the value system on which judgments are based is some kind of rationalistic calculus about utility in the outer world. Whether the curriculum is considered as subject matter, activities, or experience, emphasis falls on efficiency and control. How well does the curriculum contribute to the prescribed utility? How can its utility be demonstrated? In the latter case, good evaluation is seen as perceptive and reflective apprehension of the human complexities of the entire situation, the evaluator's dialectic is both outer and inner, and the value system on which judgments are based originates in this dual dialectic and balances personal, aesthetic, and utilitarian concerns. Regardless of how the curriculum is considered, emphasis falls on ethical living. How does the curriculum free the potentials of all participants in the situation? How can such liberation be communicated to and lived by other people?

If centering is to become the general transcendental aim of curriculum evaluation, then evaluators will gradually relinquish the technical approach to evaluation and adopt the human approach as their own orientations shift toward the human problems and possibilities at the heart of ethical living. They will gradually become aware of their inner dialectics and will enhance their perceptiveness, which makes accessible the ever-present, but often overlooked, qualities of the outer world and which puts explicit consciousness in touch with the tacit self. In developing perceptiveness they will expand the basis upon which they carry on reflective transactions through the outer dialectic with the outer world. They will become increasingly aware that good evaluation depends on refining both perceptiveness and reflectiveness and that these processes reinforce each other. Perceptiveness is a way of encountering an ever-richer variety of multiple and ambiguous data from the outer world and the tacit self. Reflectiveness is the dialogue within explicit consciousness in which the self attempts to make sense of varied perceptual data and to decide which always ambiguous actions should be taken in the always imperfect and imperfectly perceived outside world. Evaluators will come to realize there are neither complete perceptions nor perfect actions, but, lacking final answers, it is still better to try than not to try. This is perhaps the fundamental human problem of curriculum evaluation: to struggle to perceive clearly and completely, to value wisely, and to act ethically, all the while knowing that in terms of achieving all that we can hope, the struggle will ultimately fail. There are no unequivocally good actions, whatever our intentions. But the struggle is the essence of being human, for the struggle itself becomes the "curriculum" that releases potential. There is no centering without this course of study. It always has intrinsic value, although not necessarily utilitarian value. Once evaluators perceive this truth about the world, they will value their own activities by the same criteria they evaluate the curriculum. They will not look for specific results but will look to activities such as pattern-making and educating perception that are consonant with and facilitate centering.

The basic differences between the technical approach and the human approach to curriculum evaluation therefore depend primarily on the perceptiveness and the reflectiveness of the evaluator. The evaluator who pursues the goal of centering acts in general as fully human and perceives evaluees as fully human. Specific actions intended to release potential thus embody the evaluator's reflective assumptions about the centrality of autonomy in human life. The evaluator who pursues the goal of utilitarian results acts in general as less than fully human and perceives evaluees as less than fully human. Specific actions intended to warrant results thus embody the evaluator's reflective assumptions about the lack of autonomy in human life. Although certain actions or techniques are more closely associated with one approach to evaluation or the other, they do not embody that approach in and of themselves but — more accurately — reflect the orientation and assumptions of the evaluator. For instance, ethnography, the case study format, and qualitative data are usually associated with the human approach, but efforts to treat ethnographies as a science of invariant cultural structures, to use case studies to portray universals, or to analyze or interpret qualitative data as unambiguous are consistent with a technological rationality and embody assumptions about the lack of human autonomy. In contrast, behavioral goals are usually associated with the technological approach to evaluation but may under some circumstances (such as use by someone learning meditation through bio-feedback) serve the larger goal of centering and embody assumptions about the centrality of human autonomy. To be sure, the perceptive and reflective evaluator is not likely to undertake many of the same actions that the nonperceptive and nonreflective evaluator is, but some specific actions overlap both approaches to evaluation.

Because the basic differences between the two approaches depend on the perceptiveness and reflectiveness of the evaluator, this chapter will conclude by noting some salient differences within evaluators themselves. The technically oriented evaluator accepts limits on human potential and relies only on the outer dialectic (and this, unfortunately, sometimes only in attenuated form). Standing before the real mysteries of the universe, this evaluator insists they are not there, for they are of no account within a rationalistic-materialistic calculus. Thus, in general, the perceptiveness and reflectiveness of the technically oriented evaluator are less fully developed than those of the humanly oriented evaluator, who accepts no limits on human potential, relies on both the outer and the inner dialectics, and, standing in awe of the real mysteries of the universe, attempts to embrace them. The development of perceptiveness and reflectiveness helps to orient this evaluator to the fullness of human potential; in turn, this orientation expands perceptions and reflections. Both contribute to centering. In contrast to the developed perceptiveness and reflectiveness of the humanly oriented evaluator, the technically oriented evaluator tends to look but not to see, to hypothesize but not to realize, to find facts but not to make meanings, to participate but not to create, and to evaluate but not to value.

In the final analysis, then, human beings seem to consider evaluation in two different but related ways. The ordinary way views evaluation as appraisal, the determining of the worth of something. There is value in carefully and cooly calculating worth. Doing so helps us know how to live, and we should avoid all the mistakes we can. Both the technical and the human approaches to curriculum evaluation eventually get around to deciding on a value system against which appraisals can be made, although the technical often seems all too ready to accept uncritically given values, and its nominal evaluators themselves seldom actually weigh alternative value systems. Still, both approaches consider evaluation as a process of determining worth, however different they may be on how evaluation should be carried out.

The human approach, however, is more attuned to a second way of considering evaluation. This less ordinary way views evaluation as the valuing of something in the sense of celebrating it. What can always be celebrated is intrinsic worth. Intrinsic worth does not need to be calculated against some external standard, for it radiates its own warmth. For the humanly oriented evaluator, there is intrinsic worth in centering; in viewing human beings as free, autonomous meaning-makers and world-builders; in helping them perceptively and reflectively value their own inner experiences and the outer world. Instead of turning away from the problems and possibilities of human living, the curriculum evaluator can celebrate them. The humanly oriented evaluator has found there indeed is value in both seeing and joining in the celebration.

332

Notes

1. The Eight-Year Study was reported in five volumes, the first of which summarizes the entire study. See Wilford M. Aikin, *The Story of the Eight-Year Study* (New York: Harper & Bros., 1942)

2. James B. Macdonald, "A Transcendental Developmental Ideology of Education," in *Heightened Consciousness, Cultural Revolution, and Curriculum Theory*, William F. Pinar, ed. (Berkeley, Calif.: McCutchan Publishing Corporation, 1974).

3. *Ibid.*, p. 96.

4. *Ibid.*, pp. 105–6.

SEVENTEEN

Social Evaluation of Curriculum

Michael W. Apple and *Landon E. Beyer*

In this chapter, we want to demonstrate some of the inherent limitations of the usual ways educational evaluation is carried out.[1] In particular, we wish both to challenge the dominance of curriculum evaluation based on achievement test results and to suggest a set of questions and strategies that will be more responsive to the actual socioeconomic reality of schools. In so doing, we propose ways of engaging in the social evaluation of curriculum that go beyond the more individualistically and psychologically oriented models in use today.

We argue that because evaluation is a process of *placing value* on a procedure, process, goal, or outcome,[2] alternatives to the current ways we do place value on curricula can only be developed by both seeing how values now work through our activity and expanding the ways we look at these procedures, processes, goals, or outcomes to include the ideological and economic "functions" of our educational system.[3]

Our discussion construes evaluation somewhat differently than it has often been construed in the past. Evaluation is seen by many educators as demonstrating whether a specific program, text, etc. — given "the limitations of student background and ability" — is successful and then giving feedback to participants, administrators, or funding agencies about its degree of success. A comparison between the stated goals of curricular programs and how far the students have gone is not inherently wrong. After all, there may be times when goal directedness and efficiency are important. However, most of the procedures developed to deal with these concerns, while often technically sophisticated, remain relatively unreflective about the interests, values, and ideologies in the curriculum or even embodied in the concerns themselves. Given this, we take one fundamental task of evaluation in education to be unpacking what schools and curricula actually do socially.

Technical Concerns and Social Interests

Most evaluations of school curricula rely on measures of the achievement scores of pupils to determine the success of a specific curricular offering. They rest on particular assumptions regarding efficiency, cost effectiveness, ability, and mean gain in student achievement. Curricula "work" if they "produce" higher test scores, for less money, in a measurable and relatively uncomplicated way. We break down the knowledge we want to teach into atomistic units of behavior (ignoring in the process the potent practical, conceptual, and political limitations of such a reductive approach), give pre-tests, determine "ability," teach, then test, and start the whole cycle over again. The focus is on technical questions (Did we get from point A to point B?), not on whether B, or the process of getting there, is ethically or politically defensible.

This emphasis on what has been called process/product thinking has had a rather long history. For the better part of this century, educators have searched long and hard for a general set of technical procedures that would guide curriculum planning and evaluation. In large part, this has reduced itself to attempts at creating *the most efficient method* of doing curriculum work. This stress on method has not been without its negative consequences. At the same time that process/product rationality grew, the fact that curriculum planning and evaluation was through and through a political enterprise withered. The questions we asked tended to divorce ourselves and our work from the ways the unequal economic and cultural apparatus of our society operated. A "neutral" method meant both our own neutrality and that of the knowledge we selected and tested, or so it seemed.[4] The fact that the methods we employed had their roots in industry's attempts to control labor and increase productivity and profit, in the popular eugenics movement, and in maintaining particular class and status group interests became increasingly invisible. At the same time, educators seemed to assume that the development of these supposedly neutral methods would somehow eliminate the need to deal with the difficult issues of whose knowledge should be or already was preserved and transmitted in schools, and what the social impact of this knowledge and our evaluations of it would be. While a number of alternative traditions continued to try to keep this kind of political question alive, by and large the faith in the inherent neutrality of our institutions, the knowledge that was taught, and our planning and evaluation efforts was ideally suited to help legitimate the structural bases of inequality.

The key to this last sentence is the concept of legitimation. Like the late philosopher Ludwig Wittgenstein, we are claiming that the meaning of a good deal of our evaluative methods and theories is in their use. And the use in this case has often been twofold. The traditions that have come to dominate education assist in the reproduction of inequality while at the same time serving to legitimate both the institutions that recreate it and our actions within them. This is not to claim that *individual* children are not often helped by our methods and practices; nor is it to argue that all of our daily actions are misguided. Rather, we want to point to the fact that macroeconomically and macroculturally our efforts may serve functions that bear little resemblance to even our best intentions.

Part of the problem rests on the issue of neutrality. As we will see, our theories and methods of research and evaluation do not protect us as much as we might like from serving hidden social interests.

All too many evaluators and researchers tend to neglect the fact that their work already serves social interests. These interests and values are often constitutive elements of the very questions they ask. Let us give one example. In the midst of the data-gathering phase of a program to "rehabilitate" juvenile offenders, one of the questions asked was, "Why do these people steal?" A logical extension of this is the development of a program to reeducate these people. This sounds quite straightforward and neutral, does it not? However, it is here that one can begin to see values working through one's research and evaluation efforts. For, given the evident maldistribution of income in the United States (recent government reports suggest that the gap between rich and poor is increasing at approximately 7 percent per year above the inflation rate), given the massive and almost ignored unemployment and underemployment rate among minority youth, and given the intense psychological manipulation by corporate advertising to consume more and more, one could just as easily ask, "Why don't more people steal?" The question of "Who benefits?" looms large here.

Our point is not to claim neutrality for the second question; rather it is to illuminate the second-order nature of our research and evaluation questions. They have their biases in particular tacit conceptions of social justice, conceptions that tie us to social arrangements in important ways.

Redefining Our Unit of Analysis

The foregoing discussion of how the very questions we ask are connected to ideological values and outcomes points to the importance of seeing the enterprise of schooling itself as connected to these same ideological values and outcomes. Unfortunately, as we noted earlier, the very theoretical framework most educators have employed has made it difficult to face these connections honestly. Questions of "who benefits?", about what might be called the latent social effects of the curricula and social organization of schools, are not overtly dealt with in our dominant evaluative enterprise.

Let us examine this in somewhat more detail. Theory does not merely determine what we observe. It determines what we cannot observe as well. As Wright has noted, our questions "are always embedded in conceptual structures and if these structures lack certain pivotal elements . . . certain questions cannot or will not be asked." In particular, questions of what constitutes a *proper unit of analysis* are often specified by our unconscious theoretical presuppositions.[5] And it is here that we need to make serious headway if we are to understand curriculum more fully. For just as our questions do not stand alone but are connected to social relations outside of them, so too is the school itself—as an isolated entity—not a proper unit of analysis if we are interested in the social functions of curricula. If our unit of analysis is "only" the school, then the issues surrounding curriculum evaluation can stand alone and less of a serious challenge can be made to the process/product path evaluation has taken in the past. If, however, the school is interpreted as inextricably connected to powerful institutions and classes "outside" of itself, then our unit of analysis must include these connections. We are arguing, hence, that one commits a serious category error by thinking about the school as if it and its programs and problems existed independently. Such an error can have disastrous consequences for evaluation.

Thus, a first step in going beyond the usual disconnected framework, and toward a more relational analysis of curriculum and evaluation, is to accept one fundamental social fact, one that may be hard to deal with given where many of us are employed, but one that is accurate nonetheless. At one level, this can be stated easily. The way our institutions are organized and controlled is not equal. What this means is rather important. A number of lines of recent social research have devoted themselves to providing us with rather impressive documentation of the extent to which our society remains at heart unequally responsive by class, race, and gender. In brief, the evidence suggests the following: that we do not live in a meritocratic order; that as the sociologist of medicine Vicente Navarro has documented, slogans of pluralism aside, in almost every social arena from health care to anti-inflation policy one can see a pattern in which the top 20 percent of the population consistently benefit more than the bottom 80 percent;[6] that while schools may often be avenues for individual mobility (though this is more accidental than we might suppose), there has been little consistent loosening of the ties between origins and attainments through schools over time;[7] and finally that schools are not now nor have they ever been immune to social pressures, economic, racial, and gender-specific ideologies, or these patterns of differential benefits.[8]

Now we may not all agree with the social implications of this evidence; however, the accumulated evidence over the past few years has clarified how schools are not socially neutral, meritocratic institutions, tied into a pluralistic and meritocratic social order, an order which by policy and practice is organized to distribute educational and economic goods and services equally.

For schools are not isolated entities, divorced from the maintenance of economic and cultural inequality. Exactly the opposite is sometimes the case. Yet this assertion, on its own, is so general as to be less than helpful unless we become more specific about how schools are situated in this wider array of institutions.

Recent research on the social, ideological, and economic role of our educational apparatus has pointed to three activities in which schools engage. We can label these functions as assisting in accumulation, legitimation, and production. First, schools assist in the recreation of an unequally responsive economy by helping to create the conditions necessary for capital accumulation. They do this in part through their internal sorting and selecting of students by "talent," thus roughly reproducing a hierarchically organized labor force. As students are hierarchically ordered — an ordering often based on the cultural forms of dominant groups[9] — different groups of students are often taught different norms, skills, values, and dispositions by race, class, and sex. These tend to embody the values that are "required" by their projected rung on the labor market. In this way, schools help meet the needs of an economy for a stratified and at least partially socialized body of employees. Clearly, this does not mean that what goes on in schools is mechanistically determined by economic forces.[10] Just as clearly, as anyone who has worked in an inner-city school realizes, many students do not accept the values that the school teaches in this "hidden curriculum."[11] It is still essential, however, to realize that some very important ties exist between an economy and the social outcomes of schools.

Second, schools are important agencies of legitimation. That is, they distribute social ideologies and help create the conditions for their acceptance. Thus, schools tend to describe their internal workings as meritocratic (inaccurately so it seems)[12] and as contributing to widespread social justice. In this way, they foster a social belief that the major institutions of our society are

338

equally responsive by race, sex, and class. Unfortunately, as we have noted, the available data suggests that this is less the case than we might like to think.

Finally, the educational apparatus as a whole constitutes an important set of agencies for production. Our kind of economy requires high levels of technical/administrative knowledge for the expansion of markets, the artificial creation of new consumer needs, the control and division of labor, and for technical innovation to increase or hold one's share of a market or increase profit margins. Schools and universities help in the production of such knowledge. This, in part, explains why most school systems and the curricula within them are organized toward the university and why so much emphasis is placed on establishing programs for gifted students now, in a time of economic uncertainty. Students who can ultimately contribute to the production of this knowledge are sponsored by the school. Those who cannot are labelled as somehow deviant or are formally or informally tracked in schools.[13]

These three functions—accumulation, legitimation, and production—need to be understood if we are to grapple with what schools do and, especially, with what they are capable of doing. Such understandings are essential if we are to deal with problems in evaluation in a more complete, sophisticated way. One of the important facts about these functions is that they may be contradictory. That is, they may work against each other at times. For instance, education is caught between selecting and sorting an "adequately socialized" work force and at the same time acting as if it were part of an open system. The school's need to legitimate ideologies of social justice (and to make its own operation legitimate to its clientele) may, hence, be objectively at odds with the equally (and given current economic conditions, more) compelling pressure on it to serve the changing needs of industry. Only by placing our research and evaluation efforts within a more thorough analysis of these social functions, these connections, can we make progress in understanding what is happening in schools.

Making the connections between school curricula and the larger society our unit of analysis implies reorienting our methods of inquiry. First, this change in our unit of analysis would involve carefully scrutinizing a program one is evaluating in light of this wider social role, in light of the three socioeconomic functions we just examined. This means that our initial task requires that we ask what have come to be called "prior questions." Thus, for any evaluative activity in curriculum, the prior question should be, "evaluation for what social, economic, and ideological purpose?"

Let us give an example of the importance of asking the prior question of "evaluation for what social purpose?" Assume that we are engaged in the evaluation of a program to keep minority and poor teenagers in high school. We wish to ask whether and on what grounds it is "successful." But, successful according to what? As Jencks *et al.*, have shown, the economic returns for

339

blacks, as opposed to whites, who complete elementary and secondary schools is still *twice* as great for whites as for blacks.[14] Furthermore, completing secondary school gives relatively few advantages to students from economically disadvantaged backgrounds. As these researchers state: "Apparently, high school graduation pays off primarily for men from advantaged backgrounds. Men from disadvantaged backgrounds must attend college to reap large occupational benefits from their education."[15] Convincing minority and poor students to stay in school entails few economic rewards, regardless of what our commonsense assumptions lead us to expect.

This example documents a rather interesting point. In order to take seriously some claim for the retention, elimination, or modification of a curricular program, in order for our evaluation to make sense socially, our unit of analysis must be extended beyond the achievement scores of pupils. It must include the social connections between the school's role in accumulation in producing students of this type (with their probable economic trajectories) and the tacit legitimation of an ideology of opportunity (if only you finish high school everything will be all right), when the opportunity structure of the economy may preclude that as an actual statistical probability.[16]

Taking the unit of analysis to be the isolated school system, classroom, program, or achievement scores of students would preclude this kind of investigation. Yet look at what the extended socioeconomic appraisal that we have argued for does. It immediately raises the competing ideological and political claims made upon the school. It forces us to confront the latent ideological and economic outcomes of the institution and asks us to make certain that our programs, curricula, policies, research, and evaluations are not covering things that we may not want to occur. This appraisal obviously involves a good deal of debate at the level of policymaking and between the school and its varied clientele. Yet, the dominant ways we evaluate school programs tend to preclude serious consideration of competing ethical, political, or economic claims in large part because of their technical orientation and their focus on the achievement or IQ scores of the students.[17]

In the example of the evaluation of the above-mentioned dropout program, we can see how this occurs. A political and economic issue is transformed into a less powerful one. Here we are left to argue the relative merits of a specific curricular program—Are the test scores of the students raised? Do they stay in school longer?—as if this was cut off from the real distribution of power and benefits in our society. In this case, evaluators have taken the problems as defined by both the administrative managers of the institutions and elite groups in society as the major issues. Yet taking, rather than making, our problems can lead to acceptance of elite values and policies in such a way that, as Murray Edelman reminds us, the material aspects, the benefits, of these programs and policies "are likely to favor dominant groups" while the symbolic aspects of such programs and policies may tend to "falsely reassure mass publics that their interests are being protected" against dominant groups.[18] Closer scrutiny of the evidence of the social effects of such curricular programs might indicate that the problem is *not* dropouts. It is not getting students to stay in school longer. This is how the problem is defined for us. A more searching appraisal, a more intensive examination of how value is placed on it, situates the issue squarely where it belongs, in the unequal economic apparatus of the larger social order. Any curricular evaluation that ignores this misses the reality of the connections between our curricular programs and that larger society. The evaluation of the program that we have proposed — examining it in light of the connections the curriculum has to socioeconomic structures — makes it much more difficult to miss this reality.

Toward Social Evaluation Inside the School

Thus far, we have looked at curricular programs from the outside, as it were. While this has been of no small moment, we have not gone inside the school itself to examine the actual content and social relations embodied *within* the curriculum and their relation to the structure of inequality. Yet no social evaluation of curricula can be complete unless it also gets inside the black box of the school and investigates what is actually taught and what the concrete experiences of students are within the programs. In the space available here, we can only point to the kinds of issues that need to be raised, although a much more detailed analysis can be found elsewhere.[19] We urge the interested reader to pursue it further there.

Three basic areas of schooling need to be scrutinized to see the connections between curricula and ideological and economic structures. These include: (1) the daily interactions and regularities of school life — what has come to be called the *hidden curriculum* — that teach important norms and values related to, say, the world of work and to class, race, and gender divisions in our society; (2) the formal corpus of school knowledge — i.e., the overt curriculum itself — that is planned and found in the various materials and texts and filtered through teachers; and, finally, (3) the fundamental perspectives, procedures, and theories — such as social labelling practices that "blame the victim," a vulgar and reductive positivism, industrial models such as systems management, and so on — that educators use to plan, organize, and evaluate what happens in schools. Each of these elements should be examined to see to what extent the day-to-day meanings and practices that are so standard in classrooms — while often intended to help individual children — may tend to be less the instruments of help and, unfortunately, more part of a complex process of the reproduction of the unequal class, race, and gender relations in our society.[20] Because the third area—addressing the perspectives, procedures, and theories we usually employ—has already been partially discussed in our treatment of the evaluation of both the dropout and juvenile rehabilitation programs, let us turn our attention to the overt and hidden curricula.

It has become increasingly clear that a selective tradition operates in school curricula. Out of an entire universe of knowledge in history, science, social studies, language, and so on, only some is selected for teaching in our schools. Because of this, curriculum evaluation needs not only to be guided by a concern for how we might get students to acquire more knowledge (the dominant question in our efficiency-minded field), but by another set of questions as well. For *prior* to measuring whether or not students are "able" to learn or have learned a particular set of facts, skills, or dispositions, we should want to know *whose* knowledge it is, *who* selected it, and *why* it is organized and taught in this particular way, to this particular group.[21] This requires us to examine what the institution considers "legitimate" knowledge, teaching practices, and testing strategies, while we unpack their actual social outcomes. How do curriculum, teaching, and evaluation function in the accumulation, legitimation, and production roles played by the school? Is this what we as parents and educators really want to occur? Notice again that these sorts of queries require us to recapture the ethical, political, and economic sensitivity that has been lost over the years in our analysis of curriculum, as well as to take much more seriously data similar to Jencks's and Navarro's findings about the unequal returns from most of our social and cultural institutions.

But what about the hidden, not the overt, curriculum? What questions should guide our investigations in this area? Here it is important to remember that not every group receives the same tacit social messages; nor are the effects of this tacit teaching the same. Thus, the following issues are significant. What ideological norms and values does everyone get? Which are differentially taught by race, gender, and class, simply by living in the school day after day for most of one's preadult life?

Some simple examples of why we might want to interrogate the formal and informal knowledge found within the institution may be helpful here. For instance, in most schools little labor history is taught.[22] Instead, we teach military history and the history of the presidents. Women, people of color, and other minority and oppositional cultures are still strikingly misportrayed as well. The form, not only the content, of curricula—that is, the way the knowledge is organized—tends more and more to be individualized and prepackaged into standardized sets of material with one standard correct answer. It often denies or cuts short opportunities for cooperation and serious group inquiry. We also find behavior modification techniques (with their emphasis on doing exactly what someone in authority says, for a small reward) more widely in use in black, brown, and poor neighborhoods. In more economically advantaged areas, pedagogical and curricular strategies are less likely to be dominated by such techniques and are more likely to allow for intellectual curiosity, multiple answers, more flexible behavioral norms, and student-initiated projects.

We may also find that the categories and procedures we use in our curriculum organization and evaluation are also strongly related to unequal socioeconomic relations. Thus, we establish "remedial curricula" for "slow" learners and then find that being slow and being remediated is often related to the history of racial oppression and to poverty. Furthermore, we find that it is not unusual that once a student is placed in a remedial group, the objective chances of doing markedly better are very small. The label of "slow" sticks. For it seems that if we look at the macro level, when we establish "bluebird," "blackbird," and "buzzard" groups, once you are a buzzard you stay a buzzard.[23]

If these various examples are widespread (and they do seem to be), we are learning a good deal about what the overt and hidden curricula and our ways of evaluating students and programs may be doing socially. They may be, in fact, strongly related to both reproducing particular social and economic divisions in society and providing a helping ideology that legitimates these divisions.

Against Mechanistic Social Evaluation

Questions and examples of the type we just discussed are powerful tools in evaluating the school and its programs. However, these kinds of prior questions can lead to a mechanistic style of social evaluation — where we assume that the school always furthers the interests embodied by larger social tendencies favoring production, legitimation, and accumulation. This would be unfortunate. No social institution, no set of ideological forms and practices, is ever monolithic. Students, for instance, do not necessarily accept what the school teaches, nor do teachers passively acquiesce to larger pressures and tendencies. Therefore, we cannot take for granted that students are passive receptacles into which the school "pours" ideologocal content and values;[24] nor should we assume that students do not have some creative responses to the sorting and selecting functions of the school. In fact, recent research points to the critical nature of asking what students reject, because the research documents the ability of many students to reinterpret dominant ideologies in the overt and hidden curricula. Students often act in ways that make a simple conclusion about the social effects of curricula inside the black box

343

difficult to make. In much the same way, teachers often seek to reinterpret, modulate, and reject outright the dictates of others that they know are not in their students' best interests or in the interests of social justice.[25]

One thing is certain. If we are to find out all of this — what is accepted and what is rejected — if we are to really see what impact the curricula, social relations, and evaluative practices of the school have on the students themselves, evaluations based on achievement scores and other forms of testing are simply inadequate. This means a different style of evaluation, one that is more sensitive to the social role of the school, needs to be sponsored. Process/product evaluation does not enable us to get at the lived experience of students, to show *why* curricula fail, why programs are accepted or rejected, how conceptions of ability and achievement actually cover a much more complicated relationship between what a student experiences, on the one hand, and dominant ideologies and economic relations, on the other. What we need is a greater emphasis on ethnographic analyses that would show the complex interaction between the strengths of the culture the students bring with them to school, the formal and informal curricula, and the unequal society outside the institution.

The crucial importance of not relying on "objective" test or achievement data to evaluate the effects of curricula is demonstrated quite well in the ethnographic study by Paul Willis.[26] Willis focuses on a group of working-class high school students in a heavily industrialized city. He shows how, even in a school that tries to develop curricula to "meet the needs" of its students, its curricular programs fail for many students. Achievement is not raised; the students remain cynical.

Why this occurs and a large part of its actual social effect are exceptionally interesting problems and would be totally missed by an emphasis on test scores. It has less to do with the students' IQ or "ability" than we might think. Rather, it has an immense amount to do with the vibrant culture of the students themselves and their place in the social division of labor and the class structure. The knowledge that the school wants the students to learn and the hidden curriculum of punctuality, individual achievement, and authority relations are *both* rejected by the students. What the school considers legitimate knowledge bears little resemblance to the actual world of work, to life "on the street," to the facts of labor that these students experience from their parents, friends, and their own part-time jobs. Willis shows that because of this, the youth reject "book learning" and glorify physical labor and "being cool." They spend a good deal of their time in school creatively finding ways of beating the system and getting out of doing school work. By rejecting the "legitimate" culture of the school, by affirming manual work and physicality, they also affirm their own background. At the same time, they act in a way which actually constitutes a realistic assessment that, *as a class,* finishing their schooling or trying hard will not enable them to go much further than they already are.

This is a paradoxical situation, of course. By rejecting the overt curriculum, the students are rejecting "mental labor." They, thus, harden and make even more legitimate a distinction that lies at the heart of the social relations of production in an unequal economy: the separation of mental from manual labor. While they are affirming and acting on the strengths of their own lived culture, a culture that almost unconsciously recognizes the low statistical probability of high school really paying off in the end, they are also closing off whatever paths to advancement schools may, in fact, offer, and are reinforcing unfortunate ideological distinctions at one and the same time. Yet, by rejecting the authority relations of the hidden curriculum, by learning to control their own time and space and beat the system, they are also learning skills that will give them more informal control at their own workplaces later. The social effects of the hidden and overt curricula are, hence, quite complicated.

This ethnographic study does not assume a mechanistic process of domination in the school; yet at the same time it places the connections among the school, the students, the curricula, and the larger socioeconomic framework at the heart of its analysis. It even enables us to more fully answer traditional questions about curricular success or failure by not only focusing on test data but by illuminating how and why these data are produced. Social evaluations of curricular programs in our inner cities, among poor Black, Hispanic, and Native American populations, in industrialized working-class areas, in the rural areas of the south and west, and elsewhere, could profitably draw upon similar kinds of analysis.

Beyond the Maintenance of Inequalities

At the heart of the suggestions we have made here is the knowledge of what our society's institutions are like, and how school practices are related to them — in complicated and even contradictory ways. We have claimed that given this knowledge evaluators are compelled to take more seriously how the social meanings within the curriculum and the social impact of school programs work in supporting dominant groups within contemporary society in a variety of ways. Only by becoming more aware of these varied functions in which the school is called upon to engage, can we go further here. We have also warned against becoming so overly mechanistic, however, that we forget that real people, including many educators, may act against the accumulation, legitimation, and production functions of our educational institutions.

To work toward more socially responsive, democratic evaluation of curricula, several ideas must be taken more seriously than they now are by

345

evaluators. First, the unit of analysis must encompass both the complex nature of school phenomena as illuminated by ethnographic research investigations, and the larger social realities that are dynamically connected to classroom practices. This involves a fuller grasp of both educational practices and larger patterns of production and consumption in U. S. society, together with a normative framework with which these activities can be assessed.[27] An increased sensitivity to the shortcomings of an individual unit of analysis must be accompanied by an awareness of other categories of evaluative inquiry — the ethical and political, for example — if evaluation is to promote a more just society.

Second, the very language of evaluation must undergo a similar transformation. The overly psychological discourse we have inherited — discourse that emphasizes "the learner," "behavioral objectives," treatments and outcomes, the measurement of "time on task," and the like — must change as we widen our evaluative horizons. This, of course, involves an increased familiarity on the part of evaluators with modes of discourse that are not always considered central — especially the languages of politics, ethics, and aesthetics.

Third, the very real, practical concerns of teachers faced with increased pressures toward standardized outcomes, accountability and deskilling of teaching must be confronted honestly in evaluation studies. If we are to seriously work toward more fair, complete, and comprehensive evaluative practices, we must be prepared to deal with the pressures on teachers, administrators, and students to comply with criteria that have other aims. The key proposal in this regard may be to democratize the process of evaluation itself, so that teachers, students, parents, and other community members are included in the process of "placing value" on educational activities and curricular offerings. In this way the interests of nondominant groups may be represented and respected, and the ideological tendencies of dominant interests critiqued as we enlarge the circle of participants. Here as elsewhere democratizing educational practices may expose the contentious nature of curricular practices as competing groups argue over decisions based on ethical and political, as well as exclusively psychological, criteria.[28]

Fourth and last, we need to develop in greater detail than is possible here a vision of educational and social practices fostering cooperation, equality, participation, and social action to redress political injustices, as these embody key democratic actions. This involves several curricular and evaluative activities. For example, curriculum projects could explore and develop precisely those areas now excluded by formally sanctioned school knowledge. The history of women, working-class activists, alternative conceptions of science, technology, and the arts would become a focus for inquiry. Similarly, we might reorient at least a portion of our evaluative studies to emphasize student and teacher initiated inquiry into areas "selected out" by the standard curriculum, and support efforts to oppose continuing forms of domination and oppression for the nonprivileged. A positive evaluation would in that case mean not the raising of standardized test scores but the raising of students' and others' consciousness.[29]

Certainly these ideas are controversial and will involve a good deal of debate to implement. In particular, the concern of parents and teachers that their children and pupils do well on standardized tests is understandable, especially in times of fiscal uncertainty. Yet we must find ways to discuss with these groups how such concerns, while legitimate, do not really guarantee the futures we desire.[30] The concerns of this chapter have centered on who ultimately gains the most from the hidden and overt curricula and the evaluative practices found in schools. The effort to alter these so that a more just, democratic, and humane set of educational and social practices can occur will indeed necessitate protracted debate. But at least the debate will be over a substantive and not technical question: the shape of the world that is in the process of being built by all those involved in democratic practice.

Notes

1. These ideas were explored initially in Michael W. Apple and Landon E. Beyer, "Social Evaluation of Curriculum," *Educational Evaluation and Policy Analysis*, Vol. 5, 4(Winter 1983).

2. Michael W. Apple, "The Process and Ideology of Valuing in Educational Settings," *Educational Evaluation: Analysis and Responsibility*, Michael W. Apple, Michael Subkoviak, and Henry Lufler, Jr., eds. (Berkeley, Calif: McCutchan Publishing Corporation, 1974), pp. 3–34.

3. Throughout this chapter, we use the concept of the social "functions" of education. We do *not* mean to imply either that these functions are all schools do or that schools always successfully perform the social roles that they are called upon to do. As one of us has argued at length elsewhere, serious conceptual and empirical difficulties are found in a totally functional analysis of education. See Michael W. Apple, *Education and Power* (Boston: Routledge and Kegan Paul, 1982).

4. For a critique of the assumptions embedded in this search for a "neutral method," see Landon E. Beyer, "The Reconstruction of Knowledge and Educational Studies," *Journal of Education*, Vol. 168, 2(Fall 1986).

5. Erik Olin Wright, *Class Structure and Income Determination* (New York: Academic Press, 1979), pp. 57–8.

6. Vicente Navarro, *Medicine Under Captialism* (New York: Neale Watson Academic Publications, 1976), p. 91., See also Manuel Castells, *The Economic Crisis and American Society* (Princeton, N. J.: Princeton University Press, 1980).

7. Michael Olneck and James Crouse, "Myths of Meritocracy: Cognitive Skill and Adult Success in the United States." Institute for Research on Poverty Paper No. 485-78, University of Wisconsin, Madison, March 1978.

8. See Jerome Karabel and A. H. Halsey, eds., *Power and Ideology in Education* (New York: Oxford University Press, 1977).

9. See Pierre Bourdieu and Jean Claude Passeron, *Reproduction in Education, Society and Culture* (Beverly Hills, Calif.: Sage Publications, 1977); and John Ogbu, *Minority Education and Caste* (New York: Academic Press, 1978).

10. Apple, *Education and Power, op. cit.*

11. *Ibid.*, and Paul Willis, *Learning to Labour: How Working Class Kids get Working Class Jobs* (Lexington, Mass.: D. C. Heath, 1977).

12. See James Rosenbaum, *Making Inequality: The Hidden Curriculum of High School Tracking* (New York: John Wiley & Sons, Inc., 1976). On the school's role in legitimation, see John Meyer, "The Effects of Education as an Institution," *American Journal of Sociology*, 83(1977)55–77.

13. Michael W. Apple, *Ideology and Curriculum* (Boston: Routledge and Kegan Paul, 1979). On the relationship between the control of knowledge and the economy, see Harry Braverman, *Labor and Monopoly Capital* (New York: Monthly Review Press, 1974) and David Noble, *American By Design* (New York: Alfred A. Knopf, 1977).

14. Christopher Jencks *et al.*, *Who gets Ahead?* (New York: Basic Books, 1979), pp. 174–75.

15. *Ibid.*, p. 175.

16. Wright, *op. cit.*

17. Apple, *Ideology and Curriculum, op. cit.*

18. Murray Edelman, *Political Language* (New York: Academic Press, 1977), p. xxi.

19. Apple, *Ideology and Curriculum op. cit.*; Landon E. Beyer, "The Parameters of Educational Inquiry," *Curriculum Inquiry*, Vol. 16, 1(Spring 1986). See also Michael W. Apple, ed., *Cultural and Economic Reproduction in Education: Essays on Class, Ideology, and the State* (Boston: Routledge and Kegan Paul, 1982).

20. Apple, *Ideology and Curriculum, op. cit.*, p. 14.

21. *Ibid.*, p. 7.

22. Jean Anyon, "Ideology and United States History Textbooks," *Harvard Educational Review*, 49(1979).

23. See Ray Rist, *The Urban School: A Factory for Failure* (Cambridge, Mass.: M.I.T. Press, 1973); and Jeannie Oakes, *Keeping Track: How Schools Structure Inequality* (New Haven, Conn.: Yale University Press, 1985).

24. Anyone who has taught in an inner-city school knows the intense resistance that goes on. Even more subtle forms of resistance occur in more middle-class schools in many areas. See, for example, Linda McNeil, "Economic Dimensions of Social Studies Curriculum: Curriculum as Institutionalized Knowledge," unpublished Ph.D. dissertation, University of Wisconsin, Madison, 1977.

25. See Linda McNeil, *Contradictions of Control: School Structure and School Knowledge* (New York: Routledge and Kegan Paul, 1986).

26. Willis, *Learning to Labour, op. cit.*

27. Walter Feinberg, *Understanding Education* (New York: Cambridge University Press, 1983); and Landon E. Beyer, "The Parameters of Educational Inquiry," *op. cit.*

28. For a very interesting attempt to expand the discourse and methodology of evaluation, see Ernest R. House, *Evaluating with Validity* (Beverly Hills, Calif.: Sage Publications, 1980).

29. Patti Lather, "Research as Praxis," *Harvard Educational Review*, Vol. 56, 3(August 1986).

30. See Ann Bastian, Norm Fruchter, Marilyn Gittell, Colin Greer, and Kenneth Haskins, *Choosing Equality: The Case for Democratic Schooling* (Philadelphia: Temple University Press, 1986).

Biographical Sketches

MICHAEL W. APPLE is Professor of Curriculum and Instruction and Educational Policy Studies at the University of Wisconsin – Madison. His writing has focused on the relationship between curriculum and teaching and unequal power in the larger society. Among his recent books are *Ideology and Curriculum* (1979), *Education and Power* (1982, revised edition 1985), *Cultural and Economic Reproduction in Education* (1982), *Ideology and Practice in Schooling* (1983), and *Teachers and Texts: A Political Economy of Class and Gender Relations in Education* (1986).

THOMAS E. BARONE received his doctorate in 1978 from Stanford University in California. His publications reveal an interest in emancipatory educational theory and especially the relevance of aesthetic theory for curriculum concerns. He has written about and experimented with a variety of literary-style inquiry modes, including educational criticism, forms of "new journalism," critical biography, as well as novelistic storytelling. Barone is currently Associate Professor and Director of Secondary Education Programs at Northern Kentucky University in Highland Heights.

LANDON E. BEYER is Chair of the Department of Education at Knox College in Galesburg, Illinois. His research interests include the arts and

351

aesthetic theory, curriculum theory and analysis, and the social foundations of education. He has published in journals such as *Educational Theory, Curriculum Inquiry*, the *Journal of Education*, the *Journal of the Institute of Art Education*, and the *Journal of Teacher Education*. He is the author of *Knowing and Acting: Inquiry, Ideology, and Educational Studies* (1988).

DENNIS L. CARLSON received his M.A. in urban planning from the University of Washington and his Ph.D. in Educational Policy Studies from the University of Wisconsin—Madison. He is currently on the Education Faculty at Rutgers University in Newark, New Jersey. He has previously published in *Harvard Educational Review, Curriculum Inquiry, Interchange, The Journal of Curriculum Theorizing*, and *Educational Leadership*. His current research is on the role of teachers in educational renewal.

SARA E. FREEDMAN was laid off from her job as a classroom teacher after 10 years of teaching. As a member of the Boston Women's Teachers' Group, she then directed a National Institute of Education research and dissemination grant on the institutional structure of schools and its effect on teachers. She now teaches at the University of Massachusetts—Boston in the Department of Community Planning, is on the editorial board of *Radical Teacher*, and conducts workshops for teachers on workplace stress and institutional change.

HERBERT M. KLIEBARD is Professor of Curriculum and Instruction and Educational Policy Studies at the University of Wisconsin—Madison. He has delivered papers on curriculum history in Europe and Japan as well as throughout the United States. His previous books include *Language of the Classroom* (1966), *Religion and Education in America* (1969), *Teacher, Student, and Society: Perspectives on Education* (1974), and *Curriculum and Evaluation* (1977). His most recent book is *The Struggle for the American Curriculum 1893–1958* (1986).

GAIL McCUTCHEON is associate professor at Ohio State University in Columbus where she teaches and does research about action research, qualitative research, and curriculum. She taught third and fourth grades in New Mexico and New York for more than eight years, received her B.A. from the University of Mexico, M.A. from Bank Street College and her Ph.D. from Stanford University in California.

DOUGLAS D. NOBLE has been a computer programmer and a teacher in elementary, secondary and adult education, and a cofounder of an independent elementary school. He is the author of numerous critical articles on computers and education, which have been widely reprinted. His book on the history of technological ideology in American education will be published by Falmer Press in 1988. He welcomes correspondence through the Graduate School of Education and Human Development, University of Rochester, in New York.

GEORGE J. POSNER, Associate Professor of Education, Cornell University in Ithaca, New York, is the author of *Course Design: A Guide to Curriculum Development for Teachers,* third edition (with Alan Rudnitsky), and *Field Experience: A Guide to Reflective Teaching,* as well as numerous articles in curriculum development and science education. He also works extensively with New York State school districts in school improvement efforts. In addition, he has been an active member of AERA's Division B (Curriculum Studies), serving as its program chair in 1986, and a member of the editorial boards of several professional journals.

KENNETH A. SIROTNIK is currently a Research Professor in the College of Education at the University of Washington in Seattle. Previously, he spent a number of years as a senior research associate in the graduate School of Education at the University of California — Los Angeles. He has participated in many educational research studies including the nationally recognized, "A Study of Schooling." His interests and publications range broadly from topics in measurement, statistics, evaluation, and technology, to issues concerning education policy and local school improvement and change.

PHILIP H. STEEDMAN is a New Zealander who has studied at the University of Canterbury and the University of Illinois in Urbana. His research focuses on the relations between the arts and the sciences, the contemporary philosophy of science, and cybernetics. He has taught at universities in New Zealand, Australia, Canada and the United States and has published papers and reviews in a number of journals. He is currently a member of the faculty at the University of Cincinnati, Ohio.

MICHAEL J. STREIBEL is an associate Professor in the Educational Technology Program of the Department of Curriculum and Instruction at the University of Wisconsin — Madison. His current line of inquiry includes both a critical analysis of how computers are used in education and an investigation into the design of intelligent tutoring software for undergraduate science education. He also teaches a number of graduate courses in educational media, instructional design, and educational research with and about computers.

353

KENNETH N. TEITELBAUM is an Associate Professor in the Division for the Study of Teaching and Director of the Urban Teacher Preparation Program at Syracuse University in New York. His research and teaching interests include curriculum theory and history, transformations in teaching and teacher education, and social studies education. He has published in journals such as the *Journal of Curriculum Studies, History of Education Quarterly, Educational Studies, Journal of Education for Teaching,* and *Social Education.*

GEORGE WILLIS, professor of education at the University of Rhode Island, has written on a variety of curriculum issues. He is editor of *Qualitative Evaluation: Concepts and Cases in Curriculum Criticism* (1978), coauthor of *Human Services in America* (1986), a consulting editor for the *Journal of Curriculum and Supervision,* and a founding member and former president of the Society for the Study of Curriculum History.

GEORGE H. WOOD is Associate Professor of Education and Coordinator of the Institute for Democracy in Education (IDE) at Ohio University in Athens. His research and teaching interests are in the role of schooling in democratic societies. He has published in a variety of journals and books on the theory and practice of democratic education. Through the IDE, he works with classroom teachers to promote both more democratic teaching practices and more democratic schools. At Ohio University he has been named by students "University Professor" for his work as a teacher.

Name Index

Abelove, Henry, 55
Adams, R., 164
Adler, Mortimer J., 177, 186
Ahlbrand, William P., 68
Aikin, Wilford M., 333
Allender, J. S., 163
Almond, G. A., 185
Alschuler, Albert, 187
Althusser, Louis, 100, 113
Amarel, Marianne, 160, 286
Amidon, E. J., 68
Amsterdamski, Stefan, 130, 137
Angus, Jan, 70
Anthony, Susan B., 45
Anyon, Jean, 348
Apple, Michael W., 3, 14-16, 42, 54, 69, 105, 108, 113-114, 132, 133, 138, 150, 153, 164, 185, 235, 237, 283, 289, 308, 309, 310, 311, 334, 347, 348
Archambault, Reginald D., 136
Arendt, Hannah, 154, 156, 160

Aristotle, 19, 29, 126, 135
Arnold, Matthew, 120
Arnold, Thomas, 21
Aron, R., 163
Aronowitz, Stanley, 16, 52, 55, 67
Auston, J. L., 120
Avrich, Paul, 53

Baker, Eva L., 95
Barber, Benjamin, 185
Barnes, Douglas, 79, 95
Barone, Thomas E., 12, 13, 140, 164, 165
Barr, Robert, 284
Barthes, Roland, 164
Barzun, Jacques, 237
Bastian, Ann, 349
Bauch, Patricia, 67
Beardsley, Monroe, 146, 162
Becker, Henry J., 283
Beecher, Catherine, 208
Bell, Daniel, 114, 243, 244, 255, 256

General Index

Ability grouping, 183, 232, (also see tracking)
Abstract individual, 42
Accommodation, 260
Accountability systems, 112
Activity curriculum, 26-27
Aesthetic:
  attitude, 147
  content, 146-148, 154-155
  disinterestedness, 147
  experience, 146, 148
After Virtue, 223
Amalgamated Clothing Workers of America (ACWA), 35
American Educational Reserach Association (AERA), 145
American Educational Studies Association (AESA), 176-177
American Herbartian movement, 26
Another Country, 143, 147, 155, 158, 160-161
Anthropomorphized processes, 273

Antimilitarism, 44
Aptitude/Treatment Interaction studies, 151
Artificial intelligence, 243, 248
Assertive discipline, 181
Assimilation, 260
Autobiography of Malcolm X, 158

"Back to basics," 9
Best American Short Stories 1985, 161
Boston Women's Teachers' Group, 13
Brown v. Board of Education of Topeka, 323

Capital Flight, 296
Capitalism: 38, 45-46, 99-100, 109, 226
  advanced, 99, 102, 110
  advanced capitalist state, 100
  capitalist social institutions, 39
  capitalist system, 39, 43, 45

363

Journal of Curriculum Theorizing, 157

Keller Plan, 265
Knowledge, 119-135, 224-225
  traditional accounts of, 120-135
Knowledge and Control: New Directions for the Sociology of Education, 132-135
Knowledge and Curriculum, 126

"Learning how to learn," 27
Learning-oriented approach to curriculum, 81
Liberal education and the nature of knowledge, 121-122, 124, 128-130
Life and Adventures of Nicholas Nickelby, 145
Life in Classrooms, 209
Lifestyle enclaves, 228
"Likely stories," 154
Linear: 80, 82, 86
  planning approach, 89
  procedural model, 87
  technical dimension, 88
Logic of Education, 120
London School of philosophy of education, 120

"Master teachers," 232
Mastery learning, 263-264, 267, 269
Means-end rationality, 80, 274, 276
Microcomputers, 241, 259
Modes of fiction, 150-161
Milwaukee Leader, 36-37
Milwaukee School Board, 36

Nation at Risk, 172-173, 175, 289
National Commission on Excellence in Education, 185, 186, 220, 235
National Science Foundation, 185, 186
Naturalistic model for curriculum development, 140
Neo-Luddites, 307
Neo-Marxist model of the state, 100-101

"New Education Establishment," 251
"New Foundation/Academic Network," 251-252
New French Critics, 164
New Sociology of Education, 131-135
Null curriculum, 193, 194, 195

"Objective" evaluation, 324
"Objective science" of interpretation, 149
Open education, 9

Paideia Group, 185, 186
Paideia Proposal, 177
Participatory theory, 171
Pedagogical principles, 263
Phenomenology & Pedagogy, 157
Philosophy: 78
  public, 222
P-I-E model, 88
Poland, 145
Positivism, 121, 125, 130-131, 149-150, 224-225
Power and education, 4-5, 9, 13-14, 23, 133, 146, 153, 230
"Practice of possibility," 8
Praxis, 4, 10
Production system, 80
Productivity crises, 259
Programs of evaluation, 14
Progressive education, 34, 57
Progressive Education Association (PEA), 28-29
Project WILD, 202
Proletarianization of jobs, 292, 295
Protectionist theory of democracy, 171
Psychic wholeness, 228
Psychology of learning, 78
Psychotechnology, 245, 247
Public Education Information Network, 176, 186
Public schooling: 32, 34, 47-48, 64, 71, 167, 175-176